AF757693

# Private Sector Tourism in Conservation Areas in Africa

# Private Sector Tourism in Conservation Areas in Africa

Susan Snyman and Anna Spenceley

CABI

**CABI is a trading name of CAB International**

CABI
Nosworthy Way
Wallingford
Oxfordshire OX10 8DE
UK

Tel: +44 (0)1491 832111
Fax: +44 (0)1491 833508
E-mail: info@cabi.org
Website: www.cabi.org

CABI
745 Atlantic Avenue
8th Floor
Boston, MA 02111
USA

Tel: +1 (617)682-9015
E-mail: cabi-nao@cabi.org

© S. Snyman and A. Spenceley 2019. All rights reserved. No part of this publication may be reproduced in any form or by any means, electronically, mechanically, by photocopying, recording or otherwise, without the prior permission of the copyright owners.

A catalogue record for this book is available from the British Library, London, UK.

**Library of Congress Cataloging-in-Publication Data**

Names: Snyman, Susan, author. | Spenceley, Anna, author.
Title: Private sector tourism in conservation areas in Africa / Susan Snyman and Anna Spenceley.
Description: Boston, MA : CABI, 2019. | Includes bibliographical references and index.
Identifiers: LCCN 2018061262 (print) | LCCN 2019001378 (ebook) | ISBN 9781786393562 (ePDF) | ISBN 9781786393579 (ePub) | ISBN 9781786393555 (hardback)
Subjects: LCSH: Sustainable tourism--Africa. | Ecotourism--Africa. | Protected areas--Africa--Management. | Protected areas--Economic aspects--Africa. | Conservation of natural resources--Economic aspects--Africa.
Classification: LCC G155.A314 (ebook) | LCC G155.A314 S59 2019 (print) | DDC 338.4/7916--dc23

LC record available at https://lccn.loc.gov/2018061262

ISBN-13: 9781786393555 (hardback)
9781786393562 (ePDF)
9781786393579 (ePub)

Commissioning Editor: Claire Parfitt
Editorial Assistant: Tabitha Jay
Production Editor: James Bishop

Typeset by SPi, Pondicherry, India
Printed and bound in the UK by Severn, Gloucester

# Contents

# About the Authors

Susan Snyman has a PhD in Resource Economics from University of Cape Town. Having completed coursework at University of Goteborg, Sweden, the focus of her PhD research measured the socio-economic impact of high-end ecotourism in remote, rural communities adjacent to protected areas, based on over 1,700 community surveys in six southern African countries. Sue worked for Wilderness Safaris, a high-end ecotourism operator, from 2008–2018. Prior to that she worked for over a decade in ecotourism and conservation in southern Africa. Other positions include Vice-Chair of the IUCN WCPA Tourism and Protected Areas Specialist Group (TAPASG) and Coordinator of the TAPASG Communities & Heritage Working Group, working on community engagement and benefit-sharing from tourism and protected areas. Sue is currently Senior Programme Officer for the Conservation Areas and Species Programme for the IUCN Eastern and Southern African Regional Office, coordinating the Biodiversity and Protected Areas Management (BIOPAMA) programme in 24 African countries. Email: suesnyman@gmail.com

Dr Anna Spenceley is a specialist in sustainable tourism, having worked for over 20 years in developing countries on assignments promoting conservation and poverty reduction. Anna is Chair of the IUCN's World Commission on Protected Areas (WCPA) Tourism and Protected Areas Specialist Group (TAPAS Group). She sits on the board of the Global Sustainable Tourism Council (GSTC), and on the GSTC's Destination working group. She is also a Senior Research Fellow with the University of Johannesburg, and an Honorary Fellow of the University of Brighton. Anna has a substantial publication record on sustainable tourism, including being lead author on guidelines for tourism concessions in protected areas, published by both the Convention on Biological Diversity and the World Bank Group. She has also edited volumes including *Responsible Tourism: Critical issues for Conservation and Development and Tourism and Poverty Reduction: Impacts and Principles in Developing Countries.* Anna sits on the editorial board of the *Journal of Sustainable Tourism*, and of Koedoe. Website: www.anna.spenceley.co.uk; Email: annaspenceley@gmail.com

# List of Boxes

# List of Figures

# List of Tables

# Acknowledgements

We are deeply indebted to the many people who contributed towards the development of this book, and particularly those who collaborated with us on the case studies. We would also like to thank the publishers at CAB International for supporting us in this project, and a very special thanks goes to our two peer reviewers, Professor Paul Eagles and Professor Chris Rogerson, who provided invaluable advice, comments and suggestions.

# List of Acronyms

AMC – Akagera Management Company
AP – African Parks
APM – African Parks Majete Ltd
APN – African Parks Network
APZ – African Parks Zambia Ltd
ASF – African Safari Foundation
AWC – African Wildlife Capital
AWF – African Wildlife Foundation
AZC – Ahi Zameni Chemucane Association
B2B – business-to-business
B2C – business-to-customer
BEE – black economic empowerment
BML – Bale Mountain Lodge
BMNP – Bale Mountains National Park
BOT – build, operate and transfer
BRE – Barotse Royal Establishment
CBD – Convention on Biological Diversity
CBO – community-based organisation
CBNRM – community-based natural resource management
CBT – community-based tourism
CCA – community conservation area
CCL – Covane Community Lodge
CDEF – Community Development Education Fund
CEPF – Critical Ecosystem Partnership Fund
CGS – Comissão de Gestão Social
CHICOP – Chumbe Island Coral Park Limited
CI – Conservation International
CITW – Children in the Wilderness
COMESA – Common Market for Eastern and Southern Africa
CPA – communal property association
CSR – corporate social responsibility
CTC – Chemucane Tourism Company

DBO – design–build–operate
DFGFI – Dian Fossey Gorilla Fund International
DNPW – Department of National Parks and Wildlife
DUAT – Direito do Uso e Aproveitamento da Terra
DWNP – Department of Wildlife and National Parks
EIA – environmental impact assessment
EMS – environmental management system
EWCA – Ethiopian Wildlife Conservation Authority
FY – financial year
GCF – Grand Circle Foundation
GDP – gross domestic product
GEMS – Group Environmental Minimum Standards
GSNL – Greater Sossusvlei Namib Landscape
GSTC – Global Sustainable Tourism Council
HATAB – Hospitality and Tourism Association of Botswana
HWC – human–wildlife conflict
IDC – Industrial Development Corporation
IFC – International Finance Corporation
IGAD – Intergovernmental Authority on Development
IRDNC – Integrated Rural Development and Nature Conservation
IRR – internal rate of return
IUCN – International Union for the Conservation of Nature
JMB – Joint Management Board
JV – joint venture
KBA – key biodiversity area
KNP – Kruger National Park
KTP – Kgalagadi Transfrontier Park
kW – kilowatt
KWS – Kenya Wildlife Service
KZN – KwaZulu-Natal
LNP – Limpopo National Park
LPNP – Liuwa Plain National Park
MBS – Micheletti Bates Safaris
MET – Ministry of Environment
MICE – meetings, incentives, conventions and exhibitions
MPA – marine protected area
MWAP – Manda Wilderness Agriculture Project
MWCT – Manda Wilderness Community Trust
MWh – megawatt hours
MZN – Mozambique Metical
NACSO –Namibian Association of Community Support Organisations
NAD – Namibian dollar
NAO – Namibian Organic Association
NBT – nature-based tourism
NCS – Norman Carr Safaris
NEF – National Environment Fund
NGO – non-governmental organisation
NICE – Namibian Institute of Culinary Education
NRMP – Natural Resources Management Programme
NRNR – NamibRand Nature Reserve
OCT – Okavango Community Trust
OPL – One Planet Living

OWS – Okavango Wilderness Safaris
PA – protected area
PAA – protected area authority
PPP – public–private partnership
RDB – Rwanda Development Board
ROT – rehabilitate, operate and transfer
RPS – Robin Pope Safaris
SACOLA – Sabyinyo Community Livelihoods Association
SACT – South Africa College of Tourism
SADC – Southern African Development Community
SANParks – South African National Parks
SANPT – South African National Parks Trust
SDG – Sustainable Development Goal
SKNP – Singita Kruger National Park
SMART – specific, measureable, achievable, relevant and time-bound
SMME – small, medium and micro-enterprise
SRT – Save the Rhino Trust
SSC – Singita School of Cooking
TCE – tourism conservation enterprise
TFCA – transfrontier conservation area
TFPD – Transfrontier Parks Destinations
TRANSFORM – Training and Support for Resource Management Programme
TUF – tourism user fee
UNCTAD – United Nations Conference on Trade and Development
UNEP-WCMC – United Nations Environment Programme World Conservation Monitoring Centre
UNESCO – United Nations Educational, Scientific, and Cultural Organization
UNWTO – United Nations World Tourism Organization
UR – University of Rwanda
USD – United States dollar
USP – unique selling point
VCA – value chain analysis
VNP – Volcanoes National Park
WML – Witsieshoek Mountain Lodge
WS – Wilderness Safaris
WSZ – Wilderness Safaris Zimbabwe
WTM – World Travel Market
WTTC – World Travel and Tourism Council
WWF – World Wide Fund for Nature
WWT – Wilderness Wildlife Trust
ZAR – South African rand
ZAWA – Zambian Wildlife Authority

# 1

# Introduction

Tourism is seen as a powerful vehicle for economic growth and development, as well as for job creation, all over the world. It generally has low barriers to entry, a seasonal flow of visitors, a simple product and consumption at the point of production – therefore, it has significant potential as a poverty alleviation tool (Twining-Ward, 2009; United Nations, 2017). The World Bank Group (2017) states that sustainable tourism is in fact a proven tool for development, benefiting communities in destinations around the world as it is highly labour intensive, facilitates the development of new infrastructure, helps fund conservation, revitalises modern and historic cities and can contribute to international understanding. Eagles, McCool and Haynes (2002), Leung, Spenceley, Hvengaard and Buckley (2018) and Spenceley, Kohl, McArthur, Myles, Notarianni, Paleczny, Pickering and Worboys (2015) have all shown the important role that sustainable tourism can play in conservation areas. Tourism is, however, not a panacea for reducing poverty and/or for socioeconomic development. The introduction, implementation and management of tourism requires constant monitoring, management and refinement to ensure long-term, sustainable benefits for all stakeholders, as well as positive social, environmental and economic impacts. When tourism is poorly planned, it can negatively impact on parks, cities and historic or cultural monuments and can put severe pressure on local infrastructure, biodiversity conservation, resident communities and their resources (World Bank Group, 2017).

The Convention on Biological Diversity (CBD) has been addressing the area of biodiversity and tourism development since 2004, including the adoption of Guidelines on Biodiversity and Tourism Development and the production of two guideline user manuals: 'Managing tourism and biodiversity' (CBD, 2007), and 'Tourism supporting biodiversity' (CBD, 2015). Work presented to the Conference of the Parties to the CBD in 2012 concluded that the tourism sector is the largest global, market-based contributor to financing protected area (PA) systems in many countries, through entrance and other user fees, partnerships and concessions (Spenceley, Snyman and Eagles, 2017a). However, many parties to the CBD under-use tourism as a means to contribute towards the financial sustainability of PAs.

According to the World Bank (Christie, Fernandes, Messerli and Twining-Ward, 2014: 24), there are 10 main reasons to specifically develop tourism in Africa:

**1.** To spur economic development as tourism has demonstrated its economic strength and potential all over the world.
**2.** To create good jobs as tourism is a more efficient job creator than many other sectors due to the multiple downstream effects.
**3.** To build remote and developing regions as tourism is growing faster in the world's

© S. Snyman and A. Spenceley (2019). *Private Sector Tourism in Conservation Areas in Africa* (S. Snyman and A. Spenceley)

emerging and developing regions than in the rest of the world.
**4.** To accelerate reform as tourism has been shown to accelerate policy and economic reforms as political stability, good governance and an enabling business environment provide a good foundation for tourism growth (UNCTAD, 2007).
**5.** To improve infrastructure in order to attract tourists – these improvements often have positive impacts on the overall economy as well as local populations.
**6.** To increase domestic consumption and to diversify exports. Tourists' demand for goods and services (such as fuel, communication and retail) creates induced supply chain benefits.
**7.** To empower women, young people and marginalised populations because tourism is, globally, one of the few economic sectors in which women outnumber men in certain positions and are paid the same.
**8.** To preserve cultural heritage and to conserve the environment as tourism provides a source of revenue for its protection.
**9.** To promote public–private partnerships as effective tourism planning requires collaboration and partnerships between the public and private sectors.
**10.** To improve the national image, because successful tourism can change external perceptions of a country, improve intercultural understanding and create a positive frame of reference for a country.

It is argued in this volume that the private sector has the potential to provide financial sustainability to protected/conservation areas as an alternative to government allocations for financing conservation efforts, particularly in developing countries. A recent paper by Rylance, Snyman and Spenceley (2017) looked at the potential for tourism to fund PAs and found that although tourism is a significant revenue source for PA authorities in southern Africa, how it is retained and reinvested back into conservation management remains ambiguous. The lack of consistency of data related to tourism revenues provided to conservation areas in Africa makes it difficult to measure the real impact of tourism on conservation and the associated PAs and also does not allow for comparisons across the continent (Eagles *et al.*, 2002; Leung *et al.*, 2018; Rylance *et al.*, 2017; Spenceley *et al.*, 2015; Spenceley, Rylance & Laiser, 2017). The importance of sustaining tourism revenue for an individual conservation area and to a PA authority ideally will be to help underpin quality customer service, and safe and clean destinations (Spenceley *et al.*, 2015). Protected area managers need to be sensitive to business needs – for example, the timing of management operations such as burning, pest animal control, weed control and maintenance tasks can be scheduled to avoid negative experiences for visitors, which may therefore impact on financial returns (Spenceley *et al.*, 2015). Government and the private sector need to work together to optimise the benefits from tourism for conservation.

PAs, in all forms, whether formal or informal, are one way of conserving biodiversity, ecosystem services and human well-being, and are now recognised as an integral part of sustainable development strategies (Rylance *et al.*, 2017). Over the past four decades there has been a 10-fold increase in the number of PAs and with upcoming targets for all parties to the CBD needing to be met, there is likely to be even more of an increase in the near future. As the number of PAs increases, the amount of funding available to manage them has, however, remained generally stagnant (Emerton, Bishop & Thomas, 2006), and insufficient to ensure effective achievement of conservation and livelihood goals (Bovarnick, Alpizar & Schnell, 2010; Watson, Dudley, Segan & Hockings, 2014). PA financing shortfalls are most intense in developing countries and current financial needs for PAs in developing countries are thought to range between USD 1.1 billion to cover core operations and USD 2.5 billion to cover the very basic range of actions necessary to ensure that management is effective (Eagles & Hillel, 2008; Emerton *et al.*, 2006).

Traditionally, PAs were funded by public money from government. Increasingly, PA authorities do not have sufficient funds and most governments do not fund PAs fully (Adams & Infield, 2003; Buckley, 2003; Eagles, Baycetich, Chen, Dong, Halpenny, Kwan, Lenuzzi, Wang, Xiao & Zhang, 2009; Mitchell, Wooliscroft & Higham, 2013; Saayman & Saayman, 2006 in Whitelaw, King & Tolkach, 2014). However, investment in PAs and other conservation areas should be considered an investment in local economic development and in improving the quality of life of people who live in and around these areas (Rylance *et al.*, 2017). Low levels of funding to PA authorities is one of the most important threats to biodiversity conservation in Africa (de la Harpe, Fernhead, Hughes, Davies, Spenceley, Barnes, Cooper & Child, 2004). If PAs are unable to meet their ecological goals, as a result of underfunding, then it is likely that they will be unable to meet their social goals (de la Harpe *et al.*, 2004). The maintenance and expansion of PAs in Africa will require a fresh approach to fundraising and new systems for achieving financial sustainability if we are to ensure the conservation of species in the long run (Rylance *et al.*, 2017) (see Bakarr and Lockwood, 2006: 218 for a list of management principles for the establishment of PAs). According to Eagles and Hillel (2008), tourism financial flows have the potential to make much larger contributions to the management of the world's conservation estate than they currently do: this can, in part, be achieved through greater private sector investment in tourism.

Over the years, it has been shown that private sector tourism in remote, rural areas of Africa can promote local socioeconomic development (Buckley, 2010; Lapeyre, 2010; Mbaiwa & Stronza, 2010; Novelli & Scarth, 2007; Snyman, 2012a, 2012b, 2013, 2014; Spenceley, 2008). Benefits can be enhanced when accompanied by other measures such as upliftment, empowerment and education projects. It was also observed by Snyman (2012a, 2012b, 2013, 2014) and earlier noted by Adams and Infield (2003) that income generated from tourism can lead to a dynamic of competition of its own, as different stakeholders attempt to dominate access to the available revenue streams. The private sector operator wants to maximise profits, as would the community and any related government departments; 'best practice' involves maximising the benefits of all involved (including economic, environmental and social benefits), or at least satisfying their needs (Snyman, 2013).

If the aim of tourism is simple profit maximisation, then the best way is via the private sector, but if the aim is to maximise local benefits, then joint ventures (JVs) or community-based tourism (CBT) may be optimal (Spenceley, 2008; Spenceley, Rylance, Nanabhay & van der Watt, 2016). Equity mechanisms help ensure that financial benefits for responsible land custodianship are possible and can, if managed correctly, have a significant impact on rural households' social welfare in the form of community development such as health or education infrastructure, as well as poverty reduction impacts through collective revenues, and direct and indirect employment. The chosen equity or partnership arrangement will depend on the community, the private sector tourism operator, government institutions, land rights, tenure and the security of this tenure, natural resources as well as the policies, legislation and institutions in place. Land tenure rights vary from one African country to the next and are a major factor impacting on the level/degree of private sector investment that will occur. The tourism model or partnership (discussed in Chapters 2 and 3 in this volume) chosen by the private sector also depends on factors such as: the ease of access; level of service provision; social responsibilities; proximity to other conservation areas; and the state of natural resources. It is also determined by the existing and predicted future sociopolitical climate, relevant legislative procedures and existing legal frameworks, economic and political stability and the actions and interventions of key stakeholders (Castley, 2010).

## 1.1. The Scope of this Book

The focus of this book is on private sector tourism in conservation areas in sub-Saharan Africa and the various potential partnership models involving different combinations of stakeholders. Private sector tourism can take many forms, including accommodation such as hotels, lodges, game ranching, campsites and services such as transport, retail and guiding. The focus in this book is only on accommodation, and the finance and operation of lodges in sub-Saharan Africa. The reason for this focus was to specifically determine optimal partnership models for private sector tourism lodges and the various institutional arrangements that exist in terms of accommodation establishments related to conservation areas: to promote local development, while at the same time supporting biodiversity conservation. It has been argued that in more environmentally sensitive areas high-end tourism can potentially provide a low environmental impact/high economic impact model. This would, therefore, have a more positive long-term impact on sustainable development and biodiversity conservation in sub-Saharan Africa. Many of the case studies in this book are examples of high-end tourism, though middle- to lower-end models have also been included. Any tourism activities in protected or conserved areas should be compatible with the protected area's primary objective of conserving biodiversity, but also with other objectives such as the conservation of geological, historic and cultural features.

This book focuses on the role of the private sector, the different partnership models involving the private sector and how best to engage with the private sector and maximise benefits from private sector tourism in conservation areas in sub-Saharan Africa. According to Castley (2010) the development of luxury private game reserves has undoubtedly strengthened southern Africa's conservation and sustainable tourism profile. There is, however, limited academic literature specifically on private sector tourism in Africa. A number of individual studies have examined selected private sector models in Africa (e.g. Lapeyre, 2011; Snyman, 2012a, 2012b, 2014; Spenceley, 2005; Spenceley & Goodwin, 2007; Spenceley & Snyman, 2017), but only a few studies have examined the net contribution of the private sector or the variety of different partnership models which are available in different contexts and circumstances (e.g. Spenceley, 2003, 2010) and there has been no cross-country, multi-model analysis of different private sector partnership models in conservation areas in Africa. Van Wijk, Van der Duim, Lamers and Sumba (2014) noted the importance of commercial conservation tourism approaches for the work of protected areas worldwide, and in using tourism as a poverty alleviation tool in less developed countries. They focused on the potential innovative partnership opportunities between conservation non-governmental organisations (NGOs), the private sector and local communities, rather than on private sector tourism per se. This book is the first to survey, document and analyse private sector tourism lodges in conservation areas in sub-Saharan Africa with the inclusion of detailed case study analysis across the continent. It is important to note, and is clear from the case study analysis in this book, that there are no standard models, but rather a suite of approaches and options which can be tailored and adopted to different circumstances and different stakeholders. This volume presents examples of partnership models all involving the private sector, showing the economic, social and environmental impacts of each model in different countries.

To make comparisons between the case studies clear, we have applied the same structure to each. They provide background information, and then describe the institutional structure, economic, social and environmental elements, challenges and successes, lessons learned and recommendations emanating from the case study. It is not exhaustive as the number of stakeholder combinations and partnership models is extensive. It attempts, however, to offer a good overall understanding to allow for creative partnership models to be developed to benefit all stakeholders, local socioeconomic development and biodiversity conservation.

## 1.2. Users of this Book

We hope that this body of knowledge will provide a wealth of information for scholars, educators and students in their journey towards understanding how to make tourism sustainable. We further envisage that the book will be of value to people working on tourism in protected areas. The information will be of use to protected area authorities and policy makers, who can provide an enabling environment of laws, plans and regulations that promote sustainable tourism investment and operations in areas of high biodiversity. The book will also be of use to investors, tourism developers, managers and operators, who are looking to draw on existing expertise and practices, to avoid reinventing the wheel, to scale up successes and avoid pitfalls. The book will also be of value to those providing technical support to members of rural communities, who endeavour to promote a positive and fair deal from tourism partnerships, such as NGOs and technical advisors. While the geographical focus of the book is Africa, we recognise the value of south–south learning, and aspire to share experiences with other developing countries that have protected area networks which are viable for tourism development.

## 1.3. Case Study Data Sources

The case studies were compiled through a process of literature review and consultation with the private operators, technical support agencies and protected area officials who have made these enterprises happen. Based on a common structure for all the case studies, we applied an iterative process with these stakeholders to ensure that the case reflected actual conditions on the ground. Many of the stories told here have been followed, researched and encouraged by the authors for a decade or more (e.g. Anvil Bay, Damaraland, Ngala, Ndzou, Phinda, Pafuri, Rocktail Bay). They are journeys that we have been privileged to accompany, document and learn from. Others have new and evolving tales, and we welcome their incorporation in this volume.

In compiling this book, we tried to ensure their accuracy through multiple reviews by our collaborators. This volume would not have been possible without them. The book is largely a testament to their vision, drive and perseverance to establish these facilities, and also their generosity in sharing their knowledge with us, and readers of this book.

Table 1 lists all of the case studies collated here, and the contributors who made them possible.

Interestingly, the case studies included in this volume come from a variety of countries (11 different countries) and tourism companies in sub-Saharan Africa (see Table 1). At the end of each case study a summary table of the main statistics and information is included for quick reference.

## 1.4. Definition of Key Terms

In order to understand the use of various terms in this book, Table 2 provides definitions of some of the main concepts/terms used. Due to an ongoing debate related to the various terms currently in use – 'ecotourism', 'nature-based tourism', 'responsible tourism', 'sustainable tourism' and 'inclusive tourism' – this volume has chosen to simply use the word 'tourism'. In the context of this book, we describe tourism in protected areas that takes into account environmental, economic and social impacts, now and in the future.

## 1.5. Structure of this Book

Chapter 2 provides an overview of key issues relating to sustainable protected area tourism. This incorporates a review of the literature relating to tourism and conservation in Africa, the role of the private sector and its engagement with stakeholders. Background on the types of economic, social and environmental benefits that can be generated from private sector tourism investment in protected areas is described. Furthermore, an overview of challenges with private sector investment in protected areas, and with private operators themselves, is outlined.

Chapter 3 provides an overview of options for private sector partnerships in protected areas, with a range of for-profit and not-for-profit business models based on land owned by government, the private sector, communities and others. Institutional arrangements of varying degrees of complexity are explained, ranging from purely private sector operations to public private partnerships (PPPs) and joint venture partnerships. The role of philanthropy and donations from tourism to communities is also explored. In all, 18 case studies from 11 African countries illustrate the range of models observed, to share actual data from the enterprises and role players on their successes and challenges.

Chapter 4 focuses on private sector partnerships that incorporate community representation. These institutions differ considerably from purely Community-based Tourism (CBT) enterprises (this has been extensively researched previously). The chapter expands our knowledge on joint venture operations, where community entities are formal partners in the business. It also explores institutional arrangements where the management of these accommodation facilities is outsourced to the private sector. Fourteen case studies from six countries are used to illustrate these models.

In Chapter 5, we review processes that can be used to establish these partnerships in government-owned protected areas. First, we describe the steps that protected area authorities can take to establish tourism concessions and partnerships with the private sector. This is followed by suggested steps that can be used to establish tourism partnerships when the tenure for the protected area lies with a community or on privately owned land. This includes establishing new partnerships, and also retrofitting pure

**Table 1.** List of case studies and related private sector partners.

| Country | Lodge/camp | Private sector Stakeholder/ company | Contributors | Case study no. |
|---|---|---|---|---|
| Botswana | Vumbura Plains and Little Vumbura | Wilderness Safaris (WS) | Lesh Moiteela; Warren Ozorio | 29 |
| | Mombo Camp and Little Mombo | WS | Gavin Jacobs; Grant Woodrow; Warren Ozorio | 3 |
| Ethiopia | Bale Mountain Lodge | Jember Ltd | Guy Levene; Kathleen Fitzgerald | 8 |
| | Simien Lodge | Nick Crane | Nick Crane | 4 |
| Kenya | Satao Elerai | Satao Elerai Ltd | Kathleen H. Fitzgerald; Torben Rune | 31 |
| Namibia | Damaraland Camp | WS | Mike Wassung; Petru Ebersohn; Warren Ozorio | 21 |
| | Doro Nawas Camp | WS | Mike Wassung; Petru Ebersohn; Warren Ozorio | 22 |
| | Serra Cafema | WS | Mike Wassung; Petru Ebersohn; Warren Ozorio | 27 |
| | Wolwedans | NamibRand Nature Reserve | Jason Nengola | 2 |
| Malawi | Mkulumadzi Lodge | Robin Pope Safaris | Charl Grobler; Stuart Slabbert | 11 |
| | Thawale Lodge | Sunbird | Craig Hay; Stuart Slabbert | 12 |
| Mozambique | Anvil Bay Chemucane Lodge | Chemucane Tourism Company (CTC) | Steve Collins; Ricky Bell | 19 |
| | Covane Community Lodge | Scholtz Consultoria e Serviços Lda | Marina Scholtz; Luis Dinis | 25 |
| | Ndzou Camp | Eco-Micaia Lda | Andrew Kingman | 20 |
| | Nkwichi Lodge | Nkwichi Lodge | Malcolm Turner | 6 |
| Rwanda | Bisate Lodge | WS | Ingrid Baas; Chris Roche; Jomi Krobb | 1 |
| | Ruzizi Tented Lodge | Akagera Management Company | Sarah Hall | 13 |
| | Sabyinyo Silverback Lodge | Governors' Camps | Dominic Grammaticas; Kathleen Fitzgerald; Leonard Harerimana; William Mwangi | 28 |
| South Africa | Pafuri Camp | Return Africa | Peter John Massyn; Steve Collins; Bongani Baloyi | 30 |
| | Ngala Main Camp and Ngala Tented Camp | andBeyond | Andrew Nicholson; Johanthan Braack; Nikki Herbst; Les Carlisle; Aaron Jones | 10 |
| | Singita Lebombo | Singita | Andrea Ferry; Morris Ngwenyama | 14 |
| | Phinda Private Game Reserve | andBeyond | Andrew Nicholson; Virginia Bachoo; Simon Naylor; Nikki Herbst; Johanthan Braack; Les Carlisle | 26 |
| | Rocktail Camp | WS | Natalie Gouws; Patrick Boddam-Whetham; Warren Ozorio | 32 |

**Table 1.**

| Country | Lodge/camp | Private sector Stakeholder/ company | Contributors | Case study no. |
|---|---|---|---|---|
| | !Xaus Lodge | Transfrontier Park Destinations | Glynn O'Leary; Eleanor Muller | 23 |
| | Witsieshoek Mountain Lodge | Transfrontier Park Destinations | Glynn O'Leary; Eleanor Muller | 24 |
| Tanzania | Chumbe Island | Chumbe Island Coral Park Limited (CHICOP) | Sibylle Riedmiller; Ulli Kloiber; Kevin Macdonald | 7 |
| Zambia | King Lewanika Lodge | Norman Carr Safaris (In 2018, Norman Carr Safaris rebranded and is now called Time + Tide) | Dave Wilson; Stuart Slabbert | 9 |
| Zimbabwe | Davison's Camp; Little Makalolo; Linkwasha (Hwange Camps) | WS | Courtney Johnson; Warren Ozorio | 5 |

**Table 2.** Definition of key terms used.

| | |
|---|---|
| **Biodiversity** | The variability among living organisms from all sources including, inter alia, terrestrial, marine and other aquatic ecosystems and the ecological complexes of which they are a part; this includes diversity within species, between species and of ecosystems (United Nations, 1992) |
| **Community** | A social group of any size whose members reside in a specific locality, share government and may have common cultural and historic heritage/s. It can also refer to a group of individuals who interact within their immediate surroundings. A typical local community consists of business operators, public agency staff and residents, and their interactions, and can include sharing of resources, information and support as well as establishing commercial relationships between local businesses and consumers (Spenceley, 2014) |
| **Concession** | The right to use land or other property for a specified purpose, granted by a government, company or other controlling body. It can include a commercial operation and/or a piece of land (Pocket Oxford English Dictionary, 2006). A tourism concession could provide accommodation, food and beverage, recreation, education, retail and interpretive services (Eagles *et al.*, 2009). A tourism concession is defined here as 'a lease, licence, easement or permit for an operation undertaken by any party other than the protected area agency' (Thompson, Massyn, Pendry and Pastorelli, 2014) and it 'provides public service and may require some capital investment by a concessionaire for buildings, equipment and operating costs (Eagles *et al.*, 2009) |
| **Ecotourism** | Responsible travel to natural areas that conserves the environment, sustains the well-being of the local people and involves interpretation and education (The International Ecotourism Society, 2015) |
| **Joint venture** | A joint venture as 'a contractual partnership between a community or local institution and a private investor, to work together in establishing and operating a single tourism or hunting enterprise'. They add that joint ventures add cultural and ethical components to the product (Ashley and Jones, 2001: 2) |

**Table 2.**

| | |
|---|---|
| **Nature-based tourism** | All forms of tourism that use natural resources in a wild or undeveloped form – including species, habitat, landscape, scenery and fresh-water features. Nature-based tourism is travel for the purpose of enjoying undeveloped natural areas or wildlife (Goodwin, 1996) |
| **NGOs** | An NGO is an organisation not belonging to or associated with any government. |
| **Partnership** | An arrangement in which two or more individuals share the profits and liabilities of a business venture. Various arrangements are possible: all partners might share liabilities and profits equally, or some partners may have limited liability (Investopedia, 2017). Partnerships may be formal contracts and agreements or may be informal arrangements agreed upon between the various parties |
| **Private sector** | Part of the national economy that is not under direct state control |
| **Protected area** | '[A] clearly defined geographical space, recognised, dedicated and managed, through legal or other effective means, to achieve the long term conservation of nature with associated ecosystem services and cultural values' (Dudley, 2008). It is important to note that any tourism activities in protected areas should be compatible with the protected area's primary objective of conserving biodiversity. In this book the focus is on conservation and protected areas, with conservation areas being any areas of land set aside for conservation, rather than alternative land uses, whether formally or informally declared conservation areas. These areas may be government-, community-, NGO- or privately owned, or a combination of these. There are different categories of protected areas described by the International Union for the Conservation of Nature (IUCN), some of which are aligned with tourism development (Spenceley *et al*., 2017b). Protected areas are commonly called 'parks' |
| **Public–private partnership (PPP)** | An agreement between a state institution and a private party, where the private party is granted the right to access and use public assets such as land and infrastructure for its own commercial use and assumes related substantial financial, technical and operational risks. The private party receives a benefit from using the state property by charging fees to customers to whom they provide a service (adapted from National Treasury *Toolkit for tourism*, 2004) |
| **Stakeholders** | Stakeholders are persons or groups who are directly or indirectly affected by a project, as well as those who may have interests in a project and/or the ability to influence its outcome, either positively or negatively. In relation to protected areas, stakeholders may include government agencies, NGOs, the private sector, local community groups, local communities and other resource management agencies (IFC, 2012) |
| **Sustainable tourism** | Tourism that takes full account of its current and future economic, social and environmental impacts, addressing the needs of visitors, the industry, the environment and host communities (UNEP and UNWTO, 2005) |

Source: Adapted from Spenceley *et al.* (2017b)

private sector (or CBT) models into partnerships to enhance their commercial viability and social impact.

We use Chapter 6 to synthesise the best practice lessons learned from all 32 case studies, by consolidating institutional issues, economic, environmental and social considerations. We draw out the successes, challenges and lessons learned within the case studies.

Finally, in Chapter 7, we draw conclusions on the body of evidence collated, the take-home messages for readers, and pose our vision for the future of tourism in conservation areas of Africa.

## 1.6. References

Adams, W.M. & Infield, M. (2003) Who is on the gorilla's payroll? Claims on tourist revenue from a Ugandan National Park. *World Development*, 31(1), 177–190, doi: 10.1016/S0305-750X(02)00149-3.
Ashley, C. & Jones, B. (2001) Joint ventures between communities and tourism investors: experiences in southern Africa. *International Journal of Tourism Research*, 3(2), doi: 10.1002/jtr.347.
Bakarr, M.I. & Lockwood, M. (2006). Establishing Protected Areas. In Lockwood, M., Worboys, G.L. & Kothari, A. (2006). Managing Protected Areas: A Global Guide. Earthscan, London.
Bovarnick, A., Alpizar, F. & Schnell, C. (eds) (2010) *The importance of biodiversity and ecosystems in economic growth and equity in Latin America and the Caribbean: an economic valuation of ecosystems*, United Nations Development Programme, 2010. Available at http://www.undp.org/content/dam/undp/library/Environment%20and%20Energy/biodiversity/Report_ENG.pdf (accessed 4 April 2018).
Buckley, R. (2003) Pay to play in parks: an Australian policy perspective on visitor fees in public protected areas. *Journal of Sustainable Tourism*, 11(1), 56–73.
Buckley, R. (2010) *Conservation tourism*. CAB International, Wallingford, UK.
Castley, J.G. (2010) Southern and eastern Africa. In Buckley, R. (2010) *Conservation tourism* (pp. 145–175. CAB International, Wallingford, UK.
CBD (Convention on Biological Diversity) (2007) Managing tourism and biodiversity. User's manual on the CBD *Guidelines on Biodiversity and Tourism Development*. Montreal, Canada. Available at https://www.cbd.int/doc/programmes/tourism/tourism-manual-en.pdf (accessed 10 April 2018).
CBD (Convention on Biological Diversity) (2015) Tourism supporting biodiversity – a manual on applying the CBD *Guidelines on Biodiversity and Tourism Development*. Montreal, Canada. Available at https://www.cbd.int/tourism/doc/tourism-manual-2015-en.pdf (accessed 10 April 2018).
Christie, I., Fernandes, E., Messerli, H. & Twining-Ward, L. (2014) *Tourism in Africa: harnessing tourism for growth and improved livelihoods*. The World Bank, Washington, DC. Available at https://openknowledge.worldbank.org/handle/10986/18688 (accessed 16 June 2017).
de la Harpe, D., Fernhead, P., Hughes, G., Davies, R., Spenceley, A., Barnes, J., Cooper, J. & Child. B. (2004) Does commercialization of protected areas threaten conservation goals? In Suich, H. & Child, B. (eds) with Spenceley, A. (2009) *Evolution and innovation in wildlife conservation: parks and game ranches to transfrontier conservation areas* (pp. 189–216). Earthscan, UK.
Dudley, N. (ed.) (2008) *Guidelines for applying protected area management categories*. IUCN, Gland, Switzerland.
Eagles, P.F.J., McCool, S.F. & Haynes, C. (2002) *Sustainable tourism in protected areas: guidelines for planning and management.* Best Practice Protected Areas Guideline Series No. 8. IUCN, Gland, Switzerland.
Eagles, P.F.J. & Hillel, O. (2008) *Improving protected area finance through tourism*. Paper presented to the second meeting of the Ad Hoc Open-ended Working Group on Protected Areas (WGPA-2), Rome, Italy, 11–15 February 2008, in preparation for the ninth meeting of the Conference of the Parties to the Convention on Biological Diversity (COP-9) – Bonn, Germany, May 19–30 2008. Available at http://ahs.uwaterloo.ca/~eagles/documents/EaglesandHillelArticleonEconomicsandFinanceofTourisminProtectedAreas.pdf (accessed 4 April 2018).
Eagles, P.F.J., Baycetich, C.M., Chen, X., Dong, L., Halpenny, E., Kwan, P.A., Lenuzzi, J.J., Wang, X., Xiao, H. & Zhang, Y. (2009) *Guidelines for planning and management of concessions, licenses and permits for tourism in protected areas*. Tourism Planning and Management Program, University of Waterloo, Waterloo, Ontario, Canada.
Emerton, L., Bishop, J. & Thomas, L. (2006) *Sustainable financing of protected areas: a global review of challenges and options*. IUCN, Gland, Switzerland and Cambridge, UK.
Goodwin, H. (1996) In pursuit of ecotourism. *Biodiversity and Conservation*, 5, 277–292.
IFC (International Finance Corporation) (2012) Africa: the power of the private sector. *Telling our Story*, 6(4). Available at https://www.ifc.org/wps/wcm/connect/832f31004b1f9746a7a6ef08d0338960/TOSAfrica.pdf?MOD=AJPERES (accessed 5 November 2017).
Investopedia (2017) *Partnership*. Available at www.investopedia.com/terms/p/partnership.asp (accessed 12 June 2017).
Lapeyre, R. (2010) Community-based tourism as a sustainable solution to maximise impacts locally? The Tsiseb Conservancy case, Namibia. *Development Southern Africa*, 27(5), 757–772, doi: 10.1080/0376835X.2010.522837.

Lapeyre, R. (2011) Governance structures and the distribution of tourism income in Namibian communal lands: a new institutional approach. *Tijdschrift voor Economische en Sociale Geographie*, 102(3), 302–312, doi: 10.1111/j.1467-9663.2011.00665.x.

Leung, Y-F., Spenceley, A., Hvengaard, G. & Buckley, R. (2018) *Tourism and visitor management in protected areas: guidelines for sustainability*. Best Practice Protected Areas Guidelines No. 27. IUCN, Gland, Switzerland.

Mbaiwa, J.E. & Stronza, A.L. (2010) The effects of tourism development on rural livelihoods in the Okavango Delta Botswana., *Journal of Sustainable Tourism* 18(5), 635–656, doi 10.1080/09669581003653500.

Mitchell, R., Wooliscroft, B. & Higham, J. (2013) Applying sustainability in national park management: balancing public and irivate interests using a sustainable market orientation model. *Journal of Sustainable Tourism*, 2(5), 695–715.

National Treasury (2004) *Toolkit for tourism*. PPP Practice Note 1 of 2004 (p. 3). Available at http://www.ppp.gov.za/Pages/Governance.aspx?RootFolder=%2fLegal%20Aspects%2fPPP%20Toolkit%20for%20Tourism&FolderCTID=&View=%7b33F91A9E%2d68FB%2d40CC%2dB511%2d45D91A7C-C95B%7d (accessed 10 April 2018).

Novelli, M. & Scarth, A. (2007) Tourism in protected areas: integrating conservation and community development in Liwonde National Park, Malawi. *Tourism and Hospitality Planning and Development*, 4(1), 47–73, doi: 10.1080/14790530701289697.

*Pocket Oxford English Dictionary* (2006). Oxford, UK.

Rylance, A., Snyman, S. & Spenceley, A. (2017) The contribution of tourism revenue to financing protected area management in southern Africa. *Tourism Review International*, 21(2), 139–149, doi: 10.3727/154427217.

Saayman, M. & Saayman, A. (2006) Estimating the economic contribution of visitor spending in the Kruger National Park to the regional economy. *Journal of Sustainable Tourism*, 14(1), 67–81.

Snyman, S. (2012a) Ecotourism joint ventures between the private sector and communities: an updated analysis of the Torra Conservancy and Damaraland Camp partnership, Namibia. *Tourism Management Perspectives*, 4, 127–135, doi: 10.1016/j.tmp.2012.07.004.

Snyman, S. (2012b) The role of ecotourism employment in poverty reduction and community perceptions of conservation and tourism in southern Africa. *Journal of Sustainable Tourism*, 20(3), 395–416.

Snyman, S. (2013) *High-end ecotourism and rural communities in southern Africa: a socioeconomic analysis*. Unpublished PhD thesis, University of Cape Town, South Africa.

Snyman, S. (2014) Partnership between a private sector ecotourism operator and a local community in the Okavango Delta, Botswana: the case of the Okavango Community Trust and Wilderness Safaris. *Journal of Ecotourism*, 13(2–3), 110–127, doi: 10.1080/14724049.2014.980744.

Spenceley, A. (2003) *Tourism, local livelihoods and the private sector in South Africa: case studies on the growing role of the private sector in natural resources management*. Sustainable Livelihoods in South Africa Research Paper 8. Sustainable Livelihoods Southern Africa Project, Institute of Development Studies, Brighton, UK, February.

Spenceley, A. (2005) Nature-based tourism and environmental sustainability in South Africa. *Journal of Sustainable Tourism*, 13(2), 136–170.

Spenceley, A. (2008) Phinda private game reserve, South Africa. Presentation at the African Safari Lodges practitioners workshop, The Grace Hotel, Rosebank, South Africa, 19–21 May.

Spenceley, A. (2014) Tourism concession guidelines for transfrontier conservation areas in SADC. Report to GIZ / SADC. Available at: https://tfcaportal.org/sites/default/files/public-docs/tourism_concession_guidelines_sadc_tfcas_final.pdf (accessed 3 January 2019).

Spenceley, A. (2010) *Tourism product development: interventions and best practices in sub-Saharan Africa. Part 1: Synthesis; Part 2: Case studies*. World Bank, Washington, DC.

Spenceley, A. & Goodwin, H. (2007) Nature-based tourism and poverty alleviation: impacts of private sector and parastatal enterprises in and around Kruger National Park, South Africa. *Current Issues in Tourism*, 10(2 & 3), 255–277, doi: 10.2167/cit305.0.

Spenceley, A. & Snyman, S. (2017) Can a wildlife tourism company influence conservation and the development of tourism in a specific destination? *Tourism and Hospitality Research*, 17(1), 52–67.

Spenceley, A., Kohl, J., McArthur, S., Myles, P., Notarianni, M., Paleczny, D., Pickering, C. & Worboys, G.L. (2015) Visitor management. In Worboys, G.L., Lockwood, M., Kothari, A., Feary, S. & Pulsford, I. (eds) *Protected area governance and management* (pp. 715–750), ANU Press, Canberra.

Spenceley, A., Rylance, A., Nanabhay, S. and van der Watt, H. (2016) *Operational guidelines for community-based tourism in South Africa*. Department of Tourism: Republic of South Africa.

Spenceley, A., Rylance, A. & Laiser, S. (2017a) Protected area entrance fees in Tanzania: the search for competitiveness and value for money. *Koedoe* 59(1), a1442. https://doi.org/10.4102/koedoe.v59i1.1442.

Spenceley, A., Snyman, S. & Eagles, P. (2017b) *Guidelines for tourism partnerships and concessions for protected areas: generating sustainable revenues for conservation and development*. Report to the CBD. Available at https://www.cbd.int/tourism/doc/tourism-partnerships-protected-areas-web.pdf (accessed 4 April 2018).

The International Ecotourism Society (2015) *TIES announces ecotourism principles revision*. Available at https://www.ecotourism.org/news/ties-announces-ecotourism-principles-revision (accessed 5 June 2017).

Thompson, A., Massyn, P.J., Pendry, J. & Pastorelli, J. (2014) Tourism concessions in protected natural areas: guidelines for managers. United Nations Development Program. Available at: http://www.undp.org/content/undp/en/home/librarypage/environment-energy/ecosystems_and_biodiversity/tourismconcessions-in-protected-natural-areas.html (accessed 22 June 2018).

Twining-Ward, L. (2009) *Africa Region's Finance and Private Sector Development Department (AFTFP): Sub-Saharan Africa tourism industry research*. Final report for the World Bank, Washington, DC. Available at http://siteresources.worldbank.org/INTAFRSUMAFTPS/Resources/2049902-1327506860777/FinalSSATourismRpt1118.pdf (accessed 5 November 2017).

UNCTAD (United Nations Conference on Trade and Development) (2007) *World investment report: transnational corporations, extractive industries and development*. Available at http://unctad.org/en/docs/wir2007_en.pdf (accessed 24 March 2018).

UNEP and UNWTO (2005) *Making tourism more sustainable, a guide for policy makers*. UNEP and UNWTO, Madrid, Spain.

United Nations (1992) *Convention on biological diversity article 2*. Available at http://www.cbd.int/doc/legal/cbd-en.pdf (accessed 9 June 2017).

United Nations (2017) *Economic development in Africa report 2017: tourism for transformative and inclusive growth*. Available at http://unctad.org/en/PublicationsLibrary/aldcafrica2017_en.pdf (accessed 2 October 2017).

Van Wijk, J., Van der Duim, R., Lamers, M. & Sumba, D. (2014) The emergence of institutional innovations in tourism: the evolution of the African Wildlife Foundation's tourism conservation enterprises. *Journal of Sustainable Tourism*, doi: 10.1080/09669582.2014.927878.

Watson, J., Dudley, N., Segan, D. & Hockings, M. (2014) The performance and potential of protected areas. *Nature*, 515, 67–73.

Whitelaw, P.A., King, B.E. & Tolkach, D. (2014) Protected areas, conservation and tourism – financing the sustainable dream. *Journal of Sustainable Tourism*, 22(4), 584–603, doi:10.1080/09669582.2013.87344.

World Bank Group (2017) *Tourism for development: 20 reasons sustainable tourism counts for development*. Available at http://documents.worldbank.org/curated/en/558121506324624240/pdf/119954-WP-PUBLIC-SustainableTourismDevelopment.pdf (accessed 3 January 2019).

# 2

# Background

## 2.1. Tourism and the Sustainable Development Goals

The significance of tourism for biodiversity has been reflected in the Convention on Biological Diversity (CBD) since the fifth meeting of the Conference of the Parties (COP 5) in 2000, where a decision (Decision V/25) by the Parties recognised the importance of tourism for social and economic development at local, national and regional levels, up to a decision (Decision XII/11) adopted by COP 12 in 2014, which, among other things, recognises the ongoing relevance of the CBD Guidelines on Biodiversity and Tourism Development and invites Parties and other stakeholders to promote awareness of sustainable travel choices (CBD, 2016). In 2010, the Parties to the CBD adopted the Strategic Plan for Biodiversity 2010–2020 and its 20 Aichi Biodiversity Targets (UNEP-WCMC and IUCN, 2016). This has since been endorsed by multiple multilateral environmental agreements as a global framework for biodiversity. This, together with the adoption of the Sustainable Development Goals (SDGs) in 2015 (more information on tourism and the SDGs can be found in Table 3), recognise the important role of protected areas (PAs) as a key strategy for biodiversity conservation and sustainable development in the targets they contain. Tourism is of great relevance to at least 12 of the 20 Aichi Biodiversity Targets set in 2010 (Targets 1, 2, 4, 5, 8, 9, 10, 11, 12, 15, 18, 20) (CBD, 2016). With the United Nations declaring 2017 as the International Year of 'Sustainable Tourism for Development', sustainable tourism has been identified as a vital component in ensuring the achievement of the SDGs 8, 12 and 14 and the 2030 Agenda for Sustainable Development (United Nations, 2015). It also highlights the importance of tourism in terms of creating employment, driving exports and improving social welfare. This specific inclusion of tourism in some of the SDGs further highlights its global importance in terms of sustainable development. The United Nations World Tourism Organization (UNWTO) (2015) highlighted ways in which tourism contributes to each of the SDGs, and Table 3 shows the ways in which case studies in this volume contribute to them.

A recent World Bank Group paper (2017) also outlines 20 reasons sustainable tourism counts for development, grouping the reasons according to the UNWTO's five pillars of tourism for development. The case studies described in this volume highlight the pillars in Table 4, and the reasons related to them, as well as contributions to achieving the SDGs and the role that the private sector can play in terms of using tourism as a tool for conservation and development. Numerous of the above elements are highlighted in the various case studies and emphasise the importance of private sector tourism in conservation areas in Africa, and the role that sustainable

© S. Snyman and A. Spenceley (2019). *Private Sector Tourism in Conservation Areas in Africa* (S. Snyman and A. Spenceley)

**Table 3.** Linking the Sustainable Development Goals (SDGs) to case study examples.

| Goal | SDG | How does tourism have an impact? | Example |
|---|---|---|---|
| 1 NO POVERTY | End poverty in all forms everywhere | Tourism fosters economic growth and development and provides income through employment, promoting entrepreneurship and empowering disadvantaged groups | All case study examples included employment and the use of local suppliers. Many employ women |
| 2 ZERO HUNGER | End hunger, achieve food security and improved nutrition and promote sustainable agriculture | Tourism can spur agricultural productivity by promoting the production, use and sale of local produce and its full integration into the tourism value chain | Many case study examples include using local produce and engaging in community garden projects |
| 3 GOOD HEALTH AND WELL-BEING | Ensure healthy lives and promote well-being for all ages | Tourism's contribution to economic growth can have a knock-on effect on health and well-being. Tourism philanthropy can also play a role here, as can the benefits of tourism to the health of the tourist | Including through staff health programmes and tourism philanthropy contributions to community health services |
| 4 QUALITY EDUCATION | Ensure inclusive and equitable quality education and promote lifelong learning opportunities for all | Tourism can provide incentives to invest in education and vocational training as the sector requires specific skills | Tourism skills training and development, and philanthropic donations towards education, schools and scholarships |
| 5 GENDER EQUALITY | Achieve gender equality and empower all women and girls | Tourism can empower women in many ways, especially jobs and other income-generating opportunities | Many case study examples employ equal numbers of women, and some support women's groups in local communities |
| 6 CLEAN WATER AND SANITATION | Ensure availability and sustainable management of water and sanitation for all | Tourism can play a role in achieving water access and security, as well as hygiene and sanitation for all | Tourism in an area can result in improvement in water provision in local communities through philanthropic projects |

**Table 3.**

| Goal | SDG | How does tourism have an impact? | Example |
|---|---|---|---|
| 7 AFFORDABLE AND CLEAN ENERGY | Ensure access to affordable, reliable, sustainable and modern energy for all | Tourism can accelerate the shift towards renewable energy, as well as providing information on renewable energies to communities | Use of renewable energies by the private sector can educate communities about these technologies |
| 8 DECENT WORK AND ECONOMIC GROWTH | Promote sustained, inclusive and sustainable economic growth, full and productive employment and decent work for all | Tourism is one of the driving forces of global economic growth and provides access to decent work opportunities | Most case study examples had a high percentage of local community members employed |
| 9 INDUSTRY INNOVATION AND INFRASTRUCTURE | Build resilient infrastructure, promote inclusive and sustainable industrialisation and foster innovation | Tourism development relies on good public and private infrastructure and an innovative environment. Can incentivise government to upgrade infrastructure | Tourism in rural areas can stimulate government investment in infrastructure. Philanthropic donations can also support this |
| 10 REDUCED INEQUALITIES | Reduce inequality within and among countries | Tourism can be a powerful tool for community development and reduce inequalities if it engages local populations. It is an effective means for developing countries to participate in the global economy | Within countries, inequality reduced through employment, procurement and philanthropic donations |
| 11 SUSTAINABLE CITIES AND COMMUNITIES | Make cities and human settlements inclusive, safe, resilient and sustainable | Tourism has the potential to advance urban infrastructure and universal accessibility, promote regeneration of areas in decay and preserve cultural and natural heritage | Not specifically addressed as the case studies are located in protected areas. However, their economic impacts may reduce rural–urban migration |
| 12 RESPONSIBLE CONSUMPTION AND PRODUCTION | Ensure sustainable consumption and production patterns | Tourism can develop resource-efficient initiatives that result in enhanced economic, social and environmental outcomes | Through use of local suppliers of goods and services as well as through environmental management in lodges, the examples showed sustainable consumption and production. Some case studies have independent certification of their sustainability claims |

**Table 3.**

| Goal | SDG | How does tourism have an impact? | Example |
|---|---|---|---|
| 13 CLIMATE ACTION | Take urgent action to combat climate change and its impacts | By lowering energy consumption and shifting to renewable energy sources, tourism can help tackle climate change | Through environmental management systems in many of the lodges there was a reduction in energy consumption, use of renewable energy and the promotion of natural habitat conservation |
| 14 LIFE BELOW WATER | Conserve and sustainably use the oceans, seas and marine resources for sustainable development | Coastal and marine tourism rely on intact and healthy marine ecosystems, which require them to be conserved | Tourism's presence and lobbying assisted with this for case studies in marine protected areas |
| 15 LIFE ON LAND | Protect, restore and promote sustainable use of terrestrial ecosystems, sustainably manage forests, combat desertification, halt and reverse land degradation and halt biodiversity loss | Tourism can play a role in conserving biodiversity through reducing waste and consumption, conserving native fauna and flora and awareness-raising activities | Most examples engaged in environmental management systems and some form of biodiversity conservation. The presence of tourism lodges and their financial benefits to local community members tends to reduce poaching |
| 16 PEACE JUSTICE AND STRONG INSTITUTIONS | Promote peaceful and inclusive societies for sustainable development, provide access to justice for all and build effective, accountable and inclusive institutions at all levels | Tourism can foster multicultural and inter-faith tolerance and understanding | Establishment of improved governance frameworks for joint venture operations supports more stable and inclusive communities. Cultural tourism and village visits in many examples promote understanding and acceptance |
| 17 PARTNERSHIPS FOR THE GOALS | Strengthen the means of implementation and revitalise the global partnership for sustainable development | Due to the cross-sectoral nature of tourism, it can strengthen public–private partnerships (PPPs) and engage multiple stakeholders | All case study examples included partnerships of some form, most engaging multiple stakeholders |

Source: Adapted from World Tourism Organization (2015)

**Table 4.** UNWTO's 20 reasons sustainable tourism counts for development.

| |
|---|
| **Pillar 1: Sustainable economic growth** |
| Stimulates gross domestic product (GDP) growth |
| Increases international trade |
| Boosts international investment |
| Drives infrastructure development |
| Supports low income economies |
| **Pillar 2: Social inclusiveness, employment and poverty reduction** |
| Creates jobs efficiently |
| Promotes inclusive growth |
| Strengthens rural communities |
| Revitalises urban areas |
| Improves access to income via travel tech |
| Benefits women |
| Bolsters artisans |
| **Pillar 3: Resource efficiency, environmental protection and climate** |
| Facilitates conservation |
| Raises climate change awareness |
| Propels the blue economy |
| **Pillar 4: Cultural values, diversity and heritage** |
| Protects cultural sites |
| Sustains intangible culture |
| **Pillar 5: Mutual understanding, peace and security** |
| Spreads philanthropy |
| Cultivates intercultural understanding |
| Aids post-conflict recovery |

Source: World Bank Group (2017)

tourism can play in development. Tourism has also been identified as one of the 10 key sectors to evolve towards a green economy and is included as one of the initial United Nations 10-Year Framework of Programmes (10YFP) to accelerate a shift towards more sustainable consumption and production patterns (World Tourism Organization, 2014).

## 2.2. Overview of Tourism in Africa

Please note that some of this section is taken from Spenceley, Snyman and Eagles (2017a).

Tourism is one of the key industries driving change in Africa and it provides multiple opportunities for economic growth and improved livelihoods (World Tourism Organization, 2015). A World Bank study in 2013 (Christie, Fernandes, Messerli, & Twining-Ward, 2014) argued that Africa is experiencing an economic take-off, with tourism as one of the main driving sectors. Chuhan-Pole and Angwafo (2011) also highlighted the potential growth opportunities in Africa through a selection of case study examples highlighting growth experiences, building institutions and governance, leveraging sectoral advantages, boosting agricultural efficiency, engaging the private sector and improving human development. Tourism in Africa has experienced not only strong growth in terms of arrivals but also in terms of expenditures and revenues (United Nations, 2017). Since the 1990s, tourism has increasingly contributed to Africa's growth, employment and trade (United Nations, 2017). Over 30 African countries have identified tourism as a national priority within the Enhanced Integrated Framework (a multi-donor programme providing trade-related assistance to less developed countries) (World Tourism Organization, 2014). At the continental level, the African Union's Agenda 2063 and the Tourism Action Plan under its New Partnership for Africa's Development recognise tourism's importance in driving Africa's socioeconomic development and structural transformation through job creation, through catalysing growth in other productive sectors and through fostering inclusion by encouraging the participation of women and youth in the sector's activities (United Nations, 2017: 3). At the regional level, the policy frameworks of several regional economic communities, including the 2012 Protocol on Tourism of the Southern African Development Community (SADC), the Sustainable Tourism Development Strategy of the Common Market for Eastern and Southern Africa (COMESA) and the Sustainable Tourism Master Plan 2013–2023 of the Intergovernmental Authority on Development (IGAD) highlight tourism's importance in supporting socioeconomic development in Africa (United Nations, 2017: 4). At the national level, most African countries have national development plans that outline a country's vision for its future and identify planned policies and sectoral priorities, which highlight the importance of tourism (United Nations, 2017: 4).

Twining-Ward, Li, Bhammer and Wright (2018) recently reported that the tourism sector is the largest market-based contributor to financing protected areas such as national parks. In some countries, tourism depends almost exclusively on natural systems, often with wildlife as the primary attraction. They highlight that this nature-based tourism (NBT) is a powerful tool that countries can use to grow and bring jobs to local communities, generate government revenues and foreign exchange, and create new markets for entrepreneurs to sell their goods and services. Their study reported that wildlife is an essential draw for tourists who visit parks and generate economic activities that benefit local people and, therefore, for NBT to flourish, wildlife and its natural habitat must be protected and managed sustainably (Twining-Ward *et al.*, 2018). They stress that to achieve the latter, the design of conservation programmes that are socially and economically sustainable will be essential.

Despite numerous unpredictable shocks which impact on tourism in Africa, it contributed 3.1% to GDP in 2016, supporting 6 million net additional jobs in the sector (WTTC, 2017). Travel and tourism generated USD 7.6 trillion (10.2% of global GDP) and 292 million global jobs in 2016, equivalent to 1 in 10 jobs in the global economy (WTTC, 2017). Additionally, the sector accounted for 6.6% of total global exports and almost 30% of total global service exports (WTTC, 2017). The regional distribution of international tourism receipts and tourism export revenues is similar to that of tourist arrivals: from 2011 to 2014, northern Africa received on average 43% of tourism export revenues, followed by southern Africa (26%) and eastern Africa (20%) (United Nations, 2017: 17). However, when comparing export revenues with arrivals, there is an indication that southern Africa obtains more export revenues per arrival than northern Africa, indicating that an important share of the tourism product on offer in southern Africa may be more upmarket than in northern Africa (United Nations, 2017: 17). In fact, in 2014, 7 out of the top 10 most expensive lodges in the world were found in southern and eastern Africa (South African Tourism Company, 2014).

In Africa in 2016, travel and tourism directly supported over 8 million jobs (2.6% of total employment) and the total contribution (including indirect jobs) was over 20 million jobs (6.5% of total employment) (WTTC, 2017). According to the United Nations (2017) 1 in 14 jobs in Africa were generated by the tourism industry, on average, from 2011 to 2014. Mukhisa Kituyi, the secretary-general of the United Nations Conference on Trade and Development (UNCTAD) stated that 'For millions in Africa, tourism is a lifeline – its potential for driving transformative and inclusive growth must be harnessed' (United Nations, 2017). The scale of involvement of women in tourism in Africa is significant, with about 47% of hotel and restaurant employees being women (United Nations, 2017). The case studies in this volume also show a high percentage of women employed, though with differences between countries due often to cultural norms related to women being employed.

In 2016, travel and tourism investment in Africa was USD 28.5 billion (6.2% of total investment), with visitor exports of USD 40.7 billion (9.2% of total exports) generated. With respect to tourism related specifically to wildlife, according to the World Tourism Organization (2014), a typical wildlife watching tour involves on average a group of six people, lasts 10 days, has an average daily price per person of USD 433 and captures an additional USD 55 in out-of-pocket expenses per person, per day.

According to the United Nations (2017: 1) in order to better harness the potential of the tourism sector to contribute to inclusive growth, structural transformation and achievement of the SDGs, Africa should adopt policies that strengthen intersectoral linkages, boost intraregional tourism and promote peace. The United Nations (2017) report also found that tourism in Africa can be an engine for transformative and inclusive growth, as well as a complement to development strategies aimed at fostering economic diversification and structural transformation within the right policy context.

These figures highlight the important role of tourism to African economies, with predictions of increases to all these figures between 2017 and 2027 (WTTC, 2017). Understanding the role of the private sector in tourism in Africa, the focus of this book, is therefore important in terms of the long-term growth and sustainability of tourism in Africa. Epler Wood (2017) recently stressed that despite the enthusiasm around tourism's growth and increase in tourism volumes, it is important in terms of the long-term sustainability of tourism to ensure that tourism development takes into account potential negative impacts, economically, environmentally and socially, and that these should be taken into account in tourism planning from the beginning. This will also be discussed in this volume.

Along with wildlife tourism in conservation areas, a growing increase in demand for cultural tourism has been observed. Cultural tourism includes tourist visits to community villages and cultural experiences such as dancing, singing, food and other activities. A number of the case studies in this volume include some form of cultural tourism. Managing the potential negative impacts of this (see section 5.14) also needs to be taken into consideration.

## 2.3. Overview of Conservation in Africa

The original approach to conservation in Africa by colonialists and later governments was traditionally that of 'fortress conservation', which involved the exclusion of people as residents from declared PAs, the prevention of consumptive use and the minimisation of any other forms of human impact (Adams & Hulme, 2001).

Although there is currently some funding for PAs, mainly from international donors and national governments, these sources have failed to keep up with the expansion of PAs in recent years, reflecting both changing national and international development priorities and growing public sector budget constraints (Emerton, Bishop & Thomas, 2006). As discussed above, more and more, PA agencies do not have sufficient funds to support their conservation management (Buckley, 2003; Eagles, Romagosa, Buteau-Duitschaever, Havitz, Glover, & McCutcheon, 2012; Mitchell, Wooliscroft & Higham, 2013; Weaver & Lawton, 2017). As a consequence, there is increasing pressure for protected areas to enhance the value of revenue they obtain from private sources, and also to develop and diversify new sources of income (Watson, Dudley, Segan & Hockings, 2014). This has, in part, led to the introduction of different forms of tourism in a number of areas to generate income for PAs, including a range of different equity/partnership arrangements for tourism operations in conservation areas. Benefits, costs and risks from such arrangements vary depending on the agreements between the parties, and the extent of the impact on poverty reduction also varies with the chosen equity/partnership agreement. Researchers estimated in 2015 that PAs globally receive 8 billion visits a year, generating as much as USD 600 billion of tourism expenditure annually (Twining-Ward *et al.*, 2018). In contrast, less than USD 10 billion a year is spent on protecting these sites (Balmford, Green, Anderson, Beresford., Huang & Naidoo, 2015 in Twining-Ward *et al.*, 2018).

According to the International Union for Conservation of Nature (IUCN), 'a protected area is a clearly defined geographical space, recognised, dedicated and managed, through legal or other effective means, to achieve the long-term conservation of nature with associated ecosystem services and cultural values' (UNEP-WCMC and IUCN, 2016). PAs are essential for biodiversity conservation, vital to the cultures and livelihoods of indigenous peoples and local communities, and provide important ecosystems services as they deliver clean air and water, bring benefits to millions of people through tourism, and provide protection from climate change and natural disasters (UNEP-WCMC and IUCN, 2016).

According to the *Protected Planet report* (UNEP-WCMC and IUCN, 2016), ensuring a more sustainable future for people and the planet will require greater recognition of the important role that PAs play in underpinning sustainable development (Rylance, Snyman & Spenceley, 2017). There is also a need to strengthen communication of the benefits of PAs across all sectors of society to help demonstrate their economic and social values to existing and future generations (Aichi Biodiversity Target 1) (UNEP-WCMC and IUCN, 2016). Tourism can provide a means to offer value to society through the potential economic, environmental and social benefits which it can deliver.

Less than half of the world's 823 terrestrial ecoregions have at least 17% of their area in PAs and only one third of the 232 marine ecoregions have at least 10% of their area protected (Rylance *et al.*, 2017; UNEP-WCMC and IUCN, 2016). This means that less than 20% of key biodiversity areas (KBAs) are completely protected, and therefore further efforts are needed to expand PA systems to ensure that the global PA estate adequately covers areas important for biodiversity and the provision of ecosystem services to people (UNEP-WCMC and IUCN, 2016). In Africa, these figures are 16.97% for terrestrial land and 3.89% for marine areas (Protected Planet, 2018). One possible way to motivate for the expansion of PAs is to ensure that there is an economic value attached to their creation; tourism can assist in this regard and the private sector can play an important role in financing this.

Dudley (2008) noted that the land, water and natural resources in any protected area management category (i.e. from strict protection to allowed sustainable use) can be owned and/or directly managed by governmental agencies, NGOs, communities, indigenous peoples and private parties – alone or in combination. Where the community owns or has access to the land, Snyman (2013) and Lapeyre (2011) observed that many rural communities lack the necessary financial capital, business expertise and marketing channels to set up tourism operations, and then to manage and operate them. The level of community involvement will therefore vary and depends on the specific conditions of the equity arrangement; with a large amount of involvement occurring in community-based tourism (CBT), and limited, if any, in PPPs. There are some unique cases of public–private–community partnerships (such as the Makuleke contractual area in the Kruger National Park (KNP) in South Africa – see Case Study 30 and the Rocktail Camp Case Study 32 in this volume). Buckley (2010) gives an extensive overview of the role of private sector tourism in terms of conservation, highlighting the important role that private sector tourism can play in promoting biodiversity conservation. The focus of this volume is instead on the various partnership models available for private sector tourism in conservation areas in Africa, using case studies to highlight the different economic, social and environmental/conservation impacts that these different partnerships can, and do, have.

The contribution of private protected areas to a country's overall conservation objectives is something that is not well researched or understood. In part, this is due to their lack of inclusion in governments' international reporting mechanisms, such as to the Convention on Biological Diversity (CBD). In countries such as South Africa and Namibia, large tracts of land under conservation are privately owned. In other countries, private sector companies are also responsible for the protection and conservation of large tracts of land, which would potentially be utilised for other less sustainable purposes, were the private sector not managing and operating on the land. The importance of the role of the private sector in conservation, often through the utilisation of tourism as a funding mechanism, needs to be taken more seriously, with more comparable data collected related to the contribution, which is substantial. In Case Study 2, an example is shown of non-profit private sector conservation, which is another example of private sector conservation which is not well documented. The African Parks (AP) (Box 20) example is another example of private sector non-profit conservation.

In 2016, The Long Run Initiative (a non-governmental organisation – NGO – that supports private sector tourism in conservation areas, see Box 1 for more information) members collectively helped to protect more than 5.6 million acres of nature, in 27 countries, across five continents, touching the lives of over half a million people, directly supporting 207,162 community members, employing 3,800 people and investing over

**Box 1.** The Long Run Initiative

The Long Run Initiative, an NGO whose vision is that of a world in which business, nature and people are harmoniously working together for a sustainable future, brings together private sector tourism businesses working in conservation areas. In order to pursue its vision it seeks to 'support, connect and inspire nature-based business to excel in following the highest standards of sustainability encompassing Conservation, Community, Culture and Commerce (4Cs) and to collectively influence others to take up best practices for a sustainable future worldwide' (The Long Run, 2017).

USD 10 million in conservation, community and culture (The Long Run, 2017). Further research related to the contribution of private sector tourism to conservation should be a focus in the years to come in order to maximise the benefits and provide evidence to gain political and public support.

## 2.4. Overview of Tourism in Conservation Areas

Due to the extensive and unique diversity of natural resources in Africa, a large amount of tourism on the continent is in some way nature-based. In 2015, PAs were estimated to receive 8 billion visits a year, and these visits generated as much as USD 600 billion annually in tourism expenditure (Balmford *et al.*, 2015). Also, in 2015, a survey by the UNWTO estimated that 14 African countries generated an estimated USD 142 million in PA entrance fees (UNWTO, 2015). Reviewing visitor trends at 280 natural PAs in 20 countries, one study established that visitation is increasing at about 4% per year (Balmford, Beresford, Green, Naidoo, Walpole, & Manica 2009). More specifically, the same UNWTO survey found that 80% of trips sold by tour operators to Africa were for wildlife watching – making it the most important tourism segment in the region (UNWTO, 2015). This growth and scale of tourism in PAs provides numerous opportunities but brings with it a number of associated challenges (see Table 5).

Tourism has the potential to contribute directly to PAs as a global conservation strategy, and to the Aichi Biodiversity Targets adopted under the CBD that relate to conservation (Targets 11 and 12), community development (Target 18) and public awareness (Target 1) (CBD, 2010). Successful tourism in conservation areas requires the ability to develop and market tourism products based on what the conservation area has to offer, and the ability to maintain the quality of these areas for ongoing future use (Spenceley *et al.*, 2017a). The ability of a conservation area to manage tourism depends on the implementation of effective management strategies, the scale of demand for visits to the site, the staff and resources available for management of tourism and the legal and political environment covering nature protection in the country in which it is located (Font, Cochrane & Tapper, 2004). Long-term sustainability is, therefore, key. To encourage successful tourism it can, in some cases, be more efficient for the protected/conservation area to outsource tourism concessions to other stakeholders such as the private sector. In some cases it is financially advantageous for the PA to function directly as a tourism business though this is not often an option used in Africa (e.g. SANParks as a parastatal operates tourism in its parks and has a tourism unit). All organisations that create products, such as tourism experiences, must decide on the appropriate service delivery mechanism and partnership model. Tourism concessions in PAs and other conservation areas are part of a much larger system of tourism user fees (TUFs) for permitted uses in PAs, which allow each PA to raise revenues and meet goals of making the PA accessible to visitors with quality services, while meeting social and environmental objectives (Emerton *et al.*, 2006; Epler Wood, 2010; Leung *et al.*, 2018; Spenceley, Kohl, McArthur, Myles, Notarianni, Paleczny, Pickering & Worboys, 2015; Spenceley *et al.*, 2017b).

Private sector or other stakeholders' capacity to generate revenues from tourism in conservation areas will depend on their ability to attract tourists to the product. This will in turn depend on the park's location, facilities, access and the feasibility of offering services that visitors are willing to pay for which cover more than the cost of operations (Spenceley *et al.*, 2017a). The tourism potential of any conservation area

**Table 5.** Opportunities and challenges for managing private sector tourism in conservation areas.

| Opportunities | Challenges |
|---|---|
| Building a constituency of support for the conservation of nature and culture by providing outstanding and interpreted experiences that communicate the many values of conservation. Private sector tourism concessions can enhance visitor and education outcomes through good interpretation and by providing a quality visitor experience. | Conservation areas simply become another 'commodity' or resource to be exploited by an industry that is more interested in profits, access and providing new experiences than supporting conservation. This can become a threat to sustainability. |
| Through using the private sector to operate tourism in conservation areas, can increase the number of tourism products and services due to the availability of capital and related skills required to operate these, as well as allowing conservation staff to focus on their core function. Funding from government and other sources can be used for conservation activities rather than tourism activities. | Tourism demand issues because the tourism industry is highly competitive and can be seasonal and volatile. |
| Additional funding through the fees and rentals paid by the private sector contribute to funding protected areas. | This fee income is substantially less than if the services were provided directly by the protected area staff. |
| Justifying political support and better funding for conservation by recognising the importance of conservation-based tourism to local and regional economies. | The importance of conservation-based tourism leads to political support for excessive development in, or around, conservation areas. |
| Ameliorate tourism impacts through sensitive infrastructure planning, visitor impact mitigation techniques and promotion of positive impacts. | Negative impacts on the environment such as pollution (e.g. waste disposal, carbon emissions), unsustainable resource use (e.g. water) and damage to sensitive areas (e.g. through poorly developed or located infrastructure). |
| Improving the social and cultural impacts of tourism by promoting and conserving their cultural attractions, showcasing local culture (e.g. stories, craft, design, music and food), providing appropriate interpretive services and educational opportunities. | Negative impacts on local people (e.g. commodification of culture, disruption of traditional life, crime, overcrowding, displacement of local communities to accommodate tourism development, pressures caused by temporal fluctuations in levels of visitation); high cost of living and inflation resulting from tourism. |
| Stimulating local economic linkages and multipliers through local ownership of/partnerships in tourism assets, management of tourism businesses, employment, alternative livelihoods and entrepreneurship in the tourism supply chain (e.g. guiding, craft, food and beverages, and transport). | Lack of economic linkages, due to a lack of information, opportunity, access to finance, adequate policies or consistency. In some developing countries, a lack of basic education can also be a challenge. |

Source: adapted from Leung, Spenceley, Hvengaard and Buckley (2018) and Spenceley *et al.* (2017a)

depends on a variety of factors, including market demand, proximity to other popular tourism destinations, marketing and the presence of local tourism businesses and infrastructure (e.g. accommodation, catering, guiding) (Font *et al.*, 2004). In order for tourism and the associated conservation areas to be sustainable, they need to add value and demonstrate this value to stakeholders, especially local communities living in and around these areas.

For a PA to function as a tourism business, providing tourism services directly without outside contractors, the area must have the appropriate legal and policy structures. Many protected areas utilise private sector contractors because the law does not provide the park with business functions, such as the ability to set prices and retain income.

## 2.5. Role of the Private Sector

The International Finance Corporation (IFC, 2012) highlights the important role of the private sector in the growth and development of Africa, whether in creating jobs, improving infrastructure, expanding education and health care or other essential areas. According to the World Bank (Christie *et al.*, 2014), although the capital from the private sector gives value to natural and cultural assets, tourism cannot operate successfully without considerable government support: government must provide supporting infrastructure as well as the appropriate policies and institutions to create an enabling environment for private investment.

The lack of availability of sufficiently long-term local financing for tourism products and services constrains the growth of tourism in Africa (Christie *et al.*, 2014). Two consequences of a lack of domestic capital markets are: 1) foreign private investment can dominate, or 2) tourism products and services may be of a low quality, reducing destination competitiveness (Christie *et al.*, 2014). An exception to this is in Mauritius, where the success of the sugar and textile industries has allowed locals to reinvest profits in tourism (Christie *et al.*, 2014). Overcoming the challenge of exclusively foreign investment can be done through the establishment of partnerships with local communities, NGOs, companies and others. For example, the Bisate Lodge case study in this volume is an example of a foreign tourism company partnering with a local company.

An alternative view is that PA authorities regard conservation as their primary task and core competence and therefore do not (or cannot) engage in tourism. Another issue to consider is that PA revenues may not be 'ring-fenced'; instead they often need to be returned to the central fiscus whereas PA costs have to be met from the PA budget (e.g. in Mozambique and Tanzania – see Spenceley, Rylance & Laiser, 2017). It therefore makes sense to shift some costs onto the private sector, even if it means that the PA's apparent revenue is reduced by the diversion of potential visitors to the private operation. The PA will, in most cases, still receive a fee or percentage of the revenue, but not have to bear the costs (see case study examples in this volume).

The private sector can also play a role in terms of enabling knowledge exchange and the centralisation of some functions through the establishment of professional organisations, such as hotel owners or transport associations (Christie *et al.*, 2014). The private sector often has capital available for the development of new tourism ventures, as well as marketing capabilities, greater advertising opportunities, economies of scale and financial management skills.

The private sector may choose, either voluntarily or because of contractual obligations, to engage in a partnership with a community for a variety of reasons. Spenceley (2003) lists a number of reasons over and above the pure profit motive: obligations to provide benefits to rural communities through concession arrangements; the diversification of commercial activities; corporate social responsibility (CSR) and image; or market advantage. Snyman (2013) notes that successful partnerships between communities and the private sector are more likely to succeed if communities have, or establish, strong institutional structures and decision-making processes which are equitable, accountable and transparent. Ashley and Roe (2002) emphasise that when engaging with communities the private sector does, however, endure certain costs that go beyond simple financial costs to include problems of time, uncertainty and risk. Armstrong (2012) stresses that if engagements with communities are to be successful, the private sector operator needs to be ethically responsible and prepared to make a long-term commitment to the community and its development. It also takes time to build relationships and trust with a local community; both are needed to maintain relations and ensure long-term support. The private sector can certainly play an important role in initiating the development of new community institutions, facilitating and financing projects, assisting with the management of community projects and training communities to manage them independently. This can be done by the private sector transferring skills to local communities through in-house training programmes, internships and mentorships, as well as sponsoring formal training courses.

The private sector, through promotion of its own products and services, can assist in promoting a destination (e.g. the Okavango Delta) or a country (e.g. Botswana) and thereby increase overall tourism to these areas, benefiting numerous other stakeholders. Marketing, sales and advertising in the international market can be costly and the private sector's ability to invest in these can benefit numerous other businesses, communities and, sometimes, destinations and governments.

Private sector tourism is often seen as a tool to provide skills training and development to unskilled community members. One objective of private sector investment in education and training of staff is to differentiate one tourism operation from others in the area as service quality is often an outstanding feature in the tourism market (Snyman, 2013). Training and uplifting staff is also intended to increase job satisfaction and therefore staff retention, thereby lowering overall training costs and improving service levels. Partnerships which include management contracts can stipulate that the private sector provides technical assistance and transfers knowledge to local investors who do have capital but not the expertise to invest in tourism (Christie *et al.*, 2014).

There are very few examples in Africa, apart from South African National Parks (SANParks) and the iSimangaliso Wetland Park Authority, where government or parastatals have been shown to successfully implement, manage and operate tourism in conservation areas (Varghese, 2008). Largely due to the lack of the necessary commercial focus to generate sufficient revenues from natural resources, African governments and state conservation departments have been turning to the private sector to assist with the management and maintenance of conservation areas (Spenceley, 2003). The private sector appears to be better placed to identify opportunities, realise the potential of a destination, create tourism circuits, and drive forward product development and marketing of a destination and/or product. It also has the potential to adopt a range of highly effective strategies for the benefit of communities and their livelihoods (Simpson, 2008, and case study examples in this volume).

## 2.6. Private Sector Engagement with Various Stakeholders

Tourism is, however, a complex sector, with multiple stakeholders and dependent on numerous factors, both endogenous and exogenous. Stakeholders include government, the private sector, communities, NGOs, academia and national and international tourists who can determine the sustainability and success of tourism in a country. Their differing roles depend on the particular form of tourism and the level of participation required. It is important from the beginning of a tourism development to identify all relevant stakeholders and to rate them in terms of importance to the development and need to engage them in the various development, operational, management and monitoring phases. As shown in many of the case study examples in this volume, cooperation and the involvement of all stakeholders from the beginning of a tourism development project, and throughout the operation and management of it, is important to its long-term success (see Snyman, 2013; Walpole & Goodwin, 2000). This includes an agreed vision, strategy and objectives relating to tourism in the area, including achievable environmental, social and economic objectives. Defining and agreeing on all stakeholders' respective roles and responsibilities in partnerships is also crucial to success, as is defining benefit distribution plans and the structure of benefits (i.e. in kind, cash, individual, or communal). In terms of stakeholder participation, there are numerous difficulties associated with balancing all stakeholders' expectations to achieve a project that is socially and environmentally balanced, and also produces a profit (economically sustainable) (Snyman, 2013). Such difficulties are bound to lead to tensions that provoke conflicts between stakeholders. Conflict management and mitigation should, therefore, be included in partnership agreements.

The relationships between the private sector and various other stakeholders differs depending on the particular situation, but below is a summary of some of the main ways that they engage (this section is adapted from Snyman, 2013) (see Table 6, below).

### 2.6.1. Government

Government is important as a provider of the infrastructure and institutions necessary to ensure private sector investment and commitment, as well as local support. It can create the appropriate conditions for private sector investment in tourism and local supply chains by providing support and incentivising investment.

There are a number of different strategies for governments to engage in that can help to stimulate micro-enterprise, promote more business linkages and increase the number of benefits reaching the poor (see Ashley, 2006; de Boer, van Dijk & Tarimo, 2011; DFID, 1999; Tewes-Gradl, van Gaalen & Pirzer, 2014; Vedeld, Jumane, Wapalila & Songorwa, 2012). Examples of governments stimulating local micro-enterprise are the construction of craft markets close to tourism centres, skills training and development related to tourism products and facilitating engagement between local communities and the private sector.

Transparency and accountability in any government or other governing institutions involved in tourism are important in establishing the trust and support of all stakeholders. Transparency will reduce the openings for corruption and abuse of power. It is also important for government to have a multi-sectoral approach to tourism, as policies in one department may impact on other departments. For example, in the Republic of Congo changes to tourist visa processes made it difficult for tourists to get visas, which impacted on travel to the country. Unavoidably, local government support is important to the

**Table 6.** Potential impact of various stakeholders on tourism partnerships.

| | Private sector | Government | Communities | NGOs | Academia |
|---|---|---|---|---|---|
| Opportunities and willingness to form partnerships | High | Moderate, though increasing | High | Moderate, though increasing | None |
| Likelihood of contributing to conservation | Moderate, though increasing | High | Moderate | High | Low |
| Philanthropy | High | Low | Low | High | Indirect - monitoring |
| Capacity-building; skills training | High | Moderate | Low | High | Low |
| Research | Moderate | Moderate | Low | Moderate | High |
| Lobbying to government | Moderate | High | Moderate | Moderate | Low |
| Providing land and resources | High | High | High | Moderate | None |
| Providing capital | High | Moderate | Low | Moderate | None |
| Boosting local economies, linkages and multipliers | High | Moderate | High | High | Low |
| Reporting | Moderate | Low | Low | Low | High |
| Sustainability | Moderate | Moderate | Low | Moderate | N/A |
| Quality products and services | High | Moderate | Low | Moderate | None |
| Access to tourism markets | High | Low | Low | Low | None |
| Tourism marketing skills | High | Low | Low | Low | None |

long-term success of tourism in sub-Saharan Africa, but often its lack of effectiveness is due to a lack of capacity and resources.

### 2.6.2. NGOs and academia

There are numerous NGOs working in rural areas in southern Africa, such as Integrated Rural Development and Nature Conservation (IRDNC), the Namibian Association of Community Support Organisations (NACSO), the Save the Rhino Trust (SRT), the World Wide Fund for Nature (WWF), the African Safari Foundation (ASF), Conservation International (CI), the African Wildlife Foundation (AWF), African Parks (AP), The Long Run Initiative, and others.

These NGOs are involved in various fields including capacity-building, conservation, tourism, education and consultancy. The common sense of NGO involvement suggests the importance of their role in community/tourism partnerships, through focusing on empowerment and building local capacity by means of training, education, organisational support and networking, but there is a risk of unmet expectations. Community expectations raised to unrealistic levels by NGOs and thus negatively impacting on relationships with the private sector can damage relationships and have negative impacts on tourism.

NGOs can play a role in terms of providing credit (see Box 16 on Conservation Capital in this volume) and non-financial services to micro-enterprises (DFID, 1999), as well as facilitating the flow of information to communities. They can also build capacity, give advice and provide access to legal and other skills. It is important that NGOs ensure that projects are in line with community needs, involve some level of community empowerment and are not merely handouts.

Academic researchers can play an important role as providers of data and information to decision-makers trying to ensure the sustainability of tourism developments and engagements with local communities. It is important, however, that researchers are respectful towards communities, their culture, wishes and desires and that they do not unnecessarily impose themselves on local communities or use ill-conceived research questions that influence community views and cause discontent. EplerWood International (2004) highlights the role of local research institutions who partner with local businesses and build the capacity of students and professionals to deliver cost-effective services to tourism.

### 2.6.3. Communities

Tourism can be a catalyst for community development and benefits to members of rural communities by stemming rural–urban migration. Tourism can stimulate investments in infrastructure and livelihood opportunities in rural areas while increasing the demand for agricultural and artisan goods. It also employs and empowers women and provides an economic incentive for conservation for communities living with wildlife (World Bank Group, 2017). The role of communities and community members in tourism can be varied depending on community capacity, access to assets, land, skills, opportunities and their desire to be involved. Communities can form both formal and informal partnerships with governments, NGOs and the private sector. Land tenure and security are important factors in empowering local communities in their engagement with the private sector, as is business and tourism knowledge and capacity. Formal partnerships include through joint ventures, employment and other partnership models. Informal partnerships can be as suppliers of goods and services (these can also be formal), tourism philanthropy (discussed in more detail in 2.7.2.5 in this volume) and skills training and development. Examples of both formal and informal partnerships are included in the case study examples.

Cultural tourism, offered in many of the case study examples, is another way in which communities can engage in tourism. Cultural tourism can, however, result in social impacts, both positive and negative. Telfer and Sharpley (2008: 195) distinguish between social and cultural impacts. They define social impacts as the more immediate effects of tourism on local people and their lifestyles, and cultural impacts as longer-term changes occurring in the context of social values, attitudes and behaviours. Social changes are not necessarily always negative, as some local practices may themselves have been problematic. Potential positive sociocultural impacts from tourism can include building confidence, self-esteem and pride in stakeholders, especially community members. Tourists may internalise local fashions in art, music or clothing, encouraging awareness of other cultures (Telfer & Sharpley, 2008). They can also enhance cultural aspects of an area through the promotion of cultural activities and values and may lessen the out-migration of youth to urban areas (Snyman, 2012b). Potential negative social impacts which need to be borne in mind include: changes in value systems and new forms of social hierarchy which can cause conflict (Moscardo, 2008); increased pressure on health and education facilities if population in the area increases (Frechtling, 1994); fragmentation of culture through crime, prostitution and erosion of traditions (Telfer & Sharpley, 2008); and commoditisation of culture (Eagles, McCool & Haynes, 2002). The issue of choice is central to the tourism debate. It is important therefore to differentiate between constraints on land use imposed on communities, and those entered into voluntarily (Snyman, 2013). An observation by Snyman (2013) and earlier made by Eagles *et al.* (2002) is that the negative impacts of tourism tend to be more common when communities are not given choices (i.e. when they have no control over their involvement in the tourism activities – this can be mitigated when local communities are involved in the planning and management of tourism in their area).

Stakeholder engagement in partnerships with the private sector is essential to the long-term success of these partnerships. The building of trust between partners takes time and effort, but can impact greatly on the success of a partnership and, therefore, is a worthy investment. The private sector will need to invest time and energy in building these partnerships and needs to account for this in project planning.

Bramwell and Lane (2000) examined tourism partnerships that bring together a range of parties to develop tourism policies and planning (as opposed to tourism operations focused on in this volume), particularly focused on the potential for partnerships involved in tourism planning to contribute to the wider objectives of sustainable development. A key reason for the growing interest in partnerships in tourism development is the belief that tourist destinations and organisations will be able to gain a competitive advantage by bringing together the knowledge, expertise, capital and other resources of several stakeholders (Kotler *et al.*, 1993 in Bramwell and Lane, 2000).

## 2.7. Potential Benefits to be Derived from Private Sector Tourism in Africa

The potential benefits of private sector tourism in conservation areas found in the case study examples and other literature include, but are not limited to, economic (e.g. lease fees, partnerships, infrastructure development), sociocultural (e.g. employment, skills development, empowerment, local value chain linkages, philanthropy) and environmental (e.g. conservation activities, water conservation, use of renewable energy). Below is a discussion of these based on the literature, with best practices from the case study examples.

### 2.7.1. Economic benefits

Economic benefits include lease fee payments, income received from partnerships and various infrastructure developments related to tourism.

#### *2.7.1.1. Lease fees*

The private sector's payment of lease fees for operating in community and government areas can contribute substantially to local economic development. If lease fees are paid to a government, PA authority or national institution, they can benefit local communities through the investment of this income in infrastructure and development projects in the area (e.g. the building of schools, roads or clinics). The same applies if lease fees are paid to a communal institution that could choose either to invest in a communal project, such as a school or borehole, or pay out individual/household dividends which would directly impact on household income. The Torra Conservancy in Namibia has successfully made use of both individual and communal benefit distribution (see Snyman, 2012a, and Case Study 21 in this volume). Institutions do, however, need to be transparent and accountable for benefits to be equitably distributed. It is important to connect tourism benefits with the conservation area, in order for the value to be seen. During discussions in the villages in the panhandle of the Okavango Delta in Botswana, many respondents in Snyman (2014) mentioned that they were unaware of the lease fees paid by the private sector operator, Wilderness Safaris (WS) to the Community Trust representing them (see Case Study 29 in this volume, as well as the Anvil Bay Lodge Case Study 19). In such cases, the link between tourism benefits and conservation and the related tourism was broken and led to misplaced discontent with the private sector partner.

While Waylen, McGowan, Pawi Study Group and Milner-Gulland (2009) suggested that existing evidence does not clearly support the assumption that income from tourism changes local awareness and attitudes, they do indicate that further research is required. It was, however, observed during Snyman's (2013) research that the gap between the expectation and the perceived benefits delivered was significant, with unrealistic expectations being created early on in the project. The one important implication is that managing public relations may be more important than actual benefit delivery in determining the long-term viability of private sector tourism operator/community relations. This is further corroborated by Franks, Booker and Roe (2018) who concluded that giving more attention to enhancing equity, rather than directly improving livelihoods, could lead to greater contributions of PAs to human well-being, as well as better conservation.

#### *2.7.1.2. Joint ventures and other partnerships*

Joint ventures (JVs) between the private sector and local communities can promote local socioeconomic development through profit-sharing, employment, skills training and development, as well as through the empowerment of local communities to engage in business and acquire new skills (see Ashley & Jones, 2001, Lapeyre, 2011; Snyman, 2012a; Torres, Skillicorn & Nelson, 2011). The management of expectations and regular communication between stakeholders is important to the success of a JV. JVs bring together the community and its natural resources, and the private sector and its business acumen, to form a partnership which can be mutually beneficial (see Chapter 4 for more information). Kepe, Wynberg and Ellis (2005) did, however, find potential problems with JVs. These included divergent agendas of different parties, unclear roles and responsibilities of stakeholders, a lack of transparency and accountability, insufficient communication between stakeholders, unequal power distribution and lack of capacity in communities.

#### *2.7.1.3. Infrastructure development*

Infrastructural developments can have a profound impact in remote rural areas. They can be provided directly by the tourism operator, developed or upgraded by government specifically for tourism or can result from donations made by guests to philanthropic projects (see section 3.6. Voluntary payments in this volume). Infrastructure developments such as power, roads and communications can have a powerful influence on people's mobility and the choices available to them, allowing them to diversify their livelihoods and reduce the risks they face.

### 2.7.2. Social benefits

Social benefits include, among others, benefits related to formal and informal employment, skills training and development, local empowerment related to tourism development, local business linkages to entrepreneurs and small businesses resulting in local economic multipliers, and social upliftment initiatives supported by tourism philanthropy.

#### *2.7.2.1. Employment opportunities*

Employment in private sector tourism operations is one of its most important contributions to local socioeconomic development and is highlighted in all the case studies. The direct benefit of wages and salaries to household welfare goes beyond their contribution to incomes; it also allows investment in productive assets and gives tourism staff future security as well as the opportunity to diversify their livelihoods (Snyman, 2013).

Over and above the direct benefit of wages, tourism employment gives people the opportunity to develop new skills through training, allowing them to assume more control over their own development and to feel more confident in their abilities. This can empower people to initiate development or business projects for themselves, their households and their communities.

The dependency ratio found by Snyman (2013) illustrates the conduit through which wages earned by a worker translate into welfare impacts for others in remote, rural areas; on average, across six research countries (Botswana, Malawi, Namibia, South Africa, Zambia and Zimbabwe) in her study each staff member was supporting seven people.

Employment opportunities are, however, limited by the size of the operation and their impacts are affected by the number of different households employed. Having a number of staff members employed from the same family narrows employment benefits, and it would be useful to ensure hiring practices extend employment across as many households as possible (Snyman, 2013). Tourism has the ability to employ unskilled labour as well as a high proportion of women – this creates job opportunities for previously excluded people and is important in terms of equitable socioeconomic development in remote areas ('inclusive growth').

Indirect employment is also important: it results from lodges using local suppliers of goods and services, lodge staff attending schools and clinics in the area, and lodge staff spending their wages at local stores in the villages. These indirect and induced impacts can provide extensive benefits and result in tourism being more inclusive.

#### *2.7.2.2. Skills training, development and capacity-building*

Tourism is often a 'first job' for many workers. This provides them with: a) skills training and development and b) an employment history which improves their chances of getting work elsewhere if they have to leave (Snyman, 2013). Skills training and development from tourism employment or through private sector/community business partnerships can build capacity in communities (illustrated in most case study examples in this volume). Ensuring that individuals have a variety of transferable skills (such as business management skills, linguistic skills) can allow them to take advantage of opportunities in different sectors as well and, therefore, overcome the vulnerability often associated with tourism employment due to its seasonal nature (United Nations, 2017).

#### *2.7.2.3. Local empowerment*

In order to ensure the long-term success of tourism and conservation it is important that communities are empowered through them. This requires both business education and participation in decision-making processes. Tourism employment empowers local individuals by giving them the security of a permanent household income source and, frequently, new skills. Personal and community empowerment can also result from JV agreements, business partnerships, the support of local entrepreneurs and exposure to other cultures. These factors have been emphasised in Snyman and Spenceley (2012).

#### *2.7.2.4. Local linkages/value chains: suppliers of goods and services*

Tourism has the potential to offer numerous local linkages that can extend its impact beyond direct employment. The role of linkages is important in that they promote the creation of jobs and economic opportunities which, in turn, foster diversification into higher value activities and also distribute incomes more broadly (United Nations, 2017). Linkages between tourism and other productive sectors and market segments also have the potential to spur local entrepreneurship through new business opportunities (United Nations, 2017). The use of local carpenters, builders, thatchers and other technicians during construction and renovation of lodges can spread benefits further and assist in the establishment of micro-, small- and medium-sized enterprises. Ongoing maintenance of lodges is a further way to spread benefits over a longer period. Diversification into other productive sectors and activities can also assist in reducing the vulnerabilities of economies to external market dynamics while boosting productivity and increasing competitiveness (United Nations, 2017).

Over and above stimulating employment and business opportunities for local suppliers and entrepreneurs, linkages can generate multiplier effects in other economic sectors and in communities in which tourism-related activities are undertaken (Rylance and Spenceley, 2016, 2017; Snyman, 2017a; United Nations, 2017). Economic opportunities in rural areas created in the tourism sector can contribute to poverty reduction, including among women and youth, and thereby play a role in fostering social inclusion while promoting rural development, and possibly helping to stem rural–urban migration (United Nations, 2017: 45). This is specifically discussed in the context of JVs in Namibia in this volume.

Low levels of quality and variety of goods and services available, as well as numerous foreign handicraft imitations, can constrain the development of linkages (United Nations, 2017). It follows that an important part of the process is to ascertain the skills and goods available in local communities and to develop local linkages based on these. A common obstacle to broadening linkages around tourism operations is the inadequacy of skills, leaving communities unable to provide the required goods and services and unaware of tourist demands and therefore the types of goods and services to provide. This problem has been widely discussed (see e.g. Epler-Wood International, 2004; Ogutu, 2002; Rogerson, 2006; Rylance & Spenceley, 2016, 2017). Mitchell and Ashley (2010) stress the need for a multi-faceted approach to promote and increase linkages. NGOs and local government can play an important role in training and capacity-building to ensure the level of delivery and content meet the private sector tourism operators' requirements. The benefits need not be unidirectional – private sector tourism operators can benefit from local linkages through reduced transport costs, improved supply logistics and fresher produce in the case of foodstuffs (Snyman, 2013). Such linkages can also improve relationships with community neighbours as greater benefits from tourism are received.

The United Nations (2017: 76) highlights the following actions to promote linkages: 1) integrate policies on local sourcing with strategies to comply with international standards; 2) support the development of infrastructure; 3) encourage joint ventures; and 4) boost services exports.

#### *2.7.2.5. Philanthropy/donations*

Tourism can contribute to local socioeconomic development through philanthropic donations either from the tourism operator themselves or from guests who visit their operation. Donations to schools, clinics, health services and various other development projects can enhance social welfare and improve local socioeconomic conditions for communities (see Dixey, 2008; Goodwin, 2008; Honey, 2008; Scheyvens, 2009; Snyman, 2017b). A number of examples are illustrated in the case studies in this volume.

### 2.7.3. Environmental benefits

Environmental benefits relate to the potential positive impacts that tourism can have on biodiversity, either directly or indirectly. These are outlined below.

#### *2.7.3.1. Biodiversity conservation*

Revenues generated, and employment provided, by tourism can provide incentives to support the conservation of tourism resources (United Nations, 2017). A number of the case studies in this volume also illustrate direct involvement of the private sector in conservation initiatives through investments, philanthropy and raising awareness.

#### *2.7.3.2. Environmental management*

PA management plans usually provide the planning context and the environmental standards that the private sector must adhere to. Lease and concession contracts also include monitoring and reporting requirements and the need for audit processes. Environmental management systems, and certification programmes, can be used by tourism enterprises to design internal processes to minimise negative environmental impacts. Areas addressed often relate to responsible waste disposal, water conservation, use of renewable energy and carbon-offsets where fossil fuels are used.

The above points illustrate private sector tourism's important role in local socioeconomic development, increasing incomes and reducing local poverty in remote, rural areas; it is, however, not a panacea as the next section reveals.

## 2.8. Potential Challenges Associated with Private Sector Investment

Potential challenges which may arise from encouraging private sector tourism investment in conservation areas in Africa include the following.

**1.** The private sector operator may not have the same conservation incentives as the conservation or PA authority and may, therefore, not manage their operations in the most sustainable way or with biodiversity conservation as the main objective. In order to mitigate this, contracts may stipulate sustainability criteria and obligations which have to be met (Spenceley *et al.*, 2017b).

**2.** The conservation or PA authority may receive less income than they would if they managed the tourism operations themselves, though their costs will also be reduced and they will have less capital investment.

**3.** Private sector operators with a profit motive may run an operation which has negative impacts on communities and the environment which are difficult to monitor and mitigate.

**4.** The tourism industry is highly competitive; tourism can be seasonal and volatile, impacted by political, natural, economic and health issues (Spenceley *et al.*, 2017b).

**5.** A non-supportive, unclear legal framework will discourage private sector investors (Spenceley *et al.*, 2017b) or allow them to abuse existing systems and processes to the detriment of the community, environment or both.

**6.** A lack of capacity and tourism skills of conservation/PA staff to manage concessions and work with the private sector can hinder progress and lead to future conflict.

**7.** A private sector tourism operation which does not make a profit may close down, resulting in a loss of employment and a loss of income to the conservation area and/or communities.

## 2.9. Potential Challenges for the Private Sector

Although governments, communities and NGOs often appear to have negative perceptions of the private sector and its involvement in tourism in conservation areas, there are also a number of challenges which the private sector faces when engaging with governments, communities and other stakeholders in relation to the development of their tourism business. Some of these observed in the case study examples and other literature are included below (Spenceley *et al.*, 2015; Twining-Ward, 2009).

**1.** Delays in contracting, the acceptance of environmental impact assessments (EIAs), the issuing of permits/licences/concessions and other related delays in progressing the tourism operation and opening for business. The availability of capital frequently has a time limit and delaying the investment of capital can result in large financial losses for an investment, due to resulting interest payments on loans.

**2.** Unsupportive policy and legislation can hinder business development and progress. For example, requiring visas to be issued prior to arrival in a country can result in tourists being discouraged from travelling to a particular country.

**3.** Institutional issues such as excessive 'red tape', lack of flexibility, lack of understanding of the tourism market and its needs, and lack of capacity to engage with the private sector.

**4.** Access: an inability of tourists to easily access tourism products can severely impact on a private sector operation. This includes inadequate flight networks, which are not regular and at suitable times, poor road infrastructure and security issues.

**5.** A lack of tourism routes/circuits can limit tourism numbers as it can be expensive for a tourist to travel to a remote area to visit one tourism lodge. There needs to be sufficient other tourism attractions/operations in the area to allow a tourist to visit a number of places on their trip, to make the expense of getting there worth it.

**6.** Political, health and safety issues: any negative political or health perceptions of a country/area may inhibit people from travelling to a specific country/area. The need to have good governance, security and stability is important for the long-term success of tourism in conservation areas.

**7.** A lack of capacity in local communities surrounding conservation areas can make it difficult for the private sector to hire locally or to procure local goods and services, limiting the inclusiveness of tourism.

**8.** Inter- and intra-community conflict can result in issues which negatively impact on the tourism business.

**9.** Poaching and poor conservation practices of the conservation authority can result in a negative impact on the tourism product, which will impact negatively on the tourism business.

Ideally, private sector tourism in conservation areas requires a great product (which requires good conservation practices), good governance, supportive institutions, suitable infrastructure (e.g. roads, communications and services), adequate capacity, supportive access and tourism circuits.

The remainder of this book describes the various private sector partnership model options for tourism lodges in conservation areas, including case study examples to illustrate the various models, to provide data in order to understand the models and to highlight challenges, successes and lessons learned. The book ends with a general overview of the cases reviewed, as well as using extensive practical experience of the authors, to highlight some best practices in terms of private sector tourism in conservation areas in Africa.

While we have attempted to gather a diverse array of tourism accommodation case studies and to cover as many partnership models as possible, we do not claim that the book covers all alternatives and there are certainly more examples out there. We do, however, hope that the examples presented here provide learning and best practice for many situations and also hope they will guide the way to new areas of research and potential partnership options and greater long-term sustainability of tourism in conservation areas.

Through the analysis in this volume, our aim is to advance policy and support institutions by advising on the diversity of private sector tourism partnerships available and the possibility of growth, development and improvement in them. The book uses rigorous academic inquiry into private sector partnerships but also looks, through numerous case studies, at real-life examples and draws on the extensive practical experience of the authors and other colleagues who provided input and advice.

Although focused largely on sub-Saharan African case studies and examples, many of the examples in this book can be widely applied and used across the globe, in many different situations. We hope that the analysis provided will allow stakeholders to be creative in their development of tourism partnerships in conservation areas, allow more stakeholders to benefit and conservation to thrive, and contribute to local socioeconomic development and local community upliftment and empowerment.

Much has been written on the various impacts of tourism, including economic, environmental and social impacts, and direct, indirect and induced impacts, including both positive and negative aspects of these impacts. Accurately interpreting these impacts and the related statistics tends to be challenging; statistics on the economic impacts of tourism are even more difficult to interpret because of the potential direct, indirect and induced impacts that may result and the difficulty in accurately measuring all of these and ensuring that they are all accounted for. Tourism Satellite Accounts are one way of accounting for the broader impacts of tourism and a number of countries in sub-Saharan Africa (e.g. Botswana, Kenya, South Africa) have been developing these to provide a broader understanding of tourism's impact on the economy.

Tourism is often lauded for the potential local linkages it provides. Some of the case studies presented provide detailed information on local linkages, but again the induced impacts of these are generally not measured and result in a potential underestimation of the local impacts of tourism. Snyman (2017a) examined ecotourism staff (who work in conservation areas in Africa) expenditure patterns in six southern African countries and the potential local economic impact of these in remote, rural villages. She found that there was a strong, positive wide-reaching impact, illustrating the broader impacts of tourism employment beyond simply those employed. The impacts beyond this first round of spending are, however, something that has not been researched and would provide valuable information on how to extend tourism's local impacts even further.

Many of the case studies in this book rely on information supplied by private sector tourism lodge owners or managers and this could not always be audited or personally verified by the authors. Due to the confidentiality often associated with lease fees, turnover, staff wages and other financial figures, data was often provided in an aggregated form, which made per annum calculations less accurate. The data did, however, provide averages and examples of different partnerships, allowing the authors to draw reasoned conclusions to include in the analysis and best practices. It must also be borne in mind that private sector tourism, especially the high-end market, is a highly competitive industry and case study information provided on the challenges and lessons learned may not always reflect the complete story – but, again, it provides a useful qualitative understanding and examples for the different partnerships and local situations. Each situation is unique, as are the combination of stakeholders involved. This book does, therefore, not aim to be prescriptive but rather to provide information on the partnership options available, the potential challenges and the lessons learned from examples of each, using real-life examples with supporting information, statistics and analysis.

What is clear is that there is a need for more data and analysis on private sector involvement in conservation and the related tourism at a local, national and international level. As a start, baseline information is needed in destinations around the world, but particularly in Africa, to allow for an understanding of the private sector's role in tourism and conservation through private PAs and private sector partnerships with other stakeholders. We hope that this book provides a start and inspires others to take it further.

## 2.10. References

Adams, W. & Hulme, D. (2001) Changing narratives, policies and practices in African conservation. In Hulme, D. & Murphree, M. (eds) (2001) *African wildlife and livelihoods: the promise and performance of community conservation* (pp. 9–23). James Currey Ltd, Great Britain.

Armstrong, R. (2012) *An analysis of the conditions for success of community-based tourism enterprises.* International Centre for Responsible Tourism, Occasional Paper OP21. Available at https://www.cabdirect.org/cabdirect/FullTextPDF/2012/20123157768.pdf (accessed 2 February 2012).

Ashley, C. (2006) *How can governments boost the local economic impacts of tourism?* Toolkit prepared for SNV and ODI, London. Available at http://www.odi.org.uk/publications/40-can-governments-boost-local-economic-impacts-tourism (accessed 10 April 2018).

Ashley, C. & Jones, B. (2001) Joint ventures between communities and tourism investors: experiences in southern Africa. *International Journal of Tourism Research*, 3(2), doi: 10.1002/jtr.347.

Ashley, C. & Roe, E. (2002) Making tourism work for the poor: strategies and challenges in southern Africa. *Development Southern Africa*, 19(1), 61–82, doi: 10.1080/03768350220123855.

Balmford, A., Beresford, J., Green, J., Naidoo, R., Walpole, M. & Manica, A. (2009) A global perspective on trends in nature-based tourism. *PLoS Biology*, 7(6), e1000144.

Balmford, A., Green, J.M.H., Anderson, M., Beresford, J., Huang, C. & Naidoo, R. (2015) Walk on the wild side: estimating the global magnitude of visits to protected areas. *PLoS Biology*, 13(2), e1002074, doi:10.1371/journal.pbio.1002074.

Bramwell, B. & Lane, B. (eds) (2000) *Tourism collaboration and partnerships: politics, practice and sustainability.* Channel View Publications, USA.

Buckley, R.C. (2003) Pay to play in parks: an Australian policy perspective on visitor fees in public protected areas. *Journal of Sustainable Tourism*, 11(1), 56–73.

Buckley, R. (2010) *Conservation tourism.* CAB International, Wallingford, UK.

CBD (2010). 'Strategic Plan for Biodiversity 2011–2020 and the Aichi Targets'. https://www.cbd.int/doc/strategic-plan/2011-2020/Aichi-Targets-EN.pdf. Accessed 15 February 2017.

CBD (2016) *Sustainable tourism.* CBD Press Brief. Available at www.cbd.int/idb/2016 (accessed 11 November 2017).

Christie, I., Fernandes, E., Messerli, H. & Twining-Ward, L. (2014) *Tourism in Africa: harnessing tourism for growth and improved livelihoods.* The World Bank, Washington, DC. Available at https://openknowledge.worldbank.org/handle/10986/18688 (accessed 16 June 2017).

Chuhan-Pole, P. & Angwafo, M. (2011) *Yes Africa can: success stories from a dynamic continent.* The International Bank for Reconstruction and Development/The World Bank, Washington, DC.

de Boer, D., van Dijk, M.P. & Tarimo, L. (2011) Business-community partnerships: the link with sustainable local tourism development in Tanzania? *Tourism and Management Studies*, 7. Available at http://www.scielo.mec.pt/pdf/tms/n7/n7a08.pdf (accessed 6 March 2012).

DFID (Department for International Development) (1999) *Tourism and poverty elimination: untapped potential.* Summary based on report for DFID produced by Deloitte and Touche, the International Institute for Environment and Development and the Overseas Development Institute. Available at www.dfid.gov.uk/ (accessed 29 April 2011).

Dixey, L.M. (2008) The unsustainability of community tourism donor projects: lessons from Zambia. In Spenceley, A. (ed.) (2008) *Responsible tourism: critical issues for conservation and development* (pp. 323–342). Earthscan, London.

Dudley, N. (ed.) (2008) *Guidelines for applying protected area management categories*. IUCN, Gland, Switzerland.
Eagles, P.F.J., McCool, S.F. & Haynes, C. (2002) *Sustainable tourism in protected areas: guidelines for planning and management.* Best Practice Protected Areas Guideline Series No. 8. IUCN, Gland, Switzerland.
Eagles, P., Romagosa, F., Buteau-Duitschaever, W., Havitz, M., Glover, T. & McCutcheon, B. (2012) Good governance in protected areas: an evaluation of stakeholders' perceptions in British Columbia and Ontario provincial parks. *Journal of Sustainable Tourism*, 21(1), 60–79.
Emerton, L., Bishop, J. & Thomas, L. (2006) *Sustainable financing of protected areas: a global review of challenges and options*. IUCN, Gland, Switzerland and Cambridge, UK.
EplerWood International (2004) *Evaluating ecotourism as a community and economic development strategy.* The EplerWood Report. Available at www.eplerwood.com (accessed 10 February 2012).
Epler Wood, M. (2010) *Best practice for tourism concessions in protected areas: case studies from Latin America*. DAI Project 1000282. Available at https://www.academia.edu/10773205/Best_Practice_for_Tourism_Concessions_in_Protected_Areas_Cases_from_Latin_America (accessed March 2017).
Epler Wood, M. (2017) *Sustainable tourism on a finite planet: environmental, business and policy solutions*. Earthscan, UK and New York.
Font, X., Cochrane, J. and Tapper, R. (2004) *Pay per view: understanding tourism revenues for effective management plans*. Report for the WWF by Leeds Tourism Group and The Environmental Business Development Group, Leeds, UK.
Franks, P., Booker, F. & Roe, D. (2018) *Understanding and assessing equity in protected area conservation: a matter of governance, rights, social impacts and human wellbeing*. IIED Issue Paper. IIED, London.
Frechtling, D.C. (1994) Assessing the impacts of travel and tourism – measuring economic costs. In Brent Ritchie, J.R. & Goeldner, C.R. (eds) (1994). *Travel, tourism and hospitality research: a handbook for managers and researchers*, 2nd edn, Ch. 33. John Wiley & Sons, New York.
Goodwin, H. (2008) Tourism, local economic development and poverty reduction. *Applied Research in Economic Development*, 5(3), 55–64. Available at http://www.haroldgoodwin.info/uploads/ARED2008goodwin_online_v5n3_propoor_tourism.pdf (accessed 10 April 2018).
Honey, M. (2008) *Ecotourism and sustainable development: who owns paradise?* Island Press, Washington, DC.
IFC (International Finance Corporation) (2012) Africa: the power of the private sector. *Telling our Story*, 6(4). Available at https://www.ifc.org/wps/wcm/connect/832f31004b1f9746a7a6ef08d0338960/TOSAfrica.pdf?MOD=AJPERES (accessed 5 November 2017).
Kepe, T., Wynberg, R. & Ellis, W. (2005) Land reform and biodiversity conservation in South Africa: complementary or in conflict? *International Journal of Biodiversity Science and Management*, 1, 3–16, doi: 10.1080/17451590509618075.
Lapeyre, R. (2011) Governance structures and the distribution of tourism income in Namibian communal lands: a new institutional approach. *Tijdschrift voor Economische en Sociale Geographie,* 102(3), 302–312, doi: 10.1111/j.1467-9663.2011.00665.x.
Leung, Y-F., Spenceley, A., Hvengaard, G. & Buckley, R. (2018) *Tourism and visitor management in protected areas: guidelines for sustainability.* Best Practice Protected Areas Guidelines No. 27. IUCN, Gland, Switzerland.
Mitchell, J. & Ashley, C. (2010) *Tourism and poverty reduction: pathways to prosperity.* Earthscan Publications, UK.
Mitchell, R., Wooliscroft, B. & Higham, J. (2013) Applying sustainability in national park management: balancing public and private interests using a sustainable market orientation model. *Journal of Sustainable Tourism*, 21(5), 695–715.
Moscardo, G. (ed.) (2008) *Building community capacity for tourism development.* CAB International, Wallingford, UK.
Novelli, M. & Scarth, A. (2007) Tourism in protected areas: integrating conservation and community development in Liwonde National Park, Malawi. *Tourism and Hospitality Planning and Development*, 4(1), 47–73, doi: 10.1080/14790530701289697.
Ogutu, Z.A. (2002) The impact of ecotourism on livelihood and natural resource management in Eselenkei Amboseli Ecosystem, Kenya. *Land Degradation and Development*, 13, 251–256.
Protected Planet (2018) *Protected area coverage: Africa*. Available at https://www.protectedplanet.net/region/AF (accessed 3 June 2018).
Rogerson, C.M. (2006) Pro-poor local economic development in South Africa: the role of pro-poor tourism. *Local Environment*, 11(1), 37–60, doi: 10.1080/13549830500396149.

Rylance, A. & Spenceley, A. (2016) Applying inclusive business approaches to nature-based tourism in Namibia and South Africa. *Tourism: An International Interdisciplinary Journal*, 64(4), 371–383
Rylance, A. & Spenceley, A. (2017) Reducing economic leakages from tourism: value chain assessment of the tourism industry in Kasane, Botswana. *Development Southern Africa*, 24(3), 295–313.
Rylance, A., Snyman, S. & Spenceley, A. (2017) The contribution of tourism revenue to financing protected area management in southern Africa. *Tourism Review International*, 21(2), 139–149, doi: 10.3727/154427217.
Scheyvens, R. (2009) Pro-poor tourism: is there value beyond the rhetoric? *Tourism Recreation Research*, 34(2), 191–196.
Simpson, M. (2008b). The impacts of tourism initiatives on rural livelihoods and poverty reduction. In Spenceley, A. (Ed.). (2008). Responsible Tourism: Critical issues for conservation and development (pp 239–266). Earthscan, IUCN, UK.
Snyman, S. (2012a) Ecotourism joint ventures between the private sector and communities: an updated analysis of the Torra Conservancy and Damaraland Camp partnership, Namibia. *Tourism Management Perspectives*, 4, 127–135, doi: 10.1016/j.tmp.2012.07.004.
Snyman, S. (2012b) The role of ecotourism employment in poverty reduction and community perceptions of conservation and tourism in southern Africa. *Journal of Sustainable Tourism*, 20(3), 395–416.
Snyman, S. (2013) *High-end ecotourism and rural communities in southern Africa: a socioeconomic analysis.* Unpublished PhD thesis, University of Cape Town, South Africa.
Snyman, S. (2014) Partnership between a private sector ecotourism operator and a local community in the Okavango Delta, Botswana: the case of the Okavango Community Trust and Wilderness Safaris. *Journal of Ecotourism*, 13(2–3), 110–127, doi: 10.1080/14724049.2014.980744.
Snyman, S. (2017a) African tourism industry employees: expenditure patterns and comparisons with other community members. *Journal of Sustainable Tourism*, doi: 10.1080/09669582.2017.1408634.
Snyman, S. (2017b) The role of private sector ecotourism in local socio-economic development in southern Africa. *Journal of Ecotourism*, 16(3), 247–268, doi: 10.1080/14724049.2016.1226318.
Snyman, S. & Spenceley, A. (2012) Key sustainable tourism mechanisms for poverty reduction and local socio-economic development in Africa. *Africa Insight,* 42(2), 76–93.
South African Tourism Company (2014) Blog. Available at http://www.south-african-hotels.com/blog/the-most-expensive-hotels-in-the-world/ (accessed November 2017).
Spenceley, A. (2003) *Tourism, local livelihoods and the private sector in South Africa: case studies on the growing role of the private sector in natural resources management*. Sustainable Livelihoods in South Africa Research Paper 8. Sustainable Livelihoods Southern Africa project, Institute of Development Studies, Brighton UK, February.
Spenceley, A., Kohl, J., McArthur, S., Myles, P., Notarianni, M., Paleczny, D., Pickering, C. & Worboys, G.L. (2015) Visitor management. In Worboys, G.L., Lockwood, M., Kothari, A., Feary, S. & Pulsford, I. (eds) *Protected area governance and management* (pp. 715–750), ANU Press, Canberra.
Spenceley, A., Rylance, A. & Laiser, S. (2017a) Protected area entrance fees in Tanzania: the search for competitiveness and value for money. *Koedoe* 59(1), a1442. Available at https://doi.org/10.4102/koedoe.v59i1.1442.
Spenceley, A., Snyman, S. & Eagles, P. (2017b) *Guidelines for tourism partnerships and concessions for protected areas: generating sustainable revenues for conservation and development.* Report to the CBD. Available at https://www.cbd.int/tourism/doc/tourism-partnerships-protected-areas-web.pdf (accessed 4 April 2018).
Telfer, D.J. & Sharpley, R. (2008) *Tourism and development in the developing world*. Routledge, USA and Canada.
Tewes-Gradl, C., van Gaalen, M. & Pirzer, C. (2014) *Destination mutual benefit: a guide to inclusive business in tourism.* Available at https://www.giz.de/de/downloads/giz2014-en-guide-inclusive-business-tourism.pdf (accessed November 2017).
The Long Run (2017) *2016 Annual Report*. Available at https://www.thelongrun.org/2016-annual-report-released/ (accessed 4 April 2018).
Torres, R.M., Skillicorn, P. & Nelson, V. (2011) Community corporate joint ventures: an alternative model for pro-poor tourism development. *Tourism Planning and Development,* 8(3), 297–316, doi: 10.1080/21568316.2011.591158.
Twining-Ward, L. (2009) *Africa Region's Finance and Private Sector Development Department (AFTFP): Sub-Saharan Africa tourism industry research*. Final Report for the World Bank, Washington, DC. Available at http://siteresources.worldbank.org/INTAFRSUMAFTPS/Resources/2049902-1327506860777/FinalSSATourismRpt1118.pdf (accessed 5 November 2017).

Twining-Ward, L., Li, W. Bhammar, H. & Wright, E. (2018) *Supporting sustainable livelihoods through wildlife tourism. Tourism for development*. World Bank, Washington, DC. Available at https://openknowledge.worldbank.org/handle/10986/29417, license: CC BY 3.0 IGO (accessed 11 April 2018).
UNEP-WCMC and IUCN (2016) *Protected planet report 2016*. UNEP-WCMC and IUCN, Cambridge UK and Gland, Switzerland.
United Nations (2015) *Transforming our world: the 2030 agenda for sustainable development.* Available at http://www.un.org/ga/search/view_doc.asp?symbol=A/RES/70/1&Lang=E (accessed 1 October 2017).
United Nations (2017) *Economic development in Africa, report 2017: tourism for transformative and inclusive growth.* Available at http://unctad.org/en/PublicationsLibrary/aldcafrica2017_en.pdf (accessed 2 October 2017).
UNWTO (United Nations World Tourism Organization) (2015) *Towards measuring the economic value of wildlife watching tourism in Africa. Briefing paper*. Available at http://sdt.unwto.org/content/unwto-briefing-wildlife-watching-tourism-africa (accessed 23 June 2018).
Varghese, G. (2008) Public–private partnerships in South African national parks: the rationale, benefits and lessons learned. In Spenceley, A. (ed.) (2008). *Responsible tourism: critical issues for conservation and development* (pp. 69–84), Earthscan, London.
Vedeld, P., Jumane, A., Wapalila, G. & Songorwa, A. (2012) Protected areas, poverty and conflicts: a livelihoods case study of Mikumi National Park, Tanzania. *Forest Policy and Economics*, 21, 20–31, doi: 10.1016/j.forpol.2012.01.008.
Walpole, M.J. & Goodwin, H.J. (2000) Local economics of dragon tourism in Indonesia. *Annals of Tourism Research*, 27(3), 559–576, doi: 10.1016/S0160-7383(99)00088-2.
Watson, J., Dudley, N., Segan, D. & Hockings, M. (2014) The performance and potential of protected areas. *Nature*, 515, 67–73.
Waylen, K.A., McGowan, P.J.K., Pawi Study Group & Milner-Gulland, E.J. (2009) Ecotourism positively affects awareness and attitudes but not conservation behaviours: a case study at Grand Riviere, Trinidad. *Oryx,* 43(3), 343–351, doi: 10.1017/S0030605309000064.
Weaver, D. & Lawton, L. (2017) A new visitation paradigm for protected areas. *Tourism Management* 60, 140–146.
World Bank Group (2017) *Tourism for development: 20 reasons sustainable tourism counts for development.* Available at https://openknowledge.worldbank.org/bitstream/handle/10986/28388/119954-WP-PUBLIC-SustainableTourismDevelopment.pdf?sequence=1&isAllowed=y (accessed 29 September 2017).
World Tourism Organization (2014) *Towards measuring the economic value of wildlife watching tourism in Africa – a briefing paper*. UNWTO, Madrid.
World Tourism Organization (2015) *Affiliate members regional reports, volume four – tourism in Africa: a tool for development*. UNWTO, Madrid.
WTTC (World Travel & Tourism Council) (2017) *Travel & tourism: economic impact*. Available at https://www.wttc.org (accessed October 2017).

# 3

# Private Sector Partnership Options

Two main types of tourism business models for accommodation facilities in protected areas (PAs) are explored in this volume: private ownership models and community–private sector joint venture models. This chapter describes the private ownership model and the community–private–joint venture model is described in Chapter 4. Both of these chapters describe the situations where the models work well, and give examples of lodges and camps in Africa where such models are applied. For more information on different tourism partnership models see Twining-Ward, Li, Bhammer and Wright (2018).

Private tourism lodge facilities and management operations may be run by companies for profit, or by non-governmental organisations (NGOs) as not-for profit vehicles (see Figure 1).

For-profit organisations operate for the purpose of making profits and distributing profits to their owners or members (e.g. sole traders, partnerships, private limited companies, cooperatives). By contrast, non-profit organisations may make a profit, but the amount of profit that is retained is often restricted by law, resulting in the use of profit quickly. They may not distribute their property or profits to their members. In this case, profits must be used to further their public interest objectives, such as the promotion of social welfare, biodiversity conservation, economic development or education. They may be voluntary associations, trusts, NGOs or another type of entity (Spenceley, Rylance, Nanabhay & van der Watt, 2016). The land may be privately owned, or owned by a government entity, a community or an NGO. This is the simplest institutional model for the private sector to operate. The tourism venture may provide local people with employment and training opportunities, and business opportunities from the sale of goods (e.g. craft, furniture, food and drink) or services (e.g. transport, construction) to the company and its clients. However, the company is not usually obliged to do this, and the level of support to conservation and local economic development will depend on the company's level of commitment to sustainability. In some countries, there may be national policies that encourage the private sector to promote local employment and procurement (e.g. South Africa has black economic empowerment – BEE – policies, that encourage companies to emphasise opportunities for people who were disadvantaged under apartheid – see Box 2).

Six main models of private sector tourism investment in protected areas are explored in this chapter through the lens of different case studies.

1. **For-profit private sector on private land:** for example, Bisate Lodge in Rwanda (see Case Study 1 in this volume) is a privately owned and managed lodge, based in the buffer zone of Volcanoes National Park, Rwanda, on land purchased from a community cooperative.
2. **For-profit private sector on government land:** as an example, Mombo Camp in Botswana's

© S. Snyman and A. Spenceley (2019). *Private Sector Tourism in Conservation Areas in Africa* (S. Snyman and A. Spenceley)

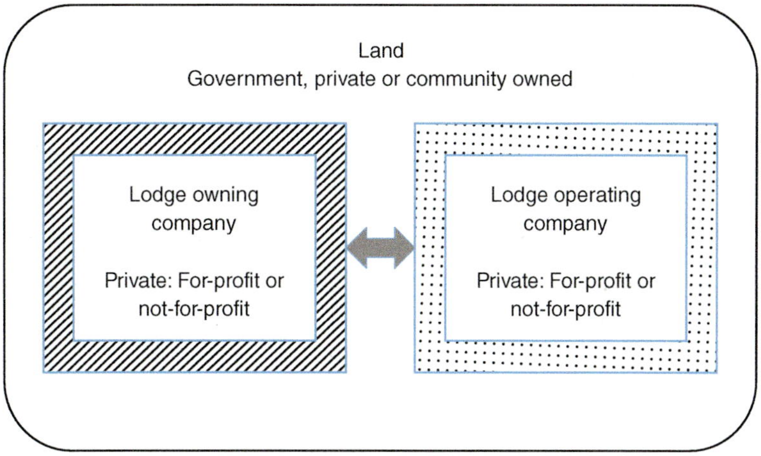


**Fig. 1.** Private ownership model.

> **Box 2.** Black economic empowerment (BEE)
>
> BEE is an affirmative action policy of the South African government that aims to redress the inequalities of apartheid. It provides certain previously disadvantaged groups of South African citizens (i.e. blacks, coloureds, Indians and Chinese) with economic privileges that were not available to them under white rule. The policy includes measures such as preferential employment, skills development, ownership, management, socioeconomic development and preferential procurement (Republic of South Africa, 2004).

Moremi Game Reserve illustrates this model (see Case Study 3 in this volume). The camp is privately owned and marketed by Okavango Wilderness Safaris (OWS) (Pty) Ltd, and based on government land with a 15-year concession lease agreement. Similarly, Nkwichi Lodge operates on land with a 50-year concession from the government of Mozambique, and runs a privately owned and managed tourism operation (see Case Study 6 in this volume).

**3. Private sector (for-profit or not-for-profit) on government, private or NGO land:** Ngala Private Game Reserve includes a safari lodge and tented camp within the Kempiana Contractual National Park in South Africa, and provides an example here. The land and infrastructure are owned by an NGO, the World Wide Fund for Nature (WWF) – South Africa (Case Study 10). The private operator, andBeyond, manages the properties. As another example from Malawi, African Parks Majete Ltd (APM) privately owns Mkulumadzi Lodge in the government-owned Majete Wildlife Reserve. APM has an agreement with the Department of National Parks and Wildlife (DNPW) to manage and develop the reserve, while the management of the lodge is outsourced by APM to a private operator, Robin Pope (see Case Study 11).

**4. Public–private partnership (PPP) on government land:** Ruzizi Tented Lodge in Rwanda is owned and operated by Akagera Management Company (AMC) and is a Rwandan registered for-profit company. AMC is a PPP, with AP holding 51% of the shares and the Rwanda Development Board 49% of the shares (Case Study 13).

**5. Private joint venture partnership on government land:** Singita Lebombo in South Africa is a joint venture of three private entities: Singita Lebombo Investment Holdings (73.6%), Kruger National Park (KNP) Staff Trust (19.8%) and Pfukani Ecotours (Pty) Ltd (6.6%). The lodge is based in Kruger National Park (KNP), under a 20-year concession agreement with South African National Parks (SANParks) (Case Study 14).

**6. Voluntary payments:** in this model, individual entrepreneurs, partnerships and collectives in communities (e.g. cooperatives) sell their products or services to tourism companies and to tourists. Tourism businesses may also provide opportunities for guests to visit communities

**Table 7.** Six private sector models.

| Model | Land ownership | Lodge ownership | Lodge management | Examples |
| --- | --- | --- | --- | --- |
| 1. For-profit private sector on private land | Private | Private | Private | Bisate Lodge, Rwanda<br>Wolwedans Lodge, Namibia |
| 2. For-profit private sector on government land | Government | Private | Private | Mombo Camps, Botswana<br>Nkwichi Lodge, Mozambique<br>WS Hwange Camps, Zimbabwe<br>Simien Lodge, Ethiopia<br>Chumbe Island, Tanzania |
| 3. Private sector (for- or not-for-profit) on government or NGO land | Government, private or NGO | Private or NGO | Private or NGO | Mkulumadzi Lodge, Malawi<br>Thawale Lodge, Malawi<br>Bale Mountain Lodge, Ethiopia<br>Ngala, South Africa<br>King Lewanika Lodge, Zambia |
| 4. PPP on government land | Government | Public–private partnership | Public–private partnership | Ruzizi Tented Lodge, Rwanda |
| 5. Private joint venture partnership on government land | Government | Private joint venture | Private joint venture | Singita Lebombo, South Africa |
| 6. Voluntary payments to communities | Any philanthropy | | | Singita Community Development Trust;<br>WWT and CITW<br>Africa Foundation |

and spend money directly on products (e.g. craft, decor and food) or services (e.g. guided tours, visits to cultural attractions and transport) (Spenceley *et al.*, 2016). Examples include the Africa Foundation (linked to andBeyond), Children in the Wilderness (CITW) and the Wilderness Wildlife Trust (WWT) (both linked to WS) (see section 3.6. Voluntary payments, in this volume).

Examples of these models operating in southern Africa included as case studies in this book are listed in Table 7, and are described in detail in this chapter.

## 3.1. For-Profit Private Sector on Private Land

### 3.1.1. Case Study 1: Bisate Lodge, Rwanda

#### Background

Bisate Lodge is a novel approach to African ecotourism. Situated on private land at 2,650 metres in the buffer zone of the Volcanoes National Park (VNP) in Rwanda, Bisate is at the heart of the biodiversity- and endemism-rich Albertine Rift. Its most celebrated wild mammal, the iconic (and endangered) mountain gorilla, is a flagship species for both tourism and conservation, and Rwanda has been instrumental in its recovery. The country harbours Africa's highest rural population density and each patch of remaining indigenous vegetation is essentially a mere island in a sea of people. Land is at an absolute premium with virtually every square metre either cultivated or inhabited. Even though some 8.5% of the country is

protected by national parks, the absolute scale of land involved is relatively small (<230,000 hectares) and the chances of park expansion and connectivity are remote. This is most apparent on the borders of the 16,000 hectare VNP which was halved in size during the 1950s and 1960s when land was excised for agriculture.

It was in this context in June 2017 that WS opened Bisate Lodge, now charging nightly rates ranging from USD 1300 t USD 1500 per person sharing per night (dependent on season). The lodge has 12 beds, as well as guides' accommodation and offers activities which include gorilla and golden monkey trekking, village visits, birding and hiking (Pers. com. Jomi Krobb, February 2019).

WS was determined to use the ecotourism project as a lever for driving park expansion, reforestation and thus enhanced biodiversity conservation and community engagement. To this end, nearly four years of planning and stakeholder engagement and consultation culminated in the purchase of 42 hectares of uninhabited agricultural land from local community members, the construction of the lodge and the employment and training of staff from the community and elsewhere. The intention is for this property not only to measure and prove the land acquisition and restoration concept but to inspire replication through future partnerships and to achieve meaningful ecosystem-level scale.

**Institutional structure**

Bisate Lodge is privately owned by a company called Imizi Ecotourism Ltd. Imizi is co-owned by Wilderness Holdings (WH) (90%) and Thousand Hills Africa (10%), a local Rwandan inbound tour operator and ground handler. WS operates, manages and markets the lodge. The uninhabited agricultural land (42 hectares) on which the lodge is built is now privately owned, having been purchased from around 103 community members, who formed a cooperative called Tuzamurane through which to engage the private sector both for the purposes of land sale (also overseen by district and national authorities) and future engagement such as employment and procurement.

Beyond the lodge itself, the broader reforestation and restoration project has grown to include many partners and contributors, from the overall park authority (the Rwanda Development Board – RDB), to NGOs including the African Wildlife Foundation (AWF) and the Dian Fossey Gorilla Fund International (DFGFI), to research institutions such as the Centre of Biodiversity Excellence at the University of Rwanda

(UR). These stakeholders variously play a part in fundraising and scientific support. Beyond this group, WS has also engaged its trade partner network of some 2,000 travel agents based worldwide in a tree-planting campaign that has engaged hundreds of tourists.

### Economic impact

Casual labour costs were approximately USD 3,000 for the six months that the lodge was operational in 2017. The land acquisition in FY2016 injected USD 475,534 into the local community through payments to community members for their land. In FY2018, a further USD 200,000 was used to purchase more land from community members. Over a two-year period USD 10,221 was paid to the community in terms of the nursery and reforestation project labour costs. USD 25,000 was used during the building of the lodge for local materials and services. As the land and the lodge are owned by the private sector, there are no lease or concession fees. Guests doing gorilla or golden monkey visits contribute to government through payment for permits (USD 1,500 per person per trek for gorilla and USD 100 for golden monkey treks).

### Social impact

WS formed an agreement with the surrounding community, which included the purchase of the initial Bisate site from 103 community members, thus injecting some USD 475,000 into the community, as well as an understanding regarding employment and training in lodge development and operation. Approximately 200 local people were temporarily employed in road and lodge construction and 24 community members have been trained as staff and are permanently employed. The camp currently employs 46 staff; of these 13 are female (28%) and 33 male (72%) (I. Baas, email, September 2017, personal communication). The high percentage of male staff is due to the large team of security staff (I. Baas, email, September 2017, personal communication). Some 37% of the staff come directly from the adjacent villages while of the remaining 63% (all with prior ecotourism experience), all but two people, are from elsewhere in Rwanda (I. Baas, email, September 2017, personal communication). Over time, it is envisaged that all staff will come from the local community. Tuzamurane, the community cooperative, was formed for equitable procurement of fresh produce and other goods from land adjacent to the site.

The salary cost to company amounts to approximately USD 21,185 per month for local Rwandan staff (I. Baas, email, February 2018, personal communication). This salary cost is approximately 40% of total monthly fixed costs. The average monthly wage is approximately USD 481 (I. Baas, email, February 2018, personal communication). All staff are provided with medical insurance for themselves as well as their spouse and children.

**Box 3.** Incorporating local culture into camp design

Rwandan fashion entrepreneur and founder of Inzuki Designs, Teta Isibo, was appointed by WS to source locally produced items in order to bring a vibrant Rwandan flair to the interior design of Bisate Lodge. Teta, named by *Forbes* as one of Africa's 30 Most Promising Young Entrepreneurs for 2017, also sourced unique items for guests to purchase at Bisate. Bisate's interior design is drawn from a variety of aspects of the Rwandan lifestyle, particularly the colourful textiles and use of texture. Many of the furnishings are decorated using *imigongo*, an art form unique to Rwanda that uses cow dung and goes back hundreds of years; the dung is mixed with soils of different colours and then painted in geometric shapes. The use of black and white cow hides also reflects the rural way of life in the villages, and volcanic stone has been used in the fireplaces to echo the volcanoes of the adjacent VNP. Bisate's sophisticated architectural and interior design is rooted in Rwandan building tradition as exemplified in the design of the royal palace of the traditional monarch. The spherical, thatched structures echo the thousands of hills that dot the Rwandan landscape. The architecture is also inspired by Bisate's amphitheatre setting.

Source: Wilderness Holdings (2017)

Besides employment (on a permanent and casual basis), Bisate Lodge has agreements with the local community to procure the items listed below at an average value of USD 1,000 per month (I. Baas, email, September 2017, personal communication):

- welcome cards for guests (a woven card);
- skewers/brochette sticks;
- different baskets such as tissue-box holders;
- balustrades for the lodge main area and rooms;
- local vegetables such as potatoes, carrots and tree tomatoes;
- milk for employees;
- firewood from exotic woodlots such as eucalyptus;
- purses for coffee gifts (a turndown gift);
- bags to sell in the curio shop;
- any sewing services necessary for the lodge;
- woodwork such as walking sticks for guests to use while trekking; and
- woodwork such as bamboo signage for the nature trail and room signs.

A total of approximately USD 40,000 per annum is also raised from guest donations and used for various community development projects (I. Baas, email, January 2018, personal communication).

#### Environmental impact

At the very heart of the Bisate project is the ambitious restoration of a plot of former agricultural land through reforestation and other measures. Although part of the park prior to the 1960s, in March 2016 when agriculture ceased there was very limited biodiversity (or even ecological) value to the land, with negligible natural vegetation and a paucity of any wild fauna. Fifty years of farming (primarily Irish potatoes, pyrethrum, beans and wheat) of this steep, subprime land ensured that what remained was essentially alien to the landscape; eucalyptus, alnus and wattle trees and terracing dug into the side of the hill were the most apparent features aside from the carefully tilled potato and pyrethrum furrows.

For the land to have any biodiversity or ecological value it was vital that a reforestation programme was implemented that allowed recovery of natural habitat. To that end, a plan introducing naturally occurring vegetation in the adjacent park and related to both altitude and aspect was put into place. Using seed and other material gathered only from outside the park, an indigenous tree nursery was established in mid-2015, and by 2018 and by 2019 more than 25,000 trees had been planted out across targeted areas of the site (Pers. Com. Jomi Krobb, February 2019). Species such as *Hagenia abyssinica*, *Dombeya torrida*, *Neoboutonia macrocalyx*, *Hypericum revolutum* and *Lobelia gibberoa* were planted on the slopes remaining from extinct volcanic cones, while the flatter land was planted with bamboo, *Arundinaria alpina*. A small team of permanent staff members oversee the nursery and day-to-day planting, while up to 20 community members are also regularly employed on a casual basis to assist with reforestation during peak planting times.

A year after agriculture had ceased and reforestation had been in place, the assemblages of birds, mammals, butterflies and other taxa had begun to show marked changes. Not only were many more species being recorded, but the kinds of species were changing. Only 20 or so bird species were recorded regularly prior to 2016, but by January 2019 more than 70 bird species had been recorded with many more forest or scrub species being added to the list of what had primarily been edge and field species. Similar, but more dramatic, trends were seen with mammals, with a number of small carnivores (serval, side-striped jackal and large grey mongoose) recolonising the land and preying on the rebounding rodent populations. Even southern tree hyrax were resident on the site by early 2017. WS is optimistic that as many as 12 bird species endemic to the Albertine Rift will move back into the area along with at least nine mammal species. Bats, butterflies, amphibians and reptiles have since been surveyed with annual follows-ups by students from UR, as well as the Karisoke Research Institute, planned to measure change over the first decade.

In addition, the lodge lives by the motto that 'every guest is a conservationist' with all visitors encouraged to spend time in the nursery and to plant a tree during their stay, thus contributing directly to the restoration of the area. This is extended to 'every guest being a philanthropist' with visitors also able to contribute towards a fund to secure more land in order to expand the park in the future.

It is in this regard that WS has formed a partnership with both the government (through the RDB) and the AWF (a non-profit conservation organisation) for further land acquisition and reforestation adjacent to the park, a project intended to increase the populations of species such as the endangered mountain gorilla and golden monkey. As part of the first official handover of AWF-owned land to the government, which took place at the park on 10 January 2018, 50 *Hagenia* seedlings from the indigenous tree nursery at Bisate Lodge were planted by a number of dignitaries to symbolise the beginning of the reforestation project. Local children from Nyabisinde Primary School recited a poem about the economic benefits of gorilla conservation and tourism for the local community and chief park warden, Prosper Uwingeli, addressed everyone regarding the importance of the land.

The camp uses a hybrid energy system of hydro-powered grid power and thermodynamic geysers; the use of reverse osmosis water systems reduces the bottled water consumption and use of plastic. The camp undergoes a biannual environmental management system (EMS) assessment to ensure compliance with WS Group Environmental Minimum Standards (GEMS).

### Successes

WS measures performance in its business through the 4Cs framework, with all four of the below components needing to work in concert for true sustainability to be achieved.

1. **Commercial:** the lodge is performing well, having achieved good occupancies over the 2017 peak season, with good forward occupancies for 2018.
2. **Community:** the lodge holds a good relationship with the surrounding community and the Tuzamurane Cooperative. Salaries, casual employment and procurement of various goods and services inject economic stimulus locally. CITW (see Case Study 16 in this volume) was started in Rwanda at Bisate Primary School in March 2018.
3. **Conservation:** the reforestation project has seen good progress, success indicated by the recolonisation of the land by numerous previously absent species, including a significant proportion of Albertine Rift endemic birds, butterflies and mammals.
4. **Culture:** the architecture and interior design of the lodge, as well as staff uniforms, guest food and other elements all reflect the proud cultural heritage of both pre-colonial and modern Rwanda.

### Challenges

Any successful or stable society or system is resistant to change, and time frames in persuading various stakeholders and authorities of the value of this new model have been longer than ideal for Bisate Lodge. The establishment of permanent infrastructure in the form of a lodge necessitates the provision of services such as roads, electricity and water which were not present before. It also injects more financial means into the local community with resultant further development and population growth around the conservation node. If this is unmanaged it can dent the biodiversity conservation gains and other aspects of the project.

Future challenges are likely to arise over time as the reforestation project progresses. These will inevitably revolve around potential human–wildlife conflict with species such as golden monkeys known to raid many of the local varieties of crops. It will be critical that the lodge operators are able to address this to the satisfaction of the community, especially if more pervasive wild species are seen to be associated with the reforestation programme.

### Lessons learned and recommendations

Comprehensive stakeholder engagement was critical: from the local community to the various levels of local government authority (cell, sector, district and province, as well as park management) to central government (land board, Rwanda Environmental Management Authority and RDB). The concept was new and as a new operator in the country without a local track record there was a need to build trust. It was also observed that more time and money should have been invested into the reforestation programme from as early as possible in order to accelerate the restoration of the property.

The access road was sited along the most logical, cost effective route, although unfortunately this has encouraged community development in line of site of the lodge, as well as in the most logical and productive areas for park expansion, thus raising costs and social upheaval in potential future phases of land acquisition.

**Table 8.** Summary – Bisate Lodge.

| | |
|---|---|
| Name of company | Imizi Ecotourism Ltd |
| Location | In the buffer zone of Volcanoes National Park (VNP), Rwanda Volcanoes National Park (VNP), Rwanda |
| Year established/opened | 2017 |
| Status of company (i.e. listed, privately owned, etc.) | Privately owned by Imizi Ecotourism Ltd |
| List of camps/lodges | Bisate Lodge (12 beds) |
| Investment/partnership option | Privately owned land purchased from community members<br>Privately owned infrastructure<br>Privately operated and managed lodge |
| Total number of staff employed | 46 |
| % local staff | 87% |
| Financial summary | The salary cost to company amounts to approximately USD 20,000 per month for local Rwandan staff<br>Community donations to development projects amount to approximately USD 40,000 per annum |

### 3.1.2. Case Study 2: Wolwedans, Namibia

#### Background

Wolwedans is a collection of camps and lodges situated in the heart of NamibRand Nature Reserve (NRNR) in the south-west of Namibia. The reserve originated in 1984 as the dream of J.A. Brückner to integrate a large number of former livestock farms and develop a wildlife sanctuary. To date, 17 former livestock farms have been rehabilitated into a single continuous natural habitat. Recognising the importance of wilderness areas, the NRNR has exclusively set aside more than 15% of its total area for wilderness.

The NRNR was registered as a non-profit private nature reserve in 1992. All landowners belonging to the reserve signed agreements and adopted a constitution, which sets the land aside for conservation, now and in the future. The reserve is financially self-sustaining, mainly through high quality, low impact tourism. Wolwedans is one of four lodges in the NRNR, all of which collect park fees.

In 2018, Wolwedans' fully inclusive rates were between Namibian dollar (NAD) 6, 950 (USD 497) and NAD 9,250 (USD 661) per person sharing, depending on the camp (Wolwedans, 2018a). Wolwedans consists of Dunes Lodge (10 beds) and Mountain View Suite (1 beds), Wolwedans Dune Camp (8 beds), the secluded Private Camp (3 beds, 3 en-suite rooms) and Boulders Safari Camp (5 beds) (Wolwedans, 2018b).

#### Institutional structure

Wolwedans was started by Mr Brückner's youngest son, Stephan, with an ethos of setting an example in sustainable tourism, the empowerment of its employees and its commitment to the conservation of NRNR. NamibRand Safaris (Pty) Ltd is the commercial operating company behind the Wolwedans Collection.

Wolwedans has adopted the 4Cs (i.e. commerce, community, conservation and culture) sustainability platform, which moulds its efforts into a comprehensive strategy. In addition to the park fee (NAD 280, USD 24) that is used for the daily reserve's operations and which goes to the NRNR, the privately owned reserve, its guests pay a foundation levy of NAD 280 (USD 24) which is channelled to the Wolwedans Foundation to offer vocational training via The Namibian Institute of Culinary Education (NICE) in Windhoek and the Desert Academy at Wolwedans. The levy is also used to cover the operational costs. Wolwedans offers Level 2 and 3 of the National Vocational Certificate in Hospitality and to date has trained and certified over 200 graduates. The conservation C is for the most part run by the NRNR, which conserves the unique ecology and wildlife of the Greater Sossusvlei Namib Landscape (GSNL). The NRNR is supported by Wolwedans through direct labour assisting with operations and policy development.

#### Economic impact

Before the NRNR, the area was home to the lucrative karakul sheep industry. This industry, which saw a boom after World War II, experienced a huge decline during the 1970s due to changing attitudes toward fur and a lack of grazing as a result of drought. The industry only employed roughly a few dozen farm workers in the same area in which now more than 300 Namibians are working. Landowners started to realise that they could make more money from tourism beds than from the volatile agriculture industry. Tourism and hospitality brought higher profits and more jobs to the area. An area that was once a backwater has become one of the most sought-after tourist destinations in Namibia.

On average, NAD 550,000 (USD 47,170) is spent on the procurement of local goods and services. Wolwedans procures 92% local goods (perishables and non-perishables) with local companies that deliver weekly to ensure fresh products. In addition, the lodge's services are locally procured.

NamibRand Safari remains the commercial entity that provides an income to the Reserve's conservation activities and contributes significantly to its operating costs. Concessionaires collect a park fee of NAD 280 (USD 24) per person per night from visitors to the Reserve. In 2016, the total income derived from this park fee collection amounted to NAD 3,822,817 (USD 331,058) of which Wolwedans collected 60% of the annual park fees in the year reported (approximately USD 198,635).

#### Social impact

The total number of staff is 99, with a total monthly salary bill of NAD 650,000 (approximately USD 55,746), and an average monthly wage of NAD 6,500 (USD 557). The majority of staff (96%) are Namibian, while only a minority (4%) are foreign. Half (50%) of the staff are women and the other half are male. Wolwedans' economic contribution to the local economy over the last 10 years is displayed in Figure 2.

Approximately NAD 2 million (USD 171,527) per annum, earned through the Foundation Levy, has been channelled to support the Wolwedans Desert Academy, a vocational school. Wolwedans also plans to begin projects in the Malthahohe community.

#### Environmental impact

Wolwedans has two solar boreholes and one diesel borehole, situated in the arrival area of the base camp. The water table is 132 metres below the surface. Water needs to be pumped on a daily basis to all the

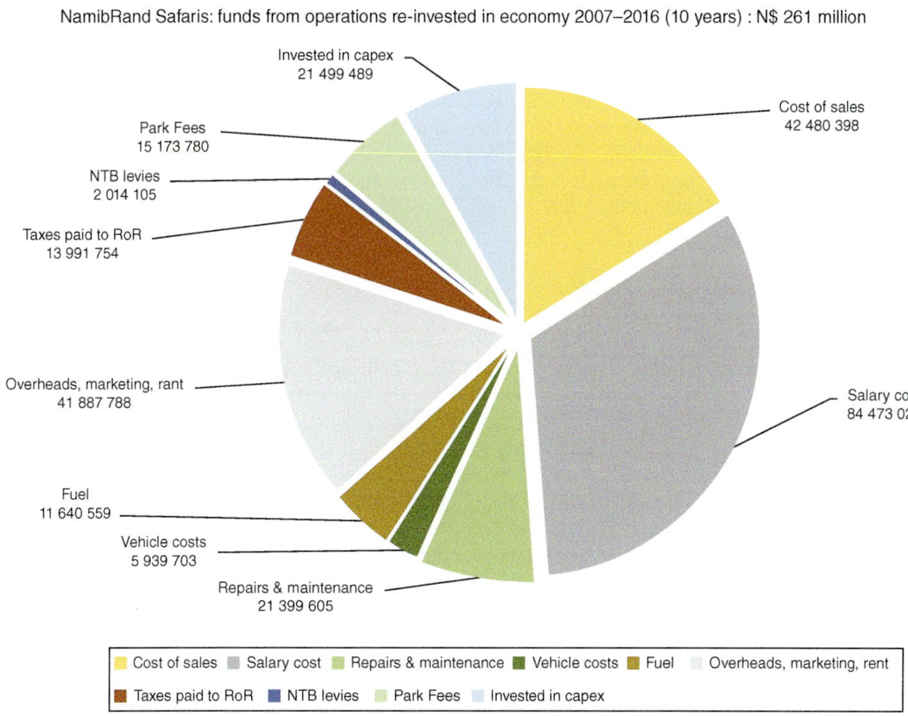


**Fig. 2.** Wolwedans' economic contribution for the past 10 years.

lodges as well as to the base village. The camps use 80,000 litres per day which is divided across the entire operation, as well as the waterholes for wildlife. The used water at Wolwedans is fed to the grey water system where it is filtered and used to water the plants at Wolwedans. The waste generated at Wolwedans is divided into two waste groups (organic and non-organic waste) which is collected at the staff base camp for pre-sorting into groups. Non-organic waste is transported to a recycling centre in Windhoek and the organic waste is provided as feed to the pigs.

Wolwedans is not connected to the national power grid, as the distance to the nearest line is more than 100 kilometres. The majority of electricity is generated by solar and backed up by generators for early morning and late evening. The installation of the solar system at the staff village cost more than NAD 5 million (USD 42,881) in 2014. Wolwedans also has a Namibian Organic Association (NOA) certified organic garden that allows their carbon footprint to be reduced as they previously used to import vegetables from Cape Town through a logistics process that would take up to 10 days. Now, guests have fresh organic salads that are less than 10 hours old.

NRNR's biodiversity and habitats are effectively managed through active monitoring and innovative, adaptive management approaches. Today, one of southern Africa's largest not-for-profit private nature reserves acts as a role model for biodiversity conservation balanced with financial sustainability.

### Successes

Wolwedans' staff come from all corners of Namibia and those based at Wolwedans are guaranteed free accommodation, electricity, water and food during their tenure. The company has seen success in having staff moving from different departments to gain new skills and has seen the successful integration of students from the Wolwedans Desert Academy into the corporate structure. The commercial entity gives NAD 2 million (USD 173,207) per annum, earned via Foundation levy to the Desert Academy. The academy teaches young Namibians all aspects of the hospitality industry including courses on housekeeping, maintenance, guiding, kitchen and administration. To date, more than 100 students have passed their exams. In June 2018, Wolwedans was awarded the acclaimed Five Flower Eco Award (Namibia), earning five flowers for all of the assessed sites: Wolwedans Dunes Lodge, Wolwedans Dune Camp, Private Camp and Boulders Safari Camp. The Collection was also awarded a newly introduced award, the Green Five Flower Achievement Award, which is given to a company that performs immeasurably high in all environmental categories. The five flowers awarded to all the camps and lodges demonstrates an above average (over 90%) achievement in the various categories and overall and shines a light on the Collections adherence to eco-tourism and its commitment to high quality, low impact tourism. The final score for each of the Collections four sites was: Dunes Lodge: 99%, Dune Camp: 99%, Private Camp: 99% and Boulders safari camp: 99%.

### Challenges

In 2011, the Wolwedans Foundation started a small, medium enterprise development initiative, with the aim of supporting motivated and driven employees to start their own business. The first recipient was a cleaner at Wolwedans, who started out as a building contractor. Due to his drive, dedication and passion, he was offered permanent employment at Wolwedans as a cleaner and later promoted to a waiter. He was offered the opportunity to start a commuter transport business that took passengers between Windhoek and northern Namibia. The support included the purchasing of the commuter bus, as well as coaching and mentoring on running a business. He started working towards owning the bus, by paying it off in monthly instalments. However, due to a lack of sustained personal commitment and mismanagement of revenue generated, the business, unfortunately, failed. This illustrates the need for business and accounting training for all potential entrepreneurs.

### Lessons learned and recommendations

It is important that existing farmers and citizens do not misinterpret the motives and actions from surrounding nature reserves. The mission and values must be clearly communicated so that the benefit for all is clearly seen. Designing community projects should keep in mind the reality on the ground for those in the communities.

**Table 9.** Summary – Wolwedans.

| | |
|---|---|
| Name of company | NamibRand Safaris (Pty) Ltd |
| Location | Namibia |
| Year established | 1995 |
| Status of company (i.e. listed, privately owned, etc.) | Private company |
| List of camps/lodges | Wolwedans Collection: Dunes Lodge (18 beds) and Mountain View Suite (2 beds), Wolwedans Dune Camp (12 beds), Private Camp (6 beds, 3 en-suite rooms), and Boulders Safari Camp |
| Investment/partnership option | Wolwedans is a private company operating on privately owned land |
| Total number of staff employed | 99 |
| % local staff | 96% |
| Financial summary | In 2016 the total income derived from the park fee collection amounted to NAD 3,822,817 (USD 331,058) of which Wolwedans collected 60% of the annual park fees in the year reported (approximately USD 198,635)<br>Total monthly salary bill of NAD 650,000 (approximately USD 55,746), and an average monthly wage of NAD 6,500 (USD 557) |

## 3.2. For-Profit Private Sector on Government Land

### 3.2.1. Case Study 3: Mombo Camp and Little Mombo, Botswana

**Background**

Mombo Camp is located on Chief's Island in the Moremi Game Reserve within the Okavango Delta of Botswana. There are two Okavango Wilderness Safaris (OWS) camps on Chief's Island: Mombo (18 beds) and Little Mombo (6 beds). Mombo is generally known to be OWS's flagship camp, and it provides a combination of very high-end quality, and a small camp, with excellent wildlife viewing in a pristine area.

In 2018, the rack rate ranged from USD 1,892 in the low season to USD 2,985 in the high season per person, per night, sharing (Wilderness Safaris, 2017a, 2017b, 2017c). In 2017 OWS started an upgrade of Mombo Camp, with an approximate capital investment of BWP 80 million (USD 7.9 million equivalent).

**Institutional structure**

The camp is privately owned by OWS Lodges (Pty) Ltd. It is marketed and managed by OWS (Pty) Ltd, which also owns and manages 19 other camps in Botswana. The infrastructure of both camps is privately owned and based on government land with a 15-year concession lease agreement (G. Woodrow, email, 2017, personal communication).

**Economic impact**

A total of over BWP 78 million (approx. USD 9.8 million) has been paid in terms of lease fees and taxes from 2009 to 2017 (FY ending February). The lease fee increases by 10% per annum, and a renewed 15 year lease includes a royalty payment of 6% of turnover per annum (Grant Woodrow, email 12 November 2018, personal communication). The company also pays a bednight levy of BWP 10 per bednight, and a tourism training levy of 0.2% turnover (Gavin Jacobs, email, 1 December 2017, personal communication). OWS is a Botswana company, and therefore revenue earned by the company is retained within Botswana and the relevant taxes are paid and retained in Botswana (Spenceley & Snyman, 2017) (see Table 10).

**Table 10.** Lease fee and tax payments to the Botswana government for Mombo, 2009–2017.

| | Total (2009–2017) |
|---|---|
| Lease fees per annum (BWP) | 10,642,776 |
| Taxes paid to government (BWP) | 67,485,638 |
| Total (BWP) | 78,136,476 |
| USD equivalent | 9,819,164 |

Source: Gavin Jacobs, email, 1 December 2017, personal communication

### Social impact

In 2017, Mombo employed 83 staff. Staff costs amounted to over BWP 58 million (approximately USD 7.1 million) between 2009 and 2017. Of this, 83% was staff pay (including salary, pension, gratuity, leave pay and incentives), while 13% was food rations and 4% was for training in 2017 (Gavin Jacobs, email, 1 December 2017, personal communication). More than 75% of the staff are local Batswana resulting in approximately BWP 52 million (approximately USD 6.3 million) being retained in Botswana and invested in local economies. Training is done both formally and informally and includes all aspects of hospitality and guiding. Training done through a visual aid training system provides staff with hospitality course certificates (Spenceley & Snyman, 2017).

### Environmental impact

Perhaps the biggest conservation achievement of OWS has been to demonstrate the value that can be attached to natural areas and their wildlife, coupled with the benefits that this has had for biodiversity conservation. The highest profile conservation activity at Mombo has been the reintroduction of white and black rhino to the area. In 2001 OWS purchased white rhino from Mokolodi Nature Reserve, and the Department of Wildlife and National Parks (DWNP) also contributed rhino from Gaborone Game Reserve. The rhino were released at Mombo in a ceremony led by the vice president of Botswana in November 2001 (Myers, Hoets & Woodrow, 2004). During that same year, the Botswana government introduced more white rhino to Moremi. Later in 2003, with the assistance of the Botswana Defence Force and DWNP, black rhino were also released at Mombo (Myers *et al.*, 2004). A government official has stated that they owe the rhino project to OWS, and it was the, '… birth of the relationship of government and private working together in conservation …' and demonstrated that they could collaborate well together. He highlighted that it was OWS that came to the government to discuss the potential for releasing rhino at Mombo and not vice versa (Spenceley & Snyman, 2017).

The environmental management of Mombo is monitored, reported and independently audited under a Global Reporting Initiative System in an annual integrated report (as are all camps managed by OWS). This approach includes indicators for energy use, water use, biodiversity, emissions, effluents and waste (Wilderness Holdings, 2017) to a higher standard of reporting than is required by the Botswana Stock Exchange (where Wilderness Holdings is listed). The camp undergoes a biannual environmental management system assessment to ensure compliance with the system. In FY2017 the camp achieved 78% compliance with the GEMS (W. Ozorio, email, August 2017, personal communication). In relation to energy consumption, the camp switched from using diesel generators to 100% solar energy in May 2012, with a backup generator on site to provide additional electricity during times of excessive demand or inclement weather conditions (W. Ozorio, email, November 2017, personal communication). Following the capital investment of approximately USD 860,000 in the solar technology plant, there was an 82% reduction in annual diesel use, from 108,981 litres to 19,309 litres. In terms of carbon emissions from electricity production, 50 tonnes of carbon dioxide were emitted directly in 2017, compared to 287 tonnes in 2012 (W. Ozorio, email, August 2017, personal communication).

The Wilderness Wildlife Trust (WWT) is a non-profit organisation (see Case Study 17 in this volume for more information), supported by WS, which supports projects that address the needs of wildlife populations, conserve endangered species, and provide education and training to local people and their communities (WWT/CITW, 2011). In 2009 a research unit was established at Mombo, providing logistical support, food and vehicle maintenance to researchers. In 2013–2014, approximately USD 411,000 was spent by OWS on biodiversity conservation research and monitoring in Botswana (Wilderness Holdings, 2014).

### Successes

Mombo has been described by one government official as the 'Rolls Royce' of tourism, from a service and standards perspective (Spenceley & Snyman, 2017), and in terms of the quality of accommodation it has been described as 'the benchmark for other camps that were built afterwards' (interview in Spenceley & Snyman, 2017). Mombo Camp has been rated in the top 10 destinations in Africa, and has won various awards from Travel and Leisure, Condé Naste (including Readers' Choice awards in 2008 and 2009 – Wilderness Safaris, 2012).

### Challenges

The fact that Mombo Camp is situated remotely on an island in the Delta has limited opportunities to offer expansive cultural tourism experiences or to actively increase local economic linkages, as villages are a great distance away. Other forms of community engagement and development therefore need to be established, including local employment and education programmes (Spenceley & Snyman, 2017).

### Lessons learned and recommendations

The Mombo and OWS case has developed over the course of 35 years, and therefore planners need to be cognisant that establishing a secure and profitable destination takes time. During this time, authorities that control land tenure have the opportunity to preferentially provide concessions and leases to operators practising sustainable and responsible tourism. The success of Mombo and the revenue generated from it has allowed OWS to invest in environmental technologies, conservation and community development in other concession areas as well, spreading benefits further (Spenceley & Snyman, 2017).

The role of responsible private sector investors and operators should be included within the list of factors that contribute towards sustainable destination development. Identifying established responsible companies, or nurturing emerging enterprises, is a role that government or protected area authorities can take. Government support through reliable, accountable institutions and policy can also stimulate private sector investment. The private sector needs to also be mindful of being responsible and operating sustainably so that their success is not unsustainability imitated. By encouraging long-term investment by such enterprises, and nurturing good communication and trusting relationships, the state, the private sector and host communities can all benefit (Spenceley & Snyman, 2017).

**Table 11.** Summary – Mombo Camp and Little Mombo.

| | |
|---|---|
| Name of company | Okavango Wilderness Safaris (OWS) Lodges (Pty) Ltd |
| Location | Okavango Delta, Botswana |
| Year established | 1991 |
| Status of company (i.e. listed, privately owned, etc.) | Privately owned by OWS Lodges (Pty) Ltd |
| List of camps/lodges | Mombo Camp (18 beds) and Little Mombo (6 beds) |
| Investment/partnership option | Government owned land<br>15-year concession lease<br>Privately owned infrastructure |
| Total number of staff employed | 83 |
| % local staff | 75% |
| Financial summary | USD 9.8 million equivalent has been paid in terms of lease fees and taxes to the government from 2009 to 2017<br>USD 6.4 million equivalent in wages to local Batswana from 2009 to 2017 |

### 3.2.2. Case Study 4: Simien Lodge, Ethiopia

#### Background

In 1975, working as logistics manager for the Oxfam/Unicef famine relief programme in Tigray, Nick Crane, took a week off to trek in the Simien Mountains in Ethiopia. This was a year before the national park was created and three years before UNESCO decided to declare the park the second World Heritage Site in the world. When Nick returned in 2001 he discovered that there were still no tourism facilities in the area. As a private investor, he felt that this was an important tourism potential that was ready to be marketed. However, it took nearly three years for the government to give permission to operate. Ethiopians were wary of foreign investment, having just emerged from 25 years of communism. Although the suspicion has lessened somewhat in the past 10 years, it is still difficult to get all ministries to cooperate with the tourism operator.

In 1978 UNESCO gave the Simiens World Heritage site status. The first World Heritage Site was Yellowstone National Park, and so when the Simiens became the second it was well deserved. The park has incredible scenery. There is an escarpment that drops vertically 2 kilometres into the watershed of the Takaze River which is one of the main tributaries of the Nile and the mountain range is an ancient volcano, formed about 40 million years ago at the northern end of the African Rift Valley. It also has unique and endemic wildlife, such as the Ethiopian wolf, the bearded Walia ibex (*Capra walie*) and the gelada mountain monkey.

In 2017, the room rack rate (including breakfast) for Simien lodge per person sharing ranged between USD 105 and USD 230 (depending on the season), with lunch and dinner rates ranging from USD 15–18 per person per meal (Simien Lodge, 2017). The lodge has 28 rooms, with a total of 60 beds.

#### Institutional structure

Initially the private sector operator teamed up with an Ethiopian partner, who had previously been general manager of the Ethiopian Wabe Schebele hotel group. The plan was that the Ethiopian partner would build and manage and the private sector operator from the UK would invest and handle the marketing abroad. However, the partnership separated in the early days as the partners had different objectives, leaving the UK investor to manage the lodge alone. The private sector operator's objective was not only to create a first-class tourism destination but also to use the lodge as a platform for community work and poverty alleviation, as he understood that cooperation with the very poor community would be vital for the success of the enterprise and found that the early tourists were happy to be involved. The private sector leases the land from the government, which owns all land in Ethiopia. The private sector operator has 43 years left on the lease plus a 20-year extension: a total of 63 years.

### Economic impact

The economic impact of the lodge in the Simien region has been extensive and it is possible to relate much of the growth of the region back to the initial investment leading to tourism flows. There were no more than 4,000 tourists a year coming to the Simiens before the lodge was built. In 2016, there were 24,000 tourists entering the park, of which about a third stayed in the lodge. If it is possible to estimate that the average tourist spends about USD 2,500 on a vacation in Ethiopia, then the extra 20,000 tourists equates to approximately USD 50 million in terms of tourism revenue. While it can be argued that this is not all spent in the Simiens, much of the marketing to get the tourists to come to Ethiopia has been handled by the lodge marketing team. Of course, most of the trip expenditure is allocated to ground transport, internal air transport and other hotels in the country.

A noticeable positive economic effect is the growth of the Simien frontier town called Debark. Before the lodge was built, Debark was a similar size to the two other small towns of Debat and St Georgis on the road north from Gonder. Ten years ago they were all very small towns with no high-rise structures, petrol stations or banks. Debark now has several banks and hotels, and last year the government decided to build a university. The construction has been rapid and in 2018 some 5,000 students will fill the classes.

Another indicator has been the number of Simien guides. When the lodge started there were only 20 guides: there are now over 80. The price for guiding has multiplied five times in this period, so it can be said that the total guiding income has increased approximately 20-fold.

Lease fees are relatively low in Ethiopia. The rent price is similar to agricultural land and the annual rent for the 16 hectares allocated to the lodge is low. However, knowing how concession fees work in other African states, the private sector company wanted to fall in line and provide a benefit for the park. A new 45-year lease between the private operator and government, with the possibility for a 20-year extension, was signed in 2015 and (at the suggestion of the company) a 3% concession fee based on turnover was agreed.

In the early years, the private sector operator was keen to reinvest in more capacity and vehicles while retaining a good cash flow. The Ethiopian partner has diminished his shareholding to just 3% as he wanted to take out his share of the profits. Net profits in recent years have been good: on average about 40% of gross revenue before accounting adjustments and tax.

### Social impact

All staff are employed from local villages. During the recruitment, the directors asked the seven local village leaders to each provide two good students to form part of the initial staff team: 10 years later they are nearly all still there. They earn fair salaries and service charges (gratuities) – probably four times what they might earn in jobs in the local town. There are 38 staff in total, with a 50:50 split between men and women. They live in the staff accommodation while on duty and when off duty they return to their home villages. Most staff are now aged about 30 and, through their employment, have been able to buy houses in town.

The staff cost is still low as an overall percentage of turnover. This is why when a downturn in tourism in late 2016 made many hotel owners decide to lay off staff, the management of Simien Lodge took the opposite view. All staff retained their jobs and it was explained that the management would ensure their livelihoods through this small dip in tourism: this could only be achieved because management had been prudent with cashflow in previous years. Bookings for later in 2017 were looking strong again and management had no intention of wanting to retrain staff, which would have incurred further costs. The staff understood the reasoning and appreciated the transparency and loyalty shown to them. Every year the managers take their staff for a 'training session' in another town in the country. This is a good opportunity for social bonding between management from the Addis Ababa sales office and the lodge staff.

The social impact on the local community cannot be underestimated. The local people defend the lodge as if it were their own property. When investors came recently proposing to build lodges along the escarpment in the prime wildlife areas, the local people declared that they would not allow it. This was in opposition to the decision of central government. There had been a relocation of 200 families from the central area of the park to an area outside the park by the government, and locals opposed the relocation of their own families to make way for 'foreigners'. By foreigners they did not mean tourists – they meant investors from Addis Ababa or outside. It is difficult to quantify how much is spent on local supplies and services, but wherever possible local supplies are purchased. In general, about 80% of food is purchased locally. This has increased over the years due to the formation of farmers' cooperatives.

### Environmental impact

The private sector operator acknowledges that it would be impossible to run a successful lodge without a high regard for the environment. Consequently, the lodge was built near to the old park entrance as it was never the wish to build in the core park wildlife areas. The park is quite small and the private sector operator felt that it would be wrong to have constructed a 'lighthouse' rather than a lodge that nestles into the hillside. During the construction stage, the boundaries of the park were extended so the lodge is now well inside the national park boundary. Grazing of domestic animals was banned around the lodge approximately five years ago which means that the gelada baboon often occupy the 16 hectares leased by the lodge.

All electricity cables are underground. Heating is by solar hot water, pumped under the floors (it is cold at night at 3,300 metres). There are two septic tanks that are alternated every year. Roof angles match those of the typical Simien dwellings. The buildings are in stone to fit in with the north Gonder architecture. All stone had to be brought in from outside the park since excavation is not allowed inside the park.

### Successes

In 2016 the lodge won the Skål Award for Rural Accommodation and in 2016 received second place in the World Travel Market (WTM) Africa Awards for poverty alleviation. In the last two years, Simien Lodge has been nominated for the 'We are Africa' awards. In recent years the lodge has:

- built eight classrooms for three local primary schools;
- manufactured hundreds of school benches through client donations;
- organised the Simien Walia run for the third year in a row with 3,000 participants receiving medals and t-shirts – this year the theme of the race was 'Save the Wolf';
- renovated the monastery that hangs on the cliff face at Saddick Amba and opened a trekking route to it.
- run conservation classes for children.

### Challenges

In one of the harshest climates in the world, in one of the remotest areas of the country and with some of the poorest people, the challenges have been obvious, including building trust with the local community. The management has succeeded through dedication and by bonding with the community. As discussed above, although the suspicion of foreigners and private sector investment has lessened somewhat in the past 10 years, it is still difficult to get all ministries to agree on various aspects related to tourism development in the country.

It is difficult to quantify how much is spent on local supplies and services, but wherever possible local suppliers are used. One of the problems, however, has been that government regulations require VAT only be charged on purchases from registered sources. This has proven difficult in the case of local farmers wanting to supply produce. The lodge has brought the farmers together into a cooperative and this appears to be a possible solution for both sides.

### Lessons learned and recommendations

It takes time and energy to build trust and confidence. Employees had to be shown that any disloyalty would be dealt with by instant dismissal, but that they would enjoy fruitful careers if they worked well and honestly.

Getting Simien communities to work together with community projects has proved not to work. There have been several community projects which started but which have failed. Private enterprise projects are generally the only ones that succeed through strict management but also with reasonable sharing and good working conditions. For example, Simien Lodge was the first company in the north of the country to introduce a private pension scheme (now merged with the government's national scheme).

**Table 12.** Summary – Simien Mountain Lodge.

| | |
|---|---|
| Name of company | Nick Crane (private individual) |
| Location | Ethiopia |
| Year established | 2004 |
| Status of company (i.e. listed, privately owned, etc.) | Private limited: Simien Park Lodges Plc |
| List of camps/lodges | Simien Mountain Lodge (28 rooms; 60 beds) |
| Investment/partnership | Private lodge ownership on government land (national park)<br>43 remaining (+20 possible extension) years for concession |
| Total number of staff employed | 38 |
| % local staff | 96% |
| Financial summary | Turnover 17.4 million Ethiopian birr (ETB) (approximately USD 744,427) in 2016 |

### 3.2.3. Case Study 5: Davison's Camp, Linkwasha Camp and Little Makalolo, Zimbabwe

#### Background

The camps belonging to WS in Hwange National Park in Zimbabwe are located in private concessions within the national park. These are Davison's Camp, Linkwasha Camp and Little Makalolo. Around the ecotourism sections of Hwange National Park (declared in 1928) are community lands, hunting concessions and to the west lies Botswana. Hwange National Park is located approximately two hours' drive from Victoria Falls and can be reached by road and air. There are a number of private tourism concessions within the national park, as well as a public access area where there are basic accommodation facilities and campsites. The camps offer game drives, game walks and village visits.

Table 13 shows the minimum and maximum fully inclusive rack rates charged per person sharing at the various camps in 2017 (Wilderness Safaris, 2017c).

### Institutional structure

WS currently operates three camps in Hwange National Park: Davisons' Camp, Linkwasha and Little Makalolo. The camps were built, and are owned, by WS, with the land being owned by government (National Parks). WS pays annual lease fees plus daily conservation fees to National Parks to operate in the area. Community and conservation projects conducted by WS are all voluntary. The Linkwasha and Makalolo concession leases, where the lodges are, were renewed in January 2009 and are for a 25-year period (ending December 2033).

### Economic impact

For the period 2015–2017, WS paid a total of USD 346,459 to National Parks in terms of lease fees and conservation fees (Wilderness Safaris Zimbabwe – WSZ – email, August 2017, personal communication). Other economic contributions include a 2% tourism levy payable to the Zimbabwe Tourism Authority amounting to USD 118,463 over the same period (WSZ, email, August 2017, personal communication).

### Social impact

A total of 170 staff are employed in the Wilderness Hwange Camps; 100% of staff are Zimbabwean, with more than 90% coming from the local community (WSZ, email, August 2017, personal communication). Staff costs (including wages, food, uniforms and training) over the period 2015–2017 amounted to USD 3.5 million, with an average of approximately USD 1.2 million per annum. The average wage for junior staff is USD 309 per month and for senior staff is USD 975 per month (WSZ, email, January 2018, personal communication). The total monthly salary cost for the camps is USD 98,305 (WSZ, email, January 2018, personal communication).

Wilderness invests an extensive amount in terms of capacity and finances in corporate social responsibility (CSR), including both community development work through their programme, Children in the Wilderness (CITW), and also conservation projects and their WWT (see Case Study 17 in this volume for more on these two independent non-profit organisations). Some of the community projects to date include: water provision through the installation of boreholes; classroom infrastructure; library development; school scholarships; solar light provision; and establishment of eco-clubs and eco-gardening.

Table 14 shows the amount spent on community development over the period 2015–2017. A large amount of this is donated by guests and other partners, including the Grand Circle Foundation (GCF). The projects are chosen in partnership with the community and are administered, facilitated and managed by CITW and WS.

A total of USD 959,748 spent on community projects and environmental education for rural children over three years is a significant investment. Wilderness also employs a full-time staff member based in Hwange National Park to engage with the community and manage all community projects and guest village visits. Another three staff members are employed, based in Victoria Falls, to manage donations, reporting and administration. The camps have bought baskets from Lupane Woman's Centre but do not buy fresh

**Table 13.** Rack rates for Hwange Camps, 2017.

| Name of camp | Minimum rack rate per person sharing | Maximum rack rate per person sharing |
|---|---|---|
| Davison's Camp (18 beds) | USD 365 | USD 605 |
| Little Makalolo (12 beds) | USD 445 | USD 805 |
| Linkwasha (18 beds) | USD 515 | USD 975 |

**Table 14.** Community payments, 2015–2017.

| Financial year | Community projects | CITW | Total community contribution |
|---|---|---|---|
| 2015 | USD 216,998 | USD 49,012 | **USD 266,010** |
| 2016 | USD 209,021 | USD 162,182 | **USD 371,203** |
| 2017 | USD 224,279 | USD 98,256 | **USD 322,535** |
| **Total** | **USD 650,298** | **USD 309,450** | **USD 959,748** |

Source: Wildnerness Holdings (2015, 2016, 2017).

produce from the communities due to a lack of the correct quality and quantity. Buying for all camps is done in Bulawayo with big suppliers such as Pick n' Pay, OK and others. In general, many products used in Zimbabwe are imported.

#### Environmental impact

WS, together with the WWT, supports the anti-poaching unit (The Scorpion Anti-Poaching Unit) in Hwange National Park, both financially and logistically, and recently (2018) spent approximately USD 50,000 on a new vehicle for the unit to assist with their patrols and logistics. Wilderness employs a full-time staff member, based in Hwange, to monitor the company's impacts on biodiversity, as well as to monitor and manage all environmental management systems. WS supports a number of conservation research projects in the park, including an Elephant Movement Study. WS also supports a water provision project in Hwange through funding staff to manage and monitor, as well as supply, diesel to pumps to pump water into various waterholes in the park.

The camps use a combination of generator inverter hybrids, grid power of hydro origin and small individual solar arrays to provide power (W. Ozorio, email, August 2017, personal communication). Coupled with this, energy efficient appliances have been used which all help to reduce generator run time in camps where hybrid systems are employed (W. Ozorio, email, August 2017, personal communication). The camps have adopted a reusable water bottle policy which ensures that the average bottled water consumption per guest remains very low, and under the target of 0.8 litres per bednight (W. Ozorio, email, August 2017, personal communication). The use of the filtered water systems has reduced bottled water consumption from 25,534 bottles in FY2007 to 6,268 bottles in FY2017 (75% positive change) (WSZ, email, August 2017, personal communication). The camps undergo a biannual environmental management system (EMS) assessment to ensure compliance with GEMS. In FY2017 the camps achieved 89% compliance with GEMS (W. Ozorio, email, August 2017, personal communication).

#### Successes

The presence of the ecotourism camps in the area, as well as the anti-poaching unit, has helped to reduce incidents of poaching, though these do still occur. The community development and CITW programmes have been extensive and made a substantial impact in terms of education, school infrastructure, provision of water and improving local livelihoods in the villages surrounding Hwange. Local employment and training has also had positive impacts.

#### Challenges

Inconsistent government policies and legislation can cause issues in terms of operating in the national park. The grading of roads and maintenance of park infrastructure is also limited, and does impact the tourism business. In recent years, poaching has had an impact on conservation and, therefore, the business.

#### Lessons learned and recommendations

Despite any contractual obligation, the ability to contribute to the lives and livelihoods of community members living adjacent to the national park has promoted more positive attitudes towards tourism and conservation. A commitment to CSR, in terms of community and conservation, is important to the long-term success of many PAs.

**Table 15.** Summary – Davison's Camp, Linkwasha Camp and Little Makalolo.

| | |
|---|---|
| Name of company | Wilderness Safaris (WS) |
| Location | Hwange National Park, Zimbabwe |
| Year established | WS began operating in Hwange in 1997 |
| Status of company (i.e. listed, privately owned, etc.) | Privately owned listed company with local indigenous partners |
| List of camps/lodges | Davison's Camp (18 beds), Little Makalolo (12 beds), Linkwasha (18 beds) |
| Investment/partnership option | Government owned land<br>25-year concession<br>Privately owned infrastructure<br>Privately managed camps |
| Total number of staff employed | 75 (for selected camps) |
| % local staff | 100% |
| Financial summary | USD 346,459 has been paid to government in terms of lease fees and conservation levies from 2015 to 2017 (3-year period)<br>USD 1.89 million in wages to local Zimbabweans from 2015 to 2017, with a monthly total salary bill of USD 66,963<br>Total of USD 635,054 paid, and/or facilitated, in terms of community development projects from 2015 to 2017<br>Total of USD 309,450 has been paid from 2015 to 2017 for environmental education projects in the villages |

### 3.2.4 Case Study 6: Nkwichi Lodge, Lake Malawi, Mozambique

### Background

Nkwichi is a 14-bed lodge located on the shores of Lake Malawi beside the 120,000-hectare Manda Wilderness Community Conservation Area of Mozambique (Turner, 2008). There are eight beaches along 4 kilometres of the Rift Valley coast (Nkwichi, 2008), and the lodge offers canoeing, bushwalks, trekking, community visits, birding, snorkelling and swimming (Mussanhane, 2008). The lodge is privately owned and managed by Nkwichi.

In 2017 the rack rates in the different types of accommodation ranged from USD 220 to 360 per person per night, sharing (M. Turner, email, 2017, personal communication).

### Institutional structure

Nkwichi Lodge has a 50-year concession for the land from the Mozambican government and the company owns the infrastructure and also manages the enterprise. To initiate the enterprise, a group of five private shareholders invested USD 500,000 in the development of the lodge (Mussanhane, 2008).

The Manda Wilderness Community Trust (MWCT) is a UK-registered charity established in 2005 (Manda Nkwichi, 2008) that has raised funds to support social and agricultural projects in the local communities around the lodge. The MWCT has supported the establishment of a community association, UMOJI, to help local people register land rights and create a community conservation area (CCA) (Mussanhane, 2008). This process received financial assistance from the Swedish Cooperative Centre (Manda Nkwichi, 2008).

The land on which the lodge is based is owned by the government (as is all land in the country), and the lodge acquired a Direito do Uso e Aproveitamento da Terra (DUAT), which is a licensed right to use the land (Mussanhane, 2008).

UMOJI is a community association with elected and traditional leaders, which uses a general assembly and executive committee in its operations. There are 16 villages within six communities populated by around 20,000 people who make up the association members. Nkwichi Lodge is a founding member of UMOJI, and is represented at each assembly (Mussanhane, 2008).

The 120,000-hectare Manda Wilderness CCA, which the lodge is adjacent to, is a conservancy fully managed by UMOJI. UMOJI has received technical support from the African Safari Lodge Foundation in its development on bidding processes, the law and negotiations (Mussanhane, 2008).

### Economic impact

The lodge has been profitable since 2006, and in 2008 the CCA was expected to generate USD 85,000 in revenue per year and provide USD 40,000 profit for the community by 2015 (Mussanhane, 2008).

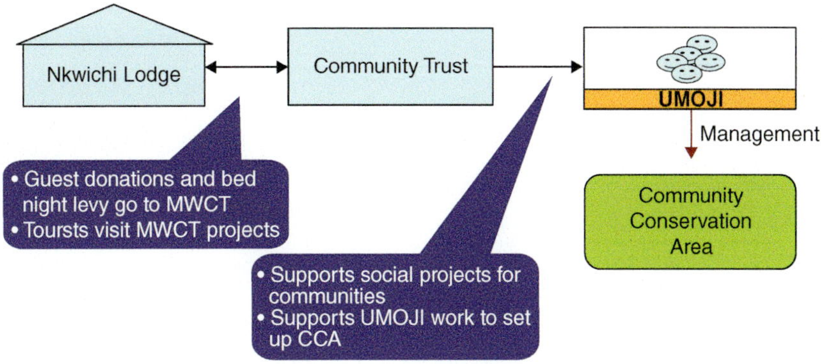


**Fig. 3.** Institutional structure of Nkwichi Lodge.
Source: Mussanhane (2008)

**Social impact**

Nkwichi Lodge permanently employs 40 local people at the lodge itself, and also employs around 29–60 contracted employees throughout the year. The average salary is USD 64 per month (which is higher than the minimum salary in the country). In 2017, 24% of the permanent staff and 21% of management were female (M. Turner, email, 2017, personal communication). It is estimated that each employee supports 15 members of their extended family (implying that the permanent employment supports 600 people directly and indirectly). There is no other formal employment available in the area, and only low levels of education, with low levels of literacy and numeracy (Mussanhane, 2008).

The MWCT raised over USD 200,000 in donations to support social projects and agricultural initiatives in the local communities. These include 11 schools, a maternity clinic, a maize mill, bridges, roads, jetties, nutrition improvement and microfinance (e.g. loans for seeds, tools and irrigation pumps) (Manda Nkwichi, 2008; Mussanhane, 2008). The social project ideas are generated by community members (Turner, 2008). Furthermore, it generates around USD 8,000 per year from tourists, and also received a USD 100,000 grant from the Ford Foundation on behalf of UMOJI (Mussanhane, 2008).

The Manda Wilderness Agriculture Project (MWAP) provides a demonstration and training centre and aims to share more ecologically sustainable agriculture in the region. The assistant manager is a local woman who is the first in the region to become permaculture qualified. Since 2002, the project has assisted over 350 local farmers to improve knowledge of agriculture and permaculture, access tools and seeds, diversify their production and improve access to markets. The project was initially funded by a grant from The Dawe Charitable Trust (Manda Nkwichi, 2008–13c) and has recently received a USD 142,500 grant from the Critical Ecosystem Partnership Fund (CEPF) to run a three-year conservation agriculture programme with the local communities (M. Turner, email, 2017, personal communication).

Local procurement of fish, craft, wood, grass, vegetables, bamboo and bricks generated USD 49,142 between 2006 and 2007 for local entrepreneurs and businesses (Mussanhane, 2008). Members of UMOJI

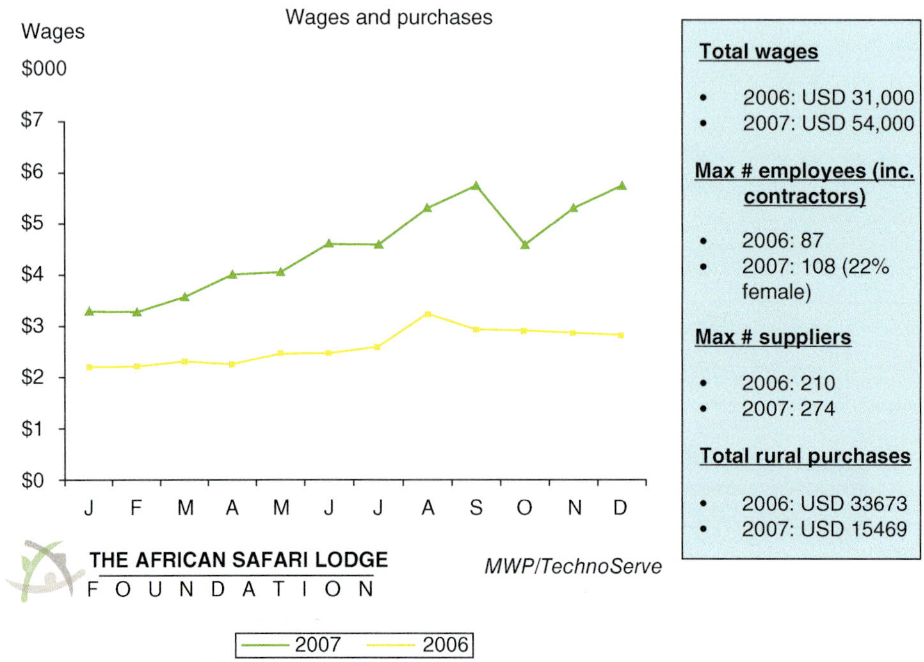


**Fig. 4.** Employment and procurement benefits.
Source: Mussanhane (2008)

have received training in agriculture (350 farmers), linkages between conservation tourism and development, leadership, law and tourism exchange trips (Mussanhane, 2008).

#### Environmental impact

Creation of a 120,000-hectare CCA is a significant positive environmental outcome of the lodge. Natural resource management committees have been established in the 16 communities to help regulate land use and, in particular, to stop hunting (Mussanhane, 2008). The communities agreed the boundaries for the CCA and obtained land titles for community land areas. The management plan for the CCA was ratified by the provincial government of Niassa in 2011 (Mussanhane, 2008; M. Turner, email, 2017, personal communication).

The lodge's electricity needs are completely powered using solar panels, though petrol water pumps are used to pump water to the chalets (M. Turner, email, 2017, personal communication).

#### Successes

Successes include the establishment of a commercially viable lodge in a remote and impoverished area of Mozambique, which has achieved financial sustainability despite global economic challenges. Injections into the local economy through wages and local supplies have enabled the creation of a number of local businesses and enterprises. Conservation has been improved through the creation of a new 120,000-hectare CCA. Improved infrastructure in the villages has increased access to health and education, especially for women and children (M. Turner, email, 2017, personal communication).

#### Challenges

There are challenges in terms of the accessibility of the lodge, but most visitors include the destination in a Malawi circuit. Employment of local people is also a challenge in terms of the low levels of education among community members, and therefore substantial training is required for new employees and also to manage the conservation area. The remote location also means that there are limited local supplies that can be procured. Human–wildlife conflict, population growth and poor natural resource management are also substantial challenges (Mussanhane, 2008).

**Table 16.** Summary – Nkwichi Lodge.

| | |
|---|---|
| Name of company | Manda Wilderness Ltd |
| Location | Manda Wilderness Community Conservation Area, Lake Malawi, Mozambique |
| Year established | 1998 |
| Status of company (i.e. listed, privately owned, etc.) | Private |
| List of camps/lodges | Nkwichi Lodge |
| Investment/partnership option | Privately owned infrastructure<br>Privately managed operations<br>Based on government owned land, within a community conservation area<br>Concession from the government through a DUAT |
| Total number of staff employed | 40 permanent employees |
| % local staff | 98% |
| Financial summary | USD 40,000 profit for the community in 2015<br>USD 200,000 raised for social projects in local communities |

### Lessons learned and recommendations

This form of enterprise can be replicated, assuming that there are high levels of donor and NGO support for community capacity-building (Mussanhane, 2008). Lessons learned include the need for appropriate background research; elaboration of a community-engagement philosophy; the importance of getting early support and permission from community members and establishing community committees and community participation; communicating with community members through a local partner or NGO; emphasising local procurement of goods, services and labour; funding community projects separately from the tourism enterprise; and working towards company and community benefits.

## 3.2.5 Case Study 7: Chumbe Island, Tanzania

### Background

From 1991 to 1994, the founder of Chumbe Island Coral Park Limited (CHICOP) successfully negotiated with the semi-autonomous government of Zanzibar/Tanzania for the western coral reef and forest of Chumbe Island to be gazetted as a marine protected area (MPA), with management entrusted to CHICOP. The company was specifically established for the purpose of developing and managing the MPA in a financially self-sustainable way, utilising ecotourism to generate revenue for all MPA operational costs and associated conservation, research and education activities. Through this, Chumbe became the first managed marine park in Tanzania, the first privately managed MPA in the world, and remains one of the very few financially self-sustainable MPAs globally.

The company objectives are not-for-profit, implementing conservation and education initiatives over more than 20 years under the framework of three iterations of management plans (1995–2005, 2006–2016, 2017–2027). Ecotourism business operations follow commercial principles for maximising revenue and promoting cost-effectiveness to ensure a sustainable revenue stream for MPA activities, exemplifying a successful business-oriented approach to sustainable and effective MPA management. CHICOP engages with a wide range of stakeholders across many different areas of the project including government agencies, fishers, local communities, schools, universities and academic institutions, NGOs and the tourism industry.

In the early 1990s, there was little awareness of the economic value of coral reefs and even the national language, Swahili, had no word for corals as they were considered to be lifeless rocks. It became CHICOP's mission, therefore, to provide environmental education to wide sectors of society. This initiative served to gain respect first of all from fishers. Educated by CHICOP's rangers, formerly fishers themselves, fishers now generally respect the park boundaries and voluntarily comply with regulations.

In 2017, the fully inclusive rack rate per person sharing ranged between USD 260 and 280, depending on the season (Chumbe Island, 2017a). This rate includes boat transfers to and from the island, accommodation, all meals and activities. There is also an option of a day trip to the island which costs USD 90 per person and includes boat transfers, lunch, soft drinks, snorkelling, guided forest walks and shared use of an ecobungalow (Chumbe Island, 2017b). There are seven bungalows on the island, accommodating 16 people.

#### Institutional structure

Though a private limited company, CHICOP is in many respects managed like an NGO, especially concerning participation of a wide variety of stakeholders, as well as detailed planning, monitoring, reporting and documentation of actions and outcomes. The company Chumbe Island Coral Park (CHICOP) is privately owned, with the land on Chumbe Island and the landing site in Zanzibar Island being leased from government.

The Chumbe MPA was established through partnerships with government and local communities and included: negotiations with seven sector ministries of the Zanzibar government; village meetings before and during project development; employment and training of community members for various project roles, including former fishers as park rangers; village leader involvement in management plans and advisory committee meetings; and the provision of wider income opportunities for local people. The strategy of providing opportunities for those who want to take them, rather than making promises, has been key to the success of working with stakeholders.

Increased understanding of the legal and institutional requirements of marine governance among government officials has also improved political support for conservation and prepared the ground for a more conducive legal framework.

Through this multi-level education approach, ecotourists have also become partners in conservation. MPA visitors participate in snorkelling, forest trail and intertidal walks, guided by well-trained rangers, and learn more about these vulnerable ecosystems.

#### Economic impact

Approximately USD 1.2 million was invested from 1991 to 1998 to develop CHICOP. Half came from the project initiator, Sibylle Riedmiller, one quarter from donor grants, while another quarter was contributed by the professional work of over 50 volunteers... Donors included GTZ, CIM, the German Tropical Forest Stamp Programme, the SADC-Environmental Education Programme, US-NOAA and Seacology.

Commercial operations started in 1998 with occupancy reaching around 70% in 2016. The annual minimum operational budget is USD 400,000. No dividends are paid out to shareholders as CHICOP operates in a not-for-profit manner. Today, CHICOP receives no financial support from government or donors and relies solely on revenue from ecotourism, which has fully funded operations since 2000. However, as no incentives are given to private PAs and other social businesses, CHICOP pays taxes like any other tourism business; these amount to around 25% of turnover. Approximately USD 34,000 per month is spent on local goods and services, with 100% spend being locally.

Land lease on the island is USD 4,873 annually, and the lease of the landing site in Zanzibar Island is USD 700 annually. CHICOP's annual contributions in taxes average over USD 100,000 annually (see Table 17 for more details related to permits and leases).

**Table 17.** Expenditure at CHICOP.

| Agency | Type | Amount | Renew date | Renewable |
|---|---|---|---|---|
| Commission for tourism | Tourism certificate<br>Management Certificate | USD 1,000<br>USD 560 | January<br>January | Annually<br>Annually |
| Commission for lands | Land lease – Chukwani | USD 700 | September | Annually |
| Commission for lands | Land lease – Chumbe | USD 4,873 | October | Annually |
| Zati | Certificate of Membership | USD 450 | January | Annually |
| Zanema | Certificate of Membership | USD 200 | January | Annually |
| Zipa | Investment license | USD 500 | January | Annually |
| Immigration department | Resident Permit (for foreign employees) | USD 2,050 | as expires (per expatriate) | 2 years |
| Department of labor | Occupation Safety<br>For foreign employees: Work permit–1st time<br>Work permit–Renew | Tsh. 1,800,000<br>USD 300<br>USD 150 | January (next due 2019)<br>as expires (per expatriate) | Every 2 years<br>Annually |
| Tanzania communications regulations authorities | Radio frequency | USD 150 | January (next due 2024) | Every 10 years |
| National insurance coorporation of tanzania ltd | Fire insurance | USD 450 | January | Annually |
| National insurance coorporation of tanzania ltd | Island insurance | USD 450 | October | Annually |
| National insurance coorporation of tanzania ltd | Workmen Compensation | Tsh. 1,637,000 | October | Annually |
| Western district council | Liquor license | USD 1,500 | December | Annual |
| Western district council | Garbage collection fee | Tsh. 30,000 | as expires | Monthly |
| Zanrec | Recycling fee | Tsh. 50,000 | as expires | Monthly |
| Zanzibar revenue board | Road License for vehicles<br>Infrastructure tax | Tsh. 20,000<br>USD 1 | Per vehicle<br>Per guest | Annually<br>Monthly |
| Zanzibar insurance corporation | Road insurance | Tsh. 120,000 | Per vehicle | Annually |

Source: Permit and licenses list from publicly available CHICOP management plan

**Environmental impact**

The reef sanctuary has become one of the most pristine coral reefs in the region, with over 470 fish species and 200 species of hard coral – 90% of all recorded in East Africa – and the forest reserve is one of the last undisturbed semi-arid 'coral rag' forests in Zanzibar, particularly after successful rat eradication in 1997. Chumbe now gives sanctuary to highly endangered endemic Aders' duikers (*Cephalophus adersi*), threatened by poaching and habitat destruction in Zanzibar. In 2000, three breeding pairs were translocated to Chumbe, supported by Zoo Munich-Hellabrunn, the Chicago Zoological Society, Fauna and Flora

International (FFI) and the WWF. Chumbe also has the world's largest known population of rare coconut crabs (*Birgus latro*) listed on the International Union for the Conservation of Nature (IUCN) Red list and, attracted by abundant fish in the sanctuary, rare roseate terns (*Sterna dougallii*) bred on Chumbe in 1994, 2006 and 2017.

On Chumbe Island, lodge establishment and operations are closely controlled and monitored in order to minimise any environmental impacts. All buildings on the island (seven ecobungalows, a visitor's centre and staff quarters) were constructed according to state-of-the-art eco-architecture including rainwater catchment, vegetative grey water filtration, composting toilets, solar water heating and photovoltaic power generation (Chumbe Island, 2017c). The walkways, nature trails and beach areas are not artificially illuminated at night: a measure taken to protect feeding and breeding patterns of nocturnal animals, such as the giant coconut crabs. For guests, individual solar powered torches are available on request. Zanzibar does not have a regional solid waste management system in place and solid waste is usually burned in the streets or thrown on illegal dumps, creating a multitude of public health concerns and environmental hazards (Chumbe Island, 2017c). Therefore, Chumbe encourages all its guests to avoid bringing plastic bags/bottles and disposable batteries to the island (Chumbe Island, 2017c). To help reduce the amount of solid waste produced, Chumbe also controls and restricts the numbers of visitors to the island and avoids the purchase of non-biodegradable products. Where possible, goods are transported in locally made, biodegradable baskets. Non-cooked fruit and vegetable waste is successfully composted on the island, while non-biodegradable waste is brought back to Zanzibar where Chumbe has been working together with a private waste operator that focuses on the collection, processing and selling of recyclable waste, both locally and internationally (Chumbe Island, 2017c). Materials imported onto Chumbe Island are carefully screened to avoid any non-indigenous elements intruding into the preserved environment.

In 2005, researchers interviewed artisanal fishers, and 94% confirmed the so-called spill-over effect of the reef sanctuary by reporting increased yields in the vicinity.

### Social impact

CHICOP's 'Education for Sustainable Development' programme for fishers, students, teachers, government officials, tourism operators and visitors has, since 1995, hosted over 7,000 schoolchildren, 1,130 teachers and 700 community members for free one-day field excursions to Chumbe Island, offering them guided forest walks and snorkelling with help for non-swimmers, especially local girls.

With 45 full-time employees and only seven rooms, CHICOP has possibly the highest employee/room ratio of any tourism business in Tanzania and employs 200% more staff than the international average for ecolodges, prioritising women and local people, including a marine biologist, educators and park rangers for park management and environmental education programmes. An impressive 93% of employees are Tanzanian and 30% are women. CHICOP also provides economic opportunities by outsourcing guest transport and providing a market for local produce. Over two-thirds of the employees come from local communities, each supporting on average of five individuals. In particular, former fishers were recruited and trained as park rangers. Provision of wider income opportunities such as agricultural products for the restaurant, building materials and handicrafts, outsourcing road and boat transport and craft services during maintenance, affect an even higher number of local people. Approximately USD 34,000 is spent monthly on local suppliers.

In 2016, CHICOP's total annual salary expenditure was over USD 200,000; the total spent on conservation and education activities was over USD 122,000.

### Successes

Chumbe is unique in the world for having created the first privately established and managed marine park on the planet, and one of the very few that are fully funded through ecotourism.

### Challenges

In the early 1990s, CHICOP was innovative in every aspect and very challenging in Zanzibar. The concept of MPAs was new to the government, which had no respective policies and legislation at that time. Thus, the business proposal required four years of negotiations with seven ministries.

There were also no architects and building contractors for ecological architecture. Thus, a professor from Braunschweig Technical University/Germany was commissioned for the design and expatriate architects were required to build on the island. There were also no qualified local staff available for any positions – no protected area rangers and no hospitality workers. Thus, professional volunteers were mobilised to train local people for many years.

**Lessons learned**

Through lessons accumulated over a period of nearly three decades, it can be concluded from this case study that privately protected marine areas supported by ecotourism can be effective and economically viable, even in a challenging political environment. Private management has strong incentives to achieve tangible on-the-ground conservation goals and cooperation with local resource users, as well as generation of income, to be cost-effective and to keep overheads down. A top ranking of CHICOP in TripAdvisor and high occupancy indicates that there is a market in the tourism industry for state-of-the-art ecodestinations that support strict conservation and sustainability principles. Close cooperation with government agencies in establishing and protecting this reserve has enhanced the understanding of environmental issues among local and national authorities.

Investment in conservation and in environmentally sound technologies, as well as the employment of additional staff for park management and environmental education programmes, raises investment and operational costs considerably, making it difficult to compete with other tourism enterprises. Income and employment for local communities, a market for local produce, developing new work skills and restocking commercial fish species in adjacent marine areas (spillover) are decisive for success. To avoid user conflicts, it is easier to preserve an area that is not used intensively for subsistence or other economic endeavours by local communities.

The establishment of the education programmes, even prior to developing the tourism infrastructure, has proven critical for success. This has enabled a wide cross-section of society (e.g. schoolchildren, teachers and fishers' groups) to visit and learn on Chumbe, gaining awareness on both the importance and role of the marine environment in their everyday lives, and the importance of MPAs and the ecosystem services being supported by Chumbe's protected habitats.

With the threats of climate change, marine conservation needs more political support from governments and the international conservation community, as well as recognition of the contributions that the private sector can make to both effective conservation area management and the livelihoods of local people on the ground. Long-term security of tenure and contracts, together with a favourable political, legal and institutional environment are needed to attract more private and community investment in marine conservation, particularly in the developing world.

**Table 18.** Summary – Chumbe Island.

| | |
|---|---|
| Name of company | Chumbe Island Coral Park Limited (CHICOP) |
| Location | Zanzibar, Tanzania |
| Year established | 1993 |
| Status of company (i.e. listed, privately owned, etc.) | Private limited company, with not-for-profit objectives |
| List of camps/lodges | Chumbe Island (7 bungalows, 16 beds) |
| Investment/partnership option | Privately owned lodge, funded by private owner, and small donor contributions for the Visitors' Centre<br>Government owned land leased to CHICOP, with exclusive management agreements for Chumbe Reef Sanctuary and Chumbe Forest Reserve |
| Total number of staff employed | 43 full-time staff |
| % local staff | 93% of employees are local and 30% women |
| Financial summary | Lodge value = USD 1.2 million invested<br>In 2016, CHICOP's total annual salary expenditure was over USD 200,000, the total spent on conservation management and education activities was over USD 122,000. All management costs are borne by CHICOP |

## 3.3. Private Sector (for- or not-for-profit) on Government, Private or NGO Land

### 3.3.1. Case Study 8: Bale Mountain Lodge, Ethiopia

**Background**

Bale Mountain Lodge (BML) is located in a clearing within the Harenna Forest of the Bale Mountains National Park (BMNP), one of the largest remaining tropical cloud forests on earth and one of Ethiopia's premier national parks (Bale Mountain Lodge, 2017a). The lodge sits below an 1,800-metre high escarpment and offers walking and horse-borne safaris, bird watching, fly fishing and game viewing. Bale Mountains National Park in the south-central part of the country hosts the world's largest Afro-alpine habitat, with 14 endemic mammal species, 57% of Ethiopia's endemic bird species and 60% of the remaining Ethiopian wolf population (there are 180–200 out of the global population of 300–350 – G. Levene, email, November 2017, personal communication). The Ethiopian wolf is the world's rarest canid and Africa's rarest carnivore.

AWF (founded as the African Wildlife Leadership Foundation in 1961), is a conservation organisation with a unique focus on Africa (van Wijk, Lamers and van der Duim, 2015). Its mission is to ensure wildlife and wild lands thrive in modern Africa. In the late 1990s, recognising the need to develop conservation enterprises that generate revenue to support conservation and communities, AWF initiated the development of conservation tourism enterprises as a mechanism to attain conservation and livelihood goals. BML is an example of this.

While Ethiopia supports a robust cultural tourism industry, its wildlife product is underdeveloped. To demonstrate the economic value of Ethiopia's protected areas, AWF started working with the Ethiopian Wildlife Conservation Authority (EWCA) to identify appropriate tourism opportunities, such as BML, that could be developed to enhance revenue for Ethiopia's protected areas. By providing quality lodging inside the parks, revenue will increase, thereby demonstrating the economic value of the parks and garnering more support from government for protected areas.

BML opened in early 2014. The lodge will ultimately accommodate 30 guests, but currently operates with eight guestrooms and a three-bedroomed house. In 2017 the fully inclusive rack rate at BML ranged between USD 190 and USD 320 per person sharing, depending on the season (Bale Mountain Lodge, 2017b). BML has different rates for residents, which in 2017 ranged between USD 150 and USD 190 per person sharing, depending on the season and only allowed to be booked no earlier than four weeks in advance (Bale Mountain Lodge, 2017b).

### Institutional structure

BML is owned and operated by a private sector company called Jember Ltd. Jember has a lease with the EWCA to operate in Bale Mountain National Park and the company was instrumental, with AWF assistance, in developing an African standard concession and lease agreement which has been adopted by the Ethiopian government as standard practice for investment in the Ethiopian national parks. Some of the financing for the lodge came from African Wildlife Capital (AWC), now called Umiliki Investments, which was founded by AWF in 2011 as Africa's first impact-investment vehicle for conservation enterprise. The company provides investment financing to small and midsize enterprises that have the capacity to make a significant conservation and socioeconomic impact, thereby positively engaging the private sector in conservation efforts. Umiliki Investments invested approximately USD 1.4 million to develop the first two ecolodges in Ethiopia's national park system: BML in BMNP and Limalimo Lodge in Simien Mountains National Park. In addition, Limalimo and AWF both separately invested in a community tourism product via Village Ways Ltd, which has developed a product south of Simien Mountain National Park. AWF invested USD 200,000 in Limalimo on top of the AWC investment. Jember Ltd borrowed USD 800,000 from AWC at 8% over eight years for BML.

Jember Ltd, which runs BML, is a conservation-driven, ethical, UK-based development company which is committed to the provision of high quality tourist facilities in Ethiopia (Bale Mountain Lodge, 2017c). For BML, 45% of the project cost is financed by Umiliki. Jember Ltd also works in close cooperation with EWCA to raise awareness of the importance of Bale Mountains National Park (Bale Mountain Lodge, 2017c) and actively addresses issues raised in the BMNP general management plan in that the lodge generates income for EWCA, employs entirely local staff, provides outreach through international marketing and visitor information and supports knowledge improvements through providing research facilities.

### Economic impact

The concession fee is a mixed system of a small annual lease fee plus a revenue-based system, where the company provides 3% of gross revenue to EWCA per year on an annual basis. USD 23,000 has been paid over the last three years to the government in terms of concession fees. Other support to the national park includes the purchase of new geo-tagging and video enabled camera equipment in support of enforcement activities, provision of personnel, temporary vehicles and food and water in support of firefighting activities, sale of local honey and handicrafts through the lodge shop and Addis-based outlets (honey value has risen from USD 3.00/kg to USD 5.50/kg in three years), and establishment of a local horse suppliers association which now supports the lodge and other tourists within the BMNP.

### Social impact

BML employs 25 staff in Bale and a further 7 in Addis Ababa (3 on a retainer basis): 13 females, 19 males. Of these, 96% of Bale-based staff are from the local community. Over the past three years, around USD 266,000 has been spent on direct staff costs with USD 188,000 being wages and the remainder being pensions, taxation, training and uniforms. A further USD 45,000 has been spent on staff food costs as the lodge provides free food and accommodation to all staff alongside paying all taxes and pension costs. All staff receive annual training. In 2017 the lodge focus was on improved environmental health and hygiene training for staff.

The lodge also values its responsible relationship with the local community and invests both time and money in community and social initiatives – of these projects a number involve financing. This includes Birr 120,000 (USD 5,500) spent on sponsoring five children from the village to complete grades 10 and 11 in the nearby town as this would be unaffordable without support, plus a further USD 4,000 and leftover construction materials used to refurbish the Rira village medical centre which had not been touched since 1974. The work included tiling the surgery, installing hot water, renewing the ceiling, replacing broken doors, windows and shutters, repainting throughout and re-shelving the dispensary. The following year the lodge committed six maintenance staff for three weeks to fit out an extension building to the same medical facility. Routinely, the lodge supports the local environmental club activities and runs an annual litter awareness and collection day. The lodge supports the local school through the end-of-year school graduation programme in which it champions education and park protection and provides some finance for writing materials and pencils. Guests also provide materials which are donated to the school in Rira or to the Mother Theresa home for mentally and physically disabled people in Goba. The lodge also collects clothes and shoes for the same cause. The approximate total investment over last three years has been around USD 18,000, including materials.

#### Environmental impact

The site is 100% eco-friendly, with power coming from its own 25 kilowatt micro-hydro power plant. Biodegradable waste is processed through a bio-gas system to provide cooking gas and firewood is sourced from sustainable plantations outside the park (Bale Mountain Lodge, 2017a).

Efficient appliances, such as heat-pump hot water heaters act as reverse refrigeration and ensure the lodge minimises its power draw (Bale Mountain Lodge, 2017d), although some of these appliances have proved hard to maintain in Ethiopia and are no longer working to optimal performance. Water is taken from the river and subjected to slow sand filtration and purification (Bale Mountain Lodge, 2017d). Water is recycled through soakaways which return the purified waste water to the soils and river (Bale Mountain Lodge, 2017a). No harsh chemicals are used; the lodge tries to use natural products whenever there is an option. All other waste is managed to prevent contamination and plastic packaging is minimised on purchase and subsequently removed after use (Bale Mountain Lodge, 2017a).

Since 2014 the lodge has sponsored 10 different research teams in and around the BMNP. Teams are provided with accommodation, food, office and research facilities and internet access for the duration of their studies, all either free or at cost, to enable affordable research in the Bale Mountains. Over this time, Munich University has discovered 22 new species of butterflies and moths and recently a viper was officially 'discovered', jointly accredited to Mississippi and Utah universities (Bale Mountain Lodge, 2017e). In August 2017, an additional Royal Society publication confirmed that a further five new frog species have also been discovered by Tim Colston of Mississippi University.

The area is also a critical water catchment for 12 to 15 million people living in the south-eastern lowlands, Somalia and Northern Kenya.

#### Successes

The establishment and operation of BML within a remote and challenging business environment has been a success, along with the sponsorship of world-class scientific research, and training and education of significant numbers of rural Ethiopians in life and technical skills, enabling many to seek work outside the BMNP.

The raising of awareness of conservation to Ethiopians through BML radio and TV exposure emphasises the protection of amazing habitats and endemic wildlife, the importance of the water towers, and also stresses the opportunities for increased tourism revenue in support of Ethiopian development.

#### Challenges

Some of the challenges observed included: competing government priorities to conservation resulting in a lack of focus and support from government stakeholders; relatively high private sector levels of debt and interest repayments restricting operating capital and cashflow for the private sector; and a volatile business and security environment which makes long-term planning difficult. Other challenges included increasing population stress in and around the BMNP resulting in increased negative activities and local community and government perceptions of available private sector funds versus the reality of cashflow in an establishing

**Table 19.** Summary – Bale Mountain Lodge.

| | |
|---|---|
| Name of company | Jember Ltd and African Wildlife Foundation |
| Location | Bale Mountain National Park, Ethiopia |
| Year established | 2014 |
| Status of company (i.e. listed, privately owned, etc.) | Jember Ltd is a private UK-based company |
| List of camps/lodges | Bale Mountain Lodge (11 rooms) |
| Investment/partnership option | Government owned land – leased on a<br>45-year concession and lease (20-year extension option thereafter)<br>Privately owned infrastructure<br>Managed by private company |
| Total number of staff employed | 32 plus the owners |
| % local staff | 94% in Bale, 100% in Addis Abba |
| Financial summary | Normal turnover around USD 450,000 to USD 550,000<br>48% EBITDA<br>USD 884,000 remaining AWC debt to end 2021 |

business. The necessity to maintain high levels of personal energy and drive to maintain focus and progress, local bureaucratic difficulties and a lack of support for small business enterprises through poor understanding of commerce and poor education levels in mid-level government posts all provide ongoing challenges to the success of the operation.

#### Lessons learned and recommendations

It was noted by the private sector operator that conservation is difficult and long term in nature and that it requires long-term commitment and drive. It was also noted that positive local relationships are key to success and should be actively developed as an integral part of any business plan. This demands trust, honesty and commitment. It was also noted that cashflow is critical. In an African environment, where volatile external factors can have a major impact on success, a strong and flexible lender relationship is required. Tourism should never promise anything which it cannot deliver: it is negative to relationships in the long run and there should be no anticipation or expectation of any thanks or gratitude from anyone, as locals will often see the problems caused for them by tourism rather than the long-term benefits. Many cynical foreigners will also assume the operator has lots of money and is 'playing at conservation' for economic reasons. In addition, conservationists often have too many projects and too much on their plate to engage as often as the private sector would like.

### 3.3.2. Case Study 9: King Lewanika Lodge, Zambia

#### Background

King Lewanika Lodge is the first permanent lodge located in Liuwa Plain National Park, Zambia. It is located on the upper Munde stream near the centre of the park. The lodge is comprised of six luxury villas including a two-bedroom family villa, with the capacity to accommodate a total of 14 guests. Norman Carr Safaris (NCS) is the management partner in the running of the lodge. In 2018, Norman Carr Safaris rebranded and is now called Time + Tide.

In 2017, the fully inclusive rack rate per person sharing started from USD 1,070 (Norman Carr Safaris, 2017).

**Institutional structure**

In 2003, the then Zambian Wildlife Authority (ZAWA), African Parks Network (APN) and the Barotse Royal Establishment (BRE) entered into a formal agreement for the long-term management of Liuwa Plain National Park (LPNP) (S. Slabbert, email, May 2017, personal communication). This partnership gave rise to African Parks Zambia Ltd (APZ), the company with the legal responsibility for managing Liuwa. Under this management agreement, APZ has been given full, delegated authority to manage LPNP for an initial term of 20 years from 31 May 2004 (S. Slabbert, email, May 2017, personal communication).

APZ has the right to develop tourism in the park and as such raised the capital to develop King Lewanika Lodge as an asset of APZ to promote tourism in the park (S. Slabbert, email, May 2017, personal communication). APZ entered into a management agreement with NCS, a private tourism operator, to assist with the design, development and ultimate operations of the lodge (S. Slabbert, email, May 2017, personal communication).

**Economic impact**

NCS pays APZ a concession fee based on a negotiated fixed rate per person that stays at the lodge per day (USD 115) (D. Wilson, email, September 2017, personal communication). This fee is made up of a concession fee (USD 60 per person per day), a park entry fee (USD 40 per person per day) and a community development fee (USD 15 per person per day) (D. Wilson, email, September 2017, personal communication). Average annual concession fees are approximately USD 50,000 and total annual staff costs are budgeted at USD 105,000.

**Social impact**

The project employed 30 local staff members during construction and employs 20 permanent staff for operations (D. Wilson, email, September 2017, personal communication). The lodge procures fresh produce locally. NCS as well as APZ have an active community development portfolio. NCS currently funds the school in Sibemi village and the Munde village sponsorship programme. These programmes are only in their second year of operation (D. Wilson, email, September 2017, personal communication). No figures were provided in terms of local procurement or community development.

### Environmental impact

The lodge works off solar for all power and water heating requirements augmented by generator, when needed (Dave Wilson, September 2017, personal communication). Waste is separated and managed by composting, incinerating and movement off site of tins and glass (D. Wilson, email, September 2017, personal communication). Grey and black water is dealt with using eco-friendly biological agents and bacteria treatments (D. Wilson, email, September 2017, personal communication).

The restoration, ongoing conservation management and law enforcement is all done by APZ in the partnership, while NCS contributes to the operational budget of APZ through the concession fee model (D. Wilson, email, September 2017, personal communication).

### Successes

The lodge opened in May 2017 but bookings are already exceeding projection (projected annual 20% occupancy) (D. Wilson, email, September 2017, personal communication).

### Challenges

The alignment of expectations between a commercial tourism operator and the hard-core conservation park management team, with operational issues such as off-road driving, waste management and promotion of the APZ conservation message versus the commercial promotion of the operator is a challenge (S. Slabbert, email, May 2017, personal communication). The two parties are working hard to create a balance between these objectives.

### Lessons learned and recommendations

There is a need for regular on-the-ground meetings and communication to ensure needs and objectives are aligned (D. Wilson, email, September 2017, personal communication). Marketing and promotional resources should be shared to leverage each other's reach. Community development objectives and resources need to be aligned, shared and combined to maximise the impacts.

**Table 20.** Summary – King Lewanika Lodge.

| | |
|---|---|
| Name of company | Norman Carr Safaris (NCS), now Time + Tide |
| Location | Liuwa Plain National Park, Zambia |
| Year established | 2017 |
| Status of company (i.e. listed, privately owned, etc.) | African Parks (AP) is a non-profit organisation<br>NCS is a privately owned company |
| List of camps/lodges | King Lewanika Lodge (14 beds) |
| Investment/partnership option | Government owned land<br>APZ have a 20-year concession<br>APZ owned infrastructure – lodge value of USD 2 million<br>NCS are the private sector operational partner |
| Total number of staff employed | APZ employs 110 permanent staff (+–100 temporary)<br>NCS employs 20 staff at King Lewanika Lodge |
| % local staff | 95% + |
| Financial summary | Lodge value USD 2 million<br>Average annual concession fees = USD 50,000<br>Total annual staff costs USD 105,000 budgeted |

### 3.3.3. Case Study 10: Ngala Safari Lodge, South Africa

#### Background

Ngala Private Game Reserve is a safari lodge within the Kempiana Contractual National Park in South Africa. The Kempiana Contractual National Park is part of Kruger National Park (KNP) and forms part of the Great Limpopo Transfrontier Conservation Area. The andBeyond Ngala Safari Lodge has 21 chalets (45 beds), while the andBeyond Ngala Tented Camp has nine luxury tents (18 beds) (andBeyond, 2017a). The reserve offers guests wildlife game drives, walking safaris, tracking adventures, photographic safaris and also rhino-ear notching safaris (to witness the capture and darting of a rhino) (andBeyond, 2017d).

In 2017 the rack rates were USD 808 for andBeyond Ngala Tented Camp, per person, per night, on a fully inclusive basis, and USD 554 per person per night at andBeyond Ngala Safari Lodge on a fully inclusive basis (andBeyond, 2017b, 2017c).

#### Institutional structure

Ngala lies within Kempiana Contractual National Park and the Safari Lodge infrastructure is owned by the World Wide Fund for Nature – South Africa (WWF-SA), an NGO. AndBeyond has a 20-year lease, that is renewable every 10 years, to use the lodge and traverse the land. Infrastructure of the Tented Lodge is privately owned by WWF-SA, while andBeyond manages both Safari and Tented Lodge.

#### Economic impact

AndBeyond's lease fees for Ngala Private Game Reserve's land are paid to WWF-SA and are used to finance conservation initiatives (e.g. expansion of other protected areas, such as the West Coast and Mountain Zebra National Parks). Any profits generated through the commercial operations are retained by andBeyond, and in turn profits are distributed to the private owners, the Enthoven and Getty families.

Traversing fees and a percentage of profits from both andBeyond Ngala Safari Lodge and andBeyond Ngala Tented Camp, flow into the South African National Parks Trust (SANPT), an NGO, for use in expanding or adding to conservation areas (Buckley & Sommer, 2001). Traversing fees are calculated taking into account the occupancy rate and the lodge accommodation revenue. For each successive year of the lease period, the annual rental escalates at a rate equal to an agreed upon consumer price index (andBeyond, 2016).

### Social impact

In 2016 Ngala Safari lodge had 102 staff, of whom 80% were drawn from local communities. The overall wage bill in 2016 was approximately USD 649,794 (ZAR 9,089,540), of which 85% was paid to people from local communities.

The Africa Foundation (formerly the Rural Investment Fund see Case Study 15 in this volume) is an independent, non-profit organisation that works to support African communities (Africa Foundation, 2016). It was established in 1992 by andBeyond (when andBeyond was called Conservation Corporation Africa) to provide a vehicle to channel donations towards community development in its lodge destinations. Currently around 95% of its projects are with andBeyond lodge communities (Nicholson, 2017). Communities are actively involved in the design, development and implementation of community projects in order to enhance buy-in, and they must demonstrate their sustainability (Spenceley, 2001).

Ngala's closest rural community of Welverdiend has benefited from social initiatives financed by the Africa Foundation over the years. These are summarised in the Table 22, and their value is estimated at ZAR 6 million (approximately USD 428,900) (V. Bachoo, email, 2017, personal communication).

### Environmental impact

Kempiana Contractual National Park was proclaimed as part of KNP on 11 March 1994 and is managed by SANParks as part of the national park. Conservation of wildlife is, therefore, undertaken by SANParks.

All lodges within the KNP, including Ngala, are required to go through a biannual audit, as prescribed by the Integrated Environmental Management of SANParks (Sowry, 2014). The ecological control officer, the relevant section ranger in the area and the general manager of the respective lodge carry out these assessments. Evaluative compliance is expected with the policies of SANParks including the national environmental legislation pertaining to sensitive areas. Reports are to be submitted to the Department of Environmental Affairs. Through these eco-audits, a lodge must obtain a score of 70% to comply with legislation, as specified by government regulation (A. Nicholson, email, 2017, personal communication).

**Table 21.** Total staff/procurement costs for Ngala Safari Lodge, 2017.

| Impact | Description/value | % local |
|---|---|---|
| **Number of staff** | | |
| Ngala Safari Lodge | 102 | 80% |
| Ngala Tented Camp | 32 | 90% |
| **Staff salaries** | ZAR 9,089,540 (USD 649,794) | 84% |
| **Procurement** | ZAR 913,012 (USD 65,270) | – |

Sources: Nicholson (2017); N. Herbst, email, 2017, Aaron Jones, 2018, personal communication

**Table 22.** Benefits provided to the local communities, through the Africa Foundation.

| Education | Health | Small business development |
|---|---|---|
| • 28 tertiary bursaries<br>• Career guidance workshops<br>• Conservation lessons and debates<br>• 10 classrooms at 3 schools<br>• Playground equipment for 4 preschools and crèches<br>• First-aid training for teachers<br>• 1 media centre with computers | • 58 toilets at schools and community centres<br>• 6 school kitchens<br>• 936 hippo water rollers<br>• 3 boreholes<br>• 1 centre for Orphaned and Vulnerable Children<br>• Rehabilitation of 2 water pumps<br>• Water tanks for clinic | • Small business training for craft market<br>• Development of craft market<br>• Small-scale farm<br>• ZAR 1000 loan towards vehicle for local taxi operator (repaid) |

Sources: Nicholson (2017), Spenceley (2001)

The audits address biosphere manipulation, wildlife management, water extraction, off-road driving, construction, energy use and waste management (solid and liquid) (Nicholson, 2017). The lodges limit their negative environmental impact by recycling their waste through a local community business; monitoring energy use and using LED lights; monitoring water use; and using cleaned wastewater to replenish waterholes and irrigate gardens (A. Nicholson, email, 2017, personal communication).

### Successes

Operating since 1992, Ngala has a 25-year history of conservation and local community beneficiation. The list of community benefits that have been generated over this period is substantial and has had a meaningful impact on the local rural community of Welverdiend (Nicholson, 2017; Spenceley, 2001). Drawing the majority of its staff from local communities, Ngala's wage payments provide significant income into the local rural economy.

Shared value has been created between andBeyond Ngala and the Welverdiend community because the majority of community members perceived that they are deriving benefits from living adjacent to a protected area and the company has more satisfied, educated and motivated staff who are more willing to conserve and protect the natural resources in the area (A. Nicholson, email, 2017, personal communication).

There was a match between senior management's ideas for strengthening the relationship between andBeyond Ngala and Welverdiend and those improvement ideas were identified by the residents of Welverdiend (A. Nicholson, email, 2017, personal communication).

Education and the allocation of Community Development Education Fund (CDEF) bursaries are recognised as the greatest benefits that Ngala provides Welverdiend, with health care, employment, empowerment and conservation also recognised (A. Nicholson, email, 2017, personal communication).

### Challenges

The real connection between ecotourism and conservation comes through participation in ownership and management, rather than through economic benefits alone. This calls for the need to engage these communities as a management partner. More value could be created in the local communities if andBeyond became more reliant on local businesses. Education has received huge attention over the last 25 years in Welverdiend, but perhaps it is time for a shift of focus towards more small business development and entrepreneurial growth. If andBeyond Ngala could start getting a meaningful volume

**Table 23.** Summary – Ngala Safari Lodge.

| | |
|---|---|
| Name of company | AndBeyond |
| Location | Kempiana Contractual National Park |
| Year established | 1992 |
| Status of company (i.e. listed, privately owned, etc.) | Land owned by WWF<br>Lodge infrastructure owned by WWF-SA<br>Lodge managed by andBeyond |
| List of camps/lodges | Ngala Safari Lodge (45 beds)<br>Ngala Tented Camp (18 beds) |
| Investment/partnership option | Ngala Safari Lodge and tented camp: fully privately owned |
| Total number of staff employed | 134 |
| % local staff | 82% |
| Financial summary | Wages of USD 649,749 in 2016, of which 85% was paid to local community members.<br>USD 428,900 in donation invested in the local Welverdiend community |

of reliable local produce from neighbouring communities, this could make a substantial difference to the community. Other challenges include the need for better communication and integration between andBeyond Ngala staff and management and the local communities (A. Nicholson, email, 2017, personal communication).

**Lessons learned and recommendations**

The case of Ngala demonstrates how a private company can actively channel donations into local community development initiatives, and how over 25 years these can make considerable positive contributions to local community members. Making the shift from philanthropy to integrating local businesses in the tourism value chain is an ongoing challenge for this company.

## 3.3.4. Case Study 11: Mkulumadzi Lodge, Malawi

**Background**

Mkulumadzi Lodge is located in Majete Wildlife Reserve, Malawi. Mkulumadzi is on the banks of the Shire River just a few kilometres from where it plunges into the Kapichira Falls. Located in the south of Malawi, Majete is an area of 70,000 hectares, part of Africa's Great Rift Valley.

The lodge has eight chalets (16 beds), each with their own bedroom, lounge and en-suite bathroom, as well as private viewing decks. The lodge offers indoor and outdoor dining with a bar, as well as a *lapa* for evening campfires and also a pool. Activities include game drives, walking, viewing hides, boating safaris and a cultural experience (Robin Pope Safaris, 2017).

The fully inclusive rack rate in 2017 per person sharing ranged between USD 350 and USD 445, depending on the season. There is also a charge of USD 20 per person per night for park fees (Robin Pope Safaris, 2017).

### Institutional structure

In March 2003, African Parks Malawi (APM) concluded an agreement with the DNPW to take on responsibility for the rehabilitation, development and management of Majete Wildlife Reserve. The agreement to manage the park was part of a PPP initiative and allowed APM total management control of Majete Wildlife Reserve. The management agreement runs for an initial term of 25 years, with an option to renew for a further 10 years. APM is a company limited by guarantee with a local board with representatives from African Parks (AP), DNPW and local businesses. APM is the private sector management partner and also provides donor funding to the project. The land is owned by the government, with APM managing the park.

APM has the right to develop tourism in the park and as such, offered a concession for the development of an upmarket lodge. This was taken up by Robin Pope Safaris (RPS), a private sector operator, which raised the capital to develop Mkulumadzi Lodge and manages the lodge. The fixed asset reverts to the ownership of APM when the concession period is complete, while moveable assets remain the property of RPS. The lodge partnership is a private company (RPS) managing the lodge for APM, a private sector management company on government land.

### Economic impact

RPS pays APM a concession fee based on a negotiated fixed rate per person staying at the lodge per day. This fee is made up of a concession fee, a percentage of profit and a park entry fee of USD 4 for locals, USD 10 for Malawian residents and USD 20 for international guests (C. Grobler, email, August 2017, personal communication). Majete Game Reserve attracted a total of 8,018 visitors in 2016 and the reserve brought in total tourism revenue of USD 411,900 (C. Grobler, email, August 2017, personal communication).

### Social impact

The project employed 50 local staff members during construction and employs 35 permanent staff for operations. The majority of staff members come from the local community, historically one of the poorest areas of Malawi. The community around Majete directly and indirectly benefits from employment or the various community projects APM and Mkulumadzi Lodge are involved in.

The lodge procures fresh produce locally (currently only 25% of needs, but it is hoping to increase this to 50% by 2018) and will use local artisans and suppliers wherever possible. The lodge promotes cultural activities in partnership with AP as part of the tourism portfolio where guests get to visit community activities in the area.

RPS as well as APM have an active community development portfolio. APM manages the Majete Scholarship Programme which, in 2016, processed and paid school fees amounting to USD 15,500, covering four university students and 100 secondary school students, and in 2017 constructed the Chiguma School, which will house 180 students (African Parks, 2017d). Other projects include bee-keeping (an important community income-generating initiative), malaria research and a tree planting project within the communities. USD 4,000 was also generated for the 19 community-based organisations (CBOs) through the sale of locally produced products including honey, woven grass material, artwork, *zitenje* (a locally made fabric) and other items (African Parks, 2017d). Mkulumadzi Lodge is involved with Pack for a Purpose, an organisation that provides travellers with up-to-date information about needed supplies for community-based projects (www.packforapurpose.org). Travellers use their luggage to take school, medical and other supplies to the communities they visit.

### Environmental impact

The restoration, ongoing conservation management and law enforcement is all done by APM while RPS contributes to the operational budget of APM through the concession fee model. RPS is responsible for the maintenance and upkeep of the road network within the concession area, and follows an environmental management plan set by APM.

The biosphere and habitat is left in as natural and unmodified a state as possible and the lodge's building style keeps in mind the visual impact of the lodge. The lodge is powered by solar power and a strict waste management plan has been implemented.

### Successes

The combination of a well-managed wildlife reserve, a secure environment and an outstanding wildlife product enabled a conducive investment climate to attract investment by a third party into a high-end lodge. RPS has invested into Majete and the 'partnership' with APM contributes significantly to the sustainability of the park as well as the lodge.

### Challenges

The alignment of expectations between a commercial tourism operator and a hard-core conservation park management team with operational issues such as the requirement or request of an operator to have an 'exclusive' wildlife area in a small reserve while the park also offers public and day visitor access is an ongoing challenge. Careful zoning and strategic road networks with daily management and communications between various operators and park users is required to ensure all users enjoy the park's offering without conflicts. The park's management and operational costs are unconditional and ever increasing while the concession agreement is based on a fixed price per guest – implying that when tourism is down, the park gets no income from its operators. There is thus a need to work towards a form of minimum annual payment to contribute towards the sustainability of the park, irrespective of tourism volumes.

### Lessons learned and recommendations

There is a need for regular on-the-ground meetings and communication to ensure needs and objectives are aligned. Increased capacity-building through external training of guides is always required. Marketing and promotional resources should be shared to leverage each other's reach. Community development objectives and resources need to be aligned, shared and combined to maximise the positive impacts.

**Table 24.** Summary – Mkulumdazi Lodge.

| | |
|---|---|
| Name of company | Robin Pope Safaris (RPS) |
| Location | Majete Wildlife Reserve, Malawi |
| Year established | APM since 2003<br>RPS since 2010 |
| Status of company (i.e. listed, privately owned, etc.) | African Parks (AP) is a non-profit organisation<br>African Parks Majete (APM) (Ltd) is a private sector management partner<br>RPS is a privately owned company |
| List of camps/lodges | Mkulumadzi (16 beds) |
| Investment/partnership option | Government owned land<br>APM has a 25-year concession<br>Lodge privately owned and run by RPS for the duration of concession. Fixed assets revert to APM at end of concession period |
| Total number of staff employed | APM has 300 staff<br>RPS at Mkulumadzi Lodge has 20 staff |
| % local staff | 95% + |
| Financial summary | Lodge value is USD 2 million |

### 3.3.5 Case Study 12: Sunbird Thawale Lodge, Malawi

#### Background

Sunbird Thawale Lodge is located in Majete Wildlife Reserve, Malawi. It is in the Lower Shire Valley, one-hour drive from Blantyre. Sunbird is the largest hotel chain in Malawi, and has four city hotels in all three regions of the country, two popular beach resorts along Lake Malawi, a mountain resort in Malawi's former capital city and a bush resort in Majete (Sunbird Hotels and Resorts, 2018). Thawale Lodge offers four twin-tented chalets, two double-tented chalets and one family chalet, all en suite (Sunbird Thawale, 2017a).

The more luxurious chalet has a unique open-air bathroom built among the rocks with a shower and a sunken bath and views of the floodlit waterhole. The lodge also has a newly built family chalet. With two en-suite rooms, a kitchenette and small living area it can sleep up to six people. A communal *lapa* with a fully staffed kitchen is available in the centre of the camp. Meals are served in the thatched restaurant and bar with a birding veranda (Sunbird Thawale, 2017a). Game drives are available at USD 25 per person (Sunbird Thawale, 2017b).

In 2017, the fully inclusive rack rate per person sharing ranged between USD 120 and USD 195 depending on the season (C. Hay, email, September 2017, personal communication).

#### Institutional structure

In March 2003, APM concluded an agreement with the DNPW to take on responsibility for the rehabilitation, development and management of Majete Wildlife Reserve. The agreement was part of a PPP initiative and allowed APM total management control of the reserve. The management agreement runs for an initial term of 25 years, with an option to renew for a further 15 years. APM is a company limited by guarantee with a local board with representatives from AP, DNPW and local businesses. APM is the private sector management partner and also provides donor funding to the project.

APM has the right to develop tourism in the park and as such raised the capital to develop Sunbird Thawale Lodge as an asset of APM to promote tourism in the park. APM entered into a management agreement with Sunbird Hotels Malawi to operate the lodge on its behalf. Sunbird Hotels is paid a management fee and APM retains the profits of the lodge.

#### Economic impact

Sunbird gets paid a management fee to operate the lodge on behalf of the park. The park receives the profits from the lodge. The lodge makes a significant contribution to the sustainability of the park annually and contributed USD 473,000 towards the operating costs of the park over the previous four years (C. Hay, email, September 2017, personal communication). Fresh produce is procured from a local supplier to the value of approximately USD 10,000 per year (C. Hay, email, September 2017, personal communication).

#### Social impact

The project employed 30 local staff members during construction and employs 15 permanent staff for operations. About 95% of these are from the local community, with 20% female and 80% male. Staff costs over a four-year period were USD 203,000 (C. Hay, email, September 2017, personal communication).

APM has a significant community development portfolio as part of park operations and manages this directly, the profits from the lodge contributing significantly to this portfolio. Activities include sponsorship of 100 scholars around the park, environmental education outreach to schools, reforestation projects, a controlled resource harvesting programme in the park and promotion of various income-generating livelihood projects such as beekeeping, production of curios and community cultural visits (C. Hay, email, September 2017, personal communication). Approximately USD 180,000 has been invested in a community extension programme at Majete over the last four years (C. Hay, email, September 2017, personal communication).

#### Environmental impact

The restoration, ongoing conservation management and law enforcement is all done by APM directly. The reserve has been fully restored to a well-stocked Big 5 park with approximately USD 500,000 invested towards this over the last four years (C. Hay, email, September 2017, personal communication).

#### Successes

Sunbird only took over the management of Thawale Lodge in February 2017 and booking projections are looking positive. Historically, the majority of visitors to Majete have been from within Malawi and the

**Table 25.** Summary – Sunbird Thawale Lodge.

| | |
|---|---|
| Name of company | Sunbird Hotels Malawi |
| Location | Majete Wildlife Reserve, Malawi |
| Year established | APM since 2003<br>Sunbird Thawale since 2017 |
| Status of company (i.e. listed, privately owned, etc.) | African Parks is a non-profit organisation.<br>Sunbird is a majority government-owned hotel chain in Malawi |
| List of camps/lodges | Sunbird Thawale Lodge (16 beds) |
| Investment/partnership option | Government owned land<br>APM has a 25-year concession<br>APM owns the lodge assets<br>Sunbird is the management partner |
| Total number of staff employed | APM has 140 staff<br>Sunbird Thawale Lodge employs 15 staff |
| % local staff | 95% + |
| Financial summary | Lodge value is USD 500,000<br>Staff costs over four-year period were USD 203,000<br>Fresh produce is procured from a local supplier to the value of approximately USD 10,000 per year |

partnership with Sunbird is expected to capitalise on this as well as take advantage of the large meetings, incentives, conventions and exhibitions (MICE) market in the city hotels (well represented by Sunbird), whose guests are looking for a 'bush break'.

#### Challenges

A large corporate mindset of hotel management versus the intimate bush lodge management needs has to be balanced. Finding a balance between the desire to rapidly expand versus the soft footprint of a bush lodge also needs to be carefully considered. Hotel catering versus lodge catering needs to be aligned to ensure guests get a suitable bush dining experience. The two parties are working hard to create a balance between these objectives.

#### Lessons learned and recommendations

There is a need for regular on-the-ground meetings and communication to ensure needs and objectives are aligned. Marketing and promotional resources should be shared to leverage each other's reach. Community development objectives and resources need to be aligned, shared and combined to maximise the impacts.

## 3.4. Public–Private Partnership on Government Land

### 3.4.1. Case Study 13: Ruzizi Tented Lodge, Rwanda

#### Background

Ruzizi Tented Lodge is located in the Akagera National Park in Rwanda. The lodge has nine tents and is privately managed by AP (African Parks, 2017a, 2017b, 2017c). Akagera National Park is central Africa's largest protected wetland and offers tourists the only Big 5 savannah experience in Rwanda.

Due to the success of Ruzizi (the lodge had 71% occupancy in its busiest month during its first full year of operation) the lodge was expanded with an additional two tents added in 2014 and Karenge

Bush Camp was also established as a seasonal 'overflow' for Ruzizi guests in 2015 (S. Hall, email, September 2017, personal communication). An impressive 30,911 paying tourists visited the park in 2016, 52% of which were Rwandan nationals, showing great national support for Akagera (African Parks, 2017d).

In 2017, the rack rate for international visitors was USD 195 for Ruzizi and USD 175 for Karenge on a full board, per person, per night sharing, basis (African Parks, 2017b, 2017c). The lodge was developed out of a demand from local tour operators for additional, alternative, accommodation options, something other than the 120-bed Akagera Game Lodge, built in the 1970s, and camping (S. Hall, email, September 2017, personal communication).

Karenge Bush Camp is a low-impact, seasonal bush camp offering six tents, with camp beds, solar lighting, full board accommodation and en-suite bucket showers and toilets (S. Hall, email, September 2017, personal communication). Due to the seasonal nature of the camp, it is not included in the case study analysis.

### Institutional structure

Both Ruzizi and Karenge are directly managed by Akagera Management Company (AMC), which is a Rwandan-registered for-profit company, with AP and the RDB as the shareholders (S. Hall, email, September 2017, personal communication). AP takes on direct responsibility for the rehabilitation and long-term management of parks and protected areas in partnership with government and communities throughout Africa, and the partnerships can take on different forms depending on the project. For more information on AP see Box 20 much later in this book. In the case of Akagera, a for-profit company was registered with AP and RDB as shareholders (S. Hall, email, September 2017, personal communication).

The lodge was funded and built by AMC, through AP, and is 100% owned and operated by AMC. AMC is a Rwandan registered company, with AP holding 51% of the shares and RDB holding 49% (S. Hall, email, September 2017, personal communication).

All 100% of the profits from both Ruzizi and Karenge go into the budget for the management of the entire park, so every stay directly contributes to the conservation of Akagera National Park (S. Hall, email, September 2017, personal communication).

### Economic impact

RDB contributes USD 250,000 per year to the project, with park-earned revenue (valued at USD 1,365,000 in 2016) generating the majority of budget funding and AP and their donor funders making up the shortfall (S. Hall, email, September 2017, personal communication). As AMC are responsible for the management of the park, no lease fees are paid to operate Ruzizi or Karenge (S. Hall, email, September 2017, personal communication).

The Howard G. Buffett Foundation, RDB, The Walton Family Foundation and the Wyss Foundation were major donor funders of Akagera Park in 2016 (African Parks, 2017d).

### Social impact

There are 19 staff at Ruzizi Tented Lodge: 0% female and 100% male (S. Hall, email, September 2017, personal communication). About 95% (18) of these are local Rwandans, and 95% of the wage expenditure (USD 80,000) goes into the local economy. Since 2010, in excess of USD 5 million has been paid in salaries to locally hired staff (African Parks, 2016).

Ruzizi Tented Lodge was built by a team of local builders and labourers and designed in-house. As far as possible, construction materials were sourced locally, as well as transport and furnishings. The exception was the thatch grass and the artisans who thatched the roof, as this particular grass and the skill of thatching were not locally available. The procurement of consumables is mostly local; vegetables are bought from a weekly market five kilometres from the park boundary and a second market 30 kilometres away supplies Rwandan tea, coffee, cheese and jams. Honey is bought from cooperatives on the boundary of the park (S. Hall, email, September 2017, personal communication). Approximately USD 1,300 per month is spent on local purchases, which is approximately 27% of total procurement (S. Hall, email, March 2018, personal communication).

A community beekeeping cooperative, COPRAMA, produced 1.4 tons of honey in 2015, and its sales through the Akagera Curio Shop and wholesale channels generated USD 4,200 in revenue for the

30 beekeepers. AMC built an additional 83 hives and another four cooperatives were established, with an additional 90 beekeepers in 2015 (African Parks, 2016).

The Umoja Women's Cooperative was provided with training on tailoring and basket weaving in 2015, and generated sales of USD 1,700, including through the Akagera Curio Shop. Akagera's park staff helped with a woodlot in Kageyo where 11,000 fruit and wood trees are grown to provide food and fuelwood. Also, the Guardian Project Goat Initiative, which was established to deter poaching of bushmeat by providing income and food for local people saw the birth of over 200 goat kids in 2015 (African Parks, 2016).

AP engages with local community members through lion sensitisation projects and environmental education (with over 1,300 local schoolchildren participating in conservation lessons in 2015 and in 2016). In 2016, 13,000 trees were planted by three schools bordering the park as part of an ongoing restoration project to reduce pressure on native vegetation (African Parks, 2017d). The community freelance guides initiative was developed in 2014. Through an open interview, selection and training process, Akagera now has 18 community freelance guides working in the park, and the cooperative earned over USD 80,000 in guiding services in 2016 (S. Hall, email, September 2017, personal communication). A small 5% of these earnings is paid back to the park in commissions, 5% is kept by the cooperative and some is set aside for training, uniforms and other expenses before sharing equally between the members (S. Hall, email, September 2017, personal communication). The government of Rwanda has shown interest in the concept for possible expansion to other parks in the country.

Community benefits from the park include casual staff wages (locally employed), the community freelance guides revenue (locally recruited guides), local purchases, environmental education programme spend (local schools bordering the park visiting the park), all amounting to approximately USD 37,300 per month (S. Hall, email, January 2018, personal communication).

### Environmental impact

AP reintroduced 18 eastern black rhino to the park in early 2017, restoring the park's Big 5 status (S. Hall, email, September 2017, personal communication). This follows the reintroduction of seven lions to the park in 2015 thanks to a 120 kilometre-long predator-proof fence (the first of its kind in Rwanda) and the lion population has increased, with the birth of 11 cubs in 2016 (African Parks, 2015, 2017a), and two additional males brought in in 2017. The park now has 19 lions. Also, over 100 grey-crowned cranes have, so far, been released into the park as part of a national rehabilitation programme that rescues them from captivity and releases them into the wild. AP has also undertaken elephant monitoring research, using GPS collars. Research work has been funded to explore the species and population densities of fish, particularly in Lake Ihema (African Parks, 2015). In 2017, a private operator, Wilderness Safaris, in partnership with AP, sponsored a shoebill survey in Akagera in order to determine the population to allow for future monitoring.

Karenge aims to create a light footprint on the park. It is a seasonal camp that is set up twice a year, for three months. At the end of the season, the tents are removed, and no construction materials are left behind (African Parks, 2017c). Karenge's water comes from a borehole at the northern exit of the park, transported by a water-bowser to the camp. Water usage is restricted since there is no running water in the camp – guests have bucket showers and toilets. Biodegradable rubbish and sewerage is dug into a pit, non-biodegradable rubbish is removed from the site. Solar lighting is provided in the camp, and solar fridges are used. Guests are briefed about staying on designated paths to reduce negative impact.

Ruzizi Tented Lodge is fully solar powered with a comprehensive system. Each tent has its own solar hot water system. Water is pumped with a solar pump from a borehole into a header tank.

### Successes

Ruzizi reached 50% average annually occupancy in its second year of operation and contributed over USD 440,000 to the park's annual budget in 2016 (S. Hall, email, September 2017, personal communication).

Internships are given to a maximum of two local students or community members for up to three months at a time. From this internship programme, three interns have subsequently been employed and one has been promoted to park receptionist (S. Hall, email, September 2017, personal communication). Ruzizi has achieved a five-star rating on TripAdvisor for three successive years (S. Hall, email, September 2017, personal communication).

**Table 26.** Summary – Ruzizi and Karenge.

| | |
|---|---|
| Name of company | Akagera Management Company |
| Location | Akagera National Park, Rwanda |
| Year established | 2012 |
| Status of company (i.e. listed, privately owned, etc.) | Private company<br>Government land<br>20-year lease |
| List of camps/lodges | Ruzizi Tented Lodge (9 tents, sleeps 20)<br>Karenge Bush Camp (6 tents, sleeps 12) |
| Investment/partnership option | Privately owned and managed by AMC whilst PPP agreement stands. 13 years remain of a 20-year PPP |
| Total number of staff employed | 19 employed at Ruzizi; 216 employed in Akagera |
| % local staff | 95% |
| Financial summary | USD 444,894 earned in 2016 and contributed to park budget |

#### Challenges

Marketing of the lodges/camps has been a challenge: Karenge is not able to be posted on TripAdvisor due to seasonality and having no fixed address (S. Hall, email, September 2017, personal communication). Length of stay is also a challenge: 70% of Akagera's total visitors are day visitors, with only 30% staying overnight across all accommodation options (S. Hall, email, September 2017, personal communication).

#### Lessons learned and recommendations

Offering internships has been beneficial both for local students and members of the community to gain experience in hospitality, and also to Ruzizi as a spare set of hands during busy periods, as well as creating a pool of potential employees (S. Hall, email, September 2017, personal communication).

Training and new menu planning every six months with a Kigali-based catering company has really helped to offer good quality, locally available meals which are often commented on by guests. Investing in the staff has been beneficial: Ian (the lodge manager in 2017) has visited other lodges both in Rwanda and internationally to gain experience (S. Hall, email, September 2017, personal communication).

## 3.5. Private Joint Venture Partnership on Government Land

### 3.5.1. Case Study 14: Singita Lebombo, South Africa

#### Background

All the information in this case study was provided by Andrea Ferry (Singita sustainability coordinator, August 2017, personal communication).

In 2000 Singita, a private sector company, entered into the SANParks Commercialisation Initiative and successfully won the bid for the Nwanetsi Concession in KNP. At almost 2 million hectares, KNP is one of the world's largest and oldest national parks, protecting diversity and abundance of species at an extraordinary scale. However, SANParks, the authority that manages the park, was (and is) a victim of

decreasing public funding, as biodiversity conservation does not rank highly on the government's list of priorities. To generate revenue in support of its conservation mandate, SANParks opened the Commercialisation Initiative. Singita recognised this as an opportunity to utilise its successful tourism model in support of the long-term conservation of an iconic and important protected area. Singita's objective for developing and operating in the park was to create, in collaboration with a substantive empowerment vehicle, a luxury wildlife tourism experience aimed primarily at attracting international visitors to South Africa and KNP. The park offered a well-known and iconic destination with which to attract these guests. In addition, Singita had an existing presence in the Sabi Sand Game Reserve which borders KNP, thus creating an attractive tourism 'circuit'. Singita believes in the 'high-end' model of higher rates and lower volumes of guests as its preferred model for operating in conservation areas.

In 2017 the fully inclusive rack rate per person sharing at Singita Lebombo was ZAR 22,750 (approximately USD 1,594) for a suite (13 suites, 26 beds). For the two-bedroomed suite (four beds) it was ZAR 68,250 (approximately USD 4,783) per night per suite (one to three guests) and for the private villa (maximum eight adults) it was ZAR 165,652 (approximately USD 11,608) per villa per night (maximum eight adults) (Singita, 2017).

### Institutional structure

Singita Kruger National Park (SKNP) Pty Ltd shareholding is as follows:

- Singita Lebombo Investment Holdings 73.6%;
- KNP Staff Trust 19.8%; and
- Pfukani Ecotours (Pty) Ltd 6.6%.

KNP Staff Trust was initially set up with the intention that employees benefit from a share scheme. However the proposal was rejected by staff as the requirement was that employees were to buy in. There are currently no transactions happening within this trust. Pfukani Ecotours is a travel company owned by Singita Lebombo (Pty) Ltd's shareholder Keith Mokoape, and was part of the BEE structuring.

SKNP signed a 20-year concession agreement with SANParks in 2000. In line with the agreement, SKNP adheres to SANParks' requirements for operating in the park including limits on the number of beds, a water quota and various other restrictions in order to protect the environment.

### Economic impact

To date, no dividends have been paid out of Singita Lebombo (Pty) Ltd. Singita pays a monthly concession fee to SANParks. In 2017, concession fees totalled ZAR 6.8 million (USD 476,524). Cumulative concession fees paid to SANParks between 2012 and 2016 totalled ZAR 43,175,412 (approximately USD 3.03 million).

### Social impact

Singita KNP employed a total of 208 people (in June 2017) with an annual staff cost in the region of ZAR 24 million (approximately USD 1.68 million). This payroll cost includes all other employee-related expenses as well. However, the average annual total payroll per annum is ZAR 11.0 million (approximately USD 770,848), and the percentage of salary per annum going to locals in the region (48%) is ZAR 5.3 million (approximately USD 371,409). The average wage per month is approximately ZAR 14,338 (USD 1,005). The total monthly value of goods and services procured locally is ZAR 208,000 (approximately USD 14,576). This amounts to ±6% of lodge operating expenses, excluding payroll, with the remainder being procured elsewhere in South Africa.

CSR initiatives are run by the Singita Community Development Trust, (see Case Study 18 in this volume) a non-profit Trust, which relies predominantly on guest donations and some contributions from the lodge. The figures discussed below are pure project spend and exclude trust administration costs.

- **Community visits:** community visits are excursions to a local village to enable guests to gain insight into daily community life and the local Tsonga culture. Guests have a chance to meet and interact with local people. Guests make a contribution when participating in a community visit, providing support to local enterprises and helping to fund the community projects Singita supports.
- **Growing to READ:** based on the positive impact of the Growing to READ programme on the preschools in communities supported by Singita Sabi Sand, SKNP decided to extend the programme to include a further cluster of 10 schools among the communities supported. This development programme is conducted in collaboration with the Education Department and the non-profit organisation, READ Educational Trust. Thriving in 10 local schools, the programme assists with teacher training and educational materials to ensure that these schools provide excellent tuition to prepare young children for formal schooling. Close to 5,000 children have received three years of teaching, under the guidance of the Growing to READ programme. The expenditure on the programme between 2014 and 2016 was ZAR 733,334 (approximately USD 66,971).
- **Singita School of Cooking (SSC):** SSC opened its doors in 2007 and today offers a 12-month course that sees 10 students drawn from local communities starting in March each year. Upon completion of the programme, students receive a NQF Level 4 qualification. Seven classes have successfully completed the course. Since opening, the programme has successfully placed 50 chefs into positions at Singita and other lodges in the Kruger Park region. It has been awarded the 2016 Trialogue Strategic CSI award and has driven an awareness and aspiration within the communities of the opportunities available within tourism. The expenditure on SSC for 2014–2016 was ZAR 1,297,792 (approximately USD 118,520).

The total amount for community projects and donations is approximately ZAR 1.6 million (USD 112,123) per annum.

### Environmental impact

From a biodiversity conservation perspective, concession fees are a major contribution to KNP funds for managing the park. Singita also contributes to anti-poaching through employment of a concession manager, provision of digital radio equipment and logistical support for the park's section ranger and his team. Singita has also assisted with research projects in the concession area. For example, SKNP has assisted SANParks and the Endangered Wildlife Trust with locations of nesting sites for southern ground hornbills and various vulture species. Biannual environmental audits are conducted by an external party which reports on the results to SANParks.

From an EMS perspective, SKNP is a member of the One Planet Living (OPL) certification programme (http://www.bioregional.com) using the 10 OPL Principles as a framework to address Care for Planet and Care for People. Its biggest success (and challenge) to date in this context was the installation of a 1 megawatt peak solar hybrid energy plant to provide 1,600 MWh of clean energy a year to power the lodges and staff villages. Permission was sought from SANParks for this project and the bureaucracy was found to be supportive. To encourage other concessionaires to move to clean renewable power supply, it would be good to see PAs make any permission/application processes clear and potentially even instigating fast-track approvals.

Recycling is a challenge in the park. Singita's recycling is taken off site to Acornhoek Municipal Recycling Facility. A success has, however, been to introduce its own water bottling plants, thus reducing plastic bottled water waste to virtually nil. A park-wide collection service and recycling processing facility would be a welcome addition to the park's services.

#### Successes

Most lodges and reserve staff are from local communities and it is in the interest of all that their homes are situated within functional and peaceful villages, and that their children are equipped to deal with modern life. This is provided through the various CSR initiatives. Supporting the establishment of micro and small businesses and maximising the purchases and use of services within the local area, in particular those for which Singita and the Trust can also provide a market, has stimulated the local economy.

The Singita Community Development Trust undertakes development programmes, namely education, enterprise development and environmental awareness, and this has had a positive impact in local communities. Local communities have started to experience benefits from living in proximity to a conservation area and it is important to ensure that they also choose a way to play a role in protecting the reserve. For example, the age-old opportunities to hunt and harvest useful plants within the reserve have been lost, but other benefits, including a flow of money/funds into the local area via employment opportunities, support for development projects as well as lodge purchases of local produce and services ensure that the reserve is seen positively. Singita has resources that it can utilise to raise an increasing amount of funding (especially through guests), thereby ensuring Singita can assist local communities.

#### Challenges

Although the concession contract was not due for renewal, in 2012 Singita applied to extend the concession tenure period and, simultaneously, reduce the concession fee payable to SANParks. The purpose of the application was twofold: to enable Singita to continue to operate a financially sustainable business, and to allow time to recoup its significant capital investment over this extended lease period. Singita was suffering financial stress caused by the knock-on effects of the global financial crisis which severely affected international guests, who tend to make up approximately 90% of Singita's occupancies. The business model at the time showed that unless the concession fees were reduced there was a risk of having to shut down, or at least mothball one of the two lodges, with a negative impact for KNP's revenue. During the open re-bid, Singita faced the risk of losing the concession. However, it was successful in extending the concession term by another 20 years and significantly reducing the concession fees to the proposed level.

In terms of community engagement, because SKNP is approximately a two-hour drive in total, through KNP, out of the park gates and then into the local communities which are in the Bushbuckridge municipality within the Ehlanzeni district of Mpumalanga, it is difficult to offer village visits for tourists. It is also difficult to coordinate local people, government departments and non-profit organisations to get involved in a systematic and organised way of supporting projects. The majority of the communities on the outskirts of SKNP are in transition from a subsistence, traditional, rural way of life to a more modern, money-based approach. This is providing challenges to many, including those who follow a more subsistence way of life who are finding that land and water restrictions are challenging, which was not the case in the past, making cattle farming difficult. They also no longer have access to wild animals and plants for subsistence purposes.

There are a limited number of jobs. The majority that do exist are provided by the lodge industry and by government. In the nearby local area, the formal employment rate is only about 20%.

#### Lessons learned and recommendations

Based on Singita's experience, lessons learned included that longer concession leases, with appropriate exit clauses for under-performance by concessionaires are favourable to operators, as they allow higher

**Table 27.** Summary – Singita Lebombo.

| | |
|---|---|
| Name of company | Singita Lebombo (Pty) Ltd |
| Location | Nwanetsi Concession, Kruger National Park (KNP), South Africa |
| Year established | 2001 |
| Status of company (i.e. listed, privately owned, etc.) | Privately owned |
| List of camps/lodges | Singita Lebombo Lodge (34 beds) and Singita Sweni Lodge (14 beds) |
| Investment/partnership option | Government owned land<br>Current status (2017) is a 20-year concession (negotiated in 2012, so 15 years remaining)<br>Privately owned infrastructure |
| Total number of staff employed | 208 |
| % local staff | 99% South African citizens and 75% of the staff are from the surrounding regions |
| Financial summary | ZAR 43,175,412 (approximately USD 3.9 million) has been paid in terms of lease fees (SANParks) (2012–2016)<br>ZAR 0 in taxes to government from SKNP due to assessed losses (2012–2016)<br>ZAR 5.3 million (approx. USD 484,018) spent on wages to local staff from SKNP.<br>ZAR 24 million/annum (approx. USD 1.68 million/annum) total staff cost |

levels of capital investment and greater likelihood of recouping this investment. In the case of a concessionaire meeting all the performance requirements, preference should be given to the existing operator when the concession contract is put up for renewal. Without prejudice to other bidders, PA authorities should consider concession applications and renewals on an individual basis to cater for the exact circumstances of the stakeholders for the particular concession. SANParks operates an excellent and professional bid process. This should be continued by KNP and mirrored by similar organisations. This professional approach has facilitated Singita's successful commercial operation in SKNP.

The remainder of this chapter looks at the contribution of the private sector through voluntary payments to communities and conservation projects in their areas of operation. These payments are not through any contractual arrangements and have been initiated by the private sector in order to support community and conservation projects. Investment in conservation and community projects can be seen as an investment in the product and long-term success of the tourism business.

## 3.6. Voluntary Payments

In terms of community partnerships and philanthropic donations, it is important that communities are not 'double-taxed': where money from tourism is spent on infrastructure and services which should have been provided by government (Snyman, 2016). It is also important that the private sector does not assume the role of government, fulfilling government functions in remote, rural areas, resulting in potential government complacency to invest in socioeconomic development if it thinks that the private sector will do it instead (Snyman, 2016). It is a fine line and can be difficult for the private sector to not get involved when community partners and neighbours are in need of basic goods and services. In many of the case study examples, it has been observed that the private sector is already fulfilling the role of government and providing government services. Future research on this contribution should be undertaken and ways to engage and partner with government should be investigated.

### 3.6.1. Case Study 15: Africa Foundation

This case study is taken from http://africafoundation.org.za/who-we-are/ (accessed 20 August 2017).

Africa Foundation is associated with ecotourism operator andBeyond and is a fund supported by donations, largely from tourists, but also through other grants. It was founded in 1992 as an independent, non-profit, tax-exempt organisation in South Africa whose purpose is to uplift, upskill and empower identified rural communities near core conservation areas. Africa Foundation owes its success largely to the long-term relationships with the communities in which it works. The foundation has a philosophy that successful projects require the community to be actively involved in the project's selection, development and subsequent running once the Foundation is no longer actively involved.

Africa Foundation aims to ensure that the greatest possible percentage of each contribution/donation goes directly to the communities it supports and that the money invested in projects is efficiently and effectively spent, ensuring the projects are sustainable. Africa Foundation attempts to ensure that all projects are managed on the ground by local champions and selected organisations that have high-quality management and donor relationships, accountability, the ability to provide comprehensive feedback and a measurable and favourable impact on the community.

By partnering with communities, governments and the private sector, Africa Foundation drives the development of sustainable projects that aim to empower communities. The Foundation believes that for true development to take place, there is a need to nurture, protect and preserve not only the natural environment and wildlife, but also people, their culture and customs. This philosophy is in line with that of andBeyond, the supporting company.

The Foundation facilitates projects identified by communities and which are grounded in their participation. It is this collaboration with community leaders and local champions that led to the four main development areas on which it focuses. These are: education, health care and clean water, as well as small business development and environment and conservation. The Foundation acts as the catalyst between local governments and local communities, with a goal to strengthen relationships and facilitate effective and sustainable project management and service delivery.

Projects are first identified by addressing community needs and are then set in motion with the community leading the way. Each project is then carefully assessed to promote success before final approval happens and fundraising begins with donors and supporters. Once the required funds are raised and successfully received, the community champions and local leaders are invited to finalise all paperwork and draw up any necessary contracts and schedules with the applicable partners and organisations who begin to work on the project. The right training, skills and resources, provided by Africa

Foundation and partner organisations, ensures projects are not only effectively implemented, but self-sustainable long after initiation. Once completed, projects are handed over to communities, who take responsibility for their success and growth. By equipping local champions with the skills and knowledge to secure additional funding of their own, they are able to build on the solid foundation Africa Foundation has put in place.

### 3.6.2 Case Study 16: Children in the Wilderness (CITW)

The creation of CITW (see http://www.childreninthewilderness.com/about-us/, accessed 20 August 2017) was an evolution of the vision of WS, which has always been that it needs to face the challenge of Africa's wildlife areas being under severe pressure. The areas in which WS operates are some of the planet's more sensitive and fragile environmental hotspots. Therefore, by focusing on children, CITW believes that they can impact significantly on the local communities in the hope of securing the future of these fragile areas.

CITW has as its overall goal the facilitation of sustainable conservation through leadership development of rural children in Africa. This is achieved in a variety of ways, from running three- to five-day eco-camps to running eco-clubs and follow-up programmes at schools within the rural communities that live on the edges of the conservation areas.

The camp programme combines leadership skills, environmental education and recreation. The programme aims at increasing children's understanding and appreciation of the diversity of natural environments. It is also designed to increase self-esteem, teach new skills and impart knowledge to rural children.

The programme's eco-clubs and follow-up programmes make use of specifically designed curricula suited to the specific country or community. In this way, CITW aims to introduce children to their wildlife heritage, build and strengthen their capabilities to cope with life's challenges and educate them with the life skills necessary to actualise their potential. Via these programmes, CITW also aims to develop leadership values among the participants, so as to create leaders who are inspired to care for their legacy and can show others the way. To achieve these goals, CITW had to start a number of other initiatives to assist children and their teachers and parents, such as school nutrition schemes, village upliftment, village vegetable gardens and school scholarships. CITW invests approximately USD 550,000 annually in environmental education and life skills projects in six southern African countries.

### 3.6.3. Case Study 17: Wilderness Wildlife Trust (WWT)

The WWT (see http://www.wildernesstrust.com, accessed 20 August 2017), an independent non-profit entity also associated with WS, supports a wide variety of projects across Africa. The projects and researchers it supports focuses its work in three key areas as follows.

1. **Research and conservation**, which includes funding species studies, monitoring of populations and understanding human–animal conflicts.
2. **Community empowerment and education**, such as community upliftment and the CITW programme (see Case Study 16).
3. **Anti-poaching and management**, including funding aerial surveys and anti-poaching units, and increasing capacity for researchers in general.

WWT contributes approximately USD 500,000 annually to community and conservation projects in Africa (Russel Friedman, WWT chairman, South Africa, August 2017, personal communication).

### 3.6.4 Case Study 18: Singita Community Development Trust

The information in this case study is taken from https://singita.com/community/ and https://singita.com/conservation/ (accessed 20 August 2017).

Conservation at Singita is encompassed by three pillars – namely, biodiversity, community and sustainability. Through the Singita Community Development Trust, Singita goes beyond the conservation

efforts required under its contractual agreements to support land rehabilitation, maintenance, wildlife monitoring and fencing security, to initiating effective and innovative anti-poaching methods, research, wildlife reintroduction, the preservation of invaluable San rock art sites and working on conservation issues beyond its boundaries.

Singita supports the notion that communities close to their reserves are key role-players in preserving the integrity of each wilderness area and its wildlife. It is, therefore, important to the company that these communities understand and benefit from the existence of the reserves. Singita's long-term, broad community development objective is to assist communities to thrive, both economically and socially. Singita employs 1,100 staff within its five regions and deliberately tries to maximise monthly purchases from local enterprises in order to play a further role in strengthening the local economy. In addition to this, the community development teams on each property coordinate active support for development initiatives. Community development programmes at Singita have three main objectives: well-educated children; the development of small enterprises; and an enhanced awareness of conservation and sustainable daily living practices among local community members.

### 3.6.5. Lessons learned

The case studies of donor-funded groups all provide examples of private sector tourism in Africa playing an active role in philanthropy, through supporting, facilitating and funding community and conservation projects in their areas of operation. Many of the larger tourism companies have formed independent foundations/organisations to facilitate these projects and the associated donations. The majority of funding comes from tourists visiting their facilities, highlighting an important additional impact of private sector tourism in Africa. Over and above the income injected into local economies from the tourism camps through lease fees, employment and the use of local suppliers of goods and services, money flows into local economies through philanthropy. Some lessons learned from the philanthropy case studies include that projects should be chosen in consultation with the local community and be something that the community wants and needs. There also needs to be transparency and accountability in the handling of all finances and the management of projects. Projects should be designed and implemented with sustainability in mind from an economic, social and environmental perspective, and should have effective monitoring and evaluation plans in place prior to implementation. Communities should be empowered and uplifted through community projects, not made dependent on tourism. Community and conservation projects should be planned and implemented, wherever possible, in partnership with other development and conservation organisations in order to maximise positive impacts. Partnerships and collaborations in philanthropic work are important to long-term sustainability.

## 3.7. Summary

This chapter has explored six models of private sector tourism investment in protected areas using different case studies.

1. For-profit private sector on private land.
2. For-profit private sector on government land.
3. Private sector (for-profit or not-for-profit) on government, private or NGO land.
4. Public private partnership on government land.
5. Private joint venture partnership on government land.
6. Voluntary payments.

The case studies demonstrate that there are many instances where private sector tourism operations make tangible conservations to conservation and local economies. Their approaches to doing this vary, as does the extent of their impact. A synthesis of the impacts is provided in Chapter 5, and the next chapter reviews a series of case studies relating to joint venture lodge ownership options.

## 3.8. References


Africa Foundation (2016) *Who we are*. Available at http://www.africafoundation.org.za/who-we-are/ (accessed 31 March 2017).

African Parks (2015) *African Parks annual report 2015: conservation at scale, African Parks*. Available at https://www.africanparks.org/about-us/financials-and-annual-reports (accessed 9 March 2017).

African Parks Annual Report: Impact Defined (2016). Available at https://www.africanparks.org/sites/default/files/uploads/resources/2017-05/2016_African_Parks_Annual_Report_Impact_Defined.pdf (accessed 2nd February 2019).

African Parks (2017a) *Akagera overview*. Available at https://www.african-parks.org/the-parks/akagera/overview (accessed 9 March 2017).

African Parks (2017b) *Akagera Ruzizi Tented Lodge*. Available at https://www.african-parks.org/the-parks/akagera/visit-the-park/ruzizi-tented-lodge (accessed 9 March 2017).

African Parks (2017c) *Akagera Karenge Bush Camp*. Available at https://www.african-parks.org/the-parks/akagera/visit-the-park/karenge-bush-camp (accessed 9 March 2017).

African Parks (2017d) *African Parks annual report 2016: impact defined*. Available at https://www.african-parks.org/sites/default/files/uploads/resources/2017-05/2016_African_Parks_Annual_Report_Impact_Defined.pdf (accessed August 2017).

andBeyond (2016) andBeyond financials 2015/16. Johannesburg: andBeyond. In: Nicholson, A. (2017) *Creating shared value: an exploratory case study assessing the shared value that a company is creating through a protected area and its unique relationship with local communities*. Thesis presented in fulfilment of the requirements for the degree of Master of Philosophy Environmental Management in the Faculty of Economic Management Sciences, Stellenbosch University, South Africa.

andBeyond (2017a) *Accommodation*. Available at http://www.andbeyond.com/ngala-safari-lodge/the-lodge/accommodations.htm (accessed 24 March 2017).

andBeyond (2017b) *Rates*. Available at http://www.andbeyond.com/ngala-tented-camp/rates-offers.htm (accessed 31 March 2017).

andBeyond (2017c) *Rates*. Available at http://www.andbeyond.com/ngala-safari-lodge/rates-offers.htm (accessed 31 March 2017).

andBeyond (2017d) *Activities at Ngala Safari Lodge*. Available at http://www.andbeyond.com/ngala-safari-lodge/activities.htm (accessed 31 March 2017).

Bale Mountain Lodge (2017a) *Information about the lodge*. Available at http://www.balemountainlodge.com/fact.html (accessed 26 August 2017).

Bale Mountain Lodge (2017b) *Rack rates*. Available at http://www.balemountainlodge.com/rate.html (accessed 26 August 2017).

Bale Mountain Lodge (2017c) *Company information*. Available at http://www.balemountainlodge.com/about.html (accessed 26 August 2017).

Bale Mountain Lodge (2017d) *Environmental information*. Available at http://www.balemountainlodge.com/eco.html (accessed 26 August 2017)

Bale Mountain Lodge (2017e) *Conservation information*. Available at http://www.balemountainlodge.com/index.html (accessed 26 August 2017).
Buckley, R.C. & Sommer, M. (2001) *Tourism and protected areas: partnerships in principle and practice*. CRC for Sustainable Tourism Research Report, Gold Coast, Queensland.
Chumbe Island (2017a) *Rack rates for overnight stays*. Available at https://chumbeisland.com/overnight-stay/ (accessed 15 October 2017).
Chumbe Island (2017b) *Rack rates for day trips*. Available at https://chumbeisland.com/day-trip/ (accessed 15 October 2017).
Chumbe Island (2017c) *Eco-operations information*. Available at https://chumbeisland.com/accommodation/eco-operations/ (accessed 15 October 2017).
Manda Nkwichi (2008–13a) *About the Trust*. Available at http://www.mandawilderness.org/about-us.html (accessed 22 August 2017).
Manda Nkwichi (2008–13b) *Education*. Available at http://www.mandawilderness.org/education.html (accessed 22 August 2017).
Manda Nkwichi (2008–13c) *Agriculture*. Available at http://www.mandawilderness.org/agriculture.html (accessed 22 August 2017).
Mussanhane, P. (2008) Manda Wilderness Project, Niassa Province, Mozambique. Presentation at the African Safari Lodges practitioners workshop, The Grace Hotel, Rosebank, South Africa, 19–21 May.
Myers, M., Hoets, P. & Woodrow, G. (2004) *Mombo: Okavango's place of plenty*. Wilderness Safaris, Gaborone, Botswana.
Nicholson, A. (2017) *Creating shared value: an exploratory case study assessing the shared value that a company is creating through a protected area and its unique relationship with local communities*. Thesis presented in fulfilment of the requirements for the degree of Master of Philosophy Environmental Management in the Faculty of Economic Management Sciences, Stellenbosch University, South Africa.
Nkwichi (2008) *The Lodge*. Available at http://www.nkwichi.com/the-lodge/ (accessed 22 August 2017).
Norman Carr Safaris (2017) Available at https://timeandtideafrica.com/norman-carr-safaris (accessed 19 September 2017).
Republic of South Africa (2004) *Government Gazette: Broad-Based Black Economic Empowerment Act, 2003*, Vol. 463(53), no. 25899. Republic of South Africa, Cape Town, 9 January 2004.
Robin Pope Safaris (2017) Available at https://www.robinpopesafaris.net/camps/mkulumadzi.php#activities (accessed 23 September 2017).
Simien Lodge (2017) *Simien Lodge room rates*. Available at http://www.simiens.com/index.php/rooms (accessed 17 August, 2017).
Singita (2017) *Singita Lebombo rates*. Available at https://singita.com/lodge/singita-lebombo-lodge/rates/ (accessed 17 August 2017).
Sowry, R. (2014) Section ranger, Kingfisherspruit, Kruger National Park. Personal interview: 10 February, Orpen, Kruger National Park, SA, cited in Nicholson, A. (2017) *Creating shared value: an exploratory case study assessing the shared value that a company is creating through a protected area and its unique relationship with local communities*. Thesis presented in fulfilment of the requirements for the degree of Master of Philosophy Environmental Management in the Faculty of Economic Management Sciences, Stellenbosch University, South Africa.
Snyman, S. (2016) The role of private sector ecotourism in local socio-economic development in southern Africa. *Journal of Ecotourism*, doi: 10.1080/14724049.2016.1226318.
Spenceley, A. (2001) *Sustainable nature-based tourism assessment*. Ngala, Ngala Private Game Reserve, 14 October.
Spenceley, A. & Snyman, S. (2017) Can a wildlife tourism company influence conservation and the development of tourism in a specific destination? *Tourism and Hospitality Research*, 17(1), 52–67.
Spenceley, A., Rylance, A., Nanabhay, S. and van der Watt, H. (2016) *Operational guidelines for community-based tourism in South Africa*. Department of Tourism, Republic of South Africa.
Sunbird Hotels and Resorts (2018) Available at https://www.sunbirdmalawi.com (accessed 3 June 2018).
Sunbird Thawale (2017a) *Lodge information*. Available at https://www.sunbirdmalawi.com/index.php/thawale (accessed 27 September 2017).
Sunbird Thawale (2017b) *Activity information*. Available at https://www.sunbirdmalawi.com/index.php/activities-thawale (accessed 27 September 2017).
Turner, M. (2008) The Manda Wilderness Project Mozambique. Presentation at the African Safari Lodges practitioners workshop, The Grace Hotel, Rosebank, South Africa, 19–21 May.

Twining-Ward, L., Li, W. Bhammar, H. & Wright, E. (2018) *Supporting sustainable livelihoods through wildlife tourism*. World Bank, Washington, DC. Available at https://openknowledge.worldbank.org/handle/10986/29417 (license: CC BY 3.0 IGO) (accessed 11 April 2018).
van Wijk, J., Lamers, M., & van der Duim, R. (2015) Promoting conservation tourism: the case of the African Wildlife Foundation's tourism conservation enterprises in Kenya. In van der Duim, R., Lamers, M. & van Wijk, J. (eds) (2015) *Institutional arrangements for conservation, development and tourism in Eastern and Southern Africa: A dynamic perspective*, pp. 203–218. Springer, Dordrecht.
Wilderness Holdings (2014) *Integrated annual report for the year ended 28 February 2014*. Wilderness Holdings, South Africa and Botswana.
Wilderness Holdings (2015) *Annual integrated report*. Wilderness Holdings, South Africa and Botswana.
Wilderness Holdings (2016) *Annual integrated report*. Wilderness Holdings, South Africa and Botswana.
Wilderness Holdings (2017) *Annual integrated report*. Wilderness Holdings, South Africa and Botswana.
Wilderness Wildlife Trust/Children in the Wilderness (WWT/CITW) (2011). Annual Report. Published by Wilderness Safaris.
Wilderness Safaris (2012) *Awards*. Available at http://www.wilderness-safaris.com/about/awards.jsp (accessed 10 January 2013).
Wilderness Safaris (2017a) *Rates*. Available at http://www.wilderness-safaris.com/camps/mombo-camp/rates (accessed 5 November 2017).
Wilderness Safaris (2017b) *Bisate Lodge rates*. Available at http://www.wilderness-safaris.com/camps/bisate-lodge/rates (accessed 17 August 2017).
Wilderness Safaris (2017c) *Hwange Camp rates*. Available at http://www.wilderness-safaris.com/camps/little-makalolo/rates http://www.wilderness-safaris.com/camps/davisons-camp/rates and http://www.wilderness-safaris.com/camps/linkwasha-camp/rates (accessed 17 August 2017).
Wolwedans (2018a) *Rates*. Available at http://www.wolwedans.com/fileadmin/Rack_Rates/RackRates-2018.pdf (accessed 6 January 2018).
Wolwedans (2018b) *Introduction*. Available at http://www.wolwedans.com/lodges-camps/introduction/ (accessed 6 January 2018).

# 4

# Joint Venture Lodge Ownership Partnership Options

Community–private sector tourism operations include operations where there is a joint venture (JV) partnership involved. The JV partnership includes two entities, with a portion of the shareholding held by a private company and a portion held by a community organisation (e.g. a community trust or other legally recognised community-based organisation). The JV may own the infrastructure (e.g. the lodge or camp facilities), and/or it may own the management company. The land on which the lodge is based may be owned by government or by a community. There is also one case of a tripartite structure, where there are three different types of partner with equity in the lodge owning company (e.g. Rocktail Camp).

Where the land is government owned, this type of business model may arise where government wants to allocate land tenure in a protected area to a community, to give them an opportunity to establish a tourism joint venture that stimulates local economic development in an impoverished area. This is embodied in the conservancy system in Namibia (see Box 4). Alternatively, a community may own land and they may want to establish a partnership with a private operator to jointly develop and/or operate a tourism camp. The tourism venture then has the potential to preferentially provide local people with equity in the JV company (and dividends when profitable), training and jobs during construction and operational phases, and revenue from selling goods or services.

In JVs, both partners contribute, have a share of ownership and receive benefits. Usually the community contributes resources that they have access to such as land, grant funding and labour. The private sector typically contributes expertise and investment, be they business and financial management expertise, marketing knowledge, existing client bases, reputation, or capital and security for commercial loans (Spenceley, Rylance, Nanabhay & van der Watt, 2016).

We identified five main types of community–private sector business model, listed below.

**1. JV lodge ownership, on government land:** for example, at Anvil Bay the government of Mozambique awarded a 50-year concession to the Ahi Zameni Chemucane Association (AZC: a community association), which in turn has a 25-year agreement with the Chemucane Tourism Company (CTC) to develop and operate a lodge. The CTC has 40% ownership by AZC, and the other 60% equity is owned by the Bell Foundation, which invested USD 2 million (Collins, 2012, 2014) (Case Study 19). Also, in Mozambique, Ndzou Lodge is located in the buffer zone of Chimanimani National Reserve, and is a joint venture between Kubatana Moribane, a local community association, and the Mozambican company Eco-Micaia Lda. The local community's

© S. Snyman and A. Spenceley (2019). *Private Sector Tourism in Conservation Areas in Africa* (S. Snyman and A. Spenceley)

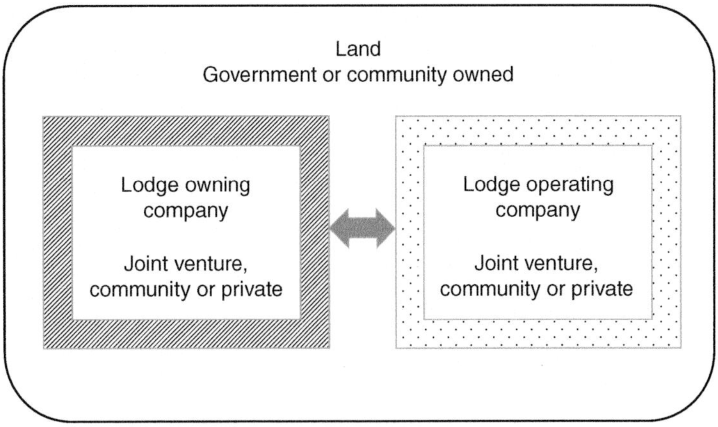


**Fig. 5.** Community–private ownership model.

> **Box 4.** Conservancies in Namibia
>
> In Namibia, wildlife is the property of the state, but under the 1996 legal amendment (Nature Conservation Amendment Act 1996), community conservancies received conditional use rights over wildlife. An important feature of the Namibian institutional framework for communal conservancies is that local rights over wildlife and tourism are entrenched in legislation; they are not mere administrative privileges that can arbitrarily be removed (Jones, 2010). The number of communal conservancies grew from 15 in 2002 to 83 in 2017 (NACSO, 2017a, 2017b).
>
> One income-generating option for conservancies is to engage in a partnership or JV with the private sector to develop ecotourism in the conservancy. JV tourism in Namibia is currently the largest overall source of benefit to the conservancies. In 2016 there were 53 JV tourism enterprises with 954 full-time and 72 part-time employees generating approximately USD 1.1 million (NACSO, 2016).

association (Kubatana Moribane) owns 60% of the business while Eco-Micaia owns 40% (Case Study 20).

**2. JV lodge ownership, on community land:** Damaraland Camp is a JV partnership between the Torra Conservancy and Wilderness Safaris (WS). The communities have been given conditional rights by the Namibian government to use the land for conservation and development. The Torra Conservancy owns 40% of the lodge and WS owns 60% (Case Study 21). Doro Nawas Camp in Namibia is owned and operated as a joint venture between the Doro !Nawas Conservancy (45% shareholding) and WS (55% shareholding). The lodge is located on land owned by the Doro !Nawas Conservancy (Case Study 22).

**3. Community owned lodge on government land, with a private management company:** Similarly, Covane Community Lodge is located in the buffer zone of the Limpopo National Park in Mozambique, and within the Great Limpopo Transfrontier Conservation Area. This community-owned lodge is managed under a seven-year contract by the company Scholtz Consultoria e Serviços Lda (Case Study 24).

**4. Community or privately owned lodge on community land:** !Xaus Lodge in the Kgalagadi Transfrontier Park in South Africa illustrates this model. It is owned by the ‡Khomani San and Mier Community Trust and managed by the private company Transfrontier Parks Destinations (TFPD) (Case Study 25). in South Africa, the land of Phinda Private Game Reserve was transferred from the private company, andBeyond, to the Mnqobokazi and Makhasa communities in 2006, following a land restoration case. The company had already established four lodges on the reserve and signed 36-year leases with each community to continue operating them (Case Study 26). Sabyinyo Silverback Lodge in Rwanda is a community owned lodge on community land. There is a management agreement between the Sabyinyo Community Livelihoods Association (SACOLA) and Governors Camp, a private operator (Case Study 28).

**5. Tripartite venture:** this type of model can be requested by the government entity in circumstances where it owns the land, and does not wish to transfer total responsibility for the capital investment to the private and community partners. We identified one camp using this model, Rocktail Camp. The camp is owned by three different parties: a black economic empowerment (BEE) company (see Box 2), a private for-profit company and the local community trust, with the government owning and managing the land (Case Study 32).

Some examples of the combinations of land ownership, lodge ownership and operating in southern Africa are outlined in Table 28.

**Table 28.** JV models.

| Model | Land ownership | Lodge ownership | Lodge management | Examples |
|---|---|---|---|---|
| 1. JV lodge ownership, on government land | Government | JV | Joint, private, or community | Ndzou camp, Mozambique<br>Anvil Bay, Mozambique<br>Vumbura and Little Vumbura Camps, Botswana |
| 2. JV lodge ownership, on community land | Community | JV | Joint, private, or community | Damaraland Camp, Namibia<br>Doro Nawas Camp, Namibia |
| 3. Community owned lodge on government land, with a private or joint venture management company | Government | Community | Joint, private | Witsieshoek, South Africa<br>Covane Community Lodge, Mozambique |
| 4. Community or privately owned lodge on community land | Community | Community or private | Private | Serra Cafema, Namibia<br>Phinda, South Africa<br>Pafuri Camp, South Africa<br>Satao Elerai, Kenya<br>Sabyinyo Silverback Lodge, Rwanda, !Xaus, South Africa |
| 5. Tripartite model | Government | Tripartite: government, private, community | Private | Rocktail Camp, South Africa |

## 4.1. Joint Venture Lodge Ownership, on Government Land

### 4.1.1. Case Study 19: Anvil Bay Chemucane Lodge, Mozambique

#### Background

Anvil Bay is a nine-chalet (18-bed) lodge situated in the Maputo Special Reserve in Mozambique. The lodge offers guests game drives, walks in the dune forest and on the beach, beach bikes, watersports (e.g. kayaks, stand-up paddle boards), snorkelling, fishing and turtle nesting walks (Anvil Bay, 2017).

The rack rate in 2017–2018 ranged from USD 384 to USD 434 during low and high seasons, based on a full board, per person, per night, sharing, basis (Anvil Bay, 2017).

**Institutional structure**

The government of Mozambique awarded a 50-year concession to the Ahi Zameni Chemucane Association (AZC), a community association, which in turn has a 25-year agreement with the Chemucane Tourism Company (CTC), a JV company, to develop and operate the lodge. The CTC has 40% ownership by AZC, which was financed by a USD 500,000 grant from the World Bank's Community Enterprise Fund, and USD 500,000 from a loan from the Ford Foundation administered by the African Safari Foundation (ASF). The other 60% equity is owned by the Bell Foundation, a non-governmental organisation (NGO), which invested USD 2 million (Collins, 2012, 2014).

Within the Maputo Special Reserve, the 809-hectare site is owned by the government of Mozambique, and the community has been awarded a special licence to develop and operate for 50 years.

**Economic impact**

The lease fee paid to the AZC is USD 30,000 per year, to cover land fees and tariffs, plus 2.5% of turnover (and a guaranteed amount of USD 15,600 per year). A bed levy of USD 6 per person per night is also paid to the community (Collins, 2012). Concession and park fees amounted to USD 13,350 (11% of expenditure: MZN 814,000) in 2016, while money paid to AZC and community levies amounted to around USD 2,412 (2% of expenditure: MZN 147,000) (S. Collins, email, 2017, personal communication).

**Social impact**

The AZC represents about 1,000 residents in three affected communities: Tsolombane, Muvukuza and Mabuluko (Collins, 2012). During the construction phase, there were 25 staff: 19 were from the communities that are part-owners of the lodge. Another seven employees were from Inhambane in Mozambique, who helped to train local people in carpentry and other construction skills. The local workers were selected during a community meeting by the community, based on their existing skills and the type of job that they were going to do. During construction, their wages ranged from between USD 115 per month for a labourer, USD 505 per month for a carpenter, and USD 710 per month for a construction supervisor (Spenceley, 2014).

Locally sourced construction materials were used where possible, including reeds for the chalet roofs. This had the unintended benefit of local people realising that grass had a value, and reduced incidents of burning (Spenceley, 2014). During construction there were also monthly trips organised for around 25 people from the three communities to visit the lodge construction site. The visitors rotated each month, so that all would have an opportunity to visit the site. Training was provided for 13 local community members in hospitality at the South Africa College of Tourism (SACT) (Spenceley, 2014).

Now that the lodge is operational, there are 29 employees, of whom 28 are Mozambican, and 22 (76%) are from the three local communities. In 2016, staff salaries were USD 55,100 (46% of operating costs: MZN 3,358 million). New local employees are identified by local community leaders, or through existing staff. Local procurement is relatively limited due to the remote location, but Anvil Bay is able to purchase seafood, dhow transport, local storage fees and small quantities of thatch for maintenance (S. Collins, email, 2017, personal communication). Staff members were trained in how to construct and maintain furniture and fittings, using sustainably resourced natural materials for furniture where possible.

#### Environmental impact

Located within a national reserve, the planning was subject to an environmental impact assessment and emphasised sustainable design. The chalets were constructed from wood from exotic trees onsite, and in order to reduce any leaching of concrete into the sand, support posts were placed in bags which were then filled with concrete. The developer took care not to cut indigenous trees, and protected tree roots running across access routes with sandbags. Water comes from a borehole (i.e. groundwater) and solar power is used for electricity (Spenceley, 2014). The lodge has a solar power 'farm' and a battery bank, that allows it to operate fully on renewable energy, unless there are three days in a row of full cloud cover. Groceries are collected by sailing a traditional dhow from the reserve to nearby Maputo where they are purchased, which reduces the use of diesel transport by car.

#### Successes

One of the key successes to the development of Anvil Bay was the long-term technical support provided by the three NGOs: the ASF Technoserve and the Peace Parks Foundation. For example, ASF helped to facilitate the partnership between the community and the private sector, provided technical advice to AZC and also facilitated funding for the community's 40% shareholding (Collins, 2014). Furthermore, the concession negotiations were speeded up by the International Finance Corporation's Anchor Investment Program (Collins, 2012).

A joint management committee was established incorporating representatives of the Ministry of Tourism, the Matituine District Government, AZC and the community (Collins, 2012).

#### Challenges

One of the challenges is the level of risk of the project. If the lodge closes, the funders will take over CTC's remaining contract rights, but AZC would retain the 50-year concession rights from the government (Collins, 2012).

It is difficult to recruit community members, because the types of skills needed by the lodge are limited in the community. Furthermore, employment of women is challenging because of attrition rates after maternity leave, or migration to South Africa (S. Collins, email, 2017, personal communication).

Constraints also relate to access to the lodge, with transfers that are not as rapid or affordable as would be liked. The lodge is considering operating an 'affordable helicopter' to address this (S. Collins, email, 2017, personal communication). A new bridge and tar road linking Maputo with the Maputo Special Reserve and Ponta d'Oura will also reduce road transfer times and costs in the future.

#### Lessons learned and recommendations

Development of JVs between community members and the private sector, and preferentially employing local people, is an important way to build local capacity and reduce poverty in remote and marginalised areas. However, it has high associated transaction costs, particularly where community members have a low basic understanding of tourism and hospitality, and lack basic education. However, this case

**Table 29.** Summary – Anvil Bay.

| | |
|---|---|
| Name of company | Chemucane Tourism Company (CTC) |
| Location | Maputo Special Reserve, Mozambique |
| Year established | 2014 |
| Status of company (i.e. listed, privately owned, etc.) | Privately owned |
| List of camps/lodges | Chemucane (18 beds) |
| Investment/partnership option | JV<br>40% ownership by Ahi Zameni Chemucane Association (community association)<br>60% ownership by Bell Foundation (NGO) |
| Total number of staff employed | 29 |
| % local staff | 96% |
| Financial summary | Concession and park fees paid to government amounted to USD 13,350, and money paid to AZC and community levies amounted to around USD 2,412 in 2016 |

demonstrates that building and operating a luxury lodge is feasible with considerable effort and energy of enlightened operators supported by adequate technical support and finance. Such initiatives are replicable in cases where substantial grant support can be identified to purchase community equity in lodge-owning companies, and to pay for preparatory and ongoing technical expertise. The long-term vision is that in 25 years the lodge should be well established in the market, will be functioning optimally, and have repaid the capital costs. The lodge will require concerted effort for the remainder of the contract to build community capacity to manage the asset themselves, or alternatively they can seek another manager. (Pers. com. S. Collins, email November 2018).

### 4.1.2. Case Study 20: Ndzou Camp, Mozambique

#### Background

Ndzou Camp is a 22-bed ecotourism development located in the Moribane Forest Reserve, in the buffer zone of the Chimanimani National Reserve in Mozambique. The camp offers accommodation in a family house (six beds), bunk room (two rooms with four bunk beds) and four rondavels (eight beds). Food and activities are linked to the forest and local culture (e.g. elephant tracking, forest walks, visits to local communities and sacred places) (A. Kingman, 2017, personal communication; Fusari, 2011).

In 2017, the rack rate for accommodation ranged between USD 8 for a bed in a bunkhouse, to USD 32 for a rondavel and USD 50 for the family house. Rates are proposed to increase to USD 10, USD 40 and USD 75, respectively, once a refurbishment is completed (A. Kingman, 2017, personal communication). There are also plans to rehabilitate two fixed tents (four beds) in the future.

#### Institutional structure

Ndzou is a JV between Kubatana Moribane, a local community association, and the Mozambican private company Eco-Micaia Lda (Eco-Micaia). The local community association (Kubatana Moribane) owns 60% of the business (i.e. Ndzou Camp Lda), while Eco-Micaia owns 40%. Eco-Micaia is the commercial (for profit) branch of the Micaia Foundation (*Fundação Micaia*), a Mozambican foundation with links in other countries (Fusari, 2011). The community's equity was financed by the Community Enterprise Fund, as part of a broader government of Mozambique and World Bank project on tourism in transfrontier conservation areas (TFCAs).

There is a management agreement (10-year validity) between Ndzou Camp and Eco-Micaia for the startup management of the camp, for the marketing and the general administration of relationships with central government and donors.

The 5.5-hectare site is owned by the government of Mozambique, and the community has a special licence to develop the land for tourism (Kingman, 2011).

#### Economic impact

When reviewed in April 2011, the financial turnover of Ndzou Camp was very low, as the camp only opened officially at the end of October 2010 (four months of operation). The monthly turnover at that time was between USD 1,000 and USD 3,200 (Fusari, 2011).

Between 2011 and 2013 the camp did good business, hosted events and had good reviews. Although turnover was low, it was sufficient to cover operational costs and Eco-Micaia's management services. However, there have been no distributable profits (A. Kingman, 2017, personal communication). To boost the economic impact on the local community, Ndzou started including a community 'levy' of USD 0.71 per occupied room per night by agreement with the association. These funds have been used to support the work of the association. From April 2017, the lodge plans to increase the levy to USD 1.43 for rondavels and USD 2.85 for the family house per night. By the end of 2017, the levy will be increased to USD 2 for a rondavel and USD 3, for the family house (A. Kingman, 2017, personal communication).

#### Social impact

Ndzou employs six full-time staff, and three to five part-time people. All of these are from the local community, and no expatriates are employed. The average wage is about USD 100 per month, which is above the government's minimum wage of MZN 5,328 per month (USD 86) (Fusari, 2011; Wageindicator.com, 2017). The construction company for the camp was based in nearby Chimoio, and mostly local workers were employed. Furthermore, all furniture for the camp was made locally by small entrepreneurs in Chimoio. Since operation, local monthly expenditures have ranged between USD 480 and USD 965 (Fusari, 2011).

Most supplies are purchased in the closest town, Chimoio (about 120 kilometres away), where the average monthly expenditure is between USD 2,410 and USD 3,215 (A. Kingman, 2017, personal communication).

Eco-Micaia developed an agreement with World Challenge (a UK-based NGO) to bring to Ndzou Camp 17 students from a girls' school in London in order to implement a pottery project and to finance the construction of a primary school in the local community (Fusari, 2011).

#### Environmental impact

In 2011, the camp had a small indigenous plant nursery that sold native plants for reforestation in the region (including in the Moribane area), including the buffer zone of the Chimanimani National Reserve (Fusari, 2011). This moved to another location because of water challenges at Ndzou Camp, but the camp retains a small seed store and a herbarium, which forms a key part of Micaia's botanical research with Kew Gardens in the UK and other partners (A. Kingman, 2017, personal communication).

#### Successes

Successes have included the development of Ndzou Camp as a joint venture between Eco-Micaia and the community association, which is still operational despite several lean years.

The camp has provided a platform for a wider engagement process in the forest zone, including the development and expansion of a honey production programme, with a market provided by the Mozambique Honey Company. Micaia has implemented several projects in the forest zone in recent years, including expansion of beekeeping, promotion of sustainable agriculture and the creation of community-managed conservation areas. Between 2016 and 2019, Micaia is contributing towards the implementation of Mozbio, a livelihoods programme funded by the World Bank through the Mozambican government. This work will include expansion of ecotourism in the Chimanimani Conservation Area (A. Kingman, 2017, personal communication). Furthermore, Micaia has also created Mozambique Eco Tours which promotes community tourism in Mozambique, including Ndzou Camp (Fusari, 2011).

There are also signs of the community having increased their responsibilities and consciousness (e.g. social and environmental) even before financial benefits from the shareholding appeared (Fusari, 2011).

#### Challenges

Initially, the community was very sceptical since they had previously had negative experiences with government entities and NGOs that promised but had not delivered. Furthermore, low literacy levels, low hospitality capacity and little understanding of financial and management aspects by local communities made it difficult to understand the financial model and partnership (e.g. the design of the business plan that was done together with the association). Biodiversity and nature conservation were initially perceived as a problem by the community rather than an opportunity, since this implied a limitation on the land to be cultivated and extracting activities in the forest (e.g. bushmeat) (Fusari, 2011). A challenge remains in maintaining the level of engagement with the community (Kingman, 2011). However, as of 2017, the community was proud and supportive of the camp, and appreciated the business challenges (A. Kingman, 2017, personal communication).

In 2013, work began to improve the main road through the area, which had made local access challenging. There were also political tensions linked to national elections followed by the outbreak of fighting between government and RENAMO (opposition party) forces. As a consequence, tourism in the area largely stopped and Ndzou was not able to maintain an events programme to encourage visitors. Now, Ndzou Camp has survived some tough years, but only just, and largely by hosting training activities as well as maintaining the core services to meet the needs of NGOs, donors, researchers and government people needing accommodation and food linked to their work in the area (A. Kingman, 2017, personal communication).

A doubling of the Moribane population over the past decade has increased the deforestation pressure on the forest, and threatens its tourism potential (A. Kingman, 2017, personal communication).

#### Lessons learned and recommendations

More easy access to financial services during the development process would have been very helpful, since raising funds and seeking investment was very time consuming. Technical assistance would have

**Table 30.** Summary – Ndzou Camp.

| | |
|---|---|
| Name of company | Eco-Micaia Lda |
| Location | Moribane Forest, Chimanimani Game Reserve (buffer zone), Mozambique |
| Year established | 2010 |
| Status of company (i.e. listed, privately owned, etc.) | Privately owned |
| List of camps/lodges | Ndzou camp: 22 beds in four rondavels, two bunk rooms, and a family house |
| Investment/partnership option | Joint venture<br>40% ownership by Kubatana Moribane community association.<br>60% ownership by Eco-Micaia |
| Total number of staff employed | Six full time |
| % local staff | 100% |
| Financial summary | No profit dividends to date (not yet profitable)<br>USD 100 per month in local wages<br>USD 2,410 and USD 3,215 per month in local expenditure |

also been relevant, especially during the preparation phase and in terms of the possibility of contracting more adequate technical officers to follow the entire process (Fusari, 2011). The time and transaction costs in order to establish the joint venture, obtain the community-equity financing and environmental approval were high.

Having been operational for eight years, Ndzou is still operating at the fringes of commercial viability. However, there are plans to expand the partnership model into other sites within the Chimanimani National Reserve, including value-added services such as trails with trained guides, and additional campsites. Micaia plans to promote the area to focus on a niche market of intrepid travellers (A. Kingman, 2017, personal communication).

## 4.2. Joint Venture Lodge Ownership, on Community Land

### 4.2.1. Case Study 21: Damaraland Camp, Namibia

Please note, the majority of this case study is adapted from Snyman (2012).

#### Background

Damaraland Camp in the Torra Conservancy (originally Ward 11) is located in the Kunene Region in north-western Namibia. The camp has 10 tents, accommodating a maximum of 20 guests. The Damaraland area offers tourists game drives and walks in beautiful desert and ancient valleys with views of the Brandberg Mountains. Unique desert elephants and desert lions can be found in the area, as well as a number of endemic birds and plants. Tourists can also experience local Nama, Damara and Riemvasmaker culture on village trips, as well as visiting ancient rock art sites in the area.

In 2017, the fully inclusive rack rate per person sharing at Damaraland Camp ranged between ZAR 4,870 (approximately USD 341) and ZAR 8,400 (approximately USD 589), depending on the season. The camp also offers a dinner, bed and breakfast rate per person sharing, for self-drive visitors, which, in 2017, ranged between ZAR 3,200 (approx. USD 224) and ZAR 6,560 (approx. USD 460) (Wilderness Safaris, 2017a).

**Institutional structure**

In Namibia, wildlife is the property of the state, but under the 1996 legal amendment (Nature Conservation Amendment Act 1996), community conservancies received conditional use rights over wildlife. An important feature of the Namibian institutional framework for communal conservancies is that local rights over wildlife and tourism are entrenched in legislation; they are not mere administrative privileges that can arbitrarily be removed (Jones, 2010). As a result, the number of communal conservancies has grown from 15 in 2002 to 83 in 2017 (NACSO, 2017a, 2017b).

One income-generating option for conservancies is to engage in a partnership or JV with the private sector to develop ecotourism in the conservancy. JV tourism in Namibia is currently the largest overall source of benefits to the conservancies. In 2016 there were 53 JV tourism enterprises with 954 full-time employees and 72 part-time employees generating approximately USD 1.1 million (NACSO, 2016). For more information on JVs see Box 4 in this volume.

The JV agreement signed in 1996 between the Torra Conservancy and WS was the first of this type between a private tourism company and a community in Namibia (Kemp, Mendelsohn & Jones, 2009). The Torra Conservancy was officially registered in June 1998. In 2000, Torra was the first conservancy to cover its own running costs, including salaries for staff, vehicle maintenance and office management (Long, 2002; Scanlon & Kull, 2009). From year 10 to year 15 of the JV partnership, WS gave the conservancy, per annum, 20% equity in Damaraland Camp until it owned 100% and chose to sell a portion back to WS to form a JV equity partnership. WS was offered and purchased 60% of the camp from the Torra Conservancy and they are now operating as equity partners with the JV leasing the land from the conservancy for a fee based on a percentage of revenue. The camp has since been upgraded, with both WS and the conservancy investing capital for the upgrade. These upgrades were initially fully funded by WS but the conservancy used cash earned from the sale of a portion of the camp back to WS to settle its portion of the shareholders' contribution in terms of the upgrade. The reinvestment of 'community capital' into the project is one of the first instances in Namibia that did not involve donor funding or loans. On 1 March 2009, the Namib Lodge Company (Pty) Ltd trading as WS and the Torra Conservancy entered into a formal equity JV and registered the company as Damaraland Camp (Pty) Ltd. The parties signed the following legal agreements: a shareholders' agreement; a lease agreement; a management agreement; and a marketing agreement. In 2010, WS assisted the conservancy to raise a bank loan of NAD 500,000 (approximately USD 62,000) based on the collateral of its shareholding in Damaraland Camp. This money was used to build Damaraland

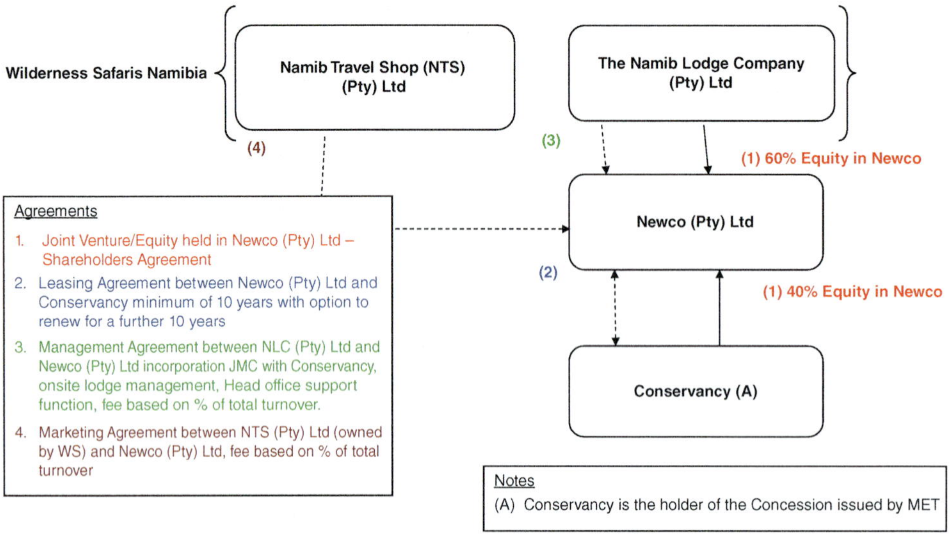


**Fig. 6.** Standard illustrative representation of legal structure of contracts/transactions between conservancies and WS Namibia.
Source: K. Jermain, email, personal communication.

Adventurer Camp – the first instance of a community raising their own funds for building purposes.

**Table 31.** Damaraland Camp lease fees.

| Damaraland Camp | Lease fees |
|---|---|
| FY2015 | USD 69,687 |
| FY2016 | USD 72,265 |
| FY2017 | USD 93,767 |
| **Total** | **USD 225,719** |

Source: Wilderness Holdings (2015, 2016, 2017)

### Economic impact

Economic contributions are made through lease fee payments, as well as supporting local community businesses (e.g. laundry and cultural activity services). USD 33,000 was paid to community members between 2015 and 2017 for goods and services (M. Wassung, email, September 2017, personal communication) and USD 225,719 was paid in terms of lease fees in the same period (see Table 31). The lease fee is 10% of turnover.

An average of approximately USD 1,522 per annum is paid to the community for local laundry services (T. Knoetze, email, March 2018, personal communication).

### Social impact

Over and above the economic benefits of the JV, the people in Torra Conservancy have gained the following: improved planning skills; insights and capacity for collaborative action; improved knowledge of their rights; broader vision for their community; and committee members on the board are empowered to make decisions and are involved in business management. WS engages in other community projects including its Children in the Wilderness (CITW) programme (for more information see Case Study 16 in this volume), library development and supporting the community school hostel. Staff at the camp receive training through an online training system called Lobster Inc., as well as through trainers visiting the camp.

The camp employs 32 staff: 19 females and 13 males, and 60% are from the local community (M. Wassung, email, September 2017, personal communication and P. Ebersohn, email, January 2018, personal communication). The average age of staff is 34. The total monthly salary bill is approximately USD 30,556, with an average wage of approximately USD 955 per staff member per month (P. Ebersohn, email, January 2018, personal communication). Staff also move between conservancies and areas for growth and advancement (M. Wassung, email, September 2017, personal communication).

### Environmental impact

The overall Namibian community-based natural resource management (CBNRM) programme has seen an increase in game numbers in conservancies, especially in the Torra Conservancy where communities are benefiting from tourism and, therefore, have an interest in conservation.

The camp uses a hybrid energy system, which combines an inverter and battery bank, connected to a small generator which operates daily during peak operational periods (W. Ozorio, email, August 2017, personal communication). This system has reduced the amount of runtime for the generator to eight hours a day.

The camp adopted a reusable water bottle policy coupled with a reverse osmosis water filtration system which ensures that the average bottled water consumption per guest remains very low, achieving an average of 0.44 litres/per bednight consumed during FY2017 (W. Ozorio, email, August 2017, personal communication). The camp undergoes a biannual environmental management system (EMS) assessment to ensure compliance with WS' Group Environmental Minimum Standards (GEMS). In FY2017 the camp achieved 99% compliance with the GEMS and is the highest performing WS camp in the region (W. Ozorio, email, August 2017, personal communication).

### Successes

This is the first instance of a community being able to use their own capital to develop a tourism product. Through the JV, numerous community members were empowered and received skills training and capacity-building. The increase in game numbers in the conservancy has been a success and added value to the conservancy. Through employment and training at Damaraland Camp many local community members have moved into management positions. Damaraland Camp has served not only as an industry skills developer but also as an anchor in the area from which the developmental ripple effects emanated to both spin-off and competitor businesses. Therefore, it has been a flagship business which has benefited the Torra Conservancy, neighbouring conservancies, the Damaraland area in general, conservation of species and the formalisation of an engagement model that has laid the foundation for the sector in Namibia, and possibly internationally (K. Jermain, email, September 2017, personal communication).

### Challenges

Initially, tourism and business capacity in the community was lacking but WS invested a large amount in staff training and capacity-building. This too has had its problems with turnover, with numerous staff being trained to management or guide levels and then leaving to work in other areas, or for other companies. Internal issues within the conservancy committee can have an impact on the partnership in terms of changing relationships. Increased game numbers can lead, and have led, to more incidences of human–wildlife conflict, especially with lions.

JVs in the form of direct leases are a success. Equity partnerships in the form of shareholding are only a success if the business is profitable, otherwise the accumulated losses have to be shared according to the shareholding, with conservancies having to supposedly pay in their share of losses (M. Wassung, email, September 2017, personal communication), though they are often unable to do this.

### Lessons learned and recommendations

There is a need for awareness-creation and further education of community members about the role of conservancies and their potential benefits as well as the role of ecotourism and implications for sustainability. A greater understanding of the tourism business and the implications, especially the risks, of shareholding to community income is also important.

**Table 32.** Summary – Damaraland Camp.

| | |
|---|---|
| Name of company | Wilderness Safaris (WS) Namibia |
| Location | Torra Conservancy,<br>Kunene region, Namibia |
| Year established | 1996 |
| Status of company (i.e. listed, privately owned, etc.) | Damaraland Camp (Pty) Ltd<br>A joint equity venture partnership between WS Namibia (60%) and the Torra Conservancy (40%) |
| List of camps/lodges | Damaraland Camp (20 beds)<br>Damaraland Adventurer Camp (8 beds) |
| Investment/partnership option | Government land leased to conservancy<br>Tenure in line with equity partnership<br>JV partnership between private sector and community conservancy |
| Total number of staff employed | 32 |
| % local staff | 65% |
| Financial summary | USD 225,719 paid in terms of lease fees to the conservancy from 2015 to 2017<br>USD 33,000 paid to community members from 2015 to 2017 for goods and services<br>USD 30,556 per month on staff salaries |

### 4.2.2. Case Study 22: Doro Nawas Camp, Namibia

### Background

The Doro !Nawas Conservancy, located in the southern part of the Kunene region in north-western Namibia, was registered in December 1999 (NACSO, 2017a, 2017b). Doro Nawas Camp, situated in the Doro !Nawas Conservancy, was opened in 2006 and has 16 rooms, accommodating a maximum of 32 guests. The camp is located in the dry Aba-Huab river valley in central Damaraland. The area has spectacular views of the Etendeka Mountains and the red sandstone cliffs of Twyfelfontein. Tourists can go on game drives, walks, village visits and visits to rock art sites at Twyfelfontein.

In 2017, the fully inclusive rack rate per person sharing at Doro Nawas Camp ranged between ZAR 3,755 (approximately USD 263) and ZAR 5,635 (approximately USD 395), depending on the season. The camp also offers a dinner, bed and breakfast rate per person sharing, for self-drive visitors, which, in 2017, ranged between ZAR 2,405 (approximately USD 169) and ZAR 4,090 (approximately USD 287) (Wilderness Safaris, 2017b).

### Institutional structure

For more background on the Namibian CBNRM programme see Case Study 21 in this volume and Box 4 (Conservancies in Namibia).

Doro Nawas Camp is a JV between private sector operator, WS, and the Doro !Nawas Conservancy. WS has a 55% shareholding in the camp, with the conservancy holding the remaining 45%. As part of the JV agreement, a Joint Management Board (JMB) was formed which includes members from the conservancy and WS.

### Economic impact

This is an equity partnership and the camp makes monthly lease payments to the conservancy as per the partnership agreement. The lease fee was previously 8% of turnover, but increased to 9% in August 2017 (T. Knoetze, email, March 2018, personal communication) (see Table 33).

An average amount of USD 10,583 per annum is spent on local community security services (T. Knoetze, email, March 2018, personal communication).

### Social impact

There are 38 staff members employed in the camp: 19 females and 19 males; 68% of the staff come from the local community (M. Wassung, email, September 2017, personal communication and P. Ebersohn, email, January 2018, personal communication). The average age of staff is 34 years. The total monthly salary bill is approximately USD 24,743, with the average monthly wage being approximately USD 651 (P. Ebersohn, email, January 2018, personal communication). Staff undergo training through online and in-person training. Staff also swap between conservancies and tourism areas for growth and advancement.

### Environmental impact

The overall Namibian CBNRM programme has seen an increase in game numbers in conservancies, including in the Doro !Nawas Conservancy.

The camp uses grid power of hydro origin and has a backup generator to ensure a constant supply of electricity (W. Ozorio, email, August 2017, personal communication). The camp has adopted a reusable water bottle policy coupled with a reverse osmosis water filtration system which ensures that the average bottled water consumption per guest remains very low, achieving

**Table 33.** Doro Nawas Camp lease fees.

| Doro Nawas Camp | Lease fees |
|---|---|
| FY2015 | USD 56,823 |
| FY2016 | USD 66,507 |
| FY2017 | USD 77,581 |
| **Total** | **USD 200,911** |

Source: Wilderness Holdings (2015, 2016, 2017)

an average of 0.34 litres/per bednight consumed during the FY2017 (W. Ozorio, email, August 2017, personal communication). The camp undergoes a biannual environmental management system (EMS) assessment to ensure compliance with WS' Group Environmental Minimum Standards (GEMS). In FY2017 the camp achieved 86% compliance with the GEMS (W. Ozorio, email, August 2017, personal communication).

### Successes

Through the JV, numerous community members have been empowered and received skills training and capacity-building. The conservancy, through education and training, has developed an understanding of the importance of game numbers and conservation to tourism (M. Wassung, email, September 2017, personal communication).

### Challenges

Initially, hospitality capacity in the community was lacking but WS has invested a large amount in staff training and capacity-building. This too has had its problems, with numerous staff being trained to management or guide levels and then leaving to work in other areas, or with other companies.

### Lessons learned and recommendations

Where communities are JV partners with an equity stake, there is a degree of risk for all stakeholders, especially if the business, for whatever reason, is not performing successfully. Another risk to the partnership is conflict within the community. In 2016 the Doro !Nawas Conservancy committee was disbanded after committee members were asked to step down by the community. There was significant discord within the community as to who should be selected as the new committee members and an agreement could not be reached. This resulted in there being no committee for an extended period and, therefore, an inability for WS to have JMB meetings with their community partner (Wilderness Holdings, 2016). These JMB meetings are a prerequisite according to the agreement between the parties which, therefore, resulted in a breach of the contract. The Ministry of Environment (MET) took over the management of the conservancy during this period. This case highlights the potential challenges resulting from private sector–community partnerships which extend beyond the actual official agreement to issues that either party may be having internally (Wilderness Holdings, 2016). The importance of a cohesive, stable community structure is also highlighted.

**Table 34.** Summary – Doro Nawas Camp.

| | |
|---|---|
| Name of company | Wilderness Safaris (WS) |
| Location | Kunene region, Namibia |
| Year established | 2006 |
| Status of company (i.e. listed, privately owned, etc.) | JV partnership between WS and the Doro !Nawas Conservancy |
| List of camps/lodges | Doro Nawas Camp (32 beds) |
| Investment/partnership option | Government land leased to conservancy<br>Tenure in line with equity partnership<br>Equity partnership between private sector and community |
| Total number of staff employed | 38 |
| % local staff | 68% |
| Financial summary | USD 220,000 lease fees to the conservancy from 2015 to 2017<br>USD 24,743 monthly cost for salaries |

## 4.3. Community Owned Lodge on Government Land, With a Private Management Company

### 4.3.1. Case Study 23: Witsieshoek Mountain Lodge, South Africa

#### Background

Witsieshoek Mountain Lodge (WML) is an 88-bed lodge in the South African section of the Maloti Drakensberg Transfrontier Conservation Area. The lodge offers three types of accommodation – 30 bungalow rooms (60 beds), eight chalets (16 beds) and a hikers' cabin (12 beds) (G. O'Leary, email, 2017, personal communication; WML, 2016a). The lodge is owned by the Batlokoa community, and is managed by TFPD, a private company, on their behalf (WML, 2016b). The lodge is a soft-adventure destination offering accommodation for hikers, mountain bikers, rock climbers and birdwatchers who wish to explore the Drakensberg Mountain.

In 2017 the rack rates in the different types of accommodation ranged from USD 39 to USD 75 per person per night, sharing (WML, 2016a).

#### Institutional structure

WML was originally built in the 1970s as a state enterprise, on the site of a stone hut built for backpackers in the 1950s by former Batlokoa King Wessels Mota. The lodge was gradually handed over by the state to King Lekunutu Mota of the local Batlokoa community in the mid-1990s when it officially became a community asset. However, management challenges prompted the traditional council to enter into an agreement with TFPD in 2010 to operate the lodge management and marketing (WML, 2016b) under a 25-year management contract (G. O'Leary, email, 2017, personal communication).

#### Economic impact

Under the management contract, the community is entitled, in lieu of rental, to receive 17% of the profit generated by the lodge or a minimum annual payment from TFPD of USD 15,000. By June 2017, despite the lodge not yet having reached profitability, TFPD had contributed an estimated USD 36,000 to the community in lieu of rental (email, G. O'Leary, 2017, personal communication).

TFPD catalysed infrastructure investment through the South African government's Department of Environmental Affairs and Tourism from the state's Public Works Programme of USD 2 million to finance renovations to the lodge from 2010, which upgraded the lodge to a four-star standard facility (O'Leary, 2014). The upgraded infrastructure is owned by the community (G. O'Leary, 2017, personal communication).

### Social impact

In addition to the rental/profit share paid to the community trust, a bed levy of 1% per night is included in the accommodation booking fee. Of the funds, 100% of those collected are disbursed through the TFPD Foundation in partnership with the local community for social upliftment and educational projects (WML, 2016a). To date, since the fund was started in 2015, the equivalent of USD 6,932 (ZAR 86,650) has been collected. The community leaders wish to build financial reserves from their lodge income, and hope to get the Foundation income to a substantial level so that they can do something '... with gravitas in the future' (E. Muller, email, 2017, personal communication).

In 2017 there were 44 full-time employees at the lodge, of whom 95% were from the Batlokoa community, or from other local communities (O'Leary, 2017).

Between 2011 and 2017, local procurement from the lodge generated USD 1.6 million for locally produced goods, and USD 1.3 million for locally sold goods (see Table 37). For example, the lodge buys furniture from a local entrepreneur, Mr Molete. Prior to 2014, Mr Molete had a micro-enterprise undertaking basic carpentry work in the local community. In 2014, on completion of the renovation of WML, Mr Molete was invited to Witsieshoek to look at sample furniture to see whether he could manufacture furniture for the lodge. After a faltering start, followed by consultation with lodge management, manufacturing errors were corrected and Mr Molete and his team have now manufactured furniture for 36 guest bedrooms, including beds, headboards, tables, chairs and mirrors. The lodge spent USD 73,600 at his business, Bolof

**Table 35.** Community benefits paid to the Batloka community (USD).

| Category | 2011 | 2012 | 2013 | 2014 | 2015 | 2016 | 2017 | TOTAL |
|---|---|---|---|---|---|---|---|---|
| Rental | 0 | 0 | 0 | 0 | 7,200 | 14,400 | 14,400 | **36,000** |
| Asset upgrades, maintenance, insurance | 9,245 | 493,434 | 486,025 | 411,612 | 403,851 | 9,790 | 26,955 | **1,840,912** |

Source: G. O'Leary, email 2017, personal communication

**Table 36.** Employment and salary benefits.

| Category | 2011 | 2012 | 2013 | 2014 | 2015 | 2016 | 2017 | TOTAL |
|---|---|---|---|---|---|---|---|---|
| Number of employees (95% local) | 26 | 26 | 28 | 35 | 36 | 38 | 44 | |
| Remuneration and benefits (USD) | 81,082 | 58,174 | 80,304 | 116,461 | 146,468 | 161,352 | 174,261 | **818,102** |

Source: O'Leary (2017)

**Table 37.** Local procurement (USD).

| Category | 2011 | 2012 | 2013 | 2014 | 2015 | 2016 | 2017 | TOTAL |
|---|---|---|---|---|---|---|---|---|
| Local origin | 22,704 | 358,496 | 352,346 | 312,047 | 341,863 | 80,211 | 104,578 | **1,572,245** |
| Local supply | 45,119 | 214,777 | 202,554 | 205,410 | 264,663 | 159,399 | 207,823 | **1,299,746** |

Source: O'Leary (2017)

Construction, during the refurbishment. To assist Mr Molete in exploring business opportunities from government agencies, the TFPD financial team assisted him to register his company on the South African government's procurement database. He now manufactures high quality lodge furniture. His workshop is in an abandoned light industrial complex in the village of Tsheseng (TFPD/TFPD Foundation, 2017: 36).

#### Environmental impact

TFPD has secured further funding of USD 1.7 million from the Department of Environmental Affairs for the Batlokoa community. This funding is for the upgrade of the infrastructure at the Sentinel Peak parking area, as well as for the rehabilitation of the eroded mountain pathways and chain ladder that provide access to the top of the Drakensberg Mountain amphitheatre.

#### Successes

Over the past seven years, the private sector manager, TFPD, has transformed a dilapidated community-owned lodge that was to be abandoned into a thriving enterprise. It generates meaningful financial returns for the community owners, and also secure full-time employment (and salaries) for 44 local people. It now has comfortable accommodation, improving occupancies, and productive and busy local staff (O'Leary, 2017). The lodge is independently certified as a sustainable tourism business by Fair Trade Tourism.

#### Challenges

As noted, communities often have a misinformed belief that private operators are making immense profits to the detriment of the community. Sometimes community members also believe that jobs are a 'right' rather than a benefit (O'Leary, 2014).

#### Lessons learned and recommendations

Private operators need to identify clearly who their relevant communities are and define and communicate clearly what community benefits are (O'Leary, 2014). Regular meetings with the community owners and a transparent sharing of information including financial results goes a long way to overcoming the challenge of 'misinformed beliefs' (G. O'Leary, email, 2017, personal communication).

**Table 38.** Summary – Witsieshoek Mountain Lodge.

| | |
|---|---|
| Name of company | Transfrontier Parks Destinations (TFPD) |
| Location | Maloti Drakensberg TFCA, South Africa |
| Year established | 2007, and redeveloped 2010–2015 |
| Status of company (i.e. listed, privately owned, etc.) | Privately managed<br>Community owned lodge |
| List of camps/lodges | WML (88 beds) |
| Investment/partnership option | Community owned land<br>Community owned lodge infrastructure (Batlokoa community)<br>Privately managed (TFPD) |
| Total number of staff employed | 44 full time, 5 part time |
| % local staff | 95% |
| Financial summary | USD 36,000 in community payments, in lieu of rental, by 2017<br>USD 6,932 in community levies paid into a trust fund<br>USD 818,102 in salaries to local people between 2011 and 2017<br>USD 1.6 million spent on locally produced goods between 2011 and 2017 |

## 4.3.2. Case Study 24: Covane Community Lodge, Mozambique

### Background

Covane Community Lodge (CCL) is located in the buffer zone of the Limpopo National Park (LNP) in Mozambique, and within the Great Limpopo Transfrontier Conservation Area. The 10-bed lodge has accommodation including chalets (8 beds), traditional Shangaan huts (15 beds) and a houseboat (4 beds), and campsites are also available. The camp is privately managed by the company Scholtz Consultoria e Serviços Lda on behalf of the Canhane community owners (CCL, undated b). Activities offered include boat-based wildlife and bird viewing (CCL, undated a), fishing and cultural tours of the Canhane village, the nearby Massingir town and market (CCL, undated c). Traditional dancers can also be organised to dance at the lodge, and weddings are also hosted (CCL, undated c, CCL undated d).

In 2017 the rack rates were USD 20 for a traditional hut or USD 50 for a chalet per unit (both B&B); USD 245 for the houseboat (self-catered, with skipper), and USD 7 per person for camping. On top of these rates is a USD 4.60 per person, per night, community levy (CCL, 2016–2017).

### Institutional structure

CCL first opened in 2004 as a community owned and managed enterprise that had been established following two years of technical support from the NGO Helvetas (now called Lupa), and financial resources from USAID (USD 50,000) and Helvetas (USD 20,000) (Spenceley, 2006). Later, on the understanding that the community was unable to achieve commercial viability, or link with source markets, technical support from Lupa, and further capital investment from the GoM's World Bank-funded Transfrontier Conservation Area project, enabled the lodge to receive further investment of USD 140,000 between 2011 and 2013, from the project's Community Enterprise Fund (World Bank, 2014). At that time, the project also tried (and failed) to find a private sector operator for the lodge. More recently, in 2014, Lupa undertook a tender process to identify a new operator and awarded a seven-year management contract to Scholtz Consultoria e Serviços Lda. The lodge was, and still is, owned by the Covane Community, through its representative association Associação Covane Community Lodge (see Figure 7).

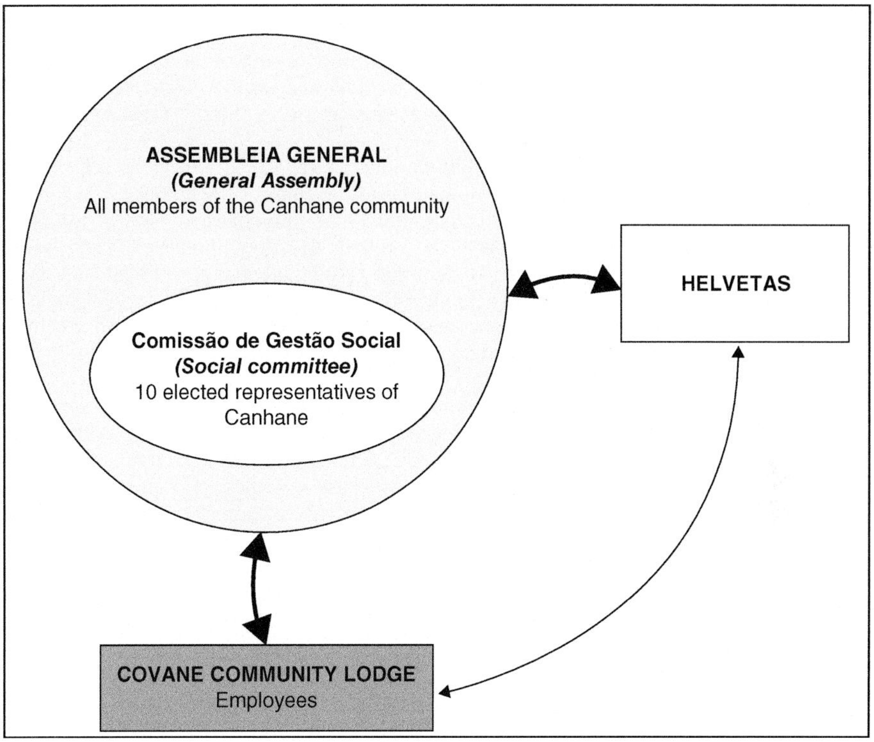


**Fig. 7.** Institutional structure of Covane Community Lodge.

The key stakeholders are described as follows (Spenceley, 2006).

- **Assembleia General:** the Assembleia General consists of all members of the Canhane community. They can approve partnerships between the lodge and private or public entities, authorise partnership agreements, projects and expansion of the lodge activities and monitor the Comissão de Gestão Social. If people move into the Canhane community, they automatically become members of the Assembleia General.
- **Comissão de Gestão Social (CGS):** the role of the CGS is to represent the interests of the Canhane community, as its elected volunteer representative. It has a bank account and can negotiate with parties to establish contracts. The committee can be re-elected by the Assembleia General every five years (Anon., undated).
- **Helvetas/Lupa:** Helvetas was a Swiss NGO that facilitated the development of the lodge. Helvetas talked to the communities about community-based tourism (CBT), potential locations for a lodge, the land law and land delimitation. The community identified a suitable location and at the suggestion of Helvetas organised the steering committee (the CGS). Helvetas transitioned to become the NGO Lupa, which is still involved (and using some of the same technical staff) in supporting Covane.

### Economic impact

The agreement between the community and private sector states that an annual rental is paid to the community, comprising an annual USD 3,000 flat fee (increasing by 5% each year) and USD 5 per bed night (increasing by 10% each year until it reaches USD 10) (L. Dinis, email, 2017, personal communication). Between July 2015 and May 2016 the community received USD 2,835 from the bed levy (Anon., undated). There is no information available on how these funds have been used.

### Social impact

The management agreement specifies that local people from Canhane are prioritised for employment opportunities. There are currently 11 staff at the lodge, of whom 9 are from the Canhane community, and 4 are from the local town of Massingir (M. Scholtz, email, 2017, personal communication).

As part of their lease agreement, the current managers have supported the development of two classrooms in the Canhane community and two houses for teachers. They are also in the process of installing a water trough for livestock (M. Scholtz, email, 2017, personal communication). The managers are responsible for supplying the water to the community, using infrastructure provided under the TFCA Community Equity Fund grant (L. Dinis, email, 2017, personal communication). Each day the lodge pumps 30,000 litres of water to the community for free, although a water purification system is needed for human consumption (M. Scholtz, email, 2017, personal communication). In 2017, Canhane village also benefited from electrification from government (L. Dinis, email, 2017, personal communication).

In 2006, the bulk of the products purchased from the local community were food and beverages (55%), followed by fuel (24%) and maintenance materials (8%). Other purchases include kitchenware, furniture, communications equipment and water (3%). The bulk of services procured from the local community were per diems for staff travelling to buy lodge provisions (24%), traditional cooking (27%), boat trips (13%), traditional dancing (12%), maintenance (12%) and the transportation of fuel (8.3%). The medicinal plant walks accounted for a small proportion of service expenditure (2%), as did accommodation (1.6%) and local labour (1%) (Spenceley, 2006). Due to the lack of local products and services available, in 2017 there was no local procurement from the Canhane community by the lodge, and only bread and fresh seasonal fruit and vegetables could be bought in the closest town of Massingir (M. Scholtz, email, 2017, personal communication).

### Environmental impact

Wildlife in the area is mainly within the sanctuary area of the LNP, but in 2006 there were hippopotamuses, crocodiles, rabbits, hares and rhino in the area. However, the lodge is not involved in their conservation.

Environmental impact assessments for the lodge development were undertaken prior to the initial development funded by USAID and Helvetas, and also the redevelopment funded by the TFCA CEF. Although there is no environmental management system in place, there is a small solar system at the office for computers and internet (M. Scholtz, email, 2017, personal communication). Water for the camp, and also the community, is pumped from the Massingir Dam.

### Successes

Successes at CCL include demonstration of how infrastructure upgrades, and contracting an external private manager can transform a struggling CBT enterprise into a commercially viable operation. Furthermore, the long-term commitment of NGOs to seek the best arrangement for the community, and evolve the approach over time, is apparent. Notably, one of the staff members who was previously involved with Helvetas, and now with Lupa, has sustained his support for the Canhane community, and the NGOs have sought additional partners and funding over the past 13 years.

The lodge is considered by the neighbouring LNP to be 'part' of the park, and the broader Great Limpopo Transfrontier Park. Therefore, travellers are only permitted to use the Giriyondo border post between

**Table 39.** Covane wages (2015–2017).

| Year | 2015 | 2016 | 2017 | Total over 3 years |
|---|---|---|---|---|
| Wage bill (Mozambican Metical (MT)) | 776,277 | 838,379 | 905,450 | MT 2,520,106 |
| Wage bill (USD equivalent) | 22,416 | 15,644 | 12,674 | USD 50,734 |

Conversions: Onanda.com 1 May each year.
Source: M. Scholtz, email, 2017, personal communication

Kruger National Park (KNP) and LNP if they have a reservation in the park, or with CCL (M. Scholtz, email, 2017, personal communication).

### Challenges

One of the challenges is the high cost of maintenance, borne by the private sector lodge managers, which over the past three years has cost an estimated USD 14,000. Additional upgrades need to be financed to provide self-catering equipment, replace thatched roofs, build staff quarters, replace the water tank, install livestock fences and upgrade the interiors. An operational challenge is the need for electricity, and the lodge will install a new transformer to provide this (M. Scholtz, email, 2017, personal communication).

### Lessons learned and recommendations

Retrofitting CBT enterprises, in order to leverage donor grants for their infrastructure, and to be privately (rather than community) managed, is viable. However, the commercial conditions need to be appropriate for the private sector to be able to establish a commercially profitable enterprise.

**Table 40.** Total staff and procurement costs.

| | 2005–2006 financial year | 2017 |
|---|---|---|
| Total number of staff | 7 | 13 |
| Number of local staff (%) | 7 (100%) | 9 (69%) |
| Total local wage bill (annual) | USD 3,948 | USD 12,674 |
| Local dependents supported (assuming 8.5 per staff) | 60 | 77 |
| Local products purchased:<br>within 21 km between 21–150 km | 26%: USD 1,582<br>54%: USD 3,285 | 0.2%<br>7% |
| Local services (dance, etc.) procured:<br>within 21 km<br>between 21–150 km | 71%: USD 919<br>26%: USD 337 | 0%<br>0 % |

Sources: M. Scholtz, email, 2017, personal communication; Spenceley (2006)

**Table 41.** Summary – Covane Community Lodge.

| | |
|---|---|
| Name of company | Scholtz Consultoria e Serviços Lda |
| Location | Limpopo National Park (LNP) buffer zone, Mozambique |
| Year established | 2004 (when run by the community) |
| Status of company (i.e. listed, privately owned, etc.) | Community owned lodge<br>Private management company |
| List of camps/lodges | CCL: chalets (8 beds), traditional Shangaan huts (15 beds), a houseboat (4 beds), and campsites |
| Investment/partnership option | Infrastructure: community owned<br>Land: government owned, DUAT to the community<br>Management company: private |
| Total number of staff employed | 13 |
| % local staff | 9 |
| Financial summary | USD 3,000 in rental paid to the community each year<br>USD 50,734 in wages to local community members between 2015 and 2017 |

### 4.3.3. Case Study 25: !Xaus Lodge, South Africa

#### Background

**Box 5.** contractual parks

A contractual park is defined as any land that is either privately owned or state owned that is managed by an agreement reached between the owner (state or private) and the National Parks Board which, legally specified in a contract, will constitute part of a 'contractual national park' and whose boundaries, its identification, ownership and status are established by contract (Reid, Fig, Magome & Leader-Williams, 2004: 378).

In South Africa, contractual national parks provide an important way in which the national protected area (PA) network can be extended by the inclusion of land that cannot be bought and/or on which mining rights will not be released (Reid *et al.*, 2004). A contractual national park usually involves the drawing up of a joint management agreement in which the rights and responsibilities of the landowners and the conservation authority that manages the land are clearly laid out. A joint management committee or board is usually constituted, including national park and land owner representatives. In both contractual park case studies in this volume, the landowner is the community, both through the land-claim process in South Africa.

!Xaus Lodge is a 24-bed community owned lodge located in the South African sector of the Kgalagadi Transfrontier Park (KTP). The lodge offers game drives, dune walks, stargazing and visits to a local bushman craft village. TFPD, a private company, manages !Xaus Lodge commercially on behalf of the ‡Khomani San and Mier communities (!Xaus Lodge, 2017b). In 2017 the rack rate was USD 350 per adult per night, sharing (!Xaus Lodge, 2017a).

### Institutional structure

In May 2002, the ‡Khomani San and Mier communities reached a historic land settlement agreement with the government of South Africa and South African National Parks (SANParks). The agreement restored land totalling 50,000 hectares in the KTP back to communities that had been displaced. The two communities then leased the land back to SANParks under a 99-year lease agreement (G. O'Leary, email, 2017, personal communication; !Xaus Lodge, 2017b).

The land is now administered as a contractual park (see Box 5) within KTP, and SANParks is responsible for its environmental management (!Xaus Lodge, 2017b).

After the first 10 years of operation in 2016, the ‡Khomani San and Mier Community Trust have received from TFPD a 17% equity stake in the lodge management company !Xaus Lodge (Pty) Ltd free of charge (TFPD, 2016b; !Xaus Lodge, 2017b). TFPD owns the other 83% (G. O'Leary, email, 2017, personal communication).

### Economic impact

!Xaus Lodge's infrastructure, which is jointly owned by the two communities, was financed through grant funding from the then South African government's Department of Environmental Affairs and Tourism. This funding of USD 520,000 was provided in terms of the !Ae!Hai Kalahari Heritage Park Agreement for the land restitution to the two communities. This amount was later supplemented as a result of TFPD's intervention by a further USD 360,000 in order to complete the lodge infrastructure sufficiently well to enable it to be opened to the public. Between 2007 and 2016 a further USD 160,000 was initiated by TFPD to renovate and upgrade the lodge for the community (G. O'Leary, email, 2017, personal communication; TFPD, 2016d).

Government returns, in terms of tax revenues and government welfare grants saved by virtue of previously unemployed people who would have qualified for these grants now being employed were estimated at USD 692,800, and SANParks received USD 325,663 in conservation fees paid by visitors and USD 55,114 in rental fees for the lodge between 2008 and 2017 (G. O'Leary, email, 2017, personal communication; !Xaus Lodge, 2017b).

The community representative organisations receive a monthly rental from the operation of the lodge based on its turnover (O'Leary, 2017). TFPD has an agreement to pay the ‡Khomani San and Mier Community Trust a percentage of gross annual turnover, which varies in relation to lodge income (i.e. 5% for turnover up to ZAR 5 m; 7.5% between ZAR 5 and ZAR 7.5 m; and 10% above ZAR 7.5 m). A minimum rental of ZAR 80,000 per annum is also applied (equivalent to USD 6,400) (G. O'Leary, email, 2018, personal communication). Between 2008 and 2017 the community owners received USD 110,228 in rental payments as well as USD 593,938 being spent on upgrades, maintenance and insurance of their lodge (O'Leary, 2017).

### Social impact

During the construction and renovation period, an estimated USD 386,000 was spent on local labour (34%) and USD 522,234 on local materials (46%) (O'Leary, 2016).

Currently, 28 people are permanently employed at !Xaus Lodge, of whom 26 (i.e. 93%) are from the local community (TFPD, 2016a). The JMB coordinates all applications as part of the employment process, so the community has a say in who works at the lodge (TFPD, 2016b). Staff salaries and benefits between 2008 and 2017 amounted to USD 883,923 (O'Leary, 2017). An example of staff training and promotion is provided in Box 6.

The lodge has also facilitated craft sales of USD 71,392 from ‡Khomani San crafters and USD 38,240 from other communities (O'Leary, 2016). A group of crafters have a 'crafting village' at the lodge where, on a monthly basis, between 12 and 16 crafters make crafts for guests' purchase, and teach their youngsters their ancient skills (TFPD, 2016c). Crafters are paid a stipend while they are at the lodge, and the lodge takes no commissions on the sale of their work (TFPD, 2016b).

The lodge spent USD 338,485 in sales of locally produced goods, and USD 966,935 in locally purchased goods made in South Africa between 2008 and 2017 (O'Leary, 2017; TFPD, 2016a). Locally produced goods include meat, wine and wood, while local services include transfers and maintenance (TFPD, 2016d).

**Box 6.** Staff case study: Melissa Mienies

Melissa Mienies joined the housekeeping team at !Xaus Lodge as a cleaner soon after it opened. Having failed her Matric (only 7.2% of the local community have passed Matric), and unable to spend another year at school, she was grateful for a job in a facility where she would be trained (only 30% of the locals have jobs). Living in the dunes at the Lodge she developed a special interest in guiding and, supported by the lodge managers, self-taught herself key information. !Xaus Lodge supported her (and three other guides) for distance training and she qualified two years ago. Mentorship and access to on-the-job training was critical to her success. She was the first female nature guide in the Kgalagadi who is a member of the local community. Her income, excluding pension benefits, accommodation and meal allowances, started, as a probationer, at USD 120 per month and today her package is USD 312 per month – a 260% increase, the majority of which has been promotion-based. Had !Xaus Lodge been built as a self-catering facility, with guests self-driving, there would not have been a job for her in the first place, let alone a wonderful opportunity to extend her horizons and prosper.

Source: TFPD (2016d)

!Xaus Lodge assists in leveraging donor funding for off-site community health, agricultural, educational and job creation projects (!Xaus Lodge, 2017b).

### Environmental impact

!Xaus operates on a 'tread-lightly' model. There is a diesel generator, but its use is limited to five hours a day, and funds are being sourced to convert the lodge to solar power. Water is desalinated on site, as well as bottled for guest consumption, with a major focus placed on teaching guests to limit water wastage. The focus on food procurement is to avoid foods that might be imported so that the 'carbon footprint' is minimised (TFPD, 2016c). The lodge encourages visitors to conserve water, using a 'primer' on water saving options. The lodge also informs guests that filling the waterhole for wildlife is prioritised over filling the guest swimming pool.

The land is managed for conservation by SANParks, as part of the broader KTP.

### Successes

!Xaus Lodge has won a series of awards for its achievements in responsible and sustainable tourism. These include winning the 2016 African Responsible Tourism Award in the category Best for Poverty Reduction as well as winning a silver award in the 2016 World Responsible Tourism Awards in London in the same category. !Xaus Lodge also received the 2010 South African Imvelo award for Best Practice Economic Impact (O'Leary, 2017). The lodge is also certified by Fair Trade in Tourism.

### Challenges

Communities often have a misinformed belief that private operators are making immense profits to the detriment of the community as soon as they see tourists arriving. Sometimes community members also believe that jobs are a 'right' rather than a benefit (O'Leary, 2014).

The physical isolation of the lodge creates immense logistical challenges for operations. These logistics are expensive to implement, and have a consequent impact on the rates charged to guests, who sometimes feel the lodge is expensive to visit.

### Lessons learned and recommendations

Private operators need to identify clearly who their relevant communities are and define and communicate clearly what the community benefits are and their value (O'Leary, 2014). Government investment in projects of this nature can generate a positive return on investment for the state if managed commercially. These projects should not be seen as welfare, but an investment in building economic capacity in rural areas.

**Table 42.** Summary – !Xaus Lodge (Pty) Ltd

| | |
|---|---|
| Name of company | Transfrontier Parks Destinations |
| Location | KTP, South Africa |
| Year established | 2007 |
| Status of company (i.e. listed, privately owned, etc.) | Private company |
| List of camps/lodges | !Xaus Lodge (12 chalets, 24 beds) |
| Investment/partnership option | Community owned contractual park land<br>Community owned lodge infrastructure, furniture and fittings<br>JV management company: 17% lodge management operating company owned by community trust and 83% owned by TFPD |
| Total number of staff employed | 28 |
| % local staff | 93% |
| Financial summary | 2007–2017: government tax revenues and grants saved: USD 692,800<br>SANParks conservation fees from visitors: USD 325,663<br>SANParks rental fees: USD 55,114<br>Community payments: USD 110,228 in rental payments, USD 593,938 in lodge upgrades, maintenance and insurance |

## 4.4. Community or Privately Owned Lodge on Community Land

### 4.4.1. Case Study 26: Phinda Private Game Reserve, South Africa

### Background

Phinda Private Game Reserve is in the Mun-ya-wana conservancy in KwaZulu-Natal (KZN), South Africa, bordering Mkhuze Game Reserve and iSimangaliso World Heritage Site. There are six luxury lodges in the reserve, operated by andBeyond: Forest Lodge (32 beds); Vlei Lodge (12 beds); Zuka Lodge (8 beds); Mountain Lodge (52 beds); Rock Lodge (12 beds); and Africa Homestead (8 beds). The camp is privately managed by andBeyond.

In 2017, the rack rate ranged from USD 506–650 for different lodges, during high and low seasons, based on a per person, per night, fully inclusive sharing basis (African Safari Group, 2017).

### Institutional structure

The institutional structure of Phinda has evolved over time, from privately owned land and infrastructure at the outset, to a mixture of community owned land with privately and community owned lodges based on it. To summarise the history, in 1994 local communities in South Africa were legally empowered to reclaim ancestral lands that had been expropriated under apartheid. In 2002, the Mnqobokazi and Makhasa communities led their claims to land within the Phinda reserve, which at that stage was privately owned. AndBeyond did not challenge the claim and received approximately USD 34.5 million from the South African government in compensation for the land and its infrastructure. In 2006, the titles to the territory and two of the six lodges located on it were transferred to the Mnqobokazi and Makhasa communities. When this transfer took place, both communities invited the company to continue its operations at Phinda. This resulted in andBeyond signing 36-year leases with each community, with an associated annual lease fee. AndBeyond has the option of renewing the partnership at the end of the 36-year period (Rylance & Spenceley, 2014).

Today, Rock and Mountain lodges are owned by andBeyond, Zuka is owned by the Gettys (a private family) and the Makhasa Community Trust owns Forest, Vlei and Homestead Lodges, and leases these to andBeyond. The company andBeyond own 2,267 hectares of the land and wildlife estate, and also has 36-year leases with Mnqobokazi community (1,140 hectares) and the Makasa community (900 hectares) (Spenceley, 2008). The company andBeyond Phinda leases 5,060.5 hectares from Makhasa Community Trust and 6,165.5 hectares from Qhubekani Mnqobokazi Community Trust. AndBeyond has the first option of renewal on the leases, which in effect gives an anticipated tenure of 72 years across 27,100 hectares of the conservancy (S. Naylor, email, 2017, personal communication). Phinda pays rental ranging from ZAR150 to ZAR295 per hectare (approximately USD 20–40) depending on the land parcel leased (Spenceley, 2008). A new piece of Makhasa Community Trust land (recently claimed by the community), called Lulubush, is about to be incorporated into the conservancy and leased by andBeyond Phinda for 36 years. Once the new area is included, the conservancy size will reach 28,717 hectares (S. Naylor, email, 2017, personal communication).

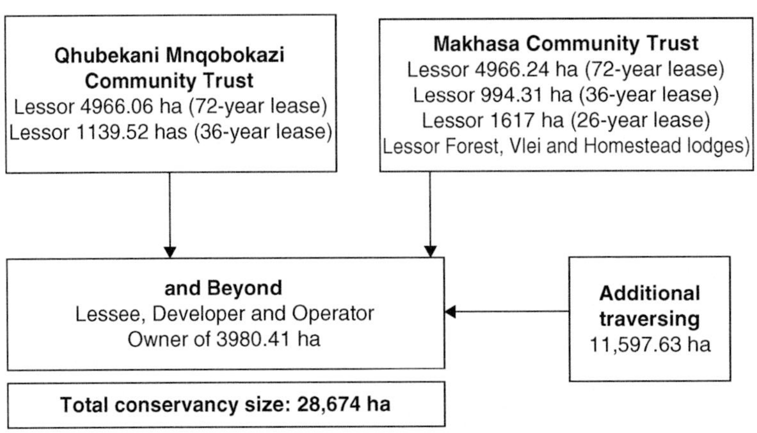


**Fig. 8.** Institutional structure of Phinda Private Game Reserve.

### Economic impact

Phinda paid approximately USD 3.56 million (ZAR 46.3 million) in lease fees to the Qhubekani Mnqobokazi and Makhasa Community Trusts between 2006 and December 2016 (S. Naylor, email, 2017, personal communication).

### Social impact

The company andBeyond Phinda currently employs 312 permanent employees, in addition to 28 fixed-term contractors for four months to two years, and 53 casual staff. The total payroll costs for the 2016/2017 costs were USD 2.49 million (ZAR 32,336,000). A large percentage of this goes into the local economy due to payment for permanent and temporary employment, as 56% of andBeyond Phinda staff are drawn from five surrounding communities. Additional employment through subcontracted builders, dance groups and maintenance companies has not been quantified (S. Naylor, email, 2017, personal communication).

Phinda's subcontractors and neighbours also contribute to local employment. The security company for the conservancy and lodge employs 95 people from local communities. Other conservancy owners and operations employ a further 67 people, of which 90% are from local communities (S. Naylor, email, 2017, personal communication).

A recent addition to skills development initiatives is the Star in Training initiative. With assistance from both community trusts, andBeyond recruits and employs young unemployed community members for a six-month period as interns. This programme exposes community members to the hospitality industry and provides skills in housekeeping, food and beverage service, cooking and front of house, among other services. Since July 2014, a total of 74 young unemployed community members completed the programme, and 15 went on to be permanently employed by Phinda. Also, 23 received fixed-term contracts, and 11 worked on a temporary/casual basis over the years. With the skills and references obtained from this programme, many young people went on to find employment in other tourist operations in the area (S. Naylor, email, 2017, personal communication).

AndBeyond is also committed to empowering local communities as business partners in the value chain. The company pursues this through its Africa Foundation, which provides upskilling, training and business development support to locals in rural communities adjacent to the conservation areas comprising and Beyond businesses. Suppliers who consistently deliver with the quality required can then provide products to other lodges within the andBeyond family (Rylance & Spenceley, 2014). The Africa Foundation has invested in the development of small businesses, including paper recycling, sewing companies to make staff uniforms, brick-making businesses, staff transport taxi operators, and making charcoal from alien invasive species, and has also built the Mbhedula craft market in Mduku (Spenceley, 2008).

The Africa Foundation (and its predecessors) has supported 86 bursaries for tertiary studies for students neighbouring Phinda between 1998 and 2008, in courses such as teaching, communications, nature conservation, business, environmental health and motor mechanics. Also, to support education, the Africa Foundation has built over 90 classrooms, three libraries and a science laboratory, and has provided over 150,000 books and educational aids and facilitated the establishment of 19 preschools. Health initiatives have included construction of a clinic at Mduku, and the refurbishment of another, HIV/AIDS awareness workshops, improved water provision and a school permaculture project (S. Naylor, email, 2017, personal communication; Spenceley, 2008).

### Environmental impact

When the company purchased land at Phinda in 1991, it began restoring farmlands that had been degraded through years of cattle farming, and the cultivation of exotic tree species (Rylance and Spenceley, 2014). It stocked the land with 15,000 head of game, and the conservation efforts have been so successful that the reserve has sold live cheetah, buffalo and white rhino to re-stock other reserves and parks in the region. The reserve formed part of the World Wide Fund for Nature (WWF) Black Rhino Range Expansion project, with animals co-owned with the provincial conservation authority, KZN Wildlife (Spenceley, 2008). In 2005, it was estimated that Phinda's operational costs associated with equipment, monitoring and staff for the black rhino were USD 2,509 per month (Spenceley & Barnes, 2005). The rhino provide Phinda's guests with safari opportunities to assist vets on rhino monitoring activities, and also conservation lessons for children from neighbouring rural schools (Spenceley & Barnes, 2005).

For environmental management systems, the company has a sustainable tourism checklist, which is used in an internal eco-audit for lodges to monitor their environmental impact. This includes categories for water and energy use, and also waste management (Spenceley, 2008).

### Successes

There are numerous successes to be learned from Phinda, not least the institutional structure that was established following the uncontested and successful land claims of the Mnqobokazi and Makhasa communities. The approach has succeeded in getting 'communities to buy into the business'. This generates benefits in areas such as wildlife poaching, which is on the rise as the region's population and poverty rates have increased. Pointing to locals' vested interest in preserving wildlife and good relations with the company, Johnathan Braack, andBeyond's sustainability manager, reports that 'We have had three rhinos poached; our neighbours had fifty. Our communities have warned us [of poaching plans] every time in advance.' Partnering with local communities thus provides andBeyond long-term security in terms of its business and wildlife conservation interests (Rylance & Spenceley, 2014).

The company combines a mechanism to channel donations into local development projects, with operational expenditure on products and services locally. Furthermore, the investment in wildlife and land management underlies a profitable commercial tourism operation.

### Challenges

An additional portion of 1,617 hectares of land was incorporated into the reserve in 2017. There is also a possibility of adding two more parcels of community land in the near future. The challenge will be for the current operations and business to be able to afford the lease and associated operational costs for these and any future additions. There is also the challenge of ensuring neighbouring communities perceive the reserve and lodges positively and continue to receive direct and indirect benefits. These benefits need to be sustained, and sufficient to meet a rapidly growing human population (S. Naylor, email, 2017, personal communication).

### Lessons learned and recommendations

The evolution of Phinda from a privately owned and managed operation to a model that includes JV operations with communities, and also direct leases with communities, has been underpinned by a strong mutually beneficial long-term relationship between the company and its neighbours. Although the model has evolved over nearly three decades, the sustainability principles are certainly replicable to other destinations.

**Table 43.** Summary – Phinda Private Game Reserve.

| | |
|---|---|
| Name of company | andBeyond |
| Location | Mun-ya-wana conservancy, KwaZulu-Natal, South Africa |
| Year established | 1991 |
| Status of company (i.e. listed, privately owned, etc.) | andBeyond, private company, lodge operator/owner |
| List of camps/lodges | Forest Lodge (32 beds), Vlei Lodge (12 beds), Zuka Lodge (8 beds), Mountain Lodge (52 beds), Rock Lodge (12 beds), and Africa Homestead (8 beds) |
| Investment/partnership option | Rock and Mountain: private ownership by andBeyond<br>Forest, Vlei and Homestead: owned by Makhasa community, and leased to andBeyond<br>Zuka Lodge: privately owned by the Gettys |
| Total number of staff employed | 312 (permanent) |
| % local staff | 56% |
| Financial summary | USD 3.56 million in lease fees to the Qhubekani Mnqobokazi and Makhasa communities from 2006 to December 2016 |

### 4.4.2. Case Study 27: Serra Cafema Camp, Namibia

#### Background

Serra Cafema Camp is situated in the Marienfluss Conservancy in northern Namibia. The conservancy was first registered in January 2001. The camp is situated on the Kunene River and offers game drives, walks, quad biking, boat trips on the Kunene River and a cultural visit to a local Himba village.

In 2017, the fully inclusive rack rate per person sharing at Serra Cafema Camp ranged between ZAR 7,660 (approximately USD 537) and ZAR 12,570 (approximately USD 881), depending on the season (Wilderness Safaris, 2017d). The camp consists of eight wood, canvas and thatched villas (Wilderness Safaris, 2017e).

#### Institutional structure

In Namibia, wildlife is the property of the state, but under the 1996 legal amendment (Nature Conservation Amendment Act 1996) community conservancies received conditional use rights over wildlife. An important feature of the Namibian institutional framework for communal conservancies is that local rights over wildlife and tourism are entrenched in legislation; they are not mere administrative privileges that can arbitrarily be removed (Jones, 2010). Accordingly, the number of communal conservancies grew from 15 in 2002 to 83 in 2017 (NACSO, 2017a, 2017b).

Serra Cafema Camp was built and is operated, managed and marketed by WS. WS pays the Marienfluss Conservancy 8% of turnover, as a lease fee (M. Wassung, email, September 2017, personal communication). In 2017, WS was investing a sum of approximately USD 220,000 to rebuild and improve the camp (M. Wassung, email, September 2017, personal communication).

#### Economic impact

As noted, as part of the lease agreement, WS pays the Marienfluss Conservancy 8% of monthly turnover as a lease fee (M. Wassung, email, September 2017, personal communication).

**Table 44.** Lease fees paid.

| | Lease fees |
|---|---|
| FY2015 | USD 95,323 |
| FY2016 | USD 90,979 |
| FY2017 | USD 103,256 |
| **Total** | **USD 289,558** |

Source: Wilderness Holdings (2015, 2016, 2017)

Due to the very remote nature of the camp, there is no opportunity to procure local goods and services as the only communities in the area are semi-nomadic Himba.

### Social impact

There are 39 staff employed in the camp: 18 females and 21 males of which 70% come from the local community (M. Wassung, email, September 2017, personal communication and P. Ebersohn, email, January 2018, personal communication). The average age of staff is 35. The total monthly salary bill is approximately USD 23,981 and the average monthly wage is approximately USD 615 (P. Ebersohn, email, January 2018, personal communication). Staff undergo training through online and in-person training.

### Environmental impact

The overall Namibian CBNRM programme has seen an increase in game numbers in conservancies, including in the Marienfluss Conservancy, with the community supportive of conservation and tourism in the area.

The camp currently uses a solar hybrid system which combines solar and generator power to electrify the camp (W. Ozorio, email, August 2017, personal communication). This system has greatly reduced the generator's operating time, however, due to the remote nature of the camp, transporting diesel to the camp presents a substantial environmental risk and logistical challenge. The camp has therefore been approved to be converted to full solar operation via a 50 kilowatt installation which was due to be commissioned June 2018 (W. Ozorio, email, August 2017, personal communication). Unfortunately, the location of the camp along the banks of the Kunene River subjects it to flooding on an almost annual basis. The back of house areas are currently being reconstructed on higher ground to prevent flood and environmental damage. The highest environmental standards will be used in the rebuild, ensuring mitigation of any negative impacts which may arise from operating this camp (W. Ozorio, email, August 2017, personal communication).

The camp undergoes a biannual EMS assessment to ensure compliance with GEMS. In FY2017 the camp achieved 59% compliance with GEMS, which was well below the required 85% (W. Ozorio, email, August 2017, personal communication). This information has been used in the camp rebuild to learn from previous experiences and seasonality in the area (W. Ozorio, email, August 2017, personal communication). Following the rebuild, the aim is to achieve 85% compliance (W. Ozorio, email, August 2017, personal communication).

**Table 45.** Summary – Serra Cafema Camp.

| | |
|---|---|
| Name of company | Wilderness Safaris (WS) |
| Location | Kunene region, Namibia |
| Year established | 2003 |
| Status of company (i.e. listed, privately owned, etc.) | Lease fee agreement between WS and Marienfluss Conservancy |
| List of camps/lodges | Serra Cafema Camp (8 villas; 16 beds) |
| Investment/partnership option | Government land leased to conservancy<br>10-year concession<br>Lease fee agreement between the private sector and community |
| Total number of staff employed | 39 |
| % local staff | 70% |
| Financial summary | USD 312,000 paid in lease fees to the conservancy from 2015 to 2017<br>USD 23,981 paid monthly for staff salaries |

**Successes**

WS has a good relationship with the Marienfluss Conservancy, with meetings held regularly and communication channels always open. This has resulted in a harmonious partnership since 2003, with the lease renewed in 2013 for 10 years and subsequently renewed for 2023–2033, which allowed WS to invest in rebuilding the camp in 2018.

**Challenges**

Initially, capacity in the community was lacking but WS invested a large amount in staff training and capacity-building. The remote location of the camp makes logistics for guests, supplies and the rebuild complicated and costly.

**Lessons learned and recommendations**

A deep understanding and education of working with local communities and cultures has been essential (M. Wassung, email, September 2017, personal communication).

### 4.4.3. Case Study 28: Sabyinyo Silverback Lodge, Rwanda

Some sections of this case study are adapted from Black and Cobbinah (2017).

**Background**

Volcanoes National Park (VNP) is in north-western Rwanda and borders Virunga National Park in the Democratic Republic of Congo and Mgahinga Gorilla National Park in Uganda. The protected area has important habitat for the endangered mountain gorillas. It is home to five of the eight volcanoes of the Virunga Mountains, which are covered in rainforest and bamboo. Sabyinyo Silverback Lodge is located about 10 kilometres from Kinigi, a small village in the north-west of Rwanda. The region's lush ecosystem provides an ideal home for the endangered mountain gorilla, golden monkey and several other endemic species, but human encroachment has led to deforestation and decreasing mountain gorilla habitat. Rwanda is one of Africa's most densely populated countries. While the mountain gorillas have made an extraordinary recovery in terms of numbers, their habitat size has remained the same. As a result, the gorilla and buffalo leave the park boundaries, which results in human–wildlife conflict (HWC).

In 2017 the rack rate for Sabyinyo Lodge ranged between USD 495 and USD 925 per adult sharing depending on the season, with the highest rate being from June to October and in December, and the lowest rate being charged in April (Governors' Camp, 2017). The lodge has 16 beds and activities from the lodge include gorilla trips, village visits, golden monkey treks, birding and hiking.

#### Institutional structure

Engaging with and ensuring the long-term commitment of communities living adjacent to VNP was recognised by the African Wildlife Foundation (AWF), a conservation NGO, and its partner the International Gorilla Conservation Project as critical to the conservation and sustainability of the park and wildlife (K. Fitzgerald, email, July 2017, personal communication). AWF assisted the local Kinigi-Nyange community in establishing Sabyinyo Silverback Lodge as a way of providing additional income and employment opportunities. Because the lodge's business is based on gorilla tourism, it further incentivises the local community to value the mountain gorillas.

AWF raised USD 750,000 on behalf of the community to develop the lodge (D. Grammaticas, email, August 2017, personal communication). The lodge itself, the fixed asset, is owned by the community. AWF then facilitated a tendering process and facilitated a partnership with Governors' Camp to operate the lodge.

SACOLA, a community organisation, was established in 2004 and the lodge was opened in 2007 under an agreement signed with the lodge operators – i.e. between Governors' Camp, a private sector operator and SACOLA. The objectives of SACOLA are the conservation of the natural resources in VNP and improvement in the livelihood of the population surrounding the park. SACOLA has 65 elected community members representing the Kinigi and Nyange areas and an executive committee of nine volunteer members that administers and distributes the lodge revenue for the benefit of the environment and local community. There are approximately 56,000 members in SACOLA (L. Harerimana, Rwanda, August 2017, personal communication).

The private lodge operator pays SACOLA 7.5% of accommodation and meal revenues as a rental and clients pay a community development levy of USD 93 per bednight to SACOLA (D. Grammaticas, email, August 2017, personal communication).

#### Economic impact

From FY2015 to FY2017 Sabyinyo Silverback Lodge generated just over USD 985,000 via rentals and community development levies for SACOLA (D. Grammaticas, email, August 2017, personal communication). An approximate monthly amount of USD 20,000 is collected from guests and paid as a rental to SACOLA as part of the partnership lease agreement. Governors pays 7.5% of accommodation and meal revenue to SACOLA as a lease fee.

#### Social impact

Rentals and community development levies paid to SACOLA are used to drive socioeconomic development, conservation initiatives and community development projects. There has been a total investment since 2006 of approximately USD 2.5 million into these socioeconomic developments, conservation initiatives and community development projects (D. Grammaticas, email, August 2017, personal communication).

To date, SACOLA's projects have included, among others (Leonard Harerimana, Rwanda, August 2017, personal communication):

- refurbishing five schools providing education to 3,200 students;
- reconstructing a local primary school including constructing 71 classrooms housing 2,500 students;

- providing school fees for 46 children from the poorest families (already covered 120 students in total);
- constructing and equipping of computer labs for the local community (60 computers);
- organising and contribution to a rural electrification project covering 3,500 homes and 25,400 people;
- building 43 homes for survivors of the genocide;
- building two villages for poor people and ex-poachers (48 houses in Kinigi and Nyange) and bringing water to these two villages;
- providing medical insurance for 4,000 people;
- building seven houses for people chased away from Tanzania;
- instigating a water project in Nyonirima;
- protecting water dispersal systems and erosion control;
- setting up a tourist 'community walk', enhancing local crafts and businesses;
- building a community cultural centre;
- constructing a local nature walk;
- constructing water tanks and water collection points for the community;
- constructing/repairing the buffalo wall along the park's edge to protect farmers' crops from marauding buffalo;
- providing support to local beekeepers;
- establishing and supporting a local pig and sheep project;
- purchasing land for a poultry project for widows of the genocide;
- creating and constructing the poultry project for widows of the genocide;
- creating carpentry and other micro-enterprise workshops for the community;
- donating over 418 cows to the poorest community members;
- constructing a health centre in the Nyange sector; and
- creating vegetable gardens for a community farming project.

All of this work is accompanied by public meetings and hearings at which the importance of conservation of the habitat of the mountain gorilla and the mountain gorilla itself is communicated and stressed. As such SACOLA is critical in helping the government communicate its conservation message to local communities (D. Grammaticas, email, August 2017, personal communication).

There are a total of 50 staff employed at Sabyinyo Lodge, 90% of whom are from the local community: 18% female and 82% male. The total monthly salary bill in 2017 was USD 38,755 and the average monthly wage was approximately USD 775 (finance, email, February 2018, personal communication). From FY2015 to FY2017 a total of USD 1,058,000 has been spent on staff costs, which includes wages, uniforms, food and training.

Approximately 97% of all procurement is local, with roughly USD 67,243 per month spent on local goods and services (finance, email, February 2018, personal communication).

### Environmental impact

Since the lodge opened, the mountain gorilla population has increased from 380 individuals in the Virunga Massif five years ago to 480 as of the last census – a 3.7% annual growth. Although not directly related to the lodge, the presence of tourism in the area and the related benefits of tourism have provided incentives to local communities to conserve the mountain gorilla.

In addition to the aforementioned SACOLA activities, Sabyinyo Silverback Lodge is also contributing to a wildlife conservation project in Gishwati Forest, a patch of natural forest situated about 50 kilometres from VNP. SACOLA provides technical advice to the Gishwati Forest Conservation Project in the development of ecotourism activities in the forest. It has helped with the creation of two hiking trails through the forest and contributed to the promotion of Gishwati Forest as an ecotourism destination. It has also provided one year of salaries and field costs for one of the tracking teams supporting the habituation and field research of a group of chimpanzees in the forest. The lodge has also provided field cameras to monitor the wildlife in Buhanga Forest (a small protected natural forest situated in Musanze area): this has confirmed the presence of serval cat in the forest (see http://www.governorscamp.com/responsible-tourism/responsible-tourism-rwanda).

EMS in the camp include all the systems that would be expected in a high-end conservation-focused lodge (D. Grammaticas, email, August 2017, personal communication).

### Successes

One success is the development of visible and needed community projects through the private sector's partnership with SACOLA. Good governance within SACOLA has ensured that the community does benefit and there is investment in community development (L. Harerimana, email, August 2017, personal communication).

### Challenges

One challenge has been in communicating the community–private sector partnership to guests staying at the lodge, including the importance of this relationship to developing and promoting positive community attitudes towards tourism and conservation (D. Grammaticas, email, August 2017, personal communication).

### Lessons learned and recommendations

SACOLA is a strong organisation with its major focus being to ensure that community members understand the links between benefits received, gorilla and habitat conservation and Sabyinyo Silverback Lodge (D. Grammaticas, email, August 2017, personal communication). SACOLA has regular community meetings with the SACOLA board, presenting all the financials to the community, including income received, how it has been used/allocated, balances remaining and the allocation of funds to priority project proposals presented by the community (L. Harerimana, email, August 2017, personal communication).

The purpose of establishing a lodge and community trusts related to it should be clearly articulated to the community as should the relationship of the lodge and trust to staff, community and tourists. The relationship between the lodge and the community trust must be clear, seen and understood, in particular in relation to benefit-sharing – for example, how a percentage of the lodge revenue is channelled through the trust and used to implement community development projects that benefit the community (Black & Cobbinah, 2017).

Community awareness programmes, using community signboards or a community education officer employed by the community trust or lodge could assist with raising awareness in the community (Black & Cobbinah, 2017). Community trusts need to have a logical, systematic and informed decision-making framework (which includes community input and which is transparent and accountable) to prioritise and allocate revenue to benefit the community, as well as conservation (Black & Cobbinah, 2017). Ensuring this can be assisted through AWF or another NGO providing long-term financial and human resources to establish, support and train community trust board members and the community at large to ensure a strong, accountable, transparent and sustainable trust. This will involve extensive capacity-building, which should be incorporated into NGO and government support programmes (Black & Cobbinah, 2017).

**Table 46.** Summary – Sabyinyo Silverback Lodge.

| | |
|---|---|
| Name of company | Governors' Camp Rwanda Ltd |
| Location | Near Volcanoes National Park (VNP), Rwanda |
| Year established/opened | 2007 |
| Status of company (i.e. listed, privately owned, etc.) | Privately owned company |
| List of camps/lodges | Sabyinyo Silverback Lodge (16 beds) |
| Investment/partnership option | Community trust-owned land and lodge infrastructure<br>35-year concession<br>Partnership between community trust (SACOLA) and private operator, Governor's Camp Rwanda Ltd<br>Private sector lodge management |
| Total number of staff employed | 50 |
| % local staff | 90% |
| Financial summary | From FY2015 to FY2017 a total of USD 985,000 was generated for SACOLA via rentals and community development levies paid by lodge guests<br>From FY2015 to FY2017 a total of USD 1,058,000 was spent on staff costs and a total of USD 985,000 was invested by SACOLA in community development projects |

### 4.4.4. Case Study 29: Vumbura Plains and Little Vumbura, Botswana

Sections of this case study are adapted from Snyman (2014).

#### Background

The tourism camps of Little Vumbura (6 tented rooms; 12 beds) and Vumbura Plains (14 rooms, 2 are family suites; 28 beds), as well as the WS Botswana training facility at Kaparota, are situated in NG 22. Kaparota was a facility specifically for training in tourism- and conservation-related jobs and focused on the company's localisation management training programme. In 2017, however, Kaparota Camp was dismantled, with the Okavango Community Trust (OCT) board given first option on all materials (L. Moiteela, email, September 2017, personal communication). Both camps offer game drives, walks, *mokoro* (traditional canoe) and other boat trips.

In 2017, the fully inclusive rack rates for the camps ranged between USD 965 and USD 2,445 per person sharing, depending on the season (Wilderness Safaris, 2017c, 2017d).

#### Institutional structure

Initially, the implementation of Community-Based Natural Resource Management (CBNRM) in Botswana was driven by the USAID-funded Natural Resources Management Programme (NRMP). Botswana officially embraced CBNRM in 1989 with the first community trust formed in 1993. The CBNRM programme was formalised into policy in July 2007 (Piet, 2007, cited in Lepper & Goebel, 2010). In order for communities to obtain a 'head lease' on land, they have to establish a legally registered community-based organisation (CBO), whose constitution shows proof of accountability and fair representation (Rozemeijer, 2009). A head lease does not give communities ownership of the land, but allows them the right to use the natural resources on the land (Rozemeijer, 2009). In general, the most common legal entity formed under the Botswanan CBNRM programme is the community trust, where trust members include all adult residents who have lived in the local area for at least five years (Simasiku, Simwanza, Tembo, Bandyopadhyay & Pavy, 2008).

Originally, Botswana's CBNRM programme differed from the programmes in Zimbabwe (CAMPFIRE) and Zambia (ADMADE) as most of the revenue was returned to the community (Boggs, 2004). The CBNRM programme was, however, revised in 2008. Under the revisions only 35% of revenue from the sale of natural resource concessions and quotas could be retained by the CBOs for their trust operations (as opposed to 100% in the past), while 65% of the funds would go to the National Environment Fund (NEF) for financing general community projects throughout the country (DeMotts & Hoon, 2012). The idea behind this change was to ensure that those communities who did not have access to valuable natural resources could still benefit from the natural resources of the country.

In 1994, the government of Botswana leased two areas of Ngamiland, NG 22 and NG 23 (Kwedi Concession), to five villages (Seronga, Gunotsoga, Eretsha, Beetsha and Gudigwa) situated in NG 11 and NG 12. This relationship was unique in Botswana as the five villages do not lie inside the concession area, but to the north of it. The OCT was formed by the five villages to administer and oversee the management of the concession agreement and the distribution of any funds acquired. It was set up in 1996 and represents the five villages in any negotiations, discussions or agreements with the private sector partners, currently (in 2017) Okavango Wilderness Safaris (OWS) and Great Plains Conservation. There is an OCT office in each of the five villages, and the OCT board includes representatives from each village. New head leases have not been awarded by government as there is currently (2018) a review of the system.

The original concession holder and operator was a safari hunting operator, Micheletti Bates Safaris (MBS), which obtained the lease from the Tawana Land Board in 1996. In 1999, MBS subleased one concession to OWS, but continued to hunt in the other concession. In 2004, OWS subleased the whole area from MBS and was then the exclusive operator, paying lease fees directly to the OCT, until Duba Plains Camp situated in NG 23 was sold to Great Plains Conservation (another private sector operator) in 2010. This case study examines only the relationship between OWS and the OCT. The camps are owned and operated by OWS, which leases the land from the OCT. A new lease was granted in 2018, with the lease period still to be confirmed, but likely to extend to 2021.

### Economic impact

WS pays a set annual lease fee to the OCT: this fee escalates by 5% each year. Payments are also made to the government in terms of taxes, royalties and enterprise licenses. Table 47 shows lease fees paid from the FY2015 (1 March) to the end of FY2017 (28 February).

### Social impact

Vumbura Plains employs 88 people: 46 females, 42 males, and Little Vumbura employs 29 staff: 21 females and 8 males – 70% of the staff come from the community (L. Moiteela, email, September 2017, personal communication). Staff undergo training through an online training system called Lobster Inc. as well as through trainers visiting the camp. The total salary bill per month in 2017 was approximately USD 87,100 and the average monthly wage was approximately USD 373 (L. Moiteela, email, January 2018, personal communication).

Staff are allowed to sell traditional baskets and jewellery in the main area which allows them to earn extra income. WS also gives donations to the community for their annual soccer tournament and ploughing their fields, and OWS built two houses in Seronga village that are housing the trust manager free of charge. Currently, OWS is providing repairs and maintenance to the trust morgue in Seronga, which was donated by OWS in 1999, and has given a business contract to a community business to the value of BWP 65,100 (USD 6,055) per annum, to transport OWS staff members (L. Moiteela, email, September 2017, personal communication). OWS has also donated a generator as a backup as Seronga has frequent intermittent power supply issues. CITW (see Case Study 16 in this volume for more information) runs eco-clubs in five schools and also supports adult empowerment clubs in two of the villages. In 2017, BWP 16,482 (USD 1,533) was donated to the adult empowerment clubs for fabric, dye and cotton (L. Moiteela, email, September 2017, personal communication) and approximately BWP 532,258

**Table 47.** Lease fees paid.

| | Lease fees |
|---|---|
| FY2015 | USD 244,027 |
| FY2016 | USD 221,305 |
| FY2017 | USD 302,070 |
| **Total** | **USD 767 402** |

Source: Wilderness Holdings (2015, 2016, 2017)

(USD 56,204) was given in total in 2017 to fund the CITW programme in Botswana. Donations of shoes, stationery and other materials have also been made to the community. Due to the remote nature of the tourism camps, it is difficult to procure goods and services from the local community. Food and other supplies are, therefore, largely bought in from Maun and procured for OWS (which operates more than 20 camps in Botswana), to a large degree from South Africa, though as more local, reliable, high-quality suppliers are establishing themselves in Maun, OWS is and will be buying more locally.

**Table 48.** Staff costs from Vumbura Plains and Little Vumbura.

| | Staff costs* |
|---|---|
| FY2015 | USD 1,590,521 |
| FY2016 | USD 1,375,240 |
| FY2017 | USD 1,387,628 |
| **Total** | **USD 4,353,389** |

*Staff costs include wages, uniforms, food, training, etc.
Source: Wilderness Holdings (2015, 2016, 2017)

### Environmental impact

Ongoing biodiversity conservation research has included supporting a research project on sable in the area. In FY2015, Vumbura Plains was the second largest consumer of generator diesel in the Wilderness Group, accounting for 13.7% of the total diesel used for the generation of power in all camps (W. Ozorio, email, August 2017, personal communication). The camp generators consumed a total of 187,384 litres of diesel over the course of a year (W. Ozorio, email, August 2017, personal communication). In July 2015, Vumbura Plains Camp was converted to 100% solar power, with the system being switched over from generator to solar power in August. The installation cost a total of BWP 9 million (approximately USD 991,190), producing a combined total of 105 kilowatts (W. Ozorio, email, August 2017, personal communication).

The use of reverse osmosis water filtration systems has reduced the bottled water consumption from 10,385 litres in FY2012 to 2,604 litres in FY2017 (W. Ozorio, email, August 2017, personal communication). The camps undergo a biannual EMS assessment to ensure compliance with WS GEMS. In FY2017 Vumbura Plains Camp achieved 92% compliance and Little Vumbura achieved 91% compliance with GEMS (W. Ozorio, email, August 2017, personal communication).

### Successes

The community received extensive lease fees over the duration of the partnership, as well as skills training and development for community members who are employed in the camps. CITW has invested a large amount in eco-clubs, adult empowerment clubs and other forms of environmental education and support in the villages. It has also sponsored two members of the OCT board to attend a national Hospitality and Tourism Association of Botswana (HATAB) meeting in order to learn about tourism and meet relevant stakeholders.

### Challenges

One of the disadvantages of the establishment of community trusts is the lack of education, training and skills of the trust members and the resultant poor institutional and financial management (Simasiku *et al.*, 2008; Snyman & Spenceley, 2012). Over the years, there have been some issues related to the transparency and accountability of the OCT board in its use of the substantial lease fee paid to it, resulting in discontent in the community and a perceived lack of benefits from tourism (Snyman, 2014). With Gudigwa Village generally feeling not equitably included, there has been some intra-community conflict which has at times also affected the partnership with the private sector. Renewal of the lease was originally due in 2011 but was delayed for various reasons; insecurity of lease tenure can also impact negatively on the partnership and private sector operations.

### Lessons learned and recommendations

Clear, transparent benefit-sharing mechanisms need to be in place with the majority of the community seeing benefits being received and establishing the link between these benefits and the associated tourism (Snyman, 2014).

Regular, ongoing meetings with the community should be in place, rather than meeting only when issues arise. The engagement of community leadership in stakeholder meetings can assist in empowering them to manage their tourism partnerships more effectively.

**Table 49.** Summary – Vumbura Plains and Little Vumbura.

| | |
|---|---|
| Name of company | Okavango Wilderness Safaris (OWS) |
| Location | Okavango Delta, Botswana |
| Year established | 2004 |
| Status of company (i.e. listed, privately owned, etc.) | Privately owned by OWS (Pty) Ltd |
| List of camps/lodges | Vumbura Plains (28 beds) and Little Vumbura (12 beds) |
| Investment/partnership option | Government owned land, giving community trust use rights<br>15-year concession<br>Privately owned infrastructure |
| Total number of staff employed | 117 |
| % local staff | 70% |
| Financial summary | USD 767,402 paid in lease fees to the OCT 2015–2017<br>USD 4.3 million paid in staff costs 2015–2017 |

### 4.4.5. Case Study 30: Pafuri Camp, South Africa

#### Background

Pafuri Camp is located in the north of KNP in South Africa, and within the Makuleke communities' Contractual National Park (see Box 5). There are three accommodation options here: Pafuri Camp (52 beds), Pafuri Walking Trails (16 beds in two camps) and the self-catering Baobab Hill Bush House (8 beds) and a private members' camp (10 beds). (B. Baloyi, email, 2017, personal communication; Return Africa; 2017a, 2017b, 2017c). The camp is privately managed by Return Africa on a concession basis with the community.

In 2017, the rack rate was USD 280 for Pafuri Camp, USD 161 for the Pafuri Walking Trail for per person, per night, sharing, and the Baobab Hill Bush House was USD 870 per night (Return Africa, 2017b, 2017c).

### Institutional structure

In 1969, the Makuleke people were forcibly removed by the state from a 26,500-hectare area that they inhabited in the north of KNP. As part of South Africa's land restitution process, formal ownership was returned to the community, who also received a development grant that was used for improvements to schools and electrification. (Elliffe, 1999; S. Collins, email, 2017, 2018 personal communication). The settlement agreement creates a community contract park jointly managed by the Makuleke Communal Property Association and SANParks (S. Collins, email, 2017, personal communication). The ownership and title of the land to the Makuleke was given back to the community on agreement that the land may be used only for conservation (Steenkamp, 1998; Steenkamp & Grossman, 2001). The Makuleke established a communal property association (CPA) representing around 15,000 community members which is the title-holder to the land in the Makuleke region of KNP. The CPA aims to promote commercial use of the land through sustainable hunting and tourism development (Collins, 2008). Hunting was permitted for the first three years following the land restitution, in order for the community to generate income while it sought commercial tourism partners (B. Baloyi, email, 2017, personal communication).

In 2003, the CPA established a USD 5.5 million concession agreement with WS to build three luxury low-impact tented lodges (Turner, 2004) on a build–operate–transfer basis (Collins, 2003; Maluleke, 2003). WS invested between USD 2.5 and USD 3.7 million in the development of Pafuri Camp adjacent to the Luvuvhu River. The 45-year agreement stated that the Makuleke would receive 8% of turnover, training, employment and some scholarships (Turner, 2004).

In 2015, after a flood in January 2013 destroyed the camp, WS sold the remaining moveable assets to Return Africa, a privately owned company which in turn renegotiated a concession with the CPA. The CPA was able to access a 0% interest loan which it used to acquire a 25% shareholding in Return Africa's Pafuri operations, and thereafter and option to take up 25% shareholding at no cost. They also receive 10% of turnover with a guaranteed minimum amount, regardless of performance (S. Collins and P.J. Massyn, email, 2017, 2018 personal communication).

All conservation activities in the contractual park are still managed by SANParks, a parastatal, which reports to a Joint Management Board (JMB).

### Economic impact

Return Africa's agreement with the Makuleke is due to pay approximately USD 170,000 in lease fees in the 2018 financial year (P.J. Massyn, email, 2017, 2018 personal communication), following payments of around USD 64,456 (ZAR 929,240) in 2015/2016 and USD 58,955 (ZAR 824,687) in 2016/17 (up to July 2017) (B. Baloyi, email, 2017, personal communication).

### Social impact

Return Africa employs approximately 52 permanent staff members, and 94% of them, including the senior management staff, are from the Makuleke community. Staff from the Makuleke community receive an approximate total of USD 298,000 in wages and related benefits annually. Return Africa also hires people locally for a variety of services including staff transport, guest transfers and infrastructure maintenance (P.J. Massyn, email, 2017, personal communication).

The Makuleke have a development trust, which administers the money made from tourism and spends it on community projects (e.g. electrification of two villages, improving schools, building a house and supporting their traditional authority) and operational costs (Collins, 2008, S. Collins, email, 2018, personal communication).

Return Africa states that the procurement of local goods and services (within a 50 kilometre radius) amounted to an annual sum during the first year of operation of USD 170,700. During the same period, Return Africa reports that it made charitable donations worth USD 27,500 towards Makuleke projects (P.J. Massyn, email, 2017, personal communication).

### Environmental impact

SANParks continues to manage the land, and reports to the JMB that was created between CPA and SANParks (Collins, 2008, S. Collins, email, 2018, personal communication.) It is guided by the Makuleke Conservation and Development Framework which replaced the 2000 management plan (S. Collins, email, 2017, personal communication).

The wetlands on the Makuleke land are a Ramsar wetland of international importance. The tourism activities have added substantial money to the SANParks conservation levy which funds conservation work in the region (S. Collins, email, 2017, personal communication).

### Successes

The Makuleke's tourism partnerships with the private sector have been groundbreaking, not least because they were based on restituted land within a national park. The evolution of the JV model and changes in partners from WS to Return Africa illustrates the empowerment of a poor rural community, which can implement decisions to work with their preferred investment partner.

This empowerment of the Makuleke has been supported by the intervention of NGOs and donor projects, including GIZ's Training and Support for Resource Management Programme (TRANSFORM) (Collins, 2008), the ASF, Webber Wentzel, the AWF and the Southern African Wildlife College (S. Collins, email, 2017, personal communication) that have supported them with technical advice. The CPA is accountable to community members and has over 15 years' experience in trying to maximise the benefits from tourism to the community, and to address conflicts and difficult decisions (Maluleke, 2014).

### Challenges

Challenges that have been faced in the past include that benefit sharing can create conflict, and that the Makuleke chief had accumulated a substantial share of the benefits (Collins, 2008). All of the benefits channelled to the chief were as a result of decisions taken by CPA constituencies to support their chief, as his salary and benefits were halted for many years as a result of a long-standing dispute with a neighbouring chief (B. Baloyi, email, 2017, personal communication). In addition, the running costs of the

**Table 50.** Summary – Pafuri Camp.

| | |
|---|---|
| Name of company | Return Africa |
| Location | Makuleke Contractual National Park, KNP, South Africa, |
| Year established | Opened in 2005 under Wilderness Safaris (WS) agreement.<br>Agreement with Return Africa since October 2015 |
| Status of company (i.e. listed, privately owned, etc.) | Return Africa: private sector operating company<br>Landowner: Makuleke Community (contractual national park) |
| List of camps/lodges | Pafuri Camp (52 beds), Pafuri Walking Trail (16 beds), Baobab Hill House (8 beds) |
| Investment/partnership option | Infrastructure owned by Makuleke CPA.<br>Return Africa has a 45-year concession agreement with the Makuleke community to operate, maintain and transfer back the facilities and to conduct tourism activities in the Makuleke Contract Park. Return Africa also has an option to develop a further 20 beds at other locations<br>SANParks: responsible for conservation |
| Total number of staff employed | 52 full-time staff at Pafuri<br>15–20 casual and seasonal staff at Pafuri |
| % local staff | 94% |
| Financial summary | Estimated USD 170,000 in lease fees to the Makuleke community in 2018 financial year |

CPA, a full-time office and half the cost of a full time park manager have used most of the funding received from the tourism operations (S. Collins, email, 2017, personal communication). Further challenges include the high number of people in the Makuleke community in relation to the value of income received from tourism activities, which is lower than they anticipated (B. Baloyi, email, 2017, personal communication).

**Lessons learned and recommendations**

The Makuleke experience demonstrates that within JVs, private partners need to integrate rural development and community empowerment into their business approach. If not, the benefit-sharing and joint management are perceived as burdens that slow the business. It is important to acknowledge that private investors are not usually rural development experts (Collins, 2008).

The fundamental requirements for successful partnerships are honest and philanthropic private sector operators, a flexible conservation authority committed to getting the community sustainable benefits and an organised and accountable community-based organisation. NGOs can also play a facilitating and mediating role between these partners. Furthermore, realistic expectations among the community must be set at the start and throughout the process and the non-tangible benefits as well as the cash benefits must be made clear. Likewise there should be clarity about the time it takes to get a large-scale ecotourism and conservation project to maturity and sustainability (Collins, 2016).

### 4.4.6. Case Study 31: Satao Elerai Lodge, Kenya

**Background**

Satao Elerai is set in a private communally owned conservancy outside of Amboseli National Park at the foot of Mount Kilimanjaro (Lamers, van der Duim, Nthiga, van Wijk & Waterreus, 2015). The Elerai Conservancy is situated within the Elerai community and is part of an important wildlife corridor between Amboseli and protected areas in Tanzania, such as Mount Kilimanjaro. Given the ecological importance of the area, AWF started negotiations with the landowners – eight families – to set aside their collective 6,000 hectares for conservation. The area was further divided into two zones, approximately 3,000 hectares each: a conservation and tourism zone; a settlement, cultivation and agricultural zone and a grazing zone.

Satao Elerai has five lodge-style suite rooms and nine to twelve deluxe mountain-facing tents (Satao Elerai, 2017a) and offers game drives, game walks, community visits and night drives. In 2017, the fully inclusive rack rate per person sharing for Satao Elerai ranged between USD 320 and USD 410, depending on the season (Satao Elerai, 2017b). Additional charges include the following (Satao Elerai, 2017b):

- ***park fees:*** adult USD 60, child (under 18) USD 45 per person per day;
- ***Elerai conservation fee:*** adult/child: USD 18 per person per night;
- ***entrance fees for Cultural Boma visit:*** USD 20 per person.

#### Institutional structure

Torben Rune, a shareholder and director of Southern Cross Safaris, a private Kenyan tour operator, was put in touch with the Elerai community by AWF to facilitate and complete the construction of the camp and run the luxury ecocamp. The early construction of the camp was done by AWF with money from donor funds, which included USAID, the Royal Netherlands Embassy, the Ford Foundation and an individual donor. Final completion of the lodge was achieved with investment by Mr Rune and Satao Elerai shareholders. The lodge opened in July 2007. The capital brought by AWF was on behalf of the community and resulted in the community owning the lodge, the fixed asset. AWF then facilitated a contract between the landowners and Southern Cross Safaris to run the lodge.

The Satao Elerai Community Wildlife Trust was established as the governance structure to govern funds earned from conservation fees (T. Rune, September 2017, personal communication). The trust consists of three members representing the eight Elerai families, Satao Elerai Ltd's group of shareholders (three members) and AWF (one member). Below the trust, the families are represented on the family committee with two people from each family, totalling 16 members. From the 16, 8 (1 per family) also sit on the management committee and the other 8 sit in one or more of five sub-committees (water, education, settlement, cultural village and conservation). Each family also has 2 to 4 administrators, a total of 17, who fulfil a supervisory role, but could be members of one or more of the committees. Through this institutional arrangement all families are represented in the committees. Membership of the trust is clear as it is the eight families who own the land.

#### Economic impact

There are four streams of income related to Satao Elerai.

**1.** The private operator pays a fixed land lease fee to each family, regardless of the occupancy of the lodge, of USD 1,068 per family per year (initially the fee was USD 712.50 per family per year with a fixed annual increment), amounting to a total of USD 8,544 per annum.
**2.** The trust fund receives a conservation fee of USD 20 per visitor per night.
**3.** A bednight fee of USD 8 per visitor per night is charged.
**4.** USD 15 is raised per visitor entering the cultural village, which is an optional activity offered to guests (guests pay USD 20, the community receives USD 15 of this).

The annual lease fee and all the bednight fees are transferred to the bank accounts of individual families, rather than a collective account. The families are free to spend their income however they choose. Occupancy in 2016 was approximately 45%, which is strong for Kenya. The community earned USD 44,375 in 2008 and by 2016 this had grown to USD 97,000 (T. Rune, email, September 2017, personal communication).

#### Social impact

The lodge employs 42 staff and the trust employs 15 staff; all are currently male employees due to Masai cultural issues (T. Rune, email, September 2017, personal communication). Of the staff, 85% come from the local community (T. Rune, email, September 2017, personal communication). The average monthly wage is approximately USD 247, with a total monthly salary cost (lodge and game scouts) of approximately USD 12,374 (T. Rune, email, March 2018, personal communication). Including wages to community members, the community income figure is estimated at a gross annual average of USD 140,000 (2016–2017) (T. Rune, email, September 2017, personal communication). The average annual amount for community donations is approximately USD 90,000, inclusive of conservation fees (T. Rune, email, March 2018, personal communication). Local procurement is highly variable and depends on the month and if there is building at the lodge.

There have been investments in school bursaries, medical payments, water provision and security. The cultural village earns approximately USD 5,000 per annum directly from *boma* entrance fees. Philanthropic investments by the private tour operator have also been undertaken, including the building and financing of a primary school for the Elerai community.

### Environmental impact

The 6,000-hectare conservancy has shown signs of recovery, with wildlife returning, wildlife numbers increasing and the rangelands improving. The main conservation outcome has been the contribution to the establishment of a wildlife corridor between Amboseli National Park and protected areas in Tanzania. An intangible benefit found by Lamers *et al.* (2015) was an increased awareness of the value of wildlife conservation, with people being more tolerant of wildlife.

### Successes

Due to the small size of the community, financial benefits have had a positive impact. The private sector partner has remained the same since inception, which allows for consistency and the development of a mutually respectful partnership. The majority of employees are from the local community. These staff members have been trained and, in many cases, advanced their careers both in the lodge and externally.

One of the key reasons for success is the commitment by the operator to conservation and community development, combined with initial support from an NGO and a meaningful partnership with the community whereby they own the lodge. This makes the tripartite relationship between AWF, the community and Satao Elerai effective.

### Challenges

A key challenge relates to equity in decision-making processes in the partnership, as well as differences in the perception of equity. At one stage during the project, three Elerai community family members were accused by the family of using their power for personal and in-family gains: the trust had an election and three new representatives were elected to represent the community on the trust board.

From the outset, all revenues and expenses have been recorded and provided to the community. However, no official audit of the trust's transactions was done. Transparency was provided with all documents being available to the community office. Community members could enter the community office at any time to see how benefits were being allocated as lists were on the wall. After six years of operation, the community and wildlife trust ordered (and paid) for an audit on all transactions, historic and present, and now official annual audits of trust operations are undertaken. There are also public annual general meetings to present financial performance.

Unauthorised grazing of cattle in the conservation area is generally under control. However, at times of extreme drought, as was experienced in 2017, isolated incidences of grazing within the conservation area have been experienced (T. Rune, email, September 2017, personal communication).

The bursary committee members and their distribution of school bursaries were seen as favouring students of particular families. For this reason, bursary payments were stopped and all families were asked to fund their own children's educations from revenues received.

In the beginning of the project, there was a boundary dispute between the eight beneficiary families and the adjacent landowner. AWF funded Ndiritu and Associates to come to site and establish the boundaries between the Pardiyo parcel of land (Elerai community) and the claimant's parcel of land. It was established that the lodge was indeed partly located on the claimant's land and so he was incorporated into the lease as a ninth lessor.

The area set aside is relatively small. The communal land in the Amboseli landscape has been subdivided. Elerai is unique. Therefore, expanding a conservancy means combining 2-, 10- or 60-acre plots, which presents a challenge. AWF set up six other conservancies in the landscape, ranging from 3,000 acres to 6,000 acres, and each conservancy wants 'their own lodge.' This is problematic as the Amboseli landscape already has too many lodges to be supported by this fragile landscape and tourism economy.

### Lessons learned and recommendations

The importance of taking the local context into account when establishing partnership arrangements is important. Lamers *et al.* (2015) found in their study of three tourism conservation enterprises (TCEs) in Kenya, including Satao Elerai, that a lack of clarity related to certain questions can seriously affect the implementation of TCEs.

Transparency in operating and maintaining the lodge and making decisions regarding benefit-sharing is important to the partnership. The Satao Elerai model has been clearly laid out and defined and so benefits are clear to both the community and the investor. This clarity has resulted in the success of the Satao Elerai model for both the community and the investor.

Partners and their representatives need to be held accountable for their decisions and actions through transparent agreements that are monitored and honoured by all parties to the agreement.

Local context changes with time and partnerships should evolve accordingly with these changing circumstances and should be adapted if required. Due diligence is, therefore, required not only in designing partnership arrangements, but also in adapting, revising and evolving them.

Given Southern Cross Safaris is an established operator, when the lodge was opened occupancy levels were relatively high. AWF opened another lodge in northern Kenya around the same time with an operator that did not already have a customer base, and it lagged far behind in occupancy.

The quid pro quo between the community obligations and the lodge is clear. If tourism is going to leverage conservation there need to be clear covenants that outline obligations and benefits tied to conservation outcomes.

AWF contracts require 85% employment by the local community. This is critical to include in the contract to ensure local employment.

**Table 51.** Summary – Satao Elerai.

| | |
|---|---|
| Name of company | Satao Elerai Ltd |
| Location | Amboseli Ecosystem, Kenya |
| Year established/opened | 2007 |
| Status of company (i.e. listed, privately owned, etc.) | Private Kenyan tour operator |
| List of camps/lodges | Satao Elerai Lodge (34 beds) |
| Investment/partnership option | Community owned land<br>Private management of the lodge<br>15-year concession<br>Community owned infrastructure, partly funded by donors, private sector and community |
| Total number of staff employed | 57 |
| % local staff | 57 direct jobs (lodge, scouts); 48 indirect jobs (women in cultural village). In total there are approximately 638 beneficiaries. 85% of staff come from the local community |
| Financial summary | USD 97,000 per year (2016–2017 figures on lease, conservation and bednight fee)<br>Including wages to community members, the community income figure is estimated at a gross annual average of USD 230,000 (2016–2017) |

## 4.5. Tripartite Venture

### 4.5.1. Case Study 32: Rocktail Camp, South Africa

#### Background

The first official protected areas in South Africa were the forest reserves of Knysna and Tsitsikamma, proclaimed in terms of the Cape Forest Act of 1888. ISimangaliso Wetland Park, where Rocktail Camp is located, is situated in KwaZulu-Natal (KZN). The park is 332,000 hectares in size and was listed as South Africa's first World Heritage Site in December 1999 in recognition of its superlative natural beauty and unique global values (iSimangaliso, 2017). No fences exist between iSimangaliso Wetland Park and the KwaMpkuane community, who live on the border of the park and from where the majority of the Rocktail Camp staff come. The community are allowed to graze their cattle and collect certain traditional plants in the park.

In 2017 the fully inclusive rack rate per person sharing at Rocktail Camp ranged between ZAR 2,900 (USD 203) and ZAR 3,555 (USD 250) (Wilderness Safaris, 2017f). The camp has 17 rooms, with 34 beds, and offers game drives, community visits, cultural experiences, diving, snorkelling, birding and walks.

#### Institutional structure

A formal JV partnership exists between WS and the KwaMpukane community. The core partnership venture in the lodge is structured through a shareholding agreement where WS owns 72.5% of the shares, the KwaMpukane Community Trust 17.5% and a BEE partner 10%. Of lodge revenue, 8.5%, as well as annual turtle viewing fees, are paid to iSimangaliso Wetland Authority (government) which owns the land and has a lease agreement with WS.

Another JV partnership exists in the communal area outside the park at Gugulesizwe. The Gugulesizwe Community Centre offers accommodation, community tours and traditional meals. WS and the KwaMpukane Community Trust are both represented by two members on the Gugulesizwe board.

This JV is structured as a partnership between the community and a private sector business where the administrative function is undertaken by WS. Dividends from both the lodge and Gugulesizwe partnerships are, however, administered solely by the KwaMpukane Community Trust in the interests of the larger KwaMpukane community, who elected them into position and nominate community projects to be supported.

### Economic impact

Lease fees are paid by the JV to iSimangaliso Wetland Authority totalling USD 236,136 from FY2015 to FY2017. This fee is based on 8.5% of revenue and increased each year from 2015 to 2017. A total of USD 30,946 was also paid to the authority for turtle viewing permits, totalling USD 267,082 paid to the authority over three years. When the camp was built at Manzengwenya inside the park, the JV received grant funding from Gijima KZN (P. Boddam-Whetham, email, September 2017, personal communication). These funds were used to complete the extension of the camp. While this money was a grant, it was elected to treat the amount as a 'soft' liability (P. Boddam-Whetham, email, September 2017, personal communication). As a result, WS has been paying off this amount to both the BEE and community partners (P. Boddam-Whetham, email, September 2017, personal communication).

### Social impact

The camp employs 34 staff: 21 females and 13 males (P. Boddam-Whetham, email, September 2017, personal communication). Of the staff, 85% come from the KwaMpukane community (P. Boddam-Whetham, email, September 2017, personal communication). Whenever additional staff are required (over peak seasons) the camp employs temporary staff from the KwaMpukane community to assist (P. Boddam-Whetham, email, September 2017, personal communication). Staff receive ongoing training and the camp runs CITW eco-clubs (see more on CITW in Case Study 16 in this volume), annual camps and other activities in the community. The camp has also supported the refurbishment of libraries at two of the community schools and has supported a medical programme which included eye and ear tests and the provision of glasses and hearing aids to community members. This amounted to approximately USD 4,082 for community development projects in 2017 and approximately USD 8,000 for CITW. The lodge buys crafts from local crafters for display in the craft centre and as decor and furnishing for the lodge. It also buys some vegetables and pineapples from the community (in 2017 this amounted to approximately USD 1,200 for the year), though this is at the beginning stages and it has not yet become sustainable for the community to supply the whole camp (N. Gouws, email, January 2018, personal communication).

### Environmental impact

The camp uses grid power and has a backup generator to ensure a constant supply of electricity. The camp has adopted a reusable water bottle policy which ensures that the average bottled water consumption per guest remains very low, achieving an average of 0.35 litres per bednight consumed during FY2017 (W. Ozorio, email, August 2017, personal communication). The camp undergoes a biannual EMS assessment to ensure compliance with WS Group GEMS. In FY2017 the camp achieved 92% compliance with GEMS (W. Ozorio, email, August 2017, personal communication).

### Successes

This is an example of a complex tourism agreement, involving numerous different stakeholders. The inclusion of a BEE partner as well as a community as shareholders is unique.

**Table 52.** Lease fee payments to the JV and park authority.

| | Lease fees paid to the JV partner* | Lease fees paid to iSimangaliso** | Fees paid to iSimangaliso for turtle viewing permits** |
|---|---|---|---|
| FY2015 | USD 12,460 | USD 80,672 | USD 11,417 |
| FY2016 | USD 8,445 | USD 69,821 | USD 7,277 |
| FY2017 | USD 10,511 | USD 85,643 | USD 12,252 |
| **Total** | **USD 31,416** | **USD 236,136** | **USD 30,946** |

Differing USD exchange rates over the years impact on the totals, which actually increased year on year in ZAR terms

Sources: *Wilderness Holdings (2015, 2016, 2017); **Wilderness Safaris (2017a, 2017b)

### Challenges

Where the protected area authority (PAA) does not fully understand tourism and the needs of the tourism industry, it can impact negatively on the success of a private sector tourism business. Lack of capacity in the community can also limit the ability of the partnership to grow and develop. Like any product, tourism must modernise in order to remain relevant. In the nature of the contracted relationship and consequent environmental impact assessment (EIA) the authority has been unhelpful in promoting 'good change' (P. Boddam-Whetham, email, September 2017, personal communication). Where there are changes in lease arrangements, PAAs also need to understand that private capital has a time limit and capital will shift to the next best investment if there are extensive delays (P. Boddam-Whetham, email, September 2017, personal communication).

### Lessons learned and recommendations

Although formalised in 2007 when Rocktail Camp was built, the relationship-building between WS and both BEE and community partners started in 2002 and pre-empted the formation of the World Heritage Site and iSimangaliso (P. Boddam-Whetham, email, September 2017, personal communication). This long relationship has built high levels of trust between the partners. This level of trust is vital for success and it has been critical that the people involved have a history and trust one another (P. Boddam-Whetham, email, September 2017, personal communication).

It is difficult to determine the empowerment impacts on the community from the JV partnership directly, though there have been a number of empowerment impacts in terms of employing locally and training local community members. The small size of the KwaMpukane community makes it easier to manage the partnership and ensure that benefits are received and seen to be received.

**Table 53.** Staff costs for Rocktail.

| | Staff costs* |
|---|---|
| FY2015 | USD 260 522 |
| FY2016 | USD 225 432 |
| FY2017 | USD 303 814 |
| **Total** | **USD 789 768** |

*Staff costs include wages, uniforms, training, food, etc.
Source: Wilderness Holdings (2015, 2016, 2017)

**Table 54.** Summary – Rocktail Camp.

| | |
|---|---|
| Name of company | Wilderness Safaris (WS) |
| Location | iSimangaliso Wetland Park, South Africa |
| Year established | 2007 |
| Status of company (i.e. listed, privately owned, etc.) | Joint venture between WS, a BEE company and KwaMpukane community, as well as a contractual agreement with iSimangaliso Wetland Authority to lease the land and to purchase turtle viewing permits |
| List of camps/lodges | Rocktail Camp (34 beds in 17 rooms) |
| Investment/partnership option | Government owned land<br>20-year concession (though there is a difference of opinion in the interpretation of the lease contract length between WS and iSimangaliso)<br>Privately owned infrastructure<br>Joint venture operating partnership which includes the private sector, community and a BEE partnership |
| Total number of staff employed | 34 |
| % local staff | 85% |
| Financial summary | USD 31,416 has been paid in fees to the BEE partner and community from FY2015 to FY2017<br>USD 236,136 has been paid in lease fees to the government, as well as USD 30,946 for turtle viewing permits from FY2015 to FY2017<br>USD 789,768 has been paid in wages and other benefits to staff from FY2015 to FY2017 |

## 4.6. Summary

This chapter has explored five models of community–private sector business.

**1.** Joint venture lodge ownership, on government land.
**2.** Joint venture lodge ownership, on community land.
**3.** Community owned lodge on government land, with a private management company.
**4.** Community or privately owned lodge on community land.
**5.** Tripartite venture.

The case studies demonstrate that there are many instances where the private sector has partnered with rural communities through the institutional arrangements of the company. While these approaches may face higher transaction costs to establish and operate than the private sector models explored in Chapter 3, they provide meaningful empowerment benefits to the rural poor. A synthesis of the impacts is provided in Chapter 6, and the next chapter describes processes to establish partnerships.

## 4.7. References

African Safari Group (2017) *Rates*. Available at https://www.andbeyond.com/our-lodges/africa/south-africa/kwazulu-natal/phinda-private-game-reserve/andbeyond-phinda-mountain-lodge/ (accessed 5 November 2017).

Anon. (undated) Community levy summary.

Anvil Bay (2017) *Rates: validity between 7 January 2017 and 6 January 2018*. Available at http://anvilbay.com/special-offers/ (accessed 8 March 2017).

Black, R. & Cobbinah, R.B. (2017) On the rim of inspiration: performance of AWF tourism enterprises in Botswana and Rwanda. *Journal of Sustainable Tourism* 25(11), 1600–1616 doi: 10.1080/09669582.2017.1296454.

Boggs, L. (2004). Community-based natural resource management in the Okavango Delta. In Fabricius, C. & Koch, E. (Eds.) with Magome, H. and Turner, S. (2004). Rights, Resources and Rural Development: Community-Based Natural Resource Management in Southern Africa (pp 147–159). Earthscan, UK.

Covane Community Lodge (2016–2017) Rate sheet. Available on http://www.covanecommunitylodge.com/assets/covane-lodge_rate-sheet_2016.pdf (accessed 30 March 2017).

CCL (Covane Community Lodge) (undated a) *Covane Community Lodge*. Available at http://www.covanecommunitylodge.com (accessed 30 March 2017).

CCL (Covane Community Lodge) (undated b) *About Covane Community Lodge*. Available at http://www.covanecommunitylodge.com/about.html (accessed 30 March 2017).

CCL (Covane Community Lodge) (undated c) *Facilities and activities*. Available at http://www.covanecommunitylodge.com/facilities.html (accessed 30 March 2017).

CCL (Covane Community Lodge) (undated d) *Destination weddings*. Available at http://www.covanecommunitylodge.com/destination-weddings.html (accessed 30 March 2017).

Collins, S. (2003) *Optimising community benefits from conservation: visual tourism versus hunting in the Makuleke Contractual Park in South Africa's Kruger National Park*. GtZ, Johannesburg.

Collins, S. (2008) The Makuleke case. *Presentation at the African Safari Lodges practitioners' workshop*, The Grace Hotel, Rosebank, South Africa, 19–21 May.

Collins, S. (2012) Ponto Chemucane Maputo Special Reserve: putting community at the centre? Technical workshop on concessioning and investment in TFCAs. Presentation at the international workshop on concessioning tourism opportunities in conservation areas and maximising rural development, Maputo, Mozambique, 19–22 March.

Collins, S. (2014) The role of NGOs facilitating tourism concessions and providing support to communities entering joint venture agreements. Technical workshop on concessioning and investment in TFCAs. Presentation at the international workshop on tourism concessions in transfrontier conservation areas in SADC, Johannesburg 1 September.

Collins, S. (2016) *No easy road. An evaluation of the Makuleke community conservation model*. African Wildlife Foundation, Nairobi, Kenya.

DeMotts, R. & Hoon, P. (2012) Whose elephants? Conserving, compensating, and competing in Northern Botswana. *Society and Natural Resources*, 25(9), 837–851, doi: 10.1080/08941920.2011.638362.

Elliffe, S. (1999) *Guidelines for the release/development of dormant state or community assets for eco-tourism development in the context of community involvement, land issues and environmental requirements.* Unpublished paper presented at the Community Public Private Partnerships Conference, 16–18 November, Johannesburg.

Fusari, A. (2011) *Ndzou Camp, Manica province, Mozambique, April 2011, report for SNV Inclusive Business Case Study.*

Governors' Camp (2017) *Sabyinyo Silverback Lodge rates.* Available at http://www.governorscamp.com/sites/default/files/uploads/Governors%20Camp%20Collection%202017%20-%20Early%20Bird%20to%2020171231%20-%20RSP.pdf (accessed 16 August 2017).

iSimangaliso (2017) *About us.* Available at https://isimangaliso.com/about-us/ (accessed 17 August 2017).

Jones, B. (2010) The evolution of Namibia's communal conservancies. In Nelson, F. (ed.) (2010) *Community rights, conservation and contested land: the politics of natural resource governance in Africa* (pp. 106–120). IUCN, Earthscan Publications, London, UK.

Kemp, L., Mendelsohn, J. & Jones, B. (2009) *The Torra Conservancy.* Namibia Nature Foundation on behalf of the Natural Resources Working Group of NACSO. Available at http://www.nacso.org.na/sites/default/files/torra_booklet.pdf (accessed 7 January 2019).

Kingman, A. (2011) Concessions and sustainability in Chimanimani: Ndzou Camp and MICAIA. Presentation at the concessioning tourism opportunities in conservation areas and maximizing rural development conference, 19–22 March, Johannesburg.

Lamers, M., van der Duim, R., Nthiga, R., van Wijk, J. & Waterreus, S. (2015) Implementing tourism conservation enterprises: a comparison of three lodges in Kenya. In van der Duim, R., Lamers, M. & van Wijk, J. (eds) (2015) *Institutional arrangements for conservation, development and tourism in eastern and southern Africa: a dynamic perspective* (pp. 219–238). Springer, Dordrecht.

Lepper, C.M. & Goebel, J.S. (2010) Community-based natural resource management, poverty alleviation and livelihood diversification: a case study from northern Botswana. *Development Southern Africa*, 27(5), 725–739, doi: 10.1080/0376835X.2010.522834.

Long, S.A. (2002). Disentangling benefits: Livelihoods, natural resource management and managing revenue from tourism. The experience of the Torra Conservancy, Namibia. DEA Research Discussion Paper 53. 22pp

Maluleke, L. (2014) The Makuleke joint venture partnerships in the GLTFCA: tourism as a nature based solution. Presentation to IUCN World Parks Congress, Sydney, Australia, 13 September.

Maluleke, M.L. (2003) Presentation by Mashangu Livingston Maluleke on behalf of the Makuleke community to the World Parks Congress, Durban, South Africa, 8–17 September.

NACSO (2016) *The state of community conservation in Namibia.* Available at http://www.nacso.org.na/sites/default/files/The%20State%20of%20Community%20Conservation%20book%202015.pdf (accessed September 2017).

NACSO (2017a) *Conservancy statistics.* Available at http://www.nacso.org.na/conservancies#statistics (accessed 19 August 2017).

NACSO (2017b) *Conservancy information.* Available at http://www.nacso.org.na/conservancies (accessed 19 August 2017).

O'Leary, G. (2014) Operating in TFCAs: the voice of experience. Presentation at the International conference on tourism concessions in transfrontier conservation areas in the Southern African Development Community, GIZ/SADC, Airport Grand Hotel, Johannesburg, South Africa, 2–3 September, 2014.

O'Leary, G. (2016) !Xaus Lodge: stakeholder returns, 9 years. Presentation at the World Travel Market, London, November 2016.

O'Leary, G. (2017) Maloti Drakensberg TFCA: sustainable tourism development and the cost of access. Presentation to the best practices workshop, Mopani Camp, Kruger National Park, February.

Reid, H., Fig, D., Magome, H. & Leader-Williams, N. (2004) Co-management of contractual national parks in South Africa: lessons from Australia. *Conservation and Society*, 2(2), 377–409.

Return Africa (2017a) *Pafuri Camp.* Available at https://www.returnafrica.com/activities/pafuri-camp/ (accessed 23 March 2017).

Return Africa (2017b) *Pafuri walking trails.* Available at https://www.returnafrica.com/activities/pafuri-walking-trails/ (accessed 23 March 2017).

Return Africa (2017c) Baobab Hill Bush Lodge. Available at https://www.returnafrica.com/activities/malateni-bush-house/ (accessed 23 March 2017).

Rozemeijer, N. (2009) CBNRM in Botswana. In Suich, H. & Child, B. (eds) with Spenceley, A. (2009) *Evolution and innovation in wildlife conservation: parks and game ranches to transfrontier conservation areas* (pp. 243–256). Earthscan, UK.

Rylance, A. and Spenceley, A. (2014) *Strong community partnership through long-term land leasing. Case study, GIZ*. German Cooperation, Endeva.
Satao Elerai (2017a) *Room information*. Available at http://sataoelerai.com/?page_id=317 (accessed 7 January 2019).
Satao Elerai (2017b) *Rates*. Available at http://sataoelerai.com/?page_id=361 (accessed 7 January 2019).
Scanlon, L.J. & Kull, C.A. (2009) Untangling the links between wildlife benefits and community-based conservation at Torra Conservancy, Namibia. *Development Southern Africa*, 26(1), 75–93, doi: 10.1080/03768350802640107.
Simasiku, P., Simivanza, H.I., Tembo, G., Bandyopadhyay, S. & Pavy, J-M. (2008) *The impact of wildlife management policies on communities and conservation in game management areas in Zambia: message to policymakers*. Natural Resources Consultative Forum. Available at https://www.researchgate.net/publication/265448373_The_Impact_of_Wildlife_Management_Policies_on_Communities_and_Conservation_in_Game_Management_Areas_in_Zambia_Message_to_Policy_Makers (accessed 7 january 2019).
Snyman, S. (2012) Ecotourism joint ventures between the private sector and communities: an updated analysis of the Torra Conservancy and Damaraland Camp partnership, Namibia. *Tourism Management Perspectives*, 4, 127–135.
Snyman, S. (2014) Partnerships between private sector ecotourism operators and local communities in the Okavango Delta, Botswana: a case study of the Okavango Community Trust and Wilderness Safaris partnership. *Journal of Ecotourism*, 13(2–3), 110–127.
Snyman, S. & Spenceley, A. (2012) Key sustainable tourism mechanisms for poverty reduction and local socio-economic development in Africa. *Africa Insight*, 42(2), 76–93.
Spenceley, A. (2006) *Sustainable nature-based tourism assessment of Covane Community Lodge*. Report to Covane Community Lodge, Helvetas and the Transboundary Protected Areas Research Initiative, January 2006.
Spenceley, A. (2008) Phinda private game reserve, South Africa. Presentation at the African Safari Lodges practitioners workshop, The Grace Hotel, Rosebank, South Africa, 19–21 May.
Spenceley, A. (2014) Aide memoire, tourism annex. TFCA II Supervision mission.
Spenceley, A. & Barnes, J. (2005) Economic analysis of rhino conservation in a land-use context within the SADC region, SADC RPRC Task 6.3–1.2 (Phase II). SADC Regional Programme for Rhino Conservation, report to IUCN-ROSA.
Spenceley, A., Rylance, A., Nanabhay, S. & van der Watt, H. (2016) *Operational guidelines for community based tourism in South Africa*. Department of Tourism, Republic of South Africa.
Steenkamp, C. (1998) The Makuleke land claim signing ceremony: harnessing social justice and conservation. *African Wildlife*, 52(4).
Steenkamp, C. & Grossman, D. (2001) People and parks: cracks in the paradigm. IUCN (World Conservation Union) policy think-tank series, No. 10, May. Available at http://www.academia.edu/1208503/People_and_parks_cracks_in_the_paradigm (accessed 7 January 2019).
TFPD (Transfrontier Parks Destinations) (2016a) *The impact of responsible tourism – part 1 !Xaus Lodge*. Available at http://www.tfpd.co.za/news/the-impact-of-responsible-tourism-part-1-xaus-lodge (accessed 23 March 2017).
TFPD (Transfrontier Parks Destinations) (2016b) *The impact of responsible tourism – part 2 !Xaus Lodge*. Available at http://www.tfpd.co.za/news/the-impact-of-responsible-tourism-part-2 (accessed 23 March 2017).
TFPD (Transfrontier Parks Destinations) (2016c) *The impact of responsible tourism – part 3 !Xaus Lodge*. Available at http://www.tfpd.co.za/news/the-impact-of-responsible-tourism-part-3 (accessed 23 March 2017).
TFPD (Transfrontier Parks Destinations) (2016d) Xaus Lodge best for poverty reduction submission, World Responsible Tourism awards at World Travel Market, London, June.
TFPD (Transfrontier Parks Destinations)/TFPD Foundation (2017) Prospectus for funding of community-owned tourism projects in South Africa, 2017.
Turner, R.L. (2004) *Communities, conservation, and tourism-based development: can community-based nature tourism live up to its promise*? Center for African Studies, Breslauer Symposium on Natural Resource Issues in Africa. Paper posted at the eScholarship Repository, University of California. Available at http://repositories.cdlib.org/cas/breslauer/turner2004a (accessed November 2004).
Wageindicator.com (2017) Minimum wages in Mozambique with effect from 01-04-2017 to 31-03-2018, updated 17-06-2017. Available at https://wageindicator.org/main/salary/minimum-wage/mozambique (accessed 5 November 2017).

Wilderness Holdings (2015) *Annual integrated report*. Available at http://www.wilderness-group.com/investor_centre/presentations/current_year (accessed September 2017).
Wilderness Holdings (2016) *Annual integrated report*. Available at http://www.wilderness-group.com/investor_centre/presentations/current_year (accessed September 2017).
Wilderness Holdings (2017) *Annual integrated report*. Available at http://www.wilderness-group.com/investor_centre/presentations/current_year (accessed September 2017).
Wilderness Safaris (2017a) *Damaraland Camp rates*. Available at http://www.wilderness-safaris.com/camps/damaraland-camp/rates (accessed on 17 August 2017)
Wilderness Safaris (2017b) *Doro Nawas Camp rates*. Available at http://www.wilderness-safaris.com/camps/doro-nawas-camp/rates (accessed 17 August 2017).
Wilderness Safaris (2017c) *Little Vumbura and Vumbura Plains rack rates*. Available at http://www.wilderness-safaris.com/camps/little-vumbura/rates and http://www.wilderness-safaris.com/camps/vumbura-plains/rates (accessed 19 August 2017).
Wilderness Safaris (2017d) *Serra Cafema Camp rates*. Available at http://www.wilderness-safaris.com/camps/serra-cafema-camp/rates (accessed 19 August 2017).
Wilderness Safaris (2017e) *Room information*. Available at http://www.wilderness-safaris.com/camps/serra-cafema-camp (accessed 27 September 2017).
Wilderness Safaris (2017f) *Rocktail Camp rates*. Available at http://www.wilderness-safaris.com/camps/rocktail-beach-camp/rates (accessed 17 August 2017).
WML (Witsieshoek Mountain Lodge) (2016a) *Rates: 1 March 2017–28 Feb 2018*. Available at http://www.witsieshoek.co.za/accommodation/rates (accessed 24 March 2017).
WML (Witsieshoek Mountain Lodge) (2016b) *About Witsieshoek and the Batloka community*. Available at http://www.witsieshoek.co.za/about (accessed 24 March 2017).
World Bank (2014) Mozambique Transfrontier Conservation Areas and Tourism Development Project (TFCATDP). Project Implementation Support Mission, 4–14 February 2014, aide memoire.
!Xaus Lodge (2017a) *!Xaus Lodge rates*. Available at http://www.xauslodge.co.za/rates (accessed 23 March 2017).
!Xaus Lodge (2017b) *How !Xaus Lodge began*. Available at http://www.xauslodge.co.za/about-us (accessed 23 March 2017).

# 5

# Processes to Develop Accommodation Partnerships in Protected Areas

This chapter has been developed from Spenceley, Snyman and Eagles (2017). It describes step-by-step processes to establish tourism accommodation partnerships that promote sustainability in protected areas. Two approaches are described: firstly, for investments in government owned protected areas, and secondly for investments on community owned land. Furthermore, the chapter outlines options for retrofitting existing tourism operations that wish to integrate a greater degree of community involvement and improve their sustainability.

## 5.1. Getting Started

Prior to the establishment of a private tourism operation is the decision as to whether a partnership is useful or not, and subsequently, to decide what type of partnership option is most suitable. Protected area authorities (PAAs) can use the flow diagram in Spenceley *et al.* (2017) (see Figure 9) to decide whether to invest in accommodation facilities themselves (insourcing) or to seek an external partner (outsourcing).

Once the decision has been made to seek a partner (or where there are no alternatives), suggested processes to develop accommodation partnerships under the different land ownership options are described below.

## 5.2. Government Owned Protected Areas

Governments can use tourism concessioning to establish partnerships with private investors for accommodation investments in protected areas (PAs). There are a number of tools available to guide PA managers through this process (e.g. Eagles, Baycetich, Chen, Dong, Halpenny, Kwan, Lenuzzi, Wang, Xiao & Zhang, 2009; Spenceley, 2014; Spenceley, Nevill, Colho & Souto, 2016a; Spenceley *et al.*, 2017; Thompson, Massyn, Pendry & Pastorelli, 2014). This section of the chapter draws heavily on each of these tools, particularly the Convention on Biological Diversity (CBD) guidelines developed by Spenceley *et al.* (2017), and summarises a process that can be used to establish new investment in sustainable tourism facilities on government land. The CBD guidelines were developed following an extensive review of existing tourism concession guidelines, tools and case studies from southern Africa and internationally, and validated through a consultative process by southern African PAAs and relevant ministries. Therefore, it is the most recent and relevant text to draw on in this book.

A tourism concession is described as 'a lease, license, easement or permit for an operation undertaken by any party other than the protected area agency' (Thompson *et al.*, 2014) and it 'provides public service and may require some capital investment by a concessionaire for

© S. Snyman and A. Spenceley (2019). *Private Sector Tourism in Conservation Areas in Africa* (S. Snyman and A. Spenceley)

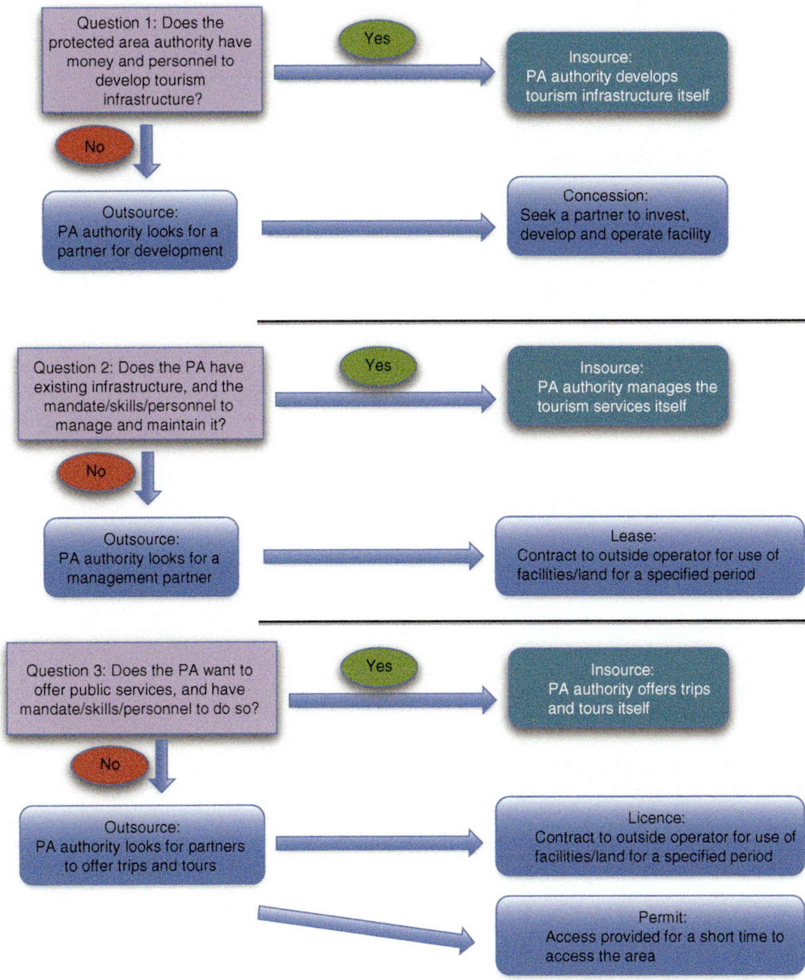


**Fig. 9.** Flow diagram for deciding the type of legal instrument to use. Source: Spenceley *et al*. (2017)

buildings, equipment and operating costs. A concession could provide accommodation, food and beverage, recreation, education, retail, and interpretive services' (Eagles *et al.*, 2009). Concessions can be designed in such a way that they promote sustainable tourism practices, by including certain conditions in concession tender documents and contracts. Table 55 summarises how tourism concession processes can address economic, environmental and social sustainability.

Concessioning processes vary between countries, and in relation to specific legislation, but there are usually three main stages used: scoping; design and feasibility; and procurement, negotiation and contracting. Suggestions regarding how to implement each of these stages are provided here.

## 5.3. Phase 1: Scoping

The scoping phase allows a PAA to establish whether tourism concessions are the right approach for a particular PA or not, and allows the PAA to develop a strategic plan for concessioning as a basis.

### 5.3.1. Motivation

The PAA should describe the reasons why it wants to develop tourism concessions, including the objectives and targets for the specific PA. These may be related to the authority's

**Table 55.** Ensuring sustainability in tourism concessions in PAs.

| Theme | Concession and partnership scoping, design and feasibility, and procurement phases |
|---|---|
| **Economic** | • Require partnership proposals to include a development plan, which indicates how concessionaries will: a) procure goods and services from local and fair-trade sources, b) employ and advance people from local and marginalised groups, and c) provide equity to local and marginalised groups.<br>• Preferentially approve agreements which directly benefit local communities/ marginalised groups.<br>• Ensure that bidders' proposals do not undermine traditional resource access rights.<br>• Educate community investors about tourism, including visitation, finance and marketing.<br>• Check investors' business models, and ensure they are realistic relating to potential bednights, revenues and employment figures.<br>• Evaluate the value for money of concession programmes, and the return on investment and internal rate of return of specific proposals, to ensure that they make financial sense to investors and PAAs.<br>• Create a framework that incorporates benefit-sharing plans for all engaged stakeholders, whether from revenue generated by the concessions for the authority, or by the concessionaire. |
| **Environmental** | • Assess the limits of acceptable use of the area in terms of tourism numbers and associated environmental impacts.<br>• Determine suitable tourism activities for the area (e.g. photographic tourism, hunting, walking trails and 4x4s).<br>• Consider impact of location and size.<br>• Consider the siting of access roads. |
| **Sociocultural** | • Ongoing engagement and open dialogue with all stakeholders.<br>• Ensure consideration of development plans in relation to respecting community access, land rights and sites of cultural importance.<br>• Assess potential opportunities for integrating local cultures and cultural activities into the tourism product in a respectful way.<br>• Provide capacity-building for community members and institutions related to tourism and business.<br>• Manage community expectations through realistic goal-setting and benefit-sharing plans.<br>• Engage local communities as to how they can be involved in the tourism product, if they would like to be. |

Source: Adapted from Spenceley *et al.* (2017), based on Casimiro and Spenceley (2012)

policies and strategies, as well as to specific particular needs at the local level (e.g. to raise finance for infrastructure, generate regular income for conservation management, transfer responsibility for tourism operations to the private sector, provide jobs and other benefits to local communities and marketing). The policies may include specific targets expected to be met by concessioning (e.g. numbers of jobs, additional revenue needed for conservation management). Motivation and targets can be identified through discussion with PAA officials, relevant ministerial staff, and also a review of key policy and strategy documents (Spenceley *et al.*, 2017). It is important for the private sector operator to be aware of these objectives and targets as they may have an impact on development and sustainability.

### 5.3.2. Previous experience

The PAA should review its existing tourism concession agreements, leases, licences or permits, and consider how the new concessions will complement or improve these. A review should be made of whether existing arrangements have worked well, or not, and how systems could be adapted to address any challenges that have been experienced in the past. It is important to take note of the type of procurement process

**Box 7.** Sustainability within South African National Parks tourism concession programme

A major objective of the concessions programme was to apply South African National Parks (SANParks) environmental regulations, and the economic empowerment of historically disadvantaged individuals and groups.
**Empowerment bids**: 20% of the points used to rate bids were allocated to empowerment plans. These in turn were weighted in relation to:

- shareholding by historically disadvantaged individuals or groups (40%);
- training and affirmative action in employment (20%);
- business and economic opportunities for local communities (40%).

**Environmental bids:** quantified monitoring targets were required for a number of environmental issues, including: road length; number of beds; water consumption (350 litres per person, per day, was specified); wastewater production; waste production; game drives and sightings (i.e. the minimum approach distance); and monitoring. Each concessionaire was required to employ an environmental control officer during construction and operation.

Source: Spenceley (2004)

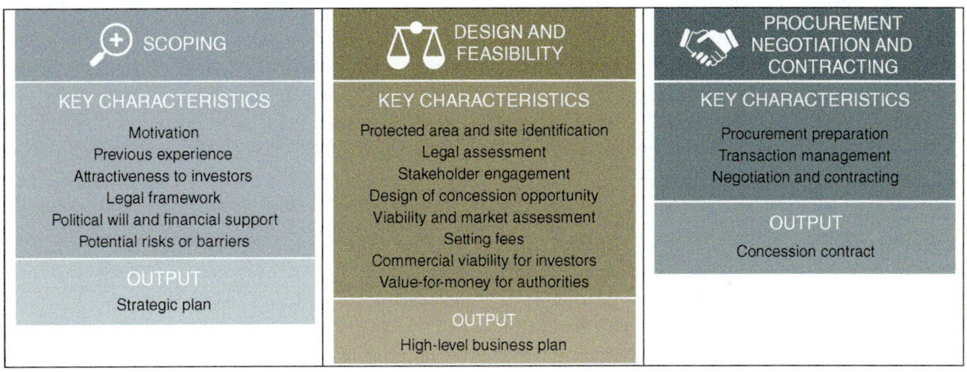


**Fig. 10.** Process for tourism concessioning in government protected areas.
Source: Spenceley *et al.* (2017)

that was followed for those concessions (e.g. tender, auction, direct award), the type of concession vehicle used (e.g. private sector, joint venture – JV – or community owned) and also the areas of success and difficulty that arose. Furthermore, the review should consider how sustainability elements were previously integrated (or not), and whether or not the revenue flowed back into conservation, as well as the level of community benefits (Spenceley *et al.*, 2017). The private sector operator also needs to be aware of the details of the procurement process to ensure transparency and also the required sustainability elements as these may impact profitability and/or the ability of the operator to meet the requirements. The confidentiality of concession processes is a substantial challenge in ensuring transparency and good governance within the approach.

If the PA already has tourism concessions or partnerships in place, the authority will already have some human resource capacity in place to design, procure and manage these. In some instances, there will be an established team with good skills and experience, while in others it will be necessary to supplement existing capacity through training or hiring additional personnel to fill any gaps (e.g. a transaction advisor). Skills needed in the concessioning team will include PA management and zoning, tourism business skills, finance and budgeting, stakeholder consultation and legal expertise (Spenceley *et al.*, 2017). The concessioning personnel will need to be adaptable and resourceful throughout the process, as the process is complex and highly likely to introduce unexpected challenges along the way.

### 5.3.3. Attractiveness to investors

The PAA should make a general assessment of how attractive the specific PA might be to investors, in order to see whether there is likely to be a market demand from investors to establish accommodation facilities in that area. Tourism investors will consider the underlying conditions of a PA before choosing to invest. They will consider its accessibility by road or air, and the level of basic infrastructure (e.g. internal roads, power, water and communications). They will also consider the aesthetic attractiveness of a site, in terms of its areas of natural and cultural interest to tourists, their unique selling propositions, and how it would link to (and add value to, or compete with) existing destinations. In Africa, investors considering developments in natural PAs will often consider wildlife and landscape against existing pollution, degradation or health concerns. Investors will also consider the riskiness of a prospect. For example, they would consider political instability (regionally, nationally and locally), potential threats (e.g. prospecting for oil or mining) and the reputability of the concessioning agency, based on the success (or failure) of previous investments. Where there are high levels of interest, the authority may already have received unsolicited bids for tourism development. Discussions with a few existing and potential tourism investors should be used to establish the level of interest and desired concession terms. If there is no interest at all, then embarking on a concessions and partnerships programme may be redundant, as it may not result in any viable bids (Spenceley *et al.*, 2017). This consultation process with the private sector is essential for ensuring a greater likelihood of a successful partnership being developed and for aligning the desires and requirements of the private sector with those of the PA. Ensuring that it is easy for private investors to invest and operate their business can also encourage private sector investment. For example, the Rwanda Development Board (RDB) provides a one-stop shop for registering a business, all in one office block in Kigali, Rwanda, making it easy to register a business and becoming operational.

### 5.3.4. Legal framework

For a PA that is being considered for tourism concessions, an officially adopted PA management plan should be in place. This should include overarching environmental and spatial context (i.e. zoning), conservation objectives and commercial options, and targets for the PA (see Lee & Middleton, 2008). The plan will indicate the level of legal protection that the area has, and this will have implications for the extent to which tourism is a priority or not. Information on key stakeholders (such as local communities) that could either be beneficiaries of concessioning, and/or who need to be consulted during the process will also be described (Spenceley *et al.*, 2017).

Laws and regulations should provide for private investment in PAs, including the ability to grant secure land tenure. Ideally, the legal framework should also permit PAAs to reinvest tourism revenues into conservation, especially conservation directly related to the PA where the tourism operation is located. The direct investment of funds into conservation in the PA where the tourism establishment is located is a direct investment back into the tourism product (fauna and flora) and is more likely to provide a motivation to the private operator as well as the park management to conserve the resources sustainably and promote further business and, therefore, greater revenue. A small review of relevant policies and laws can be made at this stage to confirm that a framework of a management plan and investment laws and regulations is in place, and that there are no major gaps or areas of conflict between them (Spenceley *et al.*, 2017).

### 5.3.5. Political will and financial support

It is vital to establish whether there is political support for partnerships and concessioning in PAs – both at a ministerial level and also within the PAA. The political environment needs to be conducive to conducting a transparent, efficient and effective process, which leads to a good contract being signed. By contrast, if there is weak governance, excessive red tape and political interference or corruption seems likely, then private investors are unlikely to be interested.

A general impression of political will can be formed through key interviews with government officials, the private sector, donors and non-governmental organisations (NGOs). Some PAAs in southern Africa self-finance their concession processes, but in others donor support has been mobilised (e.g. the World Bank Group, African Development Bank, USAID) (Spenceley *et al.*, 2017).

#### 5.3.6. Creating a strategic plan

The scoping phase should conclude with the production of a strategic plan for concessioning, which provides the context for the process. This document summarises the findings of the phase, and also specifies additional information that will be needed during the subsequent design and feasibility phase (Spenceley *et al.*, 2017).

### 5.4. Phase 2: Design and Feasibility

Phase 2 builds on the scoping activities to establish what the tourism concessioning programme will look like, including available sites, tourism products to promote, potential markets and the most favourable type of concession model to use. It should result in the development of a high-level business plan for the concessioning programme (Spenceley *et al.*, 2017).

#### 5.4.1. Protected area and site identification

The PAA should establish criteria for selecting concession sites that relate to the relative attractiveness and underlying conditions. These criteria can include the location and features (e.g. access, water availability, existing infrastructure and existing tourism), the size of the area, natural and cultural features, environmental sensitivity to tourism, social issues (e.g. local communities), land ownership and institutional issues (e.g. capacity of the PA administration to support concessionaires). Once developed, the PAA should use the criteria during site visits to rate and describe the categories, compare options and apply the criteria to identify the most viable sites (Spenceley *et al.*, 2017). It is useful at this stage to engage with the private sector to assess its requirements for a site in the specific PA (as some characteristics may vary from PA to PA) and which elements are negotiable and which are non-negotiable. The private sector, generally, has a greater amount of experience in terms of the needs and requirements to establish and operate a successful, sustainable tourism operation.

#### 5.4.2. Legal assessment

A legal assessment is needed to establish whether the conditions are viable for tourism concessions, at national and PA level, and whether the investment climate is conducive to tourism concessions. This type of assessment can be undertaken by a lawyer, or someone in the authority with a solid understanding of the law at national and protected area level (Spenceley *et al.*, 2017).

#### 5.4.3. Stakeholder engagement

A strategy should be identified for stakeholder engagement, to ensure that stakeholders are engaged at every stage of the concessioning process, and that their perspectives, knowledge and support are incorporated (Walton, Gomei & Di Carlo, 2013). Initially, the relevant stakeholders and beneficiaries should be identified and mapped. They may include institutions and representatives from government, PAAs, private sector, existing civil society groups, the academic community and also the development community. Then, for each stakeholder, decide what level of stakeholder engagement is appropriate (i.e. inform, consult, involve, collaborate or empower), and on mechanisms to engage and communicate effectively. Then begin to sensitise the stakeholders about the process and progress made so far through meetings, site visits and the media (Spenceley *et al.*, 2017). Good practices include ensuring that stakeholder expectations are managed; notifying them of updates to the process; and responding to their comments (IFC, 2007). Where local community members are involved, determine whether they need technical or other assistance to participate in the process (either in consultation processes, or in preparation to engage

**Table 56.** Legal assessment characteristics.

| National level | PA and concession level |
| --- | --- |
| • Establish whether there is an **existing legal framework for tourism concessions**.<br>• Establish whether there is **stable land tenure**, laws relating to pricing and transfer of land to the private sector, and applicable licences and permits.<br>• Identify **commitments that would be binding** on the relevant ministry and the PAA, and the roles and responsibilities of different institutions.<br>• Ensure that there is **permission to construct infrastructure** for commercial activities, such as accommodation, restaurants and retail outlets.<br>• Review regulations that may affect the **project's attractiveness to investors,** including tax liabilities, labour arrangements and legislation relating to foreign exchange, importation, competition, the tourism sector, building codes and the environment (e.g. environmental impact assessment – EIA – processes).<br>• Identify any **gaps and/or legal reforms** required. | • **Identify the authority responsible for the concession site** that would authorise the concession process and agreement<br>• **Describe the legal procedure for land applications** and approvals.<br>• Identify any **existing rights or licences** issued to the sites and adjacent areas.<br>• Identify **spatial plans** for the PA, as part of its management plan, that regulate where and how much tourism can be established.<br>• **Compile a map** of existing rights or licences. |

Source: Spenceley *et al.* (2017), adapted from Spenceley (2014)

effectively in investments) (Spenceley *et al.*, 2017). Although time-consuming, this phase is critical to long-term success and can serve to avoid future conflicts or mismatched expectations.

### 5.4.4. Viability and market assessment

The PAA conducts a situational analysis of tourism through a review of literature and consultation with identified stakeholders including the private sector. This should include a supply and demand assessment that establishes a baseline regarding the following (Spenceley, 2014).

- **Demand:** a demand study collates information on national and destination statistics regarding numbers of arrivals, source markets, demographics, length of stay, expenditure, occupancies, type of accommodation used, destinations visited, activities undertaken, trends and development objectives of the PAA.
- **Supply:** a supply study reviews information on existing and competing accommodation (including number, type, capacity, quality, rates), tour operations/guides, restaurants, transport, information and planned new tourism products, attractions and competing destinations and products.

The PAA should contact potential investors who may be experienced and interested in new sustainable tourism investments in PAs. It is useful to consider using scouting tours to other PAs, meetings at local and international trade fairs and individual meetings to engage with them. At this stage, it is useful to establish a database of existing and potential investors (including for-profit and not-for-profit private sector, and communities), and then discuss the proposed concession sites with them. These discussions can be used to establish whether the proposed PAs, sites and product types are of interest to them; competing sites and destinations; whether they would be likely to apply for a concession; what they would invest; whether the levels of infrastructure are appropriate; anticipated challenges; and risks (Spenceley *et al.*, 2016a). It is important to note that market demand may shift depending on a broad range of factors, including the political and financial climate, and also trends and fashions in travel patterns and motivations.

### 5.4.5. Design of the concession opportunity

**Concession model.** Establish the concession model that will be offered (i.e. management agreements, lease, permit, concession), its duration, and clarify who will own the assets. Establish the type of partner sought for concessions, for example (Spenceley *et al.*, 2017).

- Private sector (either for-profit or not-for profit).
- JV partnership, with community and private shareholdings.
- Tripartite public–private partnership (PPP), with a government partnership and also private sector and community partners.
- Community owned.

The type of partner will have numerous implications, including who takes the risk for a concession's capital investment (i.e. government, private sector, NGO or a host community), and also the extent of development benefits for local and host communities. These are not mutually exclusive though, and a concessions programme can encourage different types of partnership for different concession sites in a PA (Spenceley *et al.*, 2017).

A comparison of the different concession models is outlined in Table 57.

**Tourism product type.** Select the type of tourism accommodation product and associated activities that will be offered. For example, these may include luxury lodges, basic campsites or mobile camps offering wildlife viewing tours, by vehicle or foot. The type of accommodation and activities offered should be compatible with the PA management plan (Spenceley *et al.*, 2017) as well as aligning with tourist needs and requirements for the PA.

**Duration.** The concession duration to be offered should be based on the level of risk that the investor is likely to be taking (e.g. longer concessions should be offered for higher capital investments, as with accommodation). Sometimes, concessionaires who perform well can be given preferential option on a further concession term. Clarity as to the duration of the concession is important for the private sector from the start, as it will determine rates of return and payback periods.

**Risk transfer.** The PAA should decide the level of capital investment and maintenance that the concessionaire should take responsibility for. Options include build, operate and transfer (BOT), where the concessionaire is responsible for the construction costs and activities and their operation, and then transfers them to the PAA at the end of the concession period. Other forms include rehabilitate, operate and transfer (ROT), design–build–operate (DBO) and maintain and operate. PAAs can include performance bonds in contracts to ensure funds are available to invest in capital repairs and maintenance during the last few years of a contract (Spenceley *et al.*, 2017).

### 5.4.6. Setting fees

Setting a concession fee is about finding a balance between the amount the partner will gain from using the PA (a public asset) and the amount the authority earns in return. The fee-setting process should be transparent, fair and consistent. This activity should recognise that revenue is not the most important factor in PA concessions, and other factors such as public access, size and exclusivity of the area, equity, conservation and community benefits are also important. Concession fees are essentially a business expense (i.e. rental for a property, and land use) and should be set as such. Fee-setting options include the following (Thompson *et al.*, 2014).

- **Supply-driven fees** are where authorities propose reserve value/minimum fee, and offer this to the market through a competitive bidding process (e.g. tender or auction).
- **Market-driven fees** come from unsolicited applications, where a proposed fee is offered to the authority. This can be accepted, or negotiated, and then agreed (e.g. Singita, Case Study 14).
- **Revenue-based fee** formulas set fees as a percentage of gross revenue generated by the concessionaire. In southern Africa, rates are often between 6% and 10% of turnover for safari lodges in high-value PAs, combined with a minimum payment of 50% of the concession's anticipated fee. However, checking these types of fees requires strong inspection and auditing rights of an authority, and a careful definition of revenue. Per bednight fees can also be used as a proxy for a revenue-based fee (e.g. Damaraland, Case Study 21; !Xaus Lodge, Case Study 25).
- **Per-unit fees** are used where authorities wish to charge a fixed fee per unit of use, such as a set fee per hectare or per room per year.

**Table 57.** Relative benefits of outsourcing to different types of concessionaire and insourcing.

| | | Outsource | | | | Insource |
|---|---|---|---|---|---|---|
| Theme | Criteria for choosing partnership type | For-profit | Community | NGO | Joint venture | PAA |
| Financial issues | PA and government costs | Low costs to PA | Variable costs to PA | Low costs to PA | Moderate costs to PA | High costs to PA |
| | Gaining income for the PA | Moderate | Low | Moderate | Moderate | Moderate, depends on policy |
| | Expense of contract management, monitoring | High | High | Moderate | High | Low |
| | Expense of tendering procedures | High | High, variable | High | High | None |
| | Difficulty and expense of monitoring finance | High | High | Low | High | Low |
| | Ability of the PA to function like a business | Needed | Needed | Needed | Needed | Needed |
| | Expense of resolving conflicts | High | High, variable | High, variable | High | Low |
| Tourism operations | Quality of visitor services | High | Low (unless managed by for-profit subcon-tractor) | Moderate, variable | High | Moderate, depends on tourism policy |
| | Specialised tourism expertise | High | Low | Hired by NGO | High | Hired by PA |
| | PA seen as competing with private enterprise | No | Low | Low | No | High |
| | Access to new tourist markets | More access | Low access | More access | More access | Depends on PA policy |
| | Tourism workable with low visitor numbers | No | No | Yes | No | No |
| | Direct contact of PA staff with PA visitors | Low | Low | Low | Low | High |
| Socio-economic impact | Opportunity for community equity | Depends on contracts | High | High | High | High |
| | Business and job creation for local population | Moderate, variable | High | Moderate | High | High |
| | Flexibility in purchasing | High | High | High | High | Low |

**Table 57.**

| | | Outsource | | | | Insource |
|---|---|---|---|---|---|---|
| Theme | Criteria for choosing partnership type | For-profit | Community | NGO | Joint venture | PAA |
| Governance | Concession selection process open and transparent | High | High | Low | High | None |
| | Control of services by PA | Moderate | Low | Low | Moderate | High |
| | Potential source of corruption during procurement | Moderate | Moderate | Moderate | Moderate | Moderate |
| | Concessionaire's influence PA authority policy | Moderate | Low | Low | High | None |
| | Concessionaire gains political power | Moderate | Yes | Moderate | Moderate | Not a problem |
| | Power of public sector unions | Low | Low | Low | High, variable | High |
| Risk | Political influences on PA management by concessionaire | High potential | Moderate potential | Moderate potential | High potential | None, no concessionaire |
| | Liability exposure | Concessionaire | Concessionaire | Concessionaire | Concessionaire | PA |
| | Conflict over PA objectives | Moderate | High | Moderate | High | None |
| | Reversibility of decisions | Low | Low | High | Low | High |
| | Transaction costs to establish partnership | Moderate | High | Moderate | High | None |
| | Difficulty of removing a bad concessionaire | High | High | Moderate | High | None, no concessionaire |
| | Bankruptcy of the concessionaire | Problem | Problem | Problem | Problem | Not a problem |
| Human resources | Public sector union contracts | None | None | None | None | Full |
| | Employment rules and regulations | Company rules | Government rules | Company rules | Company rules | Government rules |
| | Staff working on all PA needs | Seldom | Sometimes | Sometimes | Sometimes | Not a problem |
| | Contract management expertise needed in protected area | Yes | Yes | Yes | Yes | Somewhat true |
| | Ability to use volunteers | Moderate | High | High | Moderate | Moderate |
| | Ability to obtain donations of money and time | Moderate | High | High | High | Low |

**Table 57.**

| Theme | Criteria for choosing partnership type | Outsource | | | | Insource |
|---|---|---|---|---|---|---|
| | | For-profit | Community | NGO | Joint venture | PAA |
| Environment and conservation | Likelihood of contributing to biodiversity conservation | Moderate | Low | High | Moderate | High |
| | Likelihood of applying an environmental management system (e.g. renewable energy, water conservation, recycling) | Moderate | Low | High | High | Low |
| | Likelihood of using third party certification to demonstrate 'sustainability' | High | Moderate | Moderate | High | Low |

Source: Spenceley *et al.* (2017)

These are easier to administer by an authority, but need to be set on realistic valuations of the opportunity (e.g. fees considered too high have discouraged some investors in some sites).

- **Fixed fees** can be used for small concessions, when the expected income is likely to be low, or revenues will be difficult to police.
- **Combinations** are also possible, where fixed fees are combined with revenue-based fees (e.g. Anvil Bay, Case Study 19).

If an authority wishes to establish a minimum concession fee, it can review historical fees and industry standards, and use investment analysis to determine likely profitability. The development of an acceptable internal rate of return (IRR) that will cover risks and costs associated with concession management in the PA is also important (Thompson *et al.*, 2014). It is essential to remember that the tourist operator must be able to make a profit for the operation to be viable (Spenceley *et al.*, 2017) and for them to want to invest. This may require the lease fee to be adapted over the partnership, with a revenue-based fee to start (for the first five years) and a fixed fee added once the lodge has had time to pay back some of the capital investment. See Box 8 for the African Wildlife Foundation's (AWF) experiences related to determining optimal fee structures.

### 5.4.7. Commercial viability for investors

The PAA needs to calculate whether the tourism concession is likely to be commercially viable for an investor. Developing a simple cashflow projection for a hypothetical concessionaire, and with a realistic minimum concession fee, can be used to do this. The projection will help to avoid unrealistic expectations and, if relevant, set a realistic minimum concession fee (Spenceley *et al.*, 2017).

Establish whether the concessioning will provide value for money for the PAA and compare the likely revenue that will be generated for conservation, job creation and infrastructure investment from concessioning, with alternative options or doing nothing. Importantly, consider these revenues in light of associated costs of the procurement process and managing a concession agreement (Spenceley *et al.*, 2017). Depending on the location of the site, the costs to the private sector will also vary (i.e. distance to get supplies and guests to the operation, local staff and skills available, etc.).

**Box 8.** African Wildlife Foundation (AWF) determining optimal fee structures

AWF has helped develop and facilitate the development of conservation enterprises across Africa. Over the past 15 years, AWF has supported the development of tourism facilities in Kenya, Tanzania, Ethiopia, Botswana, Rwanda, Uganda, Namibia and Zambia. These facilities have ranged in size, scale and type. All of these tourism facilities include partnerships – between communities and private sector, private sector and government agencies and communities, and private sector and government agencies. There are many ways to structure the financial benefits of a deal and this depends on the partners, their contributions and the desired outcomes. The broad categories include a fixed fee, which guarantees an amount of money regardless of the business performance, and a variable fee, a percentage of income that is performance based.

While a fixed fee model is sometimes preferred by communities as it is predictable and guaranteed, there are downsides to this model. These are twofold – the community receives the fixed fee whether the business is operating poorly or well. This means when business is running well, the community does not benefit more. When the business is doing poorly, this can also be problematic for the operator to meet payments, unless reserves have been established. A good example of this dynamic is in Kenya. In the Masai Mara landscape of southern Kenya conservancies have been set up between private landowners, the Maasai and tourism operators. It is an extraordinary case of conservation success as the conservancies are now almost larger in size than the actual reserve. In most cases, the tourism partners pay a fixed fee to the Maasai, regardless of business performance. After a few terrorism issues in Kenya in 2013 and 2014, tourism declined significantly. This meant that the tourism partners had a difficult time paying Maasai landowners; threatening to unravel a decade of conservation efforts.

At the same time, when tourism numbers are high, the Maasai do not benefit more. This reduces the incentive for conservation management. If a community and/or PAA is paid the same amount of money regardless of conservation or business performance, there is little incentive for improved conservation management. Linking the amount of payment to performance incentivises improved conservation management, enhanced marketing and overall improved product performance.

One way of ensuring predictability while simultaneously introducing a variable component is combining the two: a minimum fixed fee with a percentage of revenue. If the variable fee model is used, it is critical that the variable be based on top-line or gross revenue. A number of community–private sector tourism facilities have been set up using a percentage of net revenue as opposed to gross, and this invariably leads to conflict and, in some cases, collapse of the business. With net revenue, the operator deducts costs such as food, linens, salaries, petrol and other operational costs. There are numerous case studies where the communities do not benefit as much as they think they 'should' and blame is placed on the operator for deducting more than it should from the 'profit'. This leads to mistrust, review of the books by unqualified parties and conflict. All of this can result in additional cost and time, which negatively impacts management performance. By including a percentage of gross revenue – top-line revenue – the commercial operator and the community do not need to review the details of profit and loss. In most cases, communities and wildlife authorities lack the capacity to assess profit and loss; therefore, removing this element fosters a more positive partnership. It is easier, cleaner, and leads to a more trusting partnership. In any case, it is recommended that a third party auditor is involved in reviewing the income statements. This is standard for any serious business and helps diffuse any questions raised by communities, because an independent entity has verified the income.

Source: K. Fitzgerald, AWF

**Table 58.** Typical institutional costs of tourism concessions to PA authorities at different stages.

| Costs to institution | Scoping | Design and feasibility | Procurement |
|---|---|---|---|
| Project officer and staff | ✓ | ✓ | ✓ |
| Consultants or transaction advisor | ✓ | ✓ | ✓ |
| Expression of interest | | ✓ | |
| Stakeholder engagement | | ✓ | |
| Supporting infrastructure/upgrades | | ✓ | |
| Advertising | | | ✓ |

Source: Adapted from Spenceley *et al.* (2017)

### 5.4.8. High-level business plan for the concessioning process

This plan should conclude the design and feasibility stages and will clearly describe important elements of the concessioning (see Box 9).

## 5.5. Phase 3: Procurement, Negotiation and Contracting

This phase implements the high-level business plan and includes the preparation for the procurement (including the strategy and package, promotional materials and bidding documents), and then the transaction process itself. The phase should result in the signing of an agreed concession contract between the PAA and an investor (Spenceley *et al.*, 2017).

### 5.5.1. Procurement preparation

The PAA should develop an overall plan and identify the materials that will be used during the procurement process. These include the following (Spenceley *et al.*, 2017).

- **Description of the concession package offered to investors.** This includes elements of the high-level business plan, and also the project schedule (i.e. procurement process, concession duration, exit).
- Agreement on **the plan for the procurement strategy** to be used (e.g. open-tender, auction).
- A **plan for reaching out to investors**, which may include specific launch events, participation in international trade fairs, individual meetings with targeted operators, newspaper and magazine advertisements, social media.
- Production of **promotional materials**. In addition to glossy, attractive flyers and brochures to entice investors, these also include factsheets including basic parameters (e.g. location, size of site). Promotional materials may include press releases for the media, posters and banners for trade fairs, websites and investment portals. Technical manuals can also be produced for interested investors, with data such as land costs and acquisition procedures, construction permit costs and procedures, licenses required, labour costs and regulations (e.g. for expatriates), incentives, utility costs, relevant policies and laws, and sustainability priorities (Whyte, Perrottet, Di Fiori & Neville, 2013).

**Box 9.** Contents of a high-level business plan for concessioning

- Goals and objectives of concessioning.
- Products and services to be developed, ensuring that they are compatible with the environmental and social sensitivity of the destination.
- The concession model (i.e. management, lease, Build-Operate-Transfer, etc.), with roles and responsibilities of the authority and concessionaire, and relevant institutional arrangements.
- The business model (e.g. private sector, joint venture, community owned enterprise).
- Industry and market analysis, including supply and international, regional and domestic demand, as well as competitor and risk analyses.
- Development impact, in terms of revenue generated, jobs created, investment mobilised, natural resources protected, skills development and local economic development.
- Sustainability plan, including direct and indirect socioeconomic and cultural linkages with local communities, biodiversity conservation and environmental management.
- Project schedule, including any phased approach to releasing opportunities, the life cycle of each concession, including procurement process, duration and exit.
- Marketing plan, including product, price, promotion and place, and roles of different agencies.
- Financial plan and projections, including best-, average- and worst-case scenarios.
- Critical risks and assumptions (i.e. financial, political, environmental, social, reputational, market) and a mitigation plan.
- Monitoring and evaluation of the concession.

Sources: Legovini (2010); Spenceley (2014)

- **Development of bidding documents** and a physical or virtual 'room' to securely store data. Bidding documents would include a tender manual (i.e. rules and procedures), adverts (e.g. for expressions of interest, if the authority wants to understand the level of demand), prequalification and screening checklist, request for proposals with non-disclosure agreements, a screening checklist, and a draft contract.
- Agreement on the **bid evaluation committee**, the evaluation criteria that it will use, and the roles of its members. The committee should sign confidentiality agreements, and recuse themselves if they have a conflict of interest.

It is critical that the process is formally agreed by the PAA (and potentially at ministerial level). This is to ensure integrity and transparency in the process, and to avoid the repercussions of any political interference in the process or favouritism that may arise (Spenceley *et al.*, 2017).

### 5.5.2. Finding investors committed to the investment and sustainability

Pre-qualification stages can be used to collect information on investors' previous experience and successes with conservation and development impacts. For example, they can be asked within an expression of interest to share information on whether other enterprises have been certified by independent third parties as sustainable, or have won international awards for their efforts. References can be requested from representatives of other PAAs where they have worked, to check their track record.

It is important to provide investors with access to information gathered during the feasibility stage (e.g. the market analysis, development impact, legal analysis, etc.), and the opportunity to undertake comprehensive due diligence, to appraise the business opportunity (e.g. its assets, liabilities and commercial potential). Ideally the potential investors will be provided with opportunities to visit the site and

**Table 59.** Pros and cons of different transaction strategies.

| | Pros | Cons |
|---|---|---|
| Tender | Most transparent process.<br>Market-based system for selecting the best proposal.<br>Stimulates most investor interest.<br>Best candidate can be selected based on multiple criteria.<br>Background checks can be done. | Competitive process makes it less attractive to some investors because it reduces the chances of success.<br>Can be costly, lengthy and complicated.<br>Risk of attracting bidders with little or no experience.<br>Proposal evaluations typically done in secret. |
| Auction | Very transparent.<br>Competitive.<br>Quick and easy.<br>Stimulates investor interest.<br>Background checks can be done. | Not possible to negotiate other benefits (e.g. local benefits, jobs, contribution to conservation).<br>Difficult to conduct background checks. |
| Unsolicited bid | Greater flexibility.<br>Investor already interested.<br>No marketing and promotion required.<br>Useful if there is a lack of private sector interest.<br>Interest can be tested through a tender or auction. | Ad hoc, and reactive to bids that are provided.<br>Risk of choosing an unsuitable investor, and not getting the best deal, is potentially greater. |
| Direct negotiation | Relatively simple, quick and direct.<br>Preferred by high-ranked investors.<br>Greater flexibility.<br>No marketing and promotion required. | Not competitive.<br>Open to external criticism about transparency, favouritism and corruption.<br>Risk of choosing an unsuitable investor, and not getting the best deal, or no deal if the negotiation fails. |

Sources: Government of Zambia (2016); Investment Climate Advisory Services (2012); Spenceley *et al.* (2017)

speak with relevant stakeholders to improve their ability to make a commercially viable and realistic proposal.

The bidding documents can also be designed to encourage investors to propose how they will provide benefits for conservation and also for local communities through equity, employment and procurement. These proposals are reviewed in conjunction with a financial bid. For successful bidders, their environmental and empowerment proposal targets can be integrated into a contractual agreement and can be monitored (Spenceley *et al.*, 2017).

### 5.5.3. Transaction management

The PAA offers the concessions to the market, reviews proposals, and after negotiating with the preferred bidder, signs a concession agreement with the partner. The process uses the materials developed, and proceeds with the steps outlined in Table 60.

### 5.5.4. Negotiation and contracting

With some transaction strategies, there is very little negotiation involved and a contract is simply signed after a winner is announced (e.g. auctions, tenders where a bidder submits a signed contract). In other strategies, the negotiation can be a lengthy and complex processes (e.g. with direct negotiations), or only completed once the bidder has fulfilled the necessary conditions (e.g. obtained finance). A transaction advisor or experienced negotiator can be contracted to facilitate discussions (Spenceley *et al.*, 2017).

A PAA may have a commercial close and a financial close of the deal. The commercial close is when the concession agreement is signed by the PAA and the concessionaire. The concessionaire typically has a fixed period of time to conclude the financial arrangements with lenders and investors. Once the time has lapsed, the PAA would then have the option to cancel the concession agreement with the preferred bidder and start discussions with the reserve bidder. This is done to ensure that the PAA is not bound to a bidder that is ultimately unable to finance the project. Financial close may also include conclusion of a direct agreement between lenders and the PAA to reflect the security arrangements lenders may have over the project assets and will also govern lender step-in rights. It is important to remember that private capital is often time-bound, so if the concessioning process is too lengthy, the investor may no longer have access to the funds or may feel that it is losing money and would be better off investing the capital elsewhere.

Characteristics of a good deal include being affordable and beneficial to both parties; value for money (financial and development impacts); acceptable risk transfer; adequate technical capacity of the investor (including operations, working with communities, existing client base and promotional capability); and the promotion of sustainable tourism (Spenceley *et al.*, 2017).

## 5.6. Community Owned Protected Areas

For community owned land, the process has steps that emulate those for government PAs, but incorporates more emphasis on the establishment of an appropriate community-based institutional structure, and consultation within the community. This section is largely drawn from 'Operational guidelines for community-based tourism in South Africa' (Spenceley, Rylance, Nanabhay and van der Watt, 2016b). These guidelines were developed with an extensive review of existing community-based tourism guidelines and manuals available internationally, and through a consultative process adapted for South Africa. In this section, they are summarised and adjusted for relevance across southern Africa, and are written to guide a technical support agency (e.g. NGO or local government structure) through a process of aiding communities to develop tourism in their PAs.

For this type of PA, local community members who are stakeholders in the PA are likely to be pre-defined, under the governance framework for the PA. A 'community' may be defined as a social group of any size whose members reside in a specific locality, share government and may have a common cultural and historic heritage/s. It can also refer to a group of individuals who interact within their immediate surroundings. A typical local community consists of business operators, public agency staff and residents and their interactions, and can include sharing of

**Table 60.** Transaction steps and activities.

| Transaction step | Description | Transaction strategy: Tender | Transaction strategy: Auction | Transaction strategy: Unsolicited/ direct negotiation |
|---|---|---|---|---|
| Advertise opportunity | Place adverts in appropriate highly credible national and international newspapers, government gazettes and trade journals. Send adverts directly to investors identified during previous steps, and distribute information at international and regional trade fairs. | ✓ | ✓ | |
| Pre-qualify parties with an expression of interest in relation to key criteria (e.g. financial strength, technical and business experience, sustainability credentials) | Expressions of interest should be received, logged and secured according to the procedures required in the bidding documents. On an appointed day and time, the expressions of interest should then be produced for inspection and evaluation by the evaluation committee, according to the specified procedure, and on a pass/fail basis. Inform companies of the outcome of the pre-qualification process. | ✓ | | |
| Issue request for proposals with draft agreement, non-disclosure agreement and description of information needed from bidder | The request for proposals is made available to the bidders who passed a pre-qualification stage. Sometimes, a payment is requested from the bidders before they receive the request for proposals, which is used to help prepare bidding documents for them. | ✓ | | |
| Due diligence by bidders (site visits, bidder conference) | Access to the data 'room': to review detailed technical, legal and financial information on the concession.<br>Site visits: opportunity should be provided for each pre-qualified company to visit the concession sites, and discuss the opportunity with fully briefed PA staff, local authorities and relevant stakeholders. It is useful to use an independent practitioner to facilitate site visits, meetings and gather information on any investor concerns.<br>Bidder question and answer: the types of questions from investors may be related to background technical information or the project design, and also the transaction structure, the legal framework and allocation of risks. This process may take place by phone, email or a bidders' conference. All bidders must be treated equally, and so all responses should be shared with all of the pre-qualified bidders. | ✓ | ✓ | |

**Table 60.**

| | | Transaction strategy | | |
|---|---|---|---|---|
| Transaction step | Description | Tender | Auction | Unsolicited/ direct negotiation |
| Receive bids | Bids should be received, logged and secured according to the procedures required in the bidding documents. Bids may be requested in one envelope, two (i.e. technical and financial bids separated) or three (i.e. an additional 'empowerment' bid). | ✓ | ✓ | ✓ |
| Review bids (financial, environmental and social development bids) and select preferred bidder | On an appointed day and time, the bids should be produced for inspection and evaluation according to the specified procedure by the evaluation committee. The investors should not be present during the technical evaluation but may attend the opening of the financial bid. There should be an official transcript or minutes of the proceedings of the evaluations.<br>The winner is selected on the basis of the weighted technical/financial score or the best financial offer if the technical evaluation was pass/fail as per the request for proposals rules. At the end of the bid evaluation process, the authority communicates with all bidders. The winner is invited to finalise the contract and other project agreements. The second-placed bidder may be held in reserve for a grace period, in case agreement cannot be finalised with the preferred bidder. | ✓ | | |
| Negotiate with preferred bidder | Some processes may have some negotiation at this stage, while in other cases the bidder will have submitted a signed contract with their bid. Where there is negotiation, an experienced negotiator or transaction advisor can be useful at this stage, and there should be a climate of trust and cooperation. | ✓ | | ✓ |
| Agree management plan and sign contract | A transaction is considered finalised after the contract is signed between the contracting authority and the winning bidder. An agreed management plan should also form part of this concession agreement. | ✓ | ✓ | ✓ |

Sources: adapted from IFC (2007); Spenceley *et al.* (2016a, 2017)

resources, information and support, as well as establishing commercial relationships between local businesses and consumers. Community participation relates to the involvement and engagement of community members in decisions that affect their lives (Spenceley *et al.*, 2016b).

The community can undermine tourism success through increased poaching, crime and

**Box 10.** Elements of a typical concession contract

- Nature and scope of the concession rights (e.g. geographical area, works, services, level of exclusivity).
- Precedent conditions for entry into force.
- Duration of contract.
- Nature of property interests of parties in the concession assets (e.g. right to use an area or infrastructure).
- Maintenance of concession assets (road maintenance, access, etc.).
- Fees payable (including process for adjustments and reviews).
- Performance guarantees (e.g. service levels, occupancies).
- Monitoring, evaluation, with key performance indicators and template contract compliance checklist.
- Insurance policies.
- Limitations of liability and indemnification of the PAA.
- Force majeure (i.e. damage or destruction due to forces beyond the control of parties).
- Environmental impacts during construction, operation and commissioning.
- Right to assign concession rights to third parties.
- Restrictions/conditions on transfer of the concession.
- Restrictions/conditions on related party transactions (e.g. if the concessionaire is part of a larger group).
- Socioeconomic contributions (e.g. local equity, employment, procurement, social projects).
- Change in the law.
- Breach and cancellation processes.
- Dispute settlement provisions.
- Circumstances that a third party or the PAA could take over the operation (e.g. temporarily if there is a serious failure).
- Taxation and other fiscal matters.

Sources: Spenceley *et al.* (2017); Varghese (2008)

conflict. For this reason, long-term sustainability is aided if ecotourism *staff* are empowered and educated. Similarly, managers deciding on a model of engagement should be aware of its long-term impact on rural livelihoods. Where communities have no access to natural resources then minimising future problems can require that the operation be seen as a primary alternative livelihood but also that there should be mitigation of human–wildlife conflict (HWC) while secondary benefits to communities are also maximised (Snyman, 2013).

The process used in these areas can be described in four phases: (i) identify opportunities; (ii) design and test; (iii) set up the stakeholder structure; and (iv) develop the venture (Spenceley *et al.*, 2016b).

## 5.7. Phase 1: Identify Opportunities

This phase includes six key steps: (i) identify stakeholders and start consultation; (ii) establish goals, motivation and objectives; (iii) explore tourism product types; (iv) determine market and financial viability; (v) identify potential challenges and barriers; and (vi) decide whether to proceed or not. Activities in each of these steps are described in this section.

### 5.7.1. Identify stakeholders and start consultation

The first interactions with stakeholders are critically important as they provide the groundwork for a long-term relationship between the community and other stakeholders, including the private sector, government and other support agencies. Activities that the support agency should include are as follows.

- **Identification of key stakeholders:** establish their interest in the tourism venture, what role they would prefer and how involved they will be in the preparation, development and operational phases. A stakeholder map or diagram should be developed that shows the various stakeholders, their potential role and sphere of influence. This should include community members who are owners of the PA.
- **Outreach:** make contact with local representatives of the district authority, relevant

**Fig. 11.** Process to develop a partnership on community or private land.
Source: Spenceley *et al.* (2016b)

municipalities and the community's traditional authority. Identify what role they can play and any responsibilities they may have in relation to the design and establishment of the enterprise.

- **Introduce tourism:** describe the concept of tourism to key stakeholders and outline the various business options, types of tourism products and services, challenges and potential development benefits.
- **Decide who to consult and how:** establish which other key local stakeholders (e.g. business associations, trade unions, artisan groups and support agencies) should be consulted, and determine what their roles could be. Ensuring equal opportunities and equal voice is very important at this stage, and care needs to be taken that disadvantaged groups (the poor, females, certain minorities, the disabled) are given a chance to participate.
- **Review literature and relevant policy and legal frameworks:** collect and review local planning documents and strategies that relate to both community enterprise development and tourism, with the aim of providing a context on broader economic development plans (e.g. integrated development plans, local economic development strategies and district tourism strategies).

### 5.7.2. Establish goals, motivation and objectives

The support agency should discuss with key local stakeholders, perhaps in a workshop, their motivations, goals and objectives for supporting the tourism venture. The current level of tourism should be established by listing the existing tourism assets and resources, and also any previous experience with tourism that community members have. Discussions with community members can be used to see how motivated and driven key stakeholders are to develop new tourism ventures on their land, and also whether there are any previous negative experiences, or conflicts, that could be a risk (Spenceley *et al.*, 2016b). Some tips to troubleshoot problems and conflict in community partnerships are outlined in Box 11.

### 5.7.3. Explore tourism product types

Decide on the type of tourism product or service to develop using a combination of factors. The most important issues to consider are the community's PA resources, the likely market demand, the potential commercial viability of the accommodation product to be developed, and the level of difficulty and risk in establishing and operating the venture.

Match the resources required by the venture against the resources available within the community to determine the types of product and service that might be viable. All of the product types require adequate skills, access to finance and market access, and some more than others. For example, developing a luxury lodge in the PA will probably need extensive experience and capital investment (and so potentially a private sector partner). By contrast, a basic campsite or homestay will not require extensive experience to establish or operate, and will need very low levels of capital investment. Such sites can also be relatively quick and easy to establish. The type of facility selected influences the scale of benefits that could be realised from the development, the likelihood of success, the relevant stakeholders to engage and also the timeframe for achieving targets (Spenceley *et al.*, 2016b).

### 5.7.4. Determine market and financial viability

Market research is undertaken to establish whether there is a likely market for the tourism product and whether the tourism venture will be able to reach the markets that would buy its product. At this stage, it is important to do research including, if possible, meeting with a small group of attraction site managers and existing tourism ventures in the area (including tour operators), to find out:

- whether there are existing competitors, or if the new venture would fill a gap in the market;
- how the new product would access the market, and link directly to tourists and to tour operators and travel agents, or to an existing tourism route or circuit;
- the likely sources of customers, including domestic tourists and international tourists, and whether the trends are increasing, decreasing or stagnant.

It is important to establish whether the venture is likely to be commercially viable, and whether it is likely to be profitable within five years. At this stage, establish:

**Box 11.** Troubleshooting problems

Problems in relationships within the community and with their partners may arise from time to time. Misunderstandings can be created by:

- mismatched expectations;
- unrealistic expectations;
- competition for resources;
- miscommunication or a lack of transparency;
- weak management;
- downturn in tourism to the area or country;
- uneven power dynamics.

This is normal, and problems can often be dealt with quickly and efficiently through good communication and by tackling the problem sensitively and with the appropriate response. Early response is very important because if they are neglected, challenges may get worse over time and can ultimately lead to the failure and closure of the venture.

Source: Adapted from Spenceley *et al.* (2016b)

- the capital investment that would be required to set up the venture, including the cost of building development, equipment and training;
- how it would be financed, including from low interest or grant funding;
- the likely annual operational costs for wages, rental, utilities, insurance, supplies, services, marketing and interest on loans;
- the potential annual revenue that could be generated, based on a realistic estimate of visitors and the rate that is charged;
- the likelihood of the venture turning a profit within the first five years.

If the capital investment is very low or is a grant that does not attract interest, then achieving commercial viability should be easier. Obtaining a commercial loan can be difficult for a community entity or a community entrepreneur working alone, as banks need to secure the loans against capital (most often land or infrastructure) which such people and organisations rarely have access to. This is less of a challenge in JV partnerships as private sector companies can often provide capital investment or secure loans, and then arrange to pay back the loan from the venture's profits (Spenceley *et al.*, 2016b).

### 5.7.5. Identify potential challenges and barriers

The support agency should discuss potential challenges with key stakeholders including the local and district authorities, the tribal authorities, potential private sector partners and other key support institutions. The types of challenge may relate to political stability of the community, secure land tenure, governance within community and local structures, bureaucracy within local government departments, motivation of community members, willingness to invest time and effort, attractiveness of the area for tourism, accessibility, and levels of basic infrastructure and skills. Relevant reports should be reviewed to find out where there are barriers and how these can be resolved.

### 5.7.6. Decide whether to proceed or not

If the first phase has established: that the objectives and expectations are realistic; that it can be a well well-governed process; that the community has adequate resources and understanding of what is involved; that the venture is likely to be commercially viable; and there are no 'deal breakers' identified, then the concept can proceed to the next phase. If not, then it may be best to rethink the concept, and explore other options for economic development.

## 5.8. Phase 2: Design and Test

This phase includes 10 steps: 1) review the policy framework; 2) engage with stakeholders; 3) assess the market; 4) decide on products and services; 5) select a suitable business model; 6) choose the business format; 7) design a sustainable venture; 8) determine what resources are required; 9) assess commercial viability; and 10) decide whether to proceed or not.

### 5.8.1. Policy framework review

Review local development plans, and the PA management plan, to check that the proposed facility is aligned with them. Check the legal procedure for approving developments on the site, and the kinds of licences that will be needed (e.g. EIA). Establish whether there are land rights on areas immediately adjacent to the site, the status of other development plans in these areas, and make an evaluation of the current status of these rights or licences and their legality. Determine what licences and insurances the business itself will need to operate legally (Spenceley *et al.*, 2016b).

### 5.8.2. Engage with stakeholders

Design a stakeholder engagement plan that describes how people and specific institutions will be engaged (e.g. kept informed, consulted, involved, collaborators or empowered). These types of venture are only successful if community members are willing to engage and actively participate in the venture. Although communicating with the wider community may not be easy, getting buy-in from the majority of community members that own the PA is essential (Spenceley *et al.*, 2016b). Assessing private sector interest in a partnership with a community is also important at this stage, as well as understanding the type of partnership they would be interested in (i.e. a JV or lease agreement). It is also wise to determine the experience of private

**Box 12.** Overview of private sector JVs with local communities

**Institutional structure**

The Namibian Constitution and accompanying legislation provide for a legal institution at grass roots level and a bottom-up approach to development planning, land rights and wildlife utilisation. This arrangement provides access for the private sector to land on communal areas, specifically conservation areas that are attractive for tourism business establishment and activities. Various stakeholders at different stages of the engagement process have to come to an agreement on the utilisation of natural resources as well the envisaged benefits to the various stakeholders, in particular the local communities/conservancies. The enabling platform which legislation of conservancies creates presents both an opportunity and a challenge in terms of the efficiency and effectiveness of engagement of the stakeholders. In particular, the challenge faced by the tourism business is the various, and sometimes completely different, areas of competencies, interests and expectations. In addition, over the years a potentially destructive process has evolved where, at the beginning of negotiations between community/conservancy and private sector operators, many stakeholders are involved; however, during the period of implementation, as the partnerships evolve, only the contracted partners remain part of the process. In many cases, this situation results in the absence of ongoing monitoring and evaluation, especially by a 'watchdog' type of stakeholder. This monitoring and evaluation is necessary to review and inform process, procedures and contractual compliance. The biggest challenge the tourism operator faces is the disrupted implementation of partnership/JV contracts and, sometimes, non-contractual concerns related to the structural governance of conservancies where elected committee members serve terms which result in a high turnover of the conservancy leadership.

**Successes**

The conservancy concept has primarily afforded land and wildlife utilisation rights to rural communities. This process has entrenched a symbolic sense of ownership over land and genuine utilisation rights over natural resources. In addition, the model presents a transfer of rural development responsibility to communities. Through partnerships/JVs, especially with tourism operators, many communities have formally embraced conservation as a way of life. The communities have diversified their ways of life to embed into their customs and norms a new 'living with wildlife concept' that looks at tourism operations as one of the chosen options. Therefore, to date, due to the number of years tourism has been actively conducted in the area, the communities are well aware and understand the tourism business as 'their business' too. Tourism partnerships and JVs have not only provided jobs and skills but have also directly addressed rural-to-urban migration, especially of youth, from the conservancy areas.

Furthermore, the conservancy model indirectly creates an 'experiential multi-disciplinary learning/exposure hub' covering critical areas such as human rights, land rights, traditional authority rights, animal rights, environmental/conservation rights, constitution/governance laws, basic business management and administration, financial management skills, meeting procedures and processes, conflict resolution, development planning and tourism awareness, among many other things.

Source: K. Jermain, email, September 2017, personal communication

sector operators in terms of working with communities, their track record and any references.

### 5.8.3. Assess the market

A detailed market assessment for the tourism venture should be undertaken. This will ensure that the venture is realistic and that it can be promoted in a way that reaches the targeted clients. The assessment should consider:

- the location of the tourism venture and its proximity to tourist circuits in the country and destination;
- the patterns, profiles and interests of existing visitors to the PA;
- the specific markets that could be attracted to the facility;
- the level, nature and degree of success/problems experienced by existing tourism products that are competitors but also potential collaborators;

- the similarities and differences between the product idea and existing products in the area;
- the activities of local tour operators that bring visitors into an area, as well as coverage by international tour operators that send visitors to the region;
- existing information and promotions in the area.

This information can be obtained by the following means.

- **Reviewing existing reports and studies:** these can be obtained from local and provincial tourism authorities, enterprise development offices, chambers of commerce, tourism associations and NGOs. These reports and studies will need to describe the market, existing products and services, as well as any trends in the market.
- **Conducting visitor surveys:** these can target tourists at key locations (e.g. entrances to the PA, other popular tourist areas near the community). The results can be used to estimate the likely size of the tourism market for the venture, its value for the proposed venture, how to tailor the product and the type of travellers that will be most interested.
- **Conducting a supply and competitiveness study:** this will help to understand the current local tourism industry as well as new products and services that could add value to the destination and fill gaps in supply. Use existing reports and interviews with tourism operators to obtain the information needed. Establish whether the venture has any unique selling points (USPs) – i.e. the special reason that will make customers choose the proposed product over those of its competitors. Common USPs include the lowest price, best service and best quality, and also authentic experiences, cultural experiences and opportunities to engage with community members.
- **Identifying markets and assessing market access:** identify the target market/clients of the proposed venture and design marketing strategies to reach them. Tourism boards and bureaus and other bodies will have helpful information about current and future travel markets and segments in the country or region where the PA venture is located. Some provincial tourism authorities should be able to assist with understanding tourist travel motivation and behaviour, and can also help with marketing and promoting the operation. Business or private tourism associations can also be a valuable source of information. Attending business-to-business (B2B) or business-to-customer (B2C) events will also provide opportunities to learn and assess.

### 5.8.4. Decide on products or services to offer

Analyse the list of options for the venture that was compiled, and establish what kinds of impact it might create. Using discussions with key stakeholders, perhaps in a focus group or workshop, the support institution can rate the following selection criteria to determine the impact of different products and services that could be developed:

- **Enabling environment:** availability of resources or assets for the venture, capacity to mitigate risks, interest of relevant partners and ease of implementation, the level of competition and likelihood of success.
- **Economic impact:** likely number of new jobs, revenue and commercial viability.
- **Impact on the local environment:** likely impact on local habitats and biodiversity and natural resources (e.g. water sources). Likelihood of responsibly disposing of waste.
- **Impact on society:** likely non-financial benefits to community members, ownership/equity in the venture, institutional strengthening, governance and transparency, and benefits for women and youth.
- **Impact on culture:** likely impact on language, values and way of life. Likelihood of preservation of culture and heritage as well as renewal of cultural pride. Risk of commodification of culture and staged authenticity.

Work out which products or services have the highest ratings and then decide which should be pursued for further investigation and development. As an additional option, it may be decided that there are several products or services that could be sold in combination. An example is combining accommodation in the PA with a community tour, restaurant and sale of locally produced crafts (Spenceley *et al.*, 2016b).

### 5.8.5. Select a suitable business model

Decide on the type of business model to use for the product or service, using the guidance in Table 61.

JV partnerships between communities and the private sector provide opportunities for communities to access the financing, experience and market access of the private sector. There is a wide range of JV structures depending on the expectations and negotiation process between both parties, and the three most common are (WWF, 2014):

- **Private investment**: the private sector partner builds the operation, operates and transfers the physical assets and business to the landowner at the end of the lease agreement (e.g. the Singita Lebombo in this volume).

**Table 61.** Appropriate models for tourism products and services in community PAs.

| | Suitable models | | | |
|---|---|---|---|---|
| Criteria | Communally owned venture | JV | Community-based tourism (CBT) enterprise | Community enterprise linkages with private sector tourism businesses |
| Easy and low-risk tourist products and services (e.g. simple accommodation, village tours, craft outlets) | ✓ | | ✓ | |
| Easy and low-risk non-tourist products and services (e.g. transport, laundry, food and beverage) | | | | ✓ |
| Difficult and high-risk products and services (e.g. luxury lodge, large hotel, large/sophisticated restaurant, complex tour operator) | | ✓ | ✓ | ✓ |
| Non-tourist (or not exclusively for tourists) products that support the tourism industry (e.g. food, transport) | | | | ✓ |
| Availability of local tourism companies interested in buying products and services locally | | | | ✓ |
| Desire from community members for a collective enterprise with social benefits | ✓ | | | |
| Existence of a support institution that can advise the community | ✓ | ✓ | | |
| A target market seeking to engage with the community | ✓ | | | |
| Availability of intermediaries willing to package and distribute the tourism products (e.g. homestays) | ✓ | | | ✓ |
| Existing government-managed tourist attractions whose ownership and management can be transferred to communities (e.g. attractions and heritage sites) | ✓ | | | |

Source: Spenceley *et al.* (2016b)

- **Joint equity:** both the community and the private sector partner invest in the venture and the private sector operates (e.g. the Damaraland Camp case study in this volume). The buildings are either rented out to the private operator at a fixed fee or the community receives a proportion of revenue.
- **Management agreement:** the community invests and signs a management agreement with the private operator (e.g. Witsieshoek and !Xaus Lodge case studies in this volume).

However, JVs are not always the best choice for a community to pursue (see Table 62).

If a JV is being considered, then a critical element will be to identify and secure a partnership with a suitable private operator, preferably one with a positive long-term track record. This needs to be a company that provides investment, skills and assets to complement those of the community, and which will maximise the chances of commercial success. The community members will also need to understand the nature of the partnership, roles and responsibilities and timeframes involved. For example, it is important to appreciate that brokering JV agreements and establishing the JV can take two to three years before a venture starts construction and development (Spenceley *et al.*, 2016b). At this stage it is also important to bear in mind that private sector capital can have limits in terms of time and availability and the two need to be balanced.

A transaction advisor can play a crucial role in protecting both the community's and the private sector partner's interests. They can ensure that the community resources are valued fairly, but they can also help the private sector operator create a realistic expectation of returns within the community. This cannot be stressed enough, because the relationship between the community and the private sector partner can fail if the venture does not live up to expectations. The functions of a transaction advisor are to advise the community of the different financing and partnership options available, the process for identifying and negotiating a partnership and the realistic real value of their resources – so that they do not either undersell or oversell themselves (Spenceley *et al.*, 2016b). It is important that the transaction advisor has appropriate tourism skills,

**Table 62.** Criteria for considering or avoiding joint ventures.

| Criteria for considering JVs | Criteria for avoiding JVs |
|---|---|
| Communities are receptive and open to the concept | Communities express resistance or ambivalence |
| Private sector demand exists for the community's asset | The private sector is expected to take over government's role of community development instead of supporting it |
| The right to use the asset lies with at least one of the partners, usually the community | Communities, or another JV partner, do not have access or use rights to the asset |
| The JV concept broadly contributes to the national tourism sector goals and fits with national marketing efforts | The quality of the community's assets is not high enough |
| Land use plans and zones account for and accommodate JVs | Land use plans do not include or protect tourism investment |
| Private sector players can access finance | JVs will expose communities to dangerously high risk |
| Private sector players have responsible credentials | Private sector players do not show any willingness to operate sustainably |
| The enabling environment will protect the interests of both parties | The regulatory environment is weak and will not protect both parties |
| A reliable, experienced support sector of NGO is available | There is no experienced support sector of NGOs |

Source: WWF (2014)

knowledge, practical experience and understanding to advise appropriately as there have been many cases where communities have been ill-advised by NGOs with development experience, but no tourism experience, and expectations have been set very high. There needs to be a balance between the development experience of the support agency and the tourism experience of the private sector in order to provide the community with the best way forward.

Communities can request assistance from NGOs or government authorities to find a suitable joint venture partner, either by publicly advertising and tendering for a partner or by identifying a partner and then negotiating an agreement with them.

### 5.8.6. Choose the business format: for profit, or not for profit

Choosing the right type of entity is an important part of setting up a venture and registering it with the appropriate authorities. In some instances, it may be necessary to distinguish between the legal entity that will own the accommodation infrastructure, and the entity that will operate/manage the enterprise. There may also be a separate entity that markets the enterprise. Tourism ventures that are owned by individuals or small groups of individuals in a community generally require one legal entity only. The community should decide whether the ownership entity will be structured as a non-profit or for-profit organisation. Selecting the legal form for the community tourism venture is one decision that should not be made without the advice of legal experts in the field (Spenceley *et al.*, 2016b).

### 5.8.7. Design a sustainable venture

Sustainable ventures promote conservation of the environment through wise use of resources for construction and furnishings and appropriate architectural design and siting that minimises impacts. Sustainable design also refers to planning how the venture will be operated to ensure that local people and businesses are part of the supply chain, and decide how resources such as energy and water will be used to create the least negative environmental impact. Adopting sustainable practices makes sense for the community venture as it ensures that the business is optimally commercially viable in the long term. It also makes sense for local people involved, for whom there are tangible economic benefits through equity, employment and the supply of goods and services.

Value chain analysis (VCA) can be used to identify gaps to understand the current local linkages in the tourism value chain, and identify opportunities for the venture to build strong supply linkages in the local economy (see section 6.3.2 on local procurement). Support agencies can use the value chain approach to (Ashley, Mitchell & Spenceley, 2009):

- map the value chain, including stakeholders and where community members participate;

**Box 13.** Types of JV partners in South Africa

Private sector partners are either tourism groups (e.g. Wilderness Safaris – WS, TFPD, andBeyond) or entrepreneurs/small businesses (e.g. Coffee Shack, Mdumbi Backpackers, Bulungula Lodge). An advantage of tourism groups is that they can pool resources, have teams of specialists and benefit from economies of scale. For example, a tourism group will have only one marketing manager for many properties and can save when they supply in bulk. Entrepreneurs on the other hand are often multi skilled people who have to perform all the management and marketing functions themselves. They are almost always based within the community, since they don't have the resources to operate remotely. Unlike tourism groups who have a pool of managers they can place in the operation, an entrepreneur should be committed to the business for the full length of time it takes for the community to learn to manage it themselves. Some tourism groups have community liaison officers that are tasked with engaging with the community.

Source: Spenceley *et al.* (2016b)

**Box 14.** Tourism value chains

Value chains are described as: ' … a sequence of related business activities from the provision of specific inputs for a particular product to primary production, transformation, marketing and up to the final sale of the particular product to consumers' (GTZ, 2007). Value Chain Analysis (VCA) is used to map the value chain in order to understand how actors interact and who captures the value (Spenceley *et al.*, 2010). VCA is a valuable tool which helps to evaluate direct economic impacts and also indirect impacts on support sectors (e.g. agriculture, transport, maintenance, etc.) (Spenceley & Meyer, 2016).

The United Nations World Tourism Organization (UNWTO) states that a systematic analysis of the tourism value chain at the local destination level can be a useful tool to trace income flow in the tourism sector. This would enable an assessment of which part of tourism income goes to disadvantaged groups, while identifying possible interventions to enhance tourism's local economic impact. This can be supplemented by market assessments and working with stakeholders to identify future opportunities for engagement, supported by capacity-building (UNWTO & SNV, 2010). Some researchers have used VCA to identify challenges in strengthening local supply chains, such as poor record-keeping, limited quality and diversity of products and difficult access to local enterprises (Spenceley *et al.*, 2010), poor management, capacity and organisational difficulties of community farming projects (Rogerson, 2012) and unreliable supply due to a lack of transport options (Rylance & Spenceley, 2015). VCA has been used considerably in tourism destinations in developing countries by agencies such as the Overseas Development Institute and the International Trade Centre to establish 'pro-poor' tourism value chains, and to design interventions that can shift greater proportions of tourism revenue to the poor. A pro-poor approach to tourism value chain development can be used to generate net benefits for the poor, including cash income (e.g. through wages, selling goods or services, profits from locally owned enterprises or collective income from community-run businesses), improve access to public services (e.g. health, education, environmental management), and measure social impacts (e.g. sense of control, reduced vulnerability, cultural pride) (Ashley *et al.*, 2000).

Source: UNWTO & SNV (2010)

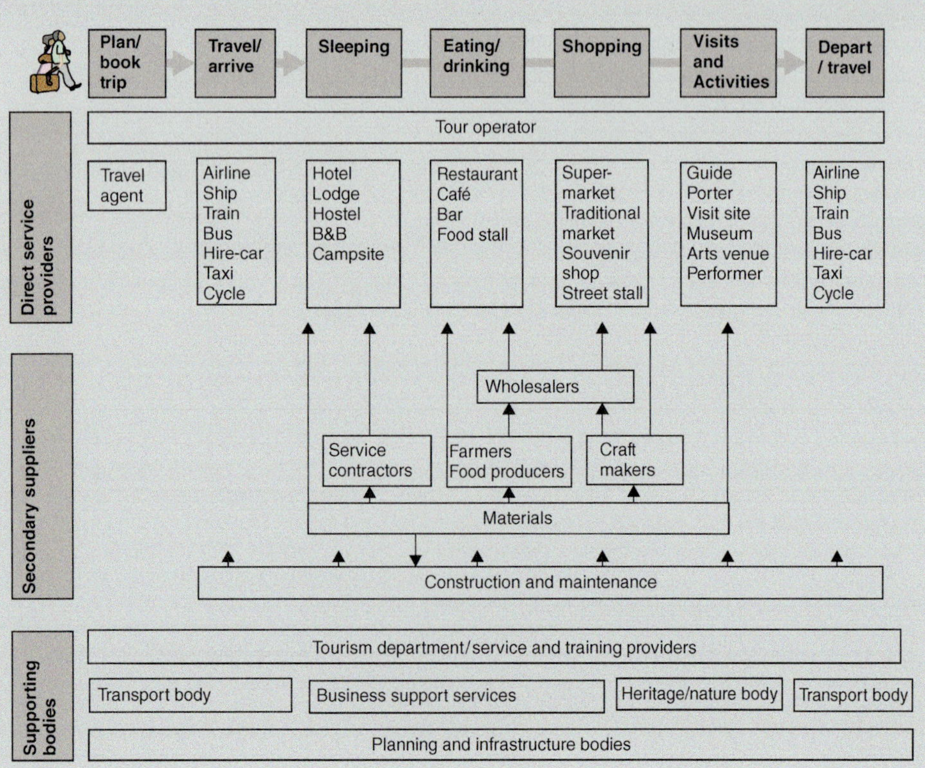

**Table 63.** Resources needed for community ventures.

| Type of resource | Description and purpose |
|---|---|
| **Land** | In the PA, with secure tenure for the accommodation facilities |
| **Financial resources** | Cashflow will be needed to sustain it during the first five years (or so) before it becomes profitable |
| • Capital investment | For infrastructure development for the venture, and to underpin the operations (e.g. roads, trails, power), and construction of the tourism accommodation |
| • Wages and consultancies | For staff and technical experts such as accountants |
| • Equipment | Vehicles, office equipment and furniture |
| • Training funds | For management and other staff in the venture and the community management entity, unless these are available for free from a support agency |
| Other operational costs | For maintenance, marketing, insurance and loan repayments |
| **Human resources** | Skills required include business acumen, product knowledge, marketing and promotion, hospitality, plus skills relating to human resource management |
| **Approvals required** | For infrastructure these include EIAs (which can be costly), business licences and labour licences |

Source: Adapted from Spenceley *et al.* (2016b)

- survey existing accommodation, restaurants, craft suppliers, excursions and entertainment to gather data and perspectives;
- track revenue flows, income to communities and barriers facing communities;
- identify opportunities and prioritise them;
- identify existing skills and resources in the community.

### 5.8.8. Determine what resources are required

Various resources will be needed to establish the community venture, and being aware of what is needed before proceeding is important in helping to create realistic expectations of the benefits from the venture (see Table 63).

If the venture requires substantial start-up investment, there are a number of potential sources:

- **Grants:** grants are sometimes provided by government programmes, philanthropic trusts, charities and NGOs that are interested in supporting initiatives that promote poverty reduction. In the past, grants for community owned ventures in southern Africa have been provided by agencies including the Ford Foundation, CESVI, local government and central government. The level of risk is very low for these grants, and agencies tend to monitor their 'returns' in terms of infrastructure developed, jobs created and numbers of people trained. In this volume, the building of Sabyinyo Silverback Lodge was supported by an AWF grant.
- **Corporate sponsorship:** some private sector businesses may want to use corporate social responsibility (CSR) investments in community businesses in their public relations materials. The level of risk is very low, and 'returns' required tend to relate to information on social improvements created.
- **Crowdfunding:** finance can be sought through internet-mediated business by raising money from a large number of people. Examples focusing on philanthropic initiatives include GlobalGiving, and microlending platforms such as Kiva and Wokai.
- **Interest-bearing loans:** loans can be made to a CBT venture if security can be provided (e.g. lease rights). Potential sources for the southern African region include the Industrial Development Corporation (IDC). Loans are associated with a level of risk that is medium to high, as 1) lenders require repayments with interest, and 2) if a CBT venture defaults on payments the security could be called in by the lender.

### 5.8.9. Assess commercial viability

A very simple cashflow forecast can be used to understand whether the venture will be commercially viable (and profitable). The cashflow framework in Table 64 can be used to get a rough estimate. It would be good to engage with a private sector operator or a support agency with experience in operating tourism businesses, to ensure an accurate cashflow forecast that is also realistic.

### 5.8.10. Decide whether to proceed or not

To decide whether to proceed or not at the end of the design and testing phase, all the information

**Box 15.** Options for financing a JV

The Thakadu Lodge in South Africa shows the diversity of funding options available.

**The community Sebolao Trust** raised USD 1 million
Grants of USD 0.6 million
USD 0.26 million from local government
USD 0.09 million from Ford Foundation
USD 0.25 million from Khula's Community Equity Fund
Interest-bearing loans of USD 0.4 million*:
USD 0.25 million from Khula's Land Empowerment Credit Facility, via IDC
USD 0.15 million from IDC (at prime)
** Lease rights ceded to IDC as security*

- **Private operator** invested USD 0.3 million

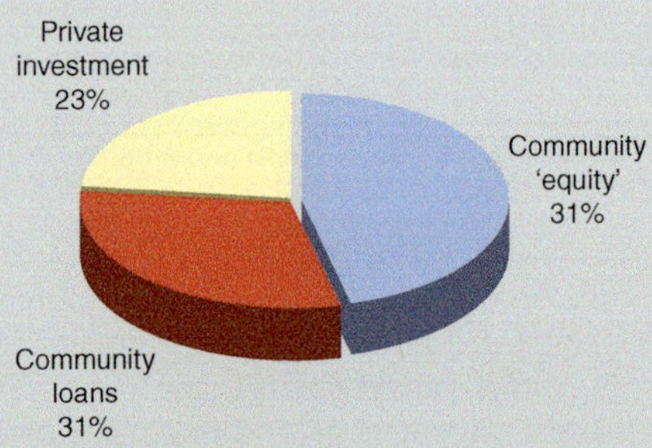


Source: Adapted from Massyn (2008) by Spenceley *et al.* (2017)

**Table 64.** Example of a simplified cashflow forecast for a CBT venture's first five years (net of VAT).

| | Start-up USD'000 | Year 1 USD'000 | Year 2 USD'000 | Year 3 USD'000 | Year 4 USD'000 | Year 5 USD'000 |
|---|---|---|---|---|---|---|
| **Cash inflows** | | | | | | |
| Owner's capital | | | | | | |
| Loans received | | | | | | |
| Grants received | | | | | | |
| Cash from sales and other operating revenue | | | | | | |
| Cash from other sources | | | | | | |
| *Total cash inflow A* | | | | | | |
| **Cash outflows** | | | | | | |
| Project costs and start-up expenses | | | | | | |
| Salaries, wages and staff costs | | | | | | |
| All other operating costs and expenses | | | | | | |
| Loan repayments | | | | | | |
| Replacement of equipment and vehicles | | | | | | |
| *Total cash outflow B* | | | | | | |
| ***NET CASHFLOW [A–B]*** | | | | | | |

Source: National Treasury (2004)

gathered by following the steps above must be shared, reviewed and explained clearly to stakeholders, especially potential private sector partners. They should be evaluated, and a decision taken as to whether the proposed venture is:

- compatible with the local policy and planning framework;
- supported by local stakeholders, who have (or will obtain) adequate capacity and skills to make it work;
- likely to have the financial, social and cultural, and environmental impacts desired by stakeholders, and that match their expectations.

If the responses to these questions are positive, then proceeding to the next phase is desirable. If not, then it is worth reconsidering the type of product or service that could be offered and/or the model proposed.

## 5.9. Phase 3: Set up the Stakeholder Structure

This section deals with the establishment of a representative oversight body or entity that represents the interest of stakeholders, and oversees how the tourism venture is developed and managed. This could be a community trust or a JV company, both of which may not be directly involved in the day-to-day management of the business but which are responsible for its ownership. Proper development of the oversight body is particularly important for development of non-profit organisations, JVs between communities and the private sector as well as cooperatives. Small-, medium- and micro-enterprises operated by a small number of community members or individual entrepreneurs do not require this additional layer of information (Spenceley *et al.*, 2016b). The activities in this phase include: (i) foster tourism awareness; (ii) develop a constitution; (iii) set up a system to distribute benefits; (iv) coordinate with support institutions and communicate with them; and (v) register the community entity.

### 5.9.1. Foster tourism awareness

Community members who understand how tourism works, the standards required and the factors that affect demand are more likely to offer successful tourism products. Capacity-building on tourism awareness will increase the community's understanding of the importance of tourism to the local economy. Some of the topics that could be covered in a tourism awareness-training programme include:

- Who are tourists?
- Where do they come from?
- Why would they want to come to your area and visit your product/service?
- What do they want to do and what don't they enjoy?
- What tourism activities or places are currently popular in the local area?
- How does a tourist decide on, select and book a holiday?
- What influences a tourist's decision to choose one tourism venture over another?
- How can the community become directly and indirectly involved in tourism?
- What competition is in the area? What are the community USPs?

These questions can either be addressed through a classroom format, field trips, workshops or a combination of these activities. Knowledge transfer from existing successful operators is useful so that community members have the chance to experience the realities of owning and operating a tourism venture.

### 5.9.2. Develop a constitution

Developing a constitution is an important first step towards setting up the structure and transparent governance. It sets out the principles, beneficiation processes and governance structures for how the oversight entity will operate. The process of developing and agreeing a constitution ensures that community members share a common vision and understanding of the objectives of the venture. The process and resulting document need to be simple and clear so that all members understand their mandates and responsibilities. Ideally, the constitution should be developed with the support of professional community facilitators combined with legal advice (Spenceley *et al.*, 2016b).

In general, a constitution should include, but not be limited to, the following:

- the purpose and objectives of the community entity;

- the form of the community entity, be it a for-profit business or a non-profit organisation;
- the membership structure of a board or trust, how can members join, leave or be expelled, and indication of the gender balance and involvement of youth;
- the roles, powers, rights and responsibilities of each member;
- the structure, roles, powers, rights and responsibilities of the management committee;
- the structures and main procedures for decision-making functions and their limitations;
- the benefit-sharing structures and processes that the structure will respect and oversee;
- how the finances and assets will be managed and reported;
- conflict resolution procedures.

The structure of the constitution will be dependent on the legal structure chosen and will be governed by different laws. Professional legal support is imperative in this process.

### 5.9.3. Design and train the community entity's management committee

Requiring community members to manage all the ownership aspects of a tourism venture is a tough undertaking, especially if few have existing experience in tourism or business. It requires significant and consistent levels of technical support and training. In consultation with the community, it is important to determine:

- the purpose and functions of the management committee;
- the scope of the committee's decision-making authority and clear procedures to make decisions and their limitations;
- the committee's reporting and communication process to the community;
- the functions and duration of each representative appointed to the committee to ensure each member serves a specific purpose;
- the benefit-sharing process (both tangible and intangible benefits), now and in the future;
- the electoral process to propose and select members of the community to the management committee;
- the process for the community to issue complaints or remove a member of the management committee.

These functions and processes should be outlined in the business's constitution. Once these have been agreed an electoral process can proceed, including:

- requesting candidates to submit application forms to confirm their candidacy;
- providing an open forum for each candidate to present themselves and their intentions to the wider community;
- facilitating an election process that is fair and transparent;
- communicating the results of the election publicly and allowing for a complaints procedure.

Support is required to fully understand the practicalities of these functions. Workshops and exposure visits are useful tools to help introduce members to their responsibilities. However, ongoing mentoring is required to build the confidence of community members. Technical support should be provided by experts with experience in tourism development, operations and marketing, business management and accounting. Training topics will include, but are not limited to:

- transparency and complaints procedures;
- communication strategy with the wider community;
- developing agendas, minutes of meetings, reporting;
- accounting and financial management;
- conducting annual general meetings.

### 5.9.4. Set up a system to distribute benefits

Stakeholders will need to be aware of the need to design a practical, transparent and well-governed mechanism for distributing benefits from tourism, and their roles and responsibilities in meeting any costs. A community entity, such as a not-for-profit trust, can be established with community members making up the membership. As part of the good governance of the entity, public elections can be held within the community to identify and vote for community representatives to manage it. Simple systems should be used to ensure that there is accountability of these representatives (and particularly of any money flowing through the entity), and that regular feedback is provided to the community through the venture and the trust (Republic of South Africa, 2015). It is also important to put in place a mechanism to ensure representation for groups who often will not get elected such as women and minorities (Spenceley *et al.*, 2016b). If the chosen partnership option is a JV with the private sector, it is important for there to be an understanding in terms of business losses and the related liability of the partners. For example, in Case Study 22 there were a number of years when the camp did not make a profit and the private sector operator funded the losses; but as JV partners the losses should be funded according to the JV by all relevant partners and communities need to be aware of this risk associated with JVs which have an equity component.

It is also important to have a clear system for allocating jobs to community members: how will community members be selected? How does one ensure that the maximum number of households are positively impacted? Clarity also needs to be sought, prior to partnerships commencing, as to the planned distribution of both tangible and intangible benefits, in order to avoid future conflict. NGO support and capacity-building can assist communities with these decisions. A clear community constitution/agreement on employment and benefit distribution is an important starting point and should be established prior to partnership discussions and engagements.

### 5.9.5. Coordinate with support institutions and communicate with them

Developing a community entity requires community facilitation, governance, legal, investment structuring and marketing skills. Whether an organisation is a local municipality or NGO it is likely that it will require additional technical support. Collaborating with other stakeholders, who have a high technical competence in a particular area and add value to the process, will increase the chances of establishing and sustaining a successful venture (Spenceley *et al.*, 2016b).

A common challenge within CBT operations is the development of unrealistic expectations of the wider community. This is often a consequence of the fact that expectations have not been managed from the outset. It is critical for the local community to understand the implications of any benefit-sharing system, including both tangible and intangible benefits. There are three key messages to communicate:

**1.** The community only benefits if the tourism business is successful and profitable.
**2.** It will not make a profit for at least the first few years, so it is a long-term vision.
**3.** The tourism establishment cannot employ everyone in the community, but indirect business linkages will have a greater impact.

Developing a clear communication strategy to ensure that the wider community is regularly informed of business progress updates, decisions, challenges and future milestones is essential. The private sector and various NGOs can play an important role in terms of building capacity in the community in relation to understanding tourism and business and this support should be provided before partnerships are established, as well as on an ongoing basis.

### 5.9.6. Register the community entity

Technical support agencies can help register the oversight body of the community entity. The registration process will be determined by which legal structure is chosen. The legal requirements for each will vary and professional legal assistance should be sought. Requirements to register the community entity will vary between countries, but may include the constitution and a registered bank account, as well as the trustees' or members' proof of identify and address (Spenceley *et al.*, 2016b). The private sector will be more likely to engage with a well-established community institution that is stable, accountable to the community and transparent.

## 5.10. Phase 4: Develop the Venture

This phase gets the entity ready for development, and includes: (i) registration of the business; (ii) market access; (iii) business planning; (iv) raising finance; (v) compliance with legal requirements; (vi) development of a human resources plan; and (vii) development of indicators. These activities are outlined below.

### 5.10.1. Register the business venture

Register the business entity that will be responsible for the day-to-day management of the tourism venture. The registration process will be determined by which legal structure is chosen, and the country of operation. The legal requirements for each will vary and professional legal assistance should be sought. Requirements to register the business entity may include the memorandum of incorporation or constitution of the entity, a registered bank account, as well as the members' proof of identify and address (Spenceley *et al.*, 2016b).

### 5.10.2. Market access

The information about target markets that was collected earlier is essential for the business plan. Once the target market is identified the next task is to decide on how the tourism product should be positioned in the market. The next step is to identify the most efficient and effective path to attract clients to the business (see Rozga & Spenceley, 2006 for a training guide). Marketing and promoting a business is a complex matter that cannot be fully dealt with at this stage in the process. However, the '4Ps' of product, price, place and promotion describe the basic analytical approach to be taken (Asker, Boronyak, Carrard & Paddon, 2010). If possible, support organisations should enlist the services of a professional tourism marketing company or specialist NGOs to develop the marketing strategy. In the case of a JV, the private sector partner will most likely have the required expertise (Spenceley *et al.*, 2016b). Use of the private sector's marketing expertise and channels can assist a great deal. Attempt should be made by the community to learn from the private sector, and to engage in internships and training programmes so that these skills can be acquired.

A successful venture of any kind should consider marketing as a continuous process to maintain its connection with customers and their presence in the market. Neglecting to market the venture or thinking that others will market on the community's behalf is risky. Therefore, sufficient training and mentorship should be provided so that management is able to understand the fundamentals and importance of continuous and innovative marketing (including social media) as well as the motivations of their target market. Budget also needs to be allocated for marketing and there should not be an underestimation of the power of word-of-mouth of tourists and, therefore, the importance of a quality experience for every tourist.

### 5.10.3. Prepare a business plan

A business plan is a step-by-step document that outlines the vision of the venture, what product or service it intends to offer and how it is intended to make the business successful. It is used as both a pragmatic document to guide the venture but also as a marketing tool to raise capital from financial institutions. A business plan will include the following elements:

- general company/venture description;
- industry background;
- competitor analysis;
- market analysis, including pricing competitiveness;
- products and services offered;
- responsible tourism practices;
- marketing plan;
- operational plan;
- management and organisation;
- start-up expenses and capitalisation;
- financial plan;
- monitoring and evaluation.

A lot of the research or the business plan should have been completed during the design and testing phase, but the venture business plan may require some additional detail. It is an important learning exercise for any business to go through, and ventures are more likely to be successful if they have written their own business plan with assistance from a business expert rather than having a plan that is produced by experts without their involvement. It is a useful problem-solving tool that assists communities to refine their expectations and ambitions for the venture (Spenceley *et al.*,

2016b). For a JV with the private sector, this plan can be developed together with input from all stakeholders.

### 5.10.4. Raise finance

The approach needed for raising funding to start a community tourism venture will vary depending upon the level of investment required. Funding is available from either commercial banks, public organisations or NGOs and is generally in the form of grants, loans or equity stakes. In the case of a JV the private sector partner may also provide a loan to the community or may invest the start-up capital. The project concept and business plan largely informs the decision of the lender. It needs to be well researched and have a realistic market assumption. Lenders are reluctant to make loans to projects that have incomplete business plans or unrealistic estimations of their success. Some of the questions that commercial banks and private sector operators may ask are (WWF, 2014):

- Will the business be viable?
- If a private partner or any other stakeholder is involved, are they credible and do they have a good track record?
- What collateral is available (e.g. to finance buildings, vehicles and other capital costs)?
- What are the current and predicted future tourism market conditions?
- Is this business profitable enough for the financier to take the risk?

In situations where the venture is solely owned by the community (there is no private sector partner), demonstrating collateral is often very difficult, making it less likely to receive commercial financing. Other small businesses may not need much start-up funding at all to get going. Depending on the scale and structure of the tourism business investment, the community may need to either finance the development of the venture or fund their equity share in the partnership. There are two routes in this regard: public development finance or a private loan (Spenceley *et al.*, 2016b).

CBT ventures tend to favour public development finance as it is usually provided at a lower rate than commercial banks and is not subject to the same stringent repayment regulations. Organisations such as international development bodies and NGOs have been the traditional funders in the past. However, these funders are increasingly demanding a stronger business case for their support and will rarely support capital investments. Therefore, a thorough and realistic business plan is extremely important. There are some examples in the case studies in this volume of innovative financing options provided by the AWF and Conservation Capital (see Box 16). The ability to optimise these mechanisms is itself dependent on a host of other factors: the quality and relevance of the conservation context; the degree and quality of engagement of the tourism facility within the management of that context; the extent to which the tourism facility demonstrates best practice in terms of environmental sustainability – including in the management of its supply chain; and – crucially – the extent to which creative and stimulating tourism products are designed that actively engage tourists in the surrounding conservation context – so that they not only enjoy it but also start to understand and empathise with it.

### 5.10.5. Comply with legal requirements

Earlier it was noted that licences and legal requirements will have to be completed before operations can begin, such as an EIA in the case of building a new tourism establishment in a PA. A legal expert should be consulted to determine which regulations apply to the operation, to prepare applications, to submit the applications and then to keep track of the applications until legal requirements are met. Complying with these requirements can cause lengthy delays if they are not dealt with in good time (Spenceley *et al.*, 2016b). If the partnership is a JV and depending on the business model used, the private sector partner may take responsibility for this; the community should, however, request to be engaged and allowed to learn from this process.

### 5.10.6. Develop and implement a human resources plan

The venture cannot employ everyone from the local community. Therefore, determining who

**Box 16.** Conservation Capital

Conservation Capital is a company working in the field of conservation enterprises and related investment financing. Since its formation in 2004, the company, together with its partners, has mobilised and structured nearly USD 250 million of finance into enterprise-driven conservation projects across more than 25 countries. Conservation Capital works primarily in Africa and Europe, but has recently started to engage in India and South America as well. The development of tourism-based conservation models has been central to many of its projects.

Conservation Capital has significant experience in the design, development and financing of private sector tourism in conservation areas. Examples of this work include the following.

- **Enhancing business models for national protected area systems:** historically, the Kenya Wildlife Service (KWS) entered into commercial contracts with third-party tourism operators on a case-by-case basis. This resulted in an unstructured portfolio of partnerships that fostered complexity, inefficiency and low returns. Conservation Capital designed a uniform commercial formula for all private sector tourism contracts that would significantly increase returns to KWS over time. Conservation Capital has since developed similar initiatives for a number of other national protected area authorities in Africa.
- **Building new conservation economies:** Ethiopia's national park system, despite the country's latent natural value, has not been developed or managed as a significant social and economic asset. Through Umiliki Investments, Conservation Capital co-financed the development of the first two ecolodges in the country's national park system – Bale Mountain Lodge in Bale Mountains National Park and Limalimo Lodge in Simien Mountains National Park. Conservation Capital also supported the Ethiopian Wildlife Conservation Authority (EWCA) to develop a national wildlife tourism strategy and ensured that global best practices in private sector tourism concessioning for national park contexts were built into the process.
- **Developing species-driven conservation tourism:** Conservation Capital designed, structured and financed the development of two premier, high-end gorilla trekking tourism lodges in both Rwanda and Uganda, both as JVs between private sector partners and host local communities. In Sabyinyo's case Conservation Capital also structured a USD 250,000 loan from a private investor – probably the first example of commercial debt ever being taken out by a local community in a conservation enterprise development context. It was repaid in less than five years. Overall, in less than 10 years, these two facilities have yielded in excess of USD 2.5 million to their host local communities, funding an impressive array of health, education, infrastructure and economic empowerment projects.
- **Structuring innovative financial incentives:** via Umiliki Investments, Conservation Capital structured a significant debt investment into one of eastern Africa's fastest-growing nature travel businesses, currently operating 21 camps and lodges in Tanzania, Zanzibar and Kenya. Attached to this investment is a pioneering rebate mechanism that enables the company to reduce the effective cost of this investment capital by up to 2% based on the development of new conservation areas and/or the introduction of incremental tourism bednights (and the economic benefits these bring) into existing but underutilised conservation landscapes.

Many lessons have been learned, but perhaps the most significant has been the fact that structuring successful stakeholder partnerships for conservation tourism needs to be done differently from those in more typical mainstream business contexts. Often these partnerships will involve all of or a combination of a government agency, a local community, a financier, the private business operator and employees – and of course the tourists themselves. Specialist value-sharing mechanisms that utilise the correct mix of 'On P&L' (revenue-based royalties, lease/concession/licence fees, etc.) drivers – that are borne by the business, and 'Off P&L' (conservation/entry fees, etc.) ones – that are borne by the tourists themselves, are required to optimise financial returns and incentives for conservation, as well as allowing the businesses themselves to flourish commercially.

Source: F. Barnard, Conservation Capital, email, December 2017, personal communication

will and will not receive employment can become extremely contentious, especially in areas of high unemployment. Support organisations need to be aware of this from the start and plan accordingly. A human resources and communication strategy can help identify potential challenges in advance and minimise community conflict (Spenceley *et al.*, 2016b). A suggested process for developing a human resources plan is outlined in Figure 12.

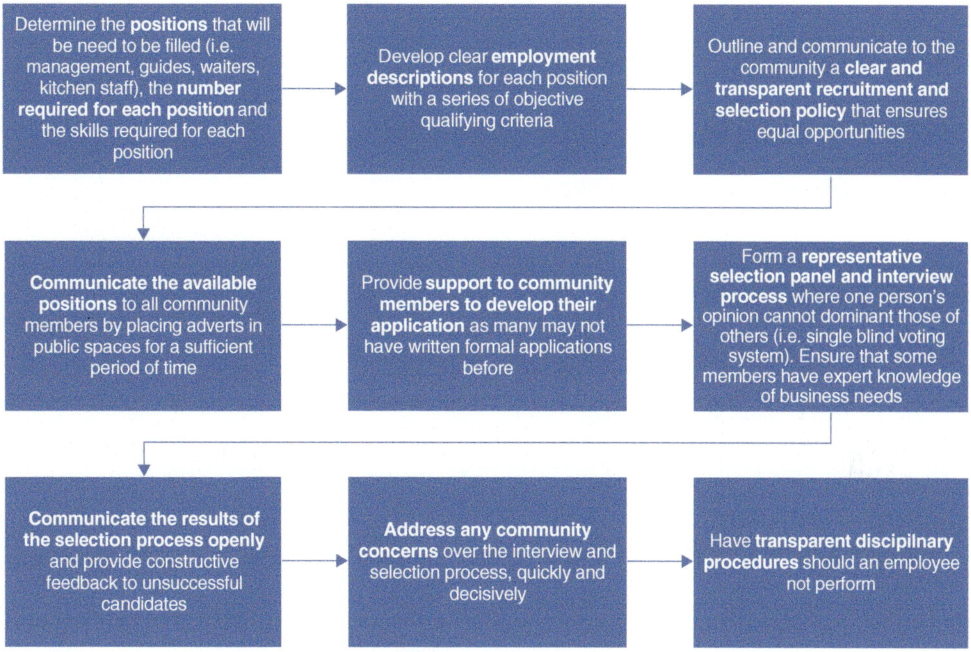


**Fig. 12.** Process of developing and implementing a human resources plan.

A venture can take the following measures to minimise community conflict during the recruitment process:

- implement the human resources plan transparently, addressing community concerns immediately, clearly and inclusively;
- ensure the recruitment process is open, the qualifying criteria are objective and the selection panel is representative;
- provide constructive feedback to unsuccessful candidates;
- emphasise the indirect employment linkages through supply chain development;
- put in place a plan for training up others in the community (particularly youth) so that they can be upskilled and can compete for jobs more effectively.

Once the employment within the venture is finalised, contracts should be agreed upon that relate to the employment descriptions, pay and benefits. Also, a period of targeted training will be required to ensure that staff members are confident and competent to fulfil their job description, and can support the running of the venture. Ensure that all members of staff – from managers to cleaners – know what they are supposed to do and how important their contributions are within the broader venture. The ILO SCORE website has useful case studies (see http://www.ilo.org/empent/Projects/score/lang--en/index.htm).

### 5.10.7. Develop indicators and baselines

At the start of the process the objective of the development of the venture should be outlined in consultation with the local community (i.e. is it to create employment, increase incomes or promote local culture?). Once the objective is agreed the next step is to determine how to track its progress. Indicators need to be an objectively verifiable means to determining progress. A useful criteria system for indicators is SMART, meaning: specific, measurable, achievable, relevant and time-bound. For each indicator a baseline (or starting point) needs to be assessed, with an assigned target by the end of the project period. In addition, a means of objectively verifying the indicator should be assigned. An example is shown in Table 65. Even where the partnership is a JV, the objectives for the tourism development need to be clearly articulated for all

**Table 65.** Indicator example.

| Measurement | Indicator | Baseline | Target | Current Status |
|---|---|---|---|---|
| Overall outcome: more decent jobs for young women in rural tourism small, medium and micro-enterprises | % of women workers promoted as a result of project interventions reporting increased job satisfaction | 0 | 90% | 50% |

relevant stakeholders, with each having a clear understanding of the objectives of the other parties. This will assist in reducing future conflict and managing the expectations of all parties in the partnership.

In summary, below are important factors to ensure a greater chance of sustainability and success in private sector/community partnerships.

- **Raising awareness.** It is important that communities are aware of all costs and benefits associated with tourism and conservation, how long benefits will take to be received, and how benefits are distributed.
- **Benefit distribution plans.** The establishment of structured, appropriate benefit distribution plans with measures of accountability and transparency. Identifying the beneficiaries of these plans and methods of distribution are also important. The possibility of a public distribution/handing over of income from tourism is one possible way of ensuring that the majority of the community sees the link between tourism and benefits.
- **Open, honest channels of communication.** Ongoing, regular communication is essential in these relationships to avoid misunderstandings, incorrect rumours, as well as for managing expectations.
- **Mitigation of human-wildlife conflict.** It is important not only to provide and increase the number of benefits, but also to mitigate the costs faced by communities in the area.
- **Education.** Higher education levels are correlated with increased incomes and more positive attitudes. It would, therefore, be advisable to promote and encourage education, through the introduction of scholarships, improved infrastructure and access to education.
- **Formal employment.** Formal employment of any kind positively impacts household incomes. The diversification of livelihoods could, therefore, assist in reducing poverty. It is important to note that there are few formal employment opportunities, other than tourism, in a number of remote, rural areas.

The main reasons for failure of partnerships include:

- internal community conflict;
- lack of transparent, accountable benefit-sharing;
- lack of communication – both internal and external;
- tourism decline, and therefore, reduced benefits.

There are many external factors which can impact on partnerships; it is, therefore, important to attempt to manage as many factors as possible to ensure a greater chance of success and sustainability.

## 5.11. Privately Owned Protected Areas

In privately owned PAs, the system of developing a new accommodation is far simpler. It can follow the same steps identified in 5.6 (community owned protected areas), but does not need the same level of community consultation, or establishment of community trusts. Ideally, the planning and development should follow best practice guidelines on sustainable construction (e.g. Mheta, Baez & O'Loughlin, 2002).

There are several internationally recognised sets of criteria, standards, indicators and certifications for sustainable tourism. Some of the tools that can be used by operational tourism concessionaires to improve sustainability include (Spenceley *et al.*, 2017):

- **Certification**: once operational, tourism businesses can apply to be independently certified as sustainable. The Global Sustainable Tourism Council (GSTC) recognises standards of certification bodies that are aligned with its criteria, and therefore credible processes.

- **Integrated reporting:** integrated reporting assists with thinking holistically and ensuring sustainability. Combining financial reporting with sustainability reporting allows companies to assess total impact and from there to assess risks, promote good practices and correct bad practices. Tourism concession contracts can stipulate reporting requirements to ensure that concessionaires integrate sustainability into their business and reporting. Tools for integrated reporting include the Global Reporting Initiative.

Where the land owner and tourism establishment owners are different, partnerships will be negotiated as above, with an establishment of objectives, contracts and reporting.

## 5.12. Retrofitting Existing Enterprises

Retrofitting existing tourism enterprises, so that they are more sustainable than originally conceived, is also a viable option. This is often required for older tourism businesses. Integrating some elements can be more costly and complex than others. For example, quick and easy interventions include improving environmental management systems, by installing water and energy-saving devices throughout an accommodation facility. More expensive options can include installation of renewable energy equipment (e.g. solar panel farms and battery banks) to remove the need for fossil fuel-based power.

In terms of community involvement, retrofitting existing models is also a possibility. The easiest options for improving community benefits from tourism are to improve the level of local employment (by preferentially employing local people) and local procurement (by preferentially sourcing products and services from local entrepreneurs and small business) (e.g. see Ashley and Haysom, 2008). More extensive changes to the institutional arrangements can also be made, to change the level of community ownership in a tourism enterprise. In order to provide communities with equity, large sums of money may be required for the community to purchase a share in an ongoing business (e.g. see Box 18). This may be provided by government or a donor agency, and is an unusual arrangement. Another option is described in Case Study 21 on Damaraland Camp, where the private sector operator gifted 20% of equity per annum to the community over a five-year period.

A more frequently observed adaptation is where a CBT owned and managed enterprise outsources the management role to the private sector. The community, or technical support agencies working with them, may realise that community members are struggling to create a commercially viable business – lacking the levels of business management, accounting skills and market linkages to generate profits. A tender process can be used to identify a private sector partner that has these capacities, and which may be able to transform a struggling community-based enterprise into a partnership that supports long-term job creation and decent wages for local people (see example in Box 19 and also Case Study 25 on !Xaus Lodge in this volume).

With all partnership options, whether government land, community land or privately owned land, there are processes to be followed to ensure a greater chance of success for the tourism operation. Communication throughout these processes is a critical aspect, as is the sharing of information and experience in order to maximise

**Box 17.** Retrofitting renewable energy equipment at Mombo Camp, Botswana

Mombo camp switched from diesel generators to 100% solar energy in May 2012, following a capital investment of approximately USD 860,000. The company predicted that during the 2014 financial year there would be a 93% (actual 92.2%) reduction in carbon emissions for Mombo because of the lack of generator emissions. This meant that the lodge would emit only 22 tonnes of carbon dioxide equivalents during the year, compared to an estimated 287 tonnes during the 2012 financial year (Wilderness Holdings, 2014).

**Box 18.** Evolving from private sector to community owned businesses: Phinda Private Game Reserve, South Africa (see Case Study 26)

The institutional structure at Phinda has evolved over time. In 1994, local communities in South Africa were legally empowered to reclaim ancestral lands that had been expropriated under apartheid. In 2002, the Mnqobokazi and Makhasa communities led their claims to land within the Phinda reserve. AndBeyond did not challenge the claim and received approximately USD 34.5 million from the South African government in compensation for the land and its infrastructure. In 2006, the titles to the territory and two of the six lodges located on it were transferred to the Mnqobokazi and Makhasa communities. When this transfer took place, both communities invited the company to continue its operations at Phinda. This resulted in andBeyond signing 36-year leases with each community, with an associated annual lease fee. AndBeyond has the option of renewing the partnership at the end of the 36-year period (Rylance and Spenceley, 2014).

**Box 19.** Outsourcing management of community-based tourism: Witsieshoek Mountain Lodge, South Africa (see Case Study 23)

Witsieshoek Mountain Lodge in South Africa was originally built in the 1970s as a state enterprise, on the site of a stone hut built for backpackers in the 1950s by former Batlokoa King Wessels Mota. The lodge was gradually handed over by the state to King Lekunutu Mota of the local Batlokoa community in the mid-1990s when it officially became a community asset. However, management challenges prompted the traditional council to enter into an agreement in 2010 with a private partner, Transfrontier Parks Destinations (TFPD), to operate the lodge management and marketing under a 25-year management contract (G. O'Leary, email, 2017, personal communication). Under the management contract, the community is entitled, in lieu of rental, to receive 17% of the profit generated by the lodge or a minimum annual payment from TFPD of USD 15,000. By June 2017, despite the lodge not yet having reached profitability, TFPD had contributed an estimated USD 36,000 to the community in lieu of rental (G. O'Leary, email, 2017, personal communication).

benefits and minimise and mitigate any negative impacts on the community and conservation.

## 5.13. Managing Tourism Development

Once the chosen land tenure and partnership model has been decided on and tourism has been developed, it is important to manage the tourism development sustainably. Table 66 provides a framework for tourism managers to manage a destination's tourism strategy.

## 5.14. Social Considerations

Telfer and Sharpley (2008) distinguish between social and cultural impacts. They define social impacts as the more immediate effects of tourism on local people and their lifestyles, and cultural impacts as longer-term changes occurring in the context of social values, attitudes and behaviours. Sociocultural changes are not necessarily always negative, as some local practices may themselves have been problematic. The focus in this volume is on social impacts. Social impacts can include empowerment, skills training and socioeconomic development, and can be both positive and negative. The case studies in this book show that the majority of private sector partnerships involve a dimension of social impacts that goes above and beyond simply benefits derived through local employment, skills training and development. Numerous private sector operators engage in philanthropic activities, either directly, through partnering with NGOs or through their guests, or a combination of these. Table 67 presents a range of social and cultural issues to consider with different institutional models.

**Table 66.** A framework for managing tourism.

| Framework | Tools |
|---|---|
| Managing stakeholder engagement to develop ownership in the tourism strategy | Ensuring adequate planning, design and location for tourism development, which is cognisant of the impacts on the local environment, local communities and resource use<br>Providing trust, space, time and an enabling business environment for innovation by the private sector<br>Research into the strengths and weaknesses of the destination in terms of developing a competitive advantage; integration of these results into the tourism's destination strategy<br>Research into the available goods, services and skills available locally; integration of these results into the design of the tourism product<br>Use of tourism consultants in the research and initial tourism development phases |
| Ensure an enabling, supportive regulatory environment for tourism investment, development and growth | Development of enabling policies, that are based on sound research and participatory development processes<br>Development of appropriate instruments and programmes to implement and regulate these policies consistently (e.g. focusing on yield, rather than tourism numbers)<br>Simplifying and supporting the development and operation of business through suitable licensing and regulatory environments<br>Vigorously tackling local and national corruption and poor governance by providing transparent and equitable solutions<br>Targeted capital infrastructure development to support tourism-related demand, and simultaneously enhancing the destination for residents through improved facilities for health care, education, transport and sanitation<br>Creating incentive and taxation instruments that support, rather than punish, commercial success |
| Ensure needed capacity and skills for servicing tourists exist | Recognising that the people living in tourism destinations are an integral part of the asset<br>Adopting participatory processes for planning and decision-making with local people<br>Providing mechanisms to ensure living, or minimum wages, across the tourism sector, in partnership with the private sector<br>Providing access to information and technical assistance to support tourism development<br>Providing access to vocational training for local people in hospitality and tourism, as well as business skills<br>Protecting the rights of workers to safe and healthy working conditions<br>Using tourism to conserve, rehabilitate and reinvigorate cultural and natural heritage and traditions<br>Skills training and workshops to increase human capital and empower local communities to manage and operate tourism in their destinations. |
| Develop and sustain a competitive advantage | Promoting value for money in tourism products and destinations, coupled with high quality service and experiences (i.e. creating a competitive advantage)<br>Establishing strong market linkages between the destination and source markets and encouraging investment in marketing and promotion<br>Promoting strong local value chains, so that local businesses can overcome barriers to engaging in tourism markets, and sell their goods and services to the tourism sector<br>Tackling and resolving conflicts as they arise, and trying to find win–win solutions<br>Avoiding negative environmental impacts where possible and mitigating damage when it occurs |

**Table 66.**

| Framework | Tools |
|---|---|
| Maintain regular and continuous monitoring and evaluation | Monitoring and evaluation of the impact of tourism, as well as other relevant policies, and providing mechanisms for feedback and adaptation<br>Monitoring and evaluating the economic and financial returns to society and local people<br>Regular appraisals of tourism development, particularly related to the destination's specific goals for tourism development<br>Assessment of whether or not the outcomes of tourism development are in line with those originally proposed<br>Adjustments to the tourism development strategy based on appraisals and assessments |

Source: adapted from Snyman (2015)

**Table 67.** Potential social and cultural issues for different institutional models.

| Community Characteristics | Pure private sector | Public–private partnership (PPP) | JV | Community-based tourism |
|---|---|---|---|---|
| **Community size** | Any size community | Any size community | Small communities | Any size community |
| **Ethnicity** | Different ethnicities | Different ethnicities | Similar ethnicity | Similar ethnicity |
| **Cohesiveness (minimal internal conflict)** | Cohesiveness not a necessity | Requires medium cohesiveness | Requires strong cohesiveness | Requires strong cohesiveness |
| **Community governance** | Good governance not essential | Good governance | Very good governance | Very good governance |
| **Support institutions** | Not required, unless there is conflict | Not required, unless there is conflict | Preferable | Required |
| **Education** | Not critical | Not critical | Preferably good | Preferably good |
| **Proximity to natural resources** | Not critical | Not critical | Preferably close | Preferably close |
| **Infrastructure** | Preferably good access and communication | Preferably good access and communication | Preferably good access and communication | Preferably good access and communication |
| **Desire for ecotourism** | Required | Required | Required | Required |
| **Leadership** | Strong leadership not essential, but preferable | Strong leadership not essential, but preferable | Strong community leadership required | Strong community leadership required |
| **Investment capital** | Not required | Not required | Required in some cases | Required in most cases |
| **Tourism knowledge and experience** | Not required, but preferable | Not required, but preferable | Preferable | Required, though can be advised |
| **Business skills/ acumen** | Not required | Not required | Preferable | Preferable |
| **HWC** | Low | Low | Medium to high | Medium to high |

Source: Snyman (2013)

## 5.15. Summary

This section has reviewed the processes to develop tourism accommodation partnerships in protected areas, whether they are in government owned or on community and privately owned land. Step-by-step processes have been elaborated, building on the knowledge previously developed by the authors, to provide guidance for future initiatives. This has included practical information on how to retrofit existing institutional structures to make them more sustainable. The next chapter provides a synthesis of best practices, and lessons learned from all the case studies in this book.

## 5.16. References

Ashley, C., Boyd, C. & Goodwin, H. (2000). Pro-poor tourism: putting poverty at the heart of the tourism agenda. ODI Natural Resource Perspectives, No. 51. Retrieved May, 3, 2013 from http://www.odi.org.uk/publications/2096-pro-poor-tourism-putting-poverty-at-heart-tourism-agenda.

Ashley, C. & Haysom, G. (2008) The development impacts of tourism supply chains: increasing impact on poverty and decreasing our ignorance. In Spenceley, A. (ed.) *Responsible tourism: critical issues for conservation and development* (pp. 129–156). Earthscan, London.

Ashley, C., Mitchell, J. & Spenceley, A. (2009) *How to assess the potential of a viable inclusive tourism intervention? Opportunity study guidelines*. Available at http://www.intracen.org/uploadedFiles/intracenorg/Content/Exporters/Sectoral_Information/Service_Exports/Tourism/Opportunity%20Studies%20Guidelines%20TPRP.pdf (accessed 14 September 2017).

Asker, S., Boronyak, L., Carrard, N. & Paddon, M. (2010) *Effective community based tourism: a best practice manual*. Griffith University, Gold Coast.

Casimiro, R. & Spenceley, A. (2012) *Tourism concessions in protected areas in Mozambique: manual for the private sector*, report USAID SPEED, 19 April 2012.

Eagles, P.F.J., Baycetich, C.M., Chen, X., Dong, L., Halpenny, E., Kwan, P.A., Lenuzzi, J.J., Wang, X., Xiao, H. & Zhang, Y. (2009) *Guidelines for planning and management of concessions, licenses and permits for tourism in protected areas.* Tourism Planning and Management Program, University of Waterloo, Waterloo, Ontario, Canada.

Government of Zambia (2016) *Guidelines and checklist in designing public private partnership (PPP) projects for wildlife conservation*. Government of Zambia, Lusaka.

GTZ (German Technical Cooperation) (2007) *Value links manual: The methodology of value chain promotion*, 1st edn. GTZ, Eschborn.

IFC (2007) *Stakeholder engagement: a good practice handbook for companies doing business in emerging markets*. IFC, Washington, DC.

Investment Climate Advisory Services (2012) *Facilitating large-scale tourism resorts in Mozambique: the tourism investment generation approach*. World Bank Group, Washington, DC.

Legovini, A. (2010) *Development Impact Evaluation Initiative: a World Bank-wide strategic approach to enhance developmental effectiveness*. World Bank, Washington, DC. Available at http://documents.worldbank.org/curated/en/689141468161083406/pdf/633220WP0DIME000Box0361513B0PUBLIC0.pdf (accessed 17 September 2018).

Lee, T. & Middleton, J. (2008) *Guidelines for management planning of protected areas*. Best Practice Protected Area Guidelines. IUCN, Cardiff.

Massyn, P.J. (2008) *Madikwe community lodges, Thakadu River Camp, Buffalo Ridge Safari Lodge*. The African Safari Lodge Foundation, Johannesburg.

Mheta, H., Baez, A.L & O'Loughlin, P. (2002) *International ecolodge guidelines*. The International Ecotourism Society, World Tourism Organization, Madrid.

National Treasury (2004) *South African public private partnership manual: National Treasury PPP practice notes issued in terms of the Public Finance Management Act: Module 1*. Available at http://www.ppp.gov.za/Legal%20Aspects/PPP%20Manual/Module%2001.pdf (accessed 17 September 2018).

Republic of South Africa (2015) *Framework for community based tourism*. Republic of South Africa, Johannesburg.

Rogerson, C. (2012) Tourism-agriculture linkages in rural South Africa: evidence from the accommodation sector. Journal of Sustainable Tourism, 20(3), 477–495.
Rozga, Z. & Spenceley, A. (2006) *Welcome to the community based tourism market access program.* UNWTO, RETOSA, September 2006.
Rylance, A. & Spenceley, A. (2016) Applying inclusive business approaches to nature-based tourism in Namibia and South Africa. Tourism: An International Interdisciplinary Journal, 64(4), 371–383.
Snyman, S. (2013) *High-end ecotourism and rural communities in southern Africa: a socioeconomic analysis*. Unpublished PhD thesis, University of Cape Town, South Africa.
Snyman, S. (2015) Strategic community participation in sustainable tourism. In McCool, S. & Bosak, K. (eds) *Reframing sustainable tourism*. Springerlink (pp. 65–80), doi: 10.1007/978-94-017-7209-9.
Spenceley, A. (2004) Responsible nature-based tourism planning in South Africa and the commercialization of Kruger National Park. In Diamantis, D. (ed.) *Ecotourism: management and assessment* (pp. 267–280). Thomson Learning, London.
Spenceley, A. (2014) *Tourism concession guidelines for transfrontier conservation areas in SADC*. Report to GIZ / SADC. Available at https://tfcaportal.org/sites/default/files/public-docs/tourism_concession_guidelines_sadc_tfcas_final.pdf (accessed 3 January 2009).
Spenceley, A. & Meyer, D. (2016) Tourism and poverty reduction: principles and impacts in developing countries. In Spenceley, A. & Meyer, D. (eds) Tourism and poverty reduction: principles and impacts in developing countries (pp. 1–23). Routledge, London and New York.
Spenceley, A, Habyalimana, S, Tusabe, R & Mariza, D. (2010) Benefits to the poor from gorilla tourism in Rwanda. Development Southern Africa, 27(5), 647–78.
Spenceley, A., Nevill, H., Coelho, C. F. & Souto, M. (2016a) *An introduction to tourism concessioning: 14 characteristics of successful programs*. World Bank Group. Available at http://documents.worldbank.org/curated/en/459431467995814879/An-introduction-to-tourism-concessioning-14-characteristics-of-successful-programs (accessed 23 June 2018).
Spenceley, A., Rylance, A., Nanabhay, S. & van der Watt, H. (2016b) *Operational guidelines for community based tourism in South Africa*. Department of Tourism, Republic of South Africa.
Spenceley, A., Snyman, S. & Eagles, P.F.J. (2017) *Guidelines for tourism partnerships and concessions for protected areas: generating sustainable revenues for conservation and development*. Report to the Convention on Biological Diversity and IUCN. Available at https://www.cbd.int/tourism/doc/tourism-partnerships-protected-areas-web.pdf (accessed 22 June 2018).
Telfer, D.J. & Sharpley, R. (2008) *Tourism and development in the developing world*. Routledge, USA and Canada.
Thompson, A., Massyn, P.J., Pendry, J. & Pastorelli, J. (2014) *Tourism concessions in protected natural areas: guidelines for managers. United Nations Development Program*. Available at http://www.undp.org/content/undp/en/home/librarypage/environment-energy/ecosystems_and_biodiversity/tourism-concessions-in-protected-natural-areas.html (accessed 22 June 2018).
UNWTO & SNV (World Tourism Organization and Netherlands Development Organization). (2010) Manual on Tourism and Poverty Alleviation. Madrid and The Hague: UNWTO/SNV
Varghese, G. (2008) Public private partnerships in South African National Parks. In Spenceley, A. (ed.) *Responsible tourism: critical issues for conservation and development* (pp. 69–84). Earthscan, UK.
Walton, A., Gomei, M. & Di Carlo, G. (2013) *Stakeholder engagement: participatory approaches for the planning and development of marine protected areas*. World Wide Fund for Nature and NOAA – National Marine Sanctuary Program. Available at http://awsassets.panda.org/downloads/stakeholder_engagement.pdf (accessed 23 June 2018).
Whyte, R., Perrottet, J., Di Fiori, V. & Nevill, H. (2013) *Global investment promotion best practices: winning tourism investment*. World Bank, Washington, DC. Available at https://openknowledge.worldbank.org/handle/10986/20766 (accessed 23 June 2018).
Wilderness Holdings (2014) Integrated annual report for the year ended 28 February 2014. Wilderness Holdings, South Africa and Botswana.
WWF (World Wide Fund for Nature) (2014) *Getting financed: 9 tips for community joint ventures in tourism*. World Bank Group, Washington, DC.

# 6

# Best Practices: Lessons Learned from the Case Studies

The 32 case studies in this volume demonstrate the rich array of approaches used to pursue sustainable tourism adopted by the private sector in protected areas (PAs) across Africa. This chapter aims to synthesise and highlight the best practices achieved and the lessons learned, and also to review the types of challenge faced. The synthesis addresses six themes: (i) institutional issues; (ii) economic issues; (iii) environmental issues; (iv) social considerations; (v) the successes and challenges of different models; and (vi) lessons learned.

## 6.1. Institutional Issues

This volume explored two main institutional models: private ownership and joint ownership (see Figure 13). A range of different institutional arrangements have been illustrated by the case studies, as were implications for benefit-sharing and sources of finance used.

### 6.1.1. Business models and institutional arrangements

Private tourism lodge facilities and management operations may be run by companies for profit, or by non-governmental organisations (NGOs) as not-for profit vehicles.

Table 68 summarises the institutional arrangements (i.e. ownership, management and land ownership) explored in the case studies for private business models. Some of the institutional arrangements are quite simple (e.g. a single company that owns and manages a lodge, based on leased private or government land such as Wolwedans, Simien Lodge, Bale Mountain Lodge, Wilderness Safaris' Hwange Camps). Others are more complex and include private sector joint venture partnerships (e.g. Bisate Lodge), or public–private partnerships (PPPs) (e.g. Ruzizi). Such partnerships can be useful in order to spread financial risk, and also to benefit from the different strengths of each collaborating partner. Some of the lodge owning and operating companies have arisen from higher-level agreements for the conservation managers of the PA in which the lodge is based (e.g. King Lewanika Lodge, Chumbe Island, Mkulumadzi). The latter arrangement is particularly noteworthy, as it illustrates how tourism investment is being used as an integral part of an overall business and revenue generation model by institutions holding co-management agreements with governments or protected area authorities (PAAs).

Table 69 summarises the institutional arrangements explored in the community–joint venture (JV) case studies. There is complexity in some of the institutional arrangements, particularly with operations in South Africa after a land restitution case and there are different owners of

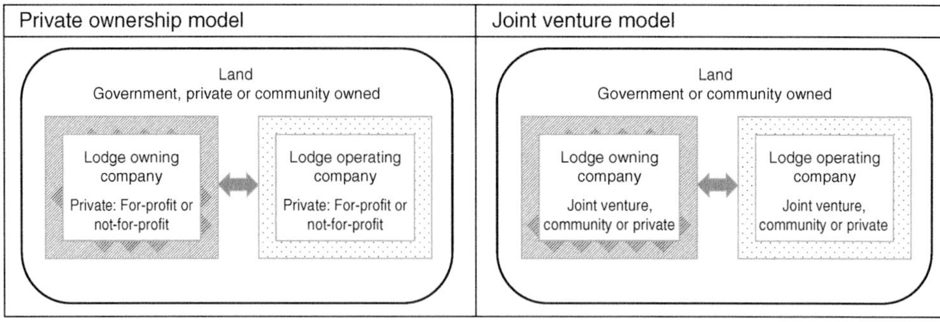


**Fig. 13.** Private and joint-venture ownership models.

**Box 20.** African Parks

African Parks (AP) is a non-profit conservation organisation that takes on direct responsibility for the rehabilitation and long-term management of PAs in partnership with governments and local communities. AP is funded through donor support, gross park income and endowment income.

Founded in 2000 in response to the dramatic decline of PAs due to poor management and lack of funding, AP utilises a business approach to conserving Africa's wildlife and remaining wild areas. While securing vast landscapes and carrying out all activities needed to protect the parks and their wildlife, AP maintains a strong focus on economic development and poverty alleviation of surrounding communities to ensure that each park is ecologically, socially and financially sustainable for the long term. The five key pillars of its model are: law enforcement; management and infrastructure; biodiversity conservation; community development; and economic impact.

Central to its PPP models is the separation of responsibilities between the government and AP. The government is the owner of the park and is responsible for legislation and policy. AP is responsible for the execution of management functions and is accountable to the government for performance. AP also establishes partnerships with private sector tourism operators to promote economic development. In 2018 it managed 14 national parks and PAs covering 10.5 million hectares in nine countries: Benin, Central African Republic, Chad, the Democratic Republic of Congo, Malawi, Mozambique, the Republic of Congo, Rwanda and Zambia.

Source: Adapted from African Parks (2018)
https://www.african-parks.org/about-us/our-story/the-african-parks-model

the land, lodge and management company (e.g. Phinda, Pafuri Camp, Rocktail Camp). There are interesting instances where governments provided land tenure to communities, and they, in turn, have developed a partnership with the private sector to operate the facilities (e.g. Ndzou Camp, Anvil Bay, Vumbura, Thawale). Similarly, a number of community owned lodges have established agreements with private management companies (e.g. !Xaus, Witsieshoek, Covane Lodge, Serra Cafema, Satao Elerai). The commercial success of these case studies illustrates the strength of models whereby communities can create commercially viable operations by either leasing the land and lodge management to a private operator, or by forming a JV partnership with them.

The case studies in this book highlight the complex diversity of potential partnership models and, therefore, institutional models: no one size fits all! Governance can include a diversity of stakeholders, including the private sector, government, communities and/or NGOs, and various combinations of these, with varying benefit-sharing and empowerment models available. The importance of stable government institutions and policy was also highlighted in terms of private sector confidence in investing in a product. It has been shown that consultation should be widespread, engaging all relevant stakeholders; it should be ongoing and regular and should, as far as possible, address the concerns of all relevant stakeholders.

**Table 68.** Private business model case studies.

| Business model | Case study examples |
|---|---|
| 1. For-profit private sector on private land | **Bisate Lodge, Rwanda:** privately owned by a company called Imizi Ecotourism Ltd, Imizi is co-owned by Wilderness Holdings (90%) and Thousand Hills Africa (10%), a local inbound tour operator and ground handler. Wilderness Safaris (WS) operates, manages and markets the lodge.<br>**Wolwedans, Namibia:** privately owned by an individual, and managed by NamibRand Safaris (Pty) Ltd. It is located on the privately owned NamibRand Nature Reserve. |
| 2. For-profit private sector on government land | **Mombo Camps, Botswana:** privately owned by Okavango Wilderness Safaris (OWS) Lodges (Pty) Ltd. Marketed and managed by OWS (Pty) Ltd. The infrastructure is privately owned and based on government land with a 15-year concession lease agreement.<br>**Nkwichi Lodge, Mozambique:** company and infrastructure privately owned by five shareholders, and privately managed. Based on government land with a 50-year concession.<br>**WS Hwange Camps, Zimbabwe:** privately owned and managed by WS. Based on land owned by government, with a 25-year lease from Zimbabwe Parks and Wildlife Management Authority.<br>**Simien Lodge, Ethiopia:** private ownership and management, based on government land with a 50-year lease agreement.<br>**Chumbe Island, Tanzania:** owned and managed by Chumbe Island Coral Park Limited (CHICOP). The company established and manages the Chumbe Island Marine PA in which it is based. The land is owned by the government. |
| 3. Private sector (for- or not-for-profit) on government or NGO land | **Mkulumadzi Lodge, Malawi:** AP Majete Ltd (APM) privately owns Mkulumadzi Lodge in the government-owned Majete Wildlife Reserve. APM has an agreement with the Department of National Parks and Wildlife (DNPW) to manage and develop the reserve. The management of the lodge is outsourced by APM to a private operator, Robin Pope Safaris.<br>**Thawale Lodge, Malawi:** owned and managed by APM, which has a board with representatives from AP, the DNPW and local businesses. APM has a 25-year agreement to manage the reserve. A private operator, Sunbird, manages the lodge for APM in return for a fee.<br>**Bale Mountain Lodge, Ethiopia:** owned and operated by a private sector company called Jember Ltd. The land in Bale Mountain National Park is leased from the Ethiopian Wildlife Conservation Authority (EWCA).<br>**Ngala, South Africa:** privately owned by WWF-SA, an NGO. The private company andBeyond has a 20-year lease to manage the lodge and traverse the land. Traversing fees and a percentage of profits flow into the South African National Parks (SANParks) Trust, an NGO, for use in expanding or adding to conservation areas. The land, in Kempiana Contractual National Park, is managed as part of the wider Kruger National Park (KNP).<br>**King Lewanika Lodge, Zambia:** owned and managed by African Parks Zambia Ltd (APZ). APZ has a 20-year agreement for management of the Liuwa Plain National Park. This arrangement emanated from a previous agreement between the then Zambian Wildlife Authority (ZAWA) (now the DNPW), the Barotse Royal Establishment (BRE), and the African Parks Network. |
| 4. PPP on government land | **Ruzizi Tented Lodge, Rwanda:** owned and operated by Akagera Management Company (AMC), a Rwandan registered for-profit company. AMC is a PPP, with AP holding 51% of the shares and Rwanda Development Board (RDB) 49% of the shares. |

**Table 68.**

| Business model | Case study examples |
|---|---|
| 5. Private joint venture partnership on government land | **Singita Lebombo, South Africa:** a joint venture of three private entities – Singita Lebombo Investment Holdings (73.6%), KNP Staff Trust (19.8%) and Pfukani Ecotours (Pty) Ltd (6.6%). The lodge is based in KNP, under a 20-year concession agreement with SANParks. |
| 6. Voluntary payments to communities | **Singita Community Development Trust, Wilderness Wildlife Trust (WWT) and Children in the Wilderness (CITW) Africa Foundation:** not-for-profit organisations. These are linked, but institutionally independent of private sector companies working in wildlife tourism. |

**Table 69.** Community JV business model case studies.

| Business model | Case study examples |
|---|---|
| 1. JV lodge ownership, on government land | **Ndzou camp, Mozambique:** a joint venture between Kubatana Moribane, a local community association (60%) and the Mozambican private company Eco-Micaia Lda (40%). Eco-Micaia has a 10-year management agreement with the JV for the management of the lodge. The land is owned by the government, and the community has a special licence to develop the land for tourism.<br>**Anvil Bay, Mozambique:** owned and managed by the Chemucane Tourism Company (CTC), which is a joint venture company of the Ahi Zameni Chemucane Association (AZC) (40% ownership) and an NGO, the Bell Foundation (60%). The community was awarded a special licence (permission to develop and operate) for 50 years by the government.<br>**Vumbura and Little Vumbura Camps, Botswana:** the lodge is managed by a private operator under a 15-year lease from a community trust, the Okavango Community Trust (OCT). The OCT, in turn, has a lease from the government to administer and oversee management of the concession area. |
| 2. JV lodge ownership on community land | **Damaraland Camp, Namibia:** owned and operated by the Namib Lodge Company (Pty) Ltd. This is a JV partnership between the Torra Conservancy (40% shareholding) and WS (60% shareholding). The Namib Lodge Company has a 10-year lease with the Torra Conservancy to manage the lodge.<br>**Doro Nawas Camp, Namibia:** owned and operated as a JV between the Doro !Nawas Conservancy (45% shareholding) and WS (55% shareholding). The company is located on land owned by the Doro !Nawas Conservancy, and the JV pays a monthly lease fee to the conservancy to use the land. |
| 3. Community owned lodge on government land, with a private or JV management company | **Witsieshoek, South Africa**: owned by the Batloka community, and managed by the private company TFPD under a 25-year management agreement.<br>**Covane Community Lodge, Mozambique:** owned by the Canhane community, and managed by the private company, Scholtz Consultoria e Serviços Lda, under a seven-year management contract. The community has a DUAT, which gives them permission to develop and operate on government land |
| 4. Community or privately owned lodge on community land | **Serra Cafema, Namibia:** Marienfluss Conservancy has conditional use rights to wildlife and tourism on the land, awarded by the state. Camp owned and operated by WS and has a 10-year lease with the conservancy<br>**Phinda, South Africa:** lodges owned by the Qhubekani Mnqobokazi and Makhasa Community Trusts. Land in the reserve owned by the Qhubekani Mnqobokazi Community Trust (21%), the Makhasa Community Trust (26%) and andBeyond (14%), with additional traversing rights to other private land (40%). Community land leased by andBeyond for environmental management and tourism, with agreements for 26–72-year leases for different parcels of land. |

**Table 69.**

| Business model | Case study examples |
|---|---|
| | **Pafuri Camp, South Africa:** land and lodge owned by the Makuleke Communal Property Association. Lodge operating company owned through a JV by Return Africa (75%) and the Makuleke CPA (25%).<br>**Satao Elerai, Kenya:** privately owned lodge on land leased from the Satao Elerai Community Wildlife Trust. The trust represents eight families and an NGO member.<br>**Sabyinyo Silverback Lodge, Rwanda:** community owned lodge on community land. Management agreement between the Sabyinyo Community Livelihoods Association (SACOLA) and Governors' Camp, a private operator.<br>**!Xaus, South Africa:** community owned lodge, managed by a JV between the ‡Khomani San and Mier Community Trust (17% shareholding) and the private company Transfrontier Parks Destinations (TFPD) (83%). Community owned land leased by the ‡Khomani San and Mier communities to SANParks for its environmental management, under a 99-year agreement. |
| 5. Tripartite model | **Rocktail Camp, South Africa:** Owners of the lodge are WS (72.5%), the KwaMpukane Community Trust (17.5%) and a black economic empowerment (BEE) partner (10%). WS has a 20-year lease from the iSimangaliso Wetland Park Authority. |

### 6.1.2. Financing partnerships

There are a number of diverse ways to secure investment capital, though the financing of tourism investments can be a big challenge. One of the major reasons for engaging the private sector is due to their ability to finance capital. As tourism is seen as a high-impact sector in most African countries, it can be among a donor's list of options to promote both conservation and sustainable development. All investors, banks and commercial lenders need to be confident that they are investing in or lending to a potentially sound, financially viable business (Spenceley *et al.*, 2017). Generally, they are concerned about mechanisms for injecting capital, mechanisms for the return of their capital, and dividends and interest payments. Equity investors are particularly concerned about protection for their investment and how they will be able to exit at the end of the investment period. Banks are especially focused on the adequacy of the project's cashflow to service debt obligations and the securities the borrower can provide. They also want to know that the project concept and business plan is sound, well researched and in line with market assumptions (World Bank Group, 2014).

The case studies demonstrate that grants from donors and governments have been the main source of investment finance for community equity in lodges. In some instances these are grants (e.g. Ndzou Camp, Covane Lodge, Mozambique), and in some instances they include low-interest loans (e.g. Anvil Bay, Mozambique). In the case of loans, the responsibility for repayments tends to fall on the private sector rather than the community partner, because the communities do not have capital to make repayments.

## 6.2. Economic Considerations

Over the past 50 years there has been considerable work and debate over the linkages between tourism and poverty reduction (see review in Spenceley & Meyer, 2012). In the 1960s and 1970s, it was understood that contributions towards development and poverty reduction 'trickled down' to generate jobs and foreign exchange earnings (Scheyvens, 2011). By the 1980s and 1990s, there was a new emphasis suggesting that unless major structural reforms of the tourism industry took place, the sector was unlikely to aid poverty reduction or reduce inequality (e.g. Britton, 1982; de Kadt, 1979; Wilkinson, 1987). Tourism was seen as a potential mechanism for impoverished and indebted countries to trade their way out of poverty (Brohman, 1996).

Bennett, Roe and Ashley (1999) proposed that the tourism sector had the potential to contribute to poverty reduction in developing countries because:

- the market comes to the producers, thus providing additional sales opportunities in the destination;
- tourism takes place in marginal areas, areas where the majority of the poor live (such as adjacent to PAs);
- tourism is generally labour intensive (although often less so than agriculture);
- intersectoral linkages can be created, especially with agriculture, artisan production and additional services, which are essential for livelihood diversification;
- tourism generally employs a high proportion of women, young people and unskilled or less-skilled individuals; a high percentage of the poorest in society fall into these categories;
- tourism has rather limited barriers to entry when compared with manufacturing or other export activities.

Research fields emerged on community-based tourism (CBT) (Spenceley, 2008; Stone & Stone, 2011; Wearing & McDonald, 2002); pro-poor tourism (Ashley, Roe & Goodwin, 2001; Hall, 2007), inclusive tourism (Mitchell and Ashley, 2010; Rylance and Spenceley, 2016; Tewes-Gradl, van Gaalen & Pirzer, 2014) and value chain analysis (VCA) (Ashley & Haysom, 2008; Ashley, Mitchell & Spenceley, 2009; Torres, 2002; Torres & Momsen, 2004), which have tourism-poverty reduction linkages (see Table 71).

Research suggests that tourism can contribute to employment and income generation (Ashley & Mitchell, 2007), gender equality (Scheyvens, 2002), education and knowledge exchange (Ashley, Roe, & Goodwin, 2001), intersectoral linkages (Belisle, 1983, 1984; Meyer, 2007; Torres, 2002), entrepreneurship and small-, medium- and micro-enterprise (SMME) development (Kirsten & Rogerson, 2002) as well as nature conservation (Saarinen, 2009; Spenceley, 2008). However, studies have warned that tourism could increase inequalities (Scheyvens, 2002, 2007), lead to the displacement of communities (Akama, 1996, 2004; Mowforth & Munt, 2009) and contribute to conflict over scarce resources (Mbaiwa & Darkoh, 2009).

The sections below examine economic impacts through reviewing the findings of our case studies, in relation to lease payments paid to communities and local employment.

### 6.2.1. Lease fee payments to communities

Among the case studies collated in this book, 16 provided data on their lease fees paid in 2017. Eight of these paid lease fees to government (or government's PAA), and collectively paid USD 2.3 million per year, with an average of USD 258,444 per annum. By comparison, eight enterprises with community leases reported average lease fees of USD 139,277 per year, and collectively they paid USD 1.1 million to their hosts (see Table 72). The contrast between the value achieved by government and community leases is stark. Two of the government lease values (Mombo Camps and Singita Lebombo) were established through a competitive bidding process as part of a tender. The community payment values are more often established through a negotiated process, sometimes brokered by an independent NGO (e.g. Covane Community Lodge, Phinda). It is interesting to ask whether community landlords might achieve higher lease fees if more of them used a competitive tender process when seeking private sector partners, or whether higher prices paid for government concessions are also a factor of better facilities or service provision.

The enterprises had different approaches to calculating the lease fees paid. These might include a fixed annual lease fee or one related to a percentage of turnover, conservation fee per visitor and bednight fees (see Table 73). While fixed fees are easy to administer, they may not be market-related, and may be inflexible and difficult to change (particularly if established by government regulations, as in Mozambique). By contrast, fees that relate to turnover or the number of clients (i.e. bednight fees) are more directly related to the success of the enterprise but require transparent reporting and audits to administer and verify.

## 6.3. Social Considerations

In relation to social considerations, the case studies looked at local employment, local procurement of goods and services, donations to community development projects and philanthropy in general. Despite there frequently being issues related to the quality and quantity of

**Table 70.** Funding sources for tourism partnerships in PAs.

| Source of finance | Description | Accessibility | Examples |
|---|---|---|---|
| Development banks or aid agencies | Investment grants; concessionary loan finance; training grants and incentives; marketing support | Private sector (for profit) | **World Bank:** community equity financed in both Ndzou Camp and Anvil Bay (Mozambique: USD 500,000 grant) through a community enterprise fund, as part of a broader Government of Mozambique and World Bank project. Grant funding of USD 140,000 to Covane Lodge for renovations.<br>**USAID:** initial finance for Covane Lodge, part-financed (USD 50,000). |
| | Finance for basic infrastructure, including roads, electrical distribution and water supply, and sometimes capital for tourism infrastructure, such as visitor centres, shops and lodges | Government and PA authorities | **International Finance Corporation (IFC)** (e.g. South Africa, Lesotho, Mozambique, Madagascar)<br>**World Bank** (e.g. Mozambique)<br>**African Development Bank** (e.g. Zambia) |
| Impact investment vehicles | Provide investment financing where there is potential for significant conservation and socioeconomic impact | Small- and medium-sized enterprises | **African Wildlife Capital (AWC):** USD 2 million was invested to develop the first two ecolodges in Ethiopia's national PA system: Bale Mountain Lodge and Limalimo Lodge. Both lodges received in excess of USD 800,000 in financing from AWC. |
| NGOs | Grants or loans brokered by NGOs for capital investment, for equity in a partnership | Communities | **AP:** provided funding to build King Lewanika (Zambia) and Thawale Lodge (Malawi).<br>**African Wildlife Foundation (AWF):** provided grants to Sabyinyo Lodge (Rwanda) and Satao Elerai (Kenya).<br>**Africa Safari Foundation (ASF):** provided a grant to establish Anvil Bay (Mozambique), Etendeka Mountain Camp (Namibia) and Thakadu River Camp (South Africa).<br>**Ford Foundation:** provided a USD 500,000 grant to Anvil Bay (Mozambique).<br>**Helvetas:** Provided a USD 20,000 towards the development of Covane Lodge (Mozambique). |
| Government grants | Grants for community infrastructure | Communities | Community land ownership and lodge equity financed through a USD 34.5 million land restitution claim at Phinda (South Africa). |
| Private investment | | Private sector (for profit) | **Bell Foundation:** the foundation's 60% equity in Anvil Bay (Mozambique) was financed by USD 2 million of private investment.<br>**WS:** private finance for infrastructure development of Damaraland Camp and Doro Nawas (Namibia). |

Source: Adapted from Spenceley *et al.* (2017); African Wildlife Foundation: http://www.awf.org/blog/building-conservation-tourism-ethiopia (accessed 14 April 2017)

**Table 71.** Themes in tourism focusing on poverty reduction.

| Terminology | Description | Reference |
|---|---|---|
| Community-based tourism | A tourism business or activity that is located within a community, it may either be privately owned or managed or operated with the involvement of the local community members. It should be able to create community linkages and adhere to responsible tourism practices that take environmental, social and cultural sustainability into account. | Spenceley *et al.* (2016) |
| Pro-poor tourism | Tourism that generates net benefits for the poor and aims to ensure that tourism growth contributes to poverty reduction. | Ashley *et al.* (2001) |
| Inclusive tourism | Transformative tourism in which marginalised groups are engaged in ethical production or consumption of tourism and the sharing of its benefits. | Scheyvens and Biddulph (2017) |
| Value chain analysis | Evaluation of a sequence of related business activities from the provision of specific inputs for a particular product to primary production, transformation, marketing and up to the final sale of the particular product to consumers. | German Technical Cooperation (2007) |

**Table 72.** Lease fees paid by accommodation in PAs, 2017.

| Payment of lease fee (and sample size) | Min. lease | Max. lease | Average | Total p/a |
|---|---|---|---|---|
| Lease fee paid to government (*n*=9) | 1,440 | 721,066 | 258,444 | 2,325,994 |
| Lease fee paid to community (*n*=8) | 3,000 | 356,000 | 139,277 | 1,114,218 |

community goods and services, the private sector operators examined were attempting to procure locally as much as possible, many with plans to increase this over time. Philanthropy and company donations to community social development projects were shown to be considerable. This can have an extensive multiplier effect, impacting many more people beyond those employed in tourism. Below is a summary of the case study data related to social considerations.

### 6.3.1. Local employment

Altogether, the 26 enterprises reporting their employment figures employed 1,683 people, and at least 1,295 were people from local communities (i.e. 77%: 1 enterprise did not report the number of local staff). Salary information was also provided by 20 operations. Their data implies an average salary of USD 1,047 per month, and that collectively the 20 tourism businesses spent USD 16.3 million in 2017 on wages for local people (see Table 74). This is a substantial amount of money reaching members of communities each month. For example, the luxury 52-bed lodge, Pafuri Camp in South Africa, employs around 52 permanent staff members, and 94% of them (including the senior management staff) are from the Makuleke community. Employees from the community receive approximately USD 298,000 in wages and related benefits annually, collectively. Return Africa also hires people locally for a variety of services including staff transport, guest transfers and infrastructure maintenance (see Case Study 30).

By contrast, Ndzou Lodge in Mozambique, a budget standard enterprise, employs six full-time and three to five part-time people, all of whom are from the local community. The average wage is about USD 100 per month, which is above the government's minimum wage of Mozambican Metical (MZN or MT) – MZN 5,328 per month (USD 86) (see Case Study 20).

Some of the enterprises demonstrate substantial contribution to the empowerment of their staff. For example, one of !Xaus Lodge's cleaning staff joined the lodge soon after it opened. Melissa Mienies developed a special interest in guiding and, supported by the lodge managers, self-taught herself key information. !Xaus Lodge supported her (and three other guides) on a distance learning course, and she

**Table 73.** Lease fee payment arrangements.

| Business model | Case study examples |
|---|---|
| 1. JV lodge ownership, on government land | **Ndzou camp, Mozambique:** a community levy of USD 0.71 per bednight is paid to Kubatana Moribane, the community association. There are plans to increase this to USD 2 per rondavel, and USD 3 per family house occupied.<br>**Anvil Bay, Mozambique:** lease fee of USD 30,000 per year (to cover land fees and tariffs), plus 2.5% of turnover (a guaranteed amount of USD 15,600 per year, and a bed levy of USD 6 per person per night is paid to the community association, Ahi Zameni Chemucane).<br>**Vumbura and Little Vumbura Camps, Botswana:** annual lease paid to Okavango Community Trust escalates by 5% per year. |
| 2. JV lodge ownership, on community land | **Damaraland Camp, Namibia:** lease fee paid to Torra Conservancy of 10% of turnover.<br>**Doro Nawas Camp, Namibia:** lease fee paid to Doro !Nawas Conservancy of 9% of turnover. |
| 3. Community owned lodge on government land, with a private or joint venture management company | **Witsieshoek, South Africa:** in lieu of rental, the Batlokoa community receives 17% of profit generated by the lodge, or a minimum payment of USD 15,000 per year.<br>**Covane Community Lodge, Mozambique:** annual rental of USD 3,000 flat fee (which increases by 5% each year), plus a USD 5 per bednight fee (increasing 10% per year until it reaches USD 10). |
| 4. Community or privately owned lodge on community land | **Serra Cafema, Namibia:** the lease fee paid to the Marienfluss Conservancy is based on 8% of turnover.<br>**Phinda, South Africa:** Phinda pays rental ranging from USD 20 to USD 40 per hectare, depending on the land parcel leased.<br>**Pafuri Camp, South Africa:** Return Africa's agreement with the Makuleke is due to pay approximately USD 170,000 in lease fees in the 2018 financial year, following payments of around USD 64,456 in 2015/2016, and USD 58,955 in 2016/2017.<br>**Satao Elerai, Kenya:** lease fees, conservation fee (USD 20 per visitor, per night), USD 8 bednight fee, USD 15 per visit to a cultural village.<br>**Sabyinyo Silverback Lodge, Rwanda:** operator pays 7.5% of accommodation and meal revenues, and clients pay a community development levy of USD 93 per bednight to the Sabyinyo Community Livelihoods Association.<br>**!Xaus, South Africa:** monthly rental to the ‡Khomani San and Mier Community Trust is based on an agreement to pay variable percentage of gross annual turnover depending on lodge income – i.e. 5% for turnover up to ZAR 5 million; 7.5% between ZAR 5 and ZAR 7.5 million; and 10% above ZAR 7.5 million. A minimum rental of ZAR 80,000 is also applied (equivalent to USD 6,400). |
| 5. Tripartite model | **Rocktail Camp, South Africa:** Lease paid to iSimangaliso Wetland Park Authority based on 8.5% revenue, in addition to turtle viewing permits. |

**Table 74.** Employment and wages, 2017.

| | Min. | Max. | Average | Total |
|---|---|---|---|---|
| Number of employees (*n*=26) | 6 | 312 | 65 | 1,683 |
| Number of local employees (*n*=25) | 6 | 176 | 52 | 1,295 |
| Salary paid individuals (USD, per month) (*n*=20) | 64 | 8,077 | 1,047 | 20,947 |

qualified as a guide. She was the first female nature guide in the Kgalagadi who is a member of the local community. Her income, excluding pension benefits, accommodation and meal allowances started, as a probationer, at USD 120 per month and today her package is USD 312 per month – a 260% increase, the majority of which has been promotion-based (see Case Study 25).

### 6.3.2. Local procurement

Thirteen of the case studies provided information on the value of their local procurement. The value of procurement ranged from nothing to USD 312,401 per month, with an average local expenditure of USD 52,625 per month. This implies that the 13 enterprises collectively spend USD 8.2 million on the procurement of local products and services each year. For example, !Xaus Lodge in the Kgalagadi Transfrontier Conservation Area in South Africa spent USD 338,485 on goods produced in local communities and USD 966,935 on locally purchased goods made in South Africa between 2008 and 2017. These locally produced goods include meat, wine and wood, while local services include transfers and maintenance (see Case Study 25).

While these collated figures seem impressive, other research indicates that local procurement by tourism lodges could be dramatically improved. For example, Rogerson (2012) assessed intersectoral linkages between agriculture and tourism in South Africa using an extensive survey of the food supply chains of 80 luxury safari operations in the country. He highlighted the tendency of high-end hotels to use imported foods rather than locally grown produce because of constraints on the availability of goods, as well as issues of reliability, quality, lack of local skills or capital, transport, health and safety concerns, prices and also the specialised nature of the foods desired by their clients. Furthermore, where proactive enterprises had attempted to develop food production projects within local communities, these had rarely succeeded. Failures were attributed to poor management, the organisational difficulties of running community farming projects and lack of capacity within many local communities. Others have also identified the challenge of economies of scale – for example, a vegetable farm that only supplies one small-scale client (e.g. one lodge) might not be commercially viable (Rylance, Spenceley, Mitchell, & Leturque, 2009).

Some tourism enterprises invest in local enterprises, so that the local enterprises can provide them with a better service. For example, Witsieshoek Mountain Lodge buys furniture from a local entrepreneur, Mr Molete. He had been undertaking basic carpentry work in the local community, but in 2014 he was invited to Witsieshoek to look at sample furniture to see whether he could manufacture furniture for the lodge. The lodge worked with him to improve early manufacturing errors, and as a result Mr Molete and his team created furniture for 36 guest bedrooms, including beds, headboards, tables, chairs and mirrors, earning USD 73,600. The lodge management company, Transfrontier Parks Destinations (TFPD), has also helped Mr Molete in exploring further business opportunities from government agencies, and in registering his company on the South African government's procurement database (see Case Study 23). In Rwanda, associated with Ruzizi Lodge, the Umoja Women's Cooperative was provided with training on tailoring and basket weaving, and generated sales of USD 1,700, including through the Akagera Curio Shop. The Akagera Management Company, which manages Ruzizi Lodge and the reserve, built 83 beehives and another four cooperatives were established, with an additional 90 beekeepers in 2015 (see Case Study 13).

### 6.3.3. Donations and philanthropy

Twelve of the case studies provided information about donations given by the lodge to local communities. The average value of these was USD 104,212, ranging from USD 7,588 (Vumbura Camps, Botswana) to USD 322,535 per year (Hwange Camps, Zimbabwe). The donations tend to be used for conservation and local community initiatives. The philanthropic programmes established by three companies are so extensive that they have established associated not-for-profit operations to raise and distribute donations. AndBeyond's charitable arm is the Africa Foundation, while WS has CITW and the Wilderness Wildlife Trust (WWT), and Singita has the Singita Community Development Trust. Over extensive periods of time, these foundations generate substantial impacts. For example, the value of the Africa Foundation's donations to communities living near Ngala in South Africa over the past 25 years is estimated at USD 428,900, with a range of educational, health and small business development programmes. Donations are raised mainly from guests visiting the andBeyond lodges across southern Africa. In initiatives supported by the Africa Foundation, communities are actively involved in the design, development and implementation of community projects in order to enhance buy-in, and they must demonstrate their sustainability (see Case Study 15). Similarly, the Africa Foundation supported 86 bursaries for tertiary studies for students neighbouring Phinda between 1998 and 2008, in courses such as teaching, communications, nature conservation, business, environmental health and motor mechanics. The Africa Foundation has built over 90 classrooms, three libraries and a science laboratory, provided over 150,000 books and educational aids, and facilitated the establishment of 19 preschools. Health initiatives have included construction of a clinic at Mduku, and refurbishment of another, HIV/AIDS awareness workshops, improved water provision and a school permaculture project (see Case Study 15). Other examples include a community levy attached to the room rate – for example, Wolwedans has earned USD 171,527 through the foundation levy, which has been channelled to support the Wolwedans Desert Academy, a vocational school.

CITW has a slightly different model of fundraising. Each year, it organises the Nedbank Tour de Tuli, which is an international cycling event within the Mapungubwe Transfrontier Conservation Area. The 300 cyclists make a donation of USD 2075 to CITW. Of the USD 750,000 income, CITW retains a profit of USD 166,666–250,000 after costs are deducted. Between 2005 and 2017, 3,770 cyclists participating in the tour raised over USD 1.7 million. At the end of 2016, these funds had been used for over 5,600 children to attend a CITW camp, for 6,000 children to participate in an eco-club programme, as well as training over 200 eco-mentors in six southern African countries (Spenceley, 2017).

## 6.4. Environmental Considerations

As the number and volume of PAs increases in order to meet their international commitments under the Aichi Targets (see Chapter 1), the amount of funding available to manage them has remained generally stagnant (Emerton *et al.*, 2006), and generally insufficient to support effective achievement of conservation and livelihood goals (Bovarnick, Fernandez-Baca, Galindo & Negret, 2010). Although tourism revenues should not be the only source of funds, because revenues for conservation tends to fluctuate with market trends (e.g. see Emerton *et al.*, 2006) the sector can certainly provide political support to conservation and serve to increase understanding of the value of parks to governments, and from there the potential economic benefits (Rylance, Snyman and Spenceley, 2017).

There has been considerable work on the environmental impacts that tourism has in protected areas (Buckley, 2010; Eagles, 2013; Mbaiwa, 2003; Wardle, Buckley, Shakeela & Castley, 2018). The case studies in this book provide illustrations of positive impacts on conservation management and environmental management systems (e.g. environmental audits, water use, waste disposal, energy use), which are synthesised here.

### 6.4.1. Conservation impacts

The enterprises based on government land pay lease/concession fees. In some PAs, these lease fees are invested directly back into conservation management of PAs in the country (e.g. Singita Lebombo, South Africa). In others, they are paid into central government coffers, and the PAs are allocated an annual budget (e.g. Nkwichi Lodge and Anvil Bay, Mozambique). In these instances, the budget allocated to a PA by government may not be related to the value of its tourism income. However, for our case studies on community land, it was not clear how the fees were spent, and to what extent money was reinvested in conservation management.

Some of the enterprises have embarked on major conservation programmes. For example, one of the case studies, Nkwichi, created a 120,000 hectare new community conservation area. Local communities agreed to the boundaries for the area and obtained land titles, and natural resource management committees were established in the 16 communities to help regulate land use, and in particular, to stop hunting (see Case Study 6). At Phinda, the company restored cattle farming and exotic tree species farmlands to natural habitats, re-stocking it with 15,000 head of game. Their efforts have been so successful in that they have been able to sell live cheetah, buffalo and white rhino to re-stock other reserves and parks in the region (see Case Study 26). In Rwanda, African Parks has reintroduced black rhino, lion and grey-crowned cranes into Akagera National Park, associated with Ruzizi Lodge. Also in Rwanda, Sabyinyo Silverback Lodge has provided one year of salaries and field costs for one of the tracking teams supporting the habituation and field research of a group of chimpanzees in the forest, and also field cameras to monitor the wildlife in Buhanga Forest (see Case Study 28). At Bisate Lodge in Rwanda, an extensive reforestation programme was established. Using seed and other material gathered only from outside the park, an indigenous tree nursery was established and more than 15,000 trees were planted between 2015 and 2017. A small permanent staff oversee the nursery and day-to-day planting, while up to 20 community members are also regularly employed on a casual basis to assist with reforestation during peak planting times. Trees have also been donated to reforest other areas around Volcanoes National Park (VNP) (see Case Study 1). Similarly, the founder of Chumbe Island Coral Park Limited (CHICOP) successfully negotiated with the semi-autonomous government of Zanzibar/Tanzania for the western coral reef and forest of Chumbe Island to be gazetted as a marine protected area (MPA), with management entrusted to CHICOP. The MPA's reef sanctuary has become one of the most pristine coral reefs in the region, with over 470 fish species and 200 species of hard coral, 90% of all recorded in East Africa, while the forest reserve is one of the last undisturbed semi-arid 'coral rag' forests in Zanzibar, particularly after successful rat eradication.

In the case of Mombo camp, donations are channelled through the WWT, a non-profit organisation. This organisation, supported by WS, helps projects that address the needs of wildlife populations, conserve endangered species and provide education and training to local people and their communities around lodges in the WS portfolio. For example, in 2009 WWT funds were used to establish a research unit in Mombo, providing logistical support, food and vehicle maintenance to researchers (see Case Study 17 and Case Study 3). In Hwange National Park, funds from the WWT and WS are used to support finances and logistics of the park's anti-poaching unit (The Scorpions) (see Case Study 5). Wildlife research efforts are also sponsored at other enterprises. For example, since 2014, Bale Mountain Lodge in Ethiopia has sponsored 10 different research teams in and around the Bale Mountains National Park (BMNP). Teams are provided with accommodation, food, office and research facilities and internet access for the duration of their studies, all either free or at cost, to enable affordable research in the Bale Mountains (see Case Study 8). The presence of tourism operations in PAs can also often serve as a deterrent to poaching due to regular movements of game drive vehicles in the area.

### 6.4.2. Environmental management systems

In terms of environmental management systems, five main categories of issues were collated: (i) environmental audits; (ii) construction impacts; (iii) energy; (iv) water use; and (v) solid waste disposal. A summary of the key issues and achievements is provided below.

- **Environmental audits:** Ngala and Singita in South Africa, Mombo and Vumbura Plains Camp in Botswana, Damaraland, Serra Cafema and Doro Nawas in Namibia WS Hwange camps in Zimbabwe and Bisate Lodge in Rwanda undertake biannual environmental audits. In the case of Ngala and Singita, this is a requirement of SANParks, the PAA. The audits address biosphere manipulation, wildlife management, water extraction, off-road driving, construction, energy use and waste management (solid and liquid). For Mombo, Vumbura Plains, Damaraland WS Hwange camps, Doro Nawas, Serra Cafema and Bisate, the audits are a condition of compliance with the Global Reporting Initiative System used by WS, and address energy use, water use, biodiversity, emissions, effluents and waste.
- **Construction impacts:** at Anvil Bay Lodge, chalets were constructed from wood

from exotic trees onsite, and in order to reduce any leaching of concrete into the sand, support posts were placed in bags which were then filled with concrete. The developer took care not to cut indigenous trees, and protected tree roots running across access routes with sandbags (see Case Study 19). A similar process was used at Forest Lodge in Phinda Reserve, as it is situated in rare sand forest. Karenge Camp in Rwanda is a seasonal camp that is set up twice a year, for three months. At the end of the season, the tents are removed and no construction materials are left behind (see Case Study 13). All WS camp examples (except Bisate) are built with non-permanent structures to allow for the removal of camps if necessary, with no structures remaining and limited impact on the environment. The use of raised wooden decks in many tourism camps also limits impacts on the environment and reduces the camp's environmental footprint.

- **Energy:** several enterprises emphasised energy conservation and the use of renewable sources, to reduce their carbon impact (and reduce operational costs). For example, Singita Lebombo installed a 1 megawatt peak solar hybrid energy plant to provide 1,600 MWh of clean energy annually, which is used to power the lodges and staff villages (see Case Study 14). Bale Mountain Lodge in Ethiopia is 100% eco-friendly with power coming from its own 25 kilowatt micro-hydro power plant. Biodegradable waste is processed through its biogas system to provide cooking gas and firewood is sourced from sustainable plantations outside the national park (see Case Study 8). Mombo Camp switched from using diesel generators to 100% solar energy in May 2012, with a backup generator. Its capital investment of approximately USD 860,000 in the solar system led to an 82% reduction in annual diesel use, from 108,981 litres to 19,309 litres per annum. In terms of carbon emissions from electricity production, 50 tonnes of carbon dioxide were emitted directly in 2017, compared to 287 tonnes in 2012 (see Case Study 3), and a similar retrofit has been applied at Vumbura (see Case Study 29). Nkwichi Lodge's electricity needs are completely powered using solar panels, though petrol water pumps are used to pump water to the chalets (see Case Study 6). Anvil Bay Lodge in Mozambique has a solar power 'farm' and a battery bank that allows the lodge to operate fully on renewable energy, unless there are three days in a row of full cloud cover (see Case Study 19), and both Ruzizi Tented Lodge in Rwanda and King Lewanika Lodge in Zambia are also fully solar powered (see Case Study 13 and Case Study 9). Using a different source of renewable energy, Bisate Lodge in Rwanda camp uses a hybrid energy system of hydro-powered grid power and thermodynamic geysers (see Case Study 1).
- **Water:** !Xaus Lodge is located in the desert, and therefore water conservation is a major focus. Water is desalinated on site for use throughout the lodge, including in bottles for guest consumption, and there is a major focus placed on teaching guests to limit water wastage. The lodge also informs guests that filling the waterhole for wildlife is prioritised over filling the guest swimming pool (see Case Study 25). At Bale Mountain Lodge, water is taken from the river and subjected to slow sand filtration and purification. Water is recycled through soakaways which return the purified waste water to the soils and river (see Case Study 8). WS lodges have systematically reduced the amount of bottled water used. For example, at Vumbura Plains, the use of reverse osmosis water filtration systems reduced the bottled water consumption from 10,385 litres in 2012 to 2,604 litres in 2017 (see Case Study 29). Damaraland Camp has also adopted a reusable water bottle policy coupled with a reverse osmosis water filtration system which ensures that the average bottled water consumption per guest remains very low, achieving an average of 0.44 litres/per bednight consumed during 2017 (see Case Study 21). Similarly, the group's Hwange Camps reduced the bottled water consumption from 25,534 bottles in FY2007 to 6,268 bottles in 2017 (see Case Study 5).
- **Solid waste:** most of the enterprises attempt to reduce solid waste disposal through recycling. There is variable success, depending on the level of local recycling

**Box 21.** Tackling bottled water use in the Okavango Delta

Wilderness Holdings has installed on-site water purification systems at its camps, with refillable drinking bottles provided for guests.

This has led to significant improvements, with a 53% reduction in bottled water use since 2012 (i.e. 467,485 fewer bottles), and a group average of 0.72 litres of bottled water used per bednight during 2016.

The overall volume of water consumed in camps in the Okavango Delta of Botswana was reduced between 2015 and 2016 by 8%.

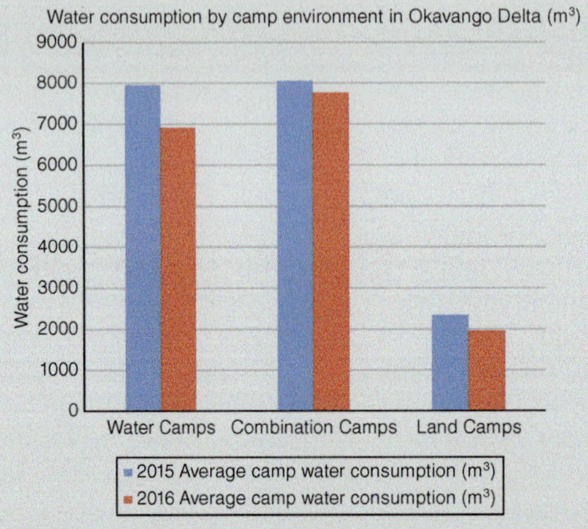


Source: Wilderness Holdings Integrated Annual Report for the year ended 28 February 2016, Warren Ozorio, Wilderness Safaris, personal communication

services – whether private sector or by municipalities. For example, at King Lewanika Lodge in Zambia, waste is separated and managed by composting, incinerating and movement of tins and glass off site (see Case Study 9). The bottled water use initiatives undertaken by WS lodges (see above) have achieved impressive reductions in the use of single-use plastic (see Box 21).

## 6.5. Successes and Challenges

A diverse range of successes are profiled within the case studies in this volume. These include the following.

- **Transformation** of dilapidated community owned lodges into commercially viable enterprises (Witsieshoek, South Africa; Covane Lodge, Mozambique).
- **Partnerships with local communities** that provide the private sector with long-term security in terms of business and wildlife conservation (Phinda, South Africa; Return Africa, South Africa) and, for communities, an increase in the likelihood of an operation continuing during 'lean' years (Ndzou, Mozambique).
- **Long-term technical support and commitment** (i.e. 15–20 years), including securing financial support for community partnerships by partners (Anvil Bay, Mozambique; Covane Lodge, Mozambique; Pafuri Camp, South Africa).
- **Meaningful financial returns** provided to community members in rural, impoverished areas (Witsieshoek, South Africa; Nkwichi, Mozambique) including through lease fees (Vumbura, Botswana) and procurement (Singita, South Africa), employment and salaries (Witsieshoek, South Africa).
- **Empowerment and training** of community members (Damaraland, Namibia) including internships (Ruzizi, Rwanda; Wolwedans, Namibia), career progression (Phinda, South Africa; Wolwedans, Namibia), vocational training (Wolwedans) and getting 'communities to buy into the business' (Phinda, South Africa).

- **Long-term programmes of community benefits** (i.e. wages, procurement, philanthropy) that create meaningful improvements in local communities (Ngala, South Africa).
- **Improved community access to health and education**, especially for women and children (Phinda, South Africa; Nkwichi, Mozambique; Vumbura, Botswana; Hwange Camps, Zimbabwe; Simien Lodge, Ethiopia).
- **Increased environmental awareness** among communities (Ndzou, Mozambique; Damaraland and Doro Nawas, Namibia; Chumbe, Tanzania).
- **Sponsorship of academic research** on wildlife and conservation (Phinda, South Africa; Mombo, Botswana; Bale Mountain Lodge, Ethiopia).
- **Enhanced protection of wildlife** by community members because of their vested interest and good relations with the private sector (Phinda, South Africa; Damaraland and Doro Nawas, Namibia).
- **Improved conservation and wildlife management in natural areas** (Mombo, Botswana; Nkwichi, Mozambique; Phinda, South Africa; Singita, South Africa), with increased wildlife numbers (Damaraland, Namibia; Mombo, Botswana) and reduced poaching (Phinda, South Africa; Hwange Camps, Zimbabwe) and new conservation areas (Nkwichi, Mozambique; Chumbe, Tanzania).
- **Achieving independent sustainable tourism certification** (Witsieshoek, South Africa; !Xaus, South Africa; Wolwedans, Namibia).

Of course, there are also a considerable number of challenges faced. These include the following.

- **Inconsistent government policies** and legislation (Hwange Camps, Zimbabwe).
- **Volatile business and security environments** that make long-term planning difficult (Bale Mountain Lodge, Ethiopia).
- **Where a PA authority does not fully understand tourism** and the needs of the tourism industry, it impacts negatively on a private sector tourism business's success (Rocktail, South Africa).
- **Misinformed beliefs** among community members about the profitability of tourism (Witsieshoek, South Africa; !Xaus, South Africa), and suspicions about foreigners and private sector investment (Simien Lodge, Ethiopia).
- **Perceptions of biodiversity and nature conservation** as a problem by the community rather than an opportunity, due to limitations on cultivation, extraction of natural resources and human–wildlife conflict (HWC) (Ndzou, Mozambique).
- **Alignment of expectations** between a commercial tourism operator and the conservation park management team with operational issues such as off-road driving and waste management (King Lewanika, Zambia; Mkulumadzi, Malawi).
- **Unrealistic expectations** of the size of financial benefits, and the number of beneficiaries (Witsieshoek, South Africa; Pafuri Camp, South Africa) coupled with limited available jobs in high population areas (Singita, South Africa; Bale Mountain Lodge, Ethiopia).
- **Rights vs benefits**, and community members thinking jobs are a 'right' rather than a benefit (Witsieshoek, South Africa; !Xaus, South Africa).
- **Coordination** of local people, government departments and non-profit organisations to get involved in a systematic and organised way to support projects (Singita, South Africa).
- **Communicating partnerships to guests**, including the importance of the relationship between developing and promoting positive community attitudes towards tourism and conservation (Sabyinyo Lodge, Rwanda).
- **Recruitment of community members for employment**, because the types of skills needed by the lodge are limited in rural areas (Anvil Bay, Mozambique; Chumbe, Tanzania).
- **Community members with low literacy levels**, low hospitality capacity and little understanding of financial and management aspects. Substantial training is required (Ndzou, Mozambique; Nkwichi, Mozambique; Vumbura, Botswana).
- **Losing employees** to other companies following investment in their training (Damaraland, Namibia; Doro Nawas, Namibia).
- **Employment of women** is challenged because of attrition rates after maternity leave

(Anvil Bay, Mozambique) and due to cultural issues (Satao Elerai, Kenya).

- **Limited opportunities for local procurement or services in highly remote and underdeveloped areas** (Mombo, Botswana; Damaraland, Namibia; Ngala, South Africa; Nkwichi, Mozambique).
- **Transparency and accountability** of community trusts financial management (Pafuri Camp, South Africa; Vumbura, Botswana).
- **Conflict created by benefit-sharing** where elites capture an unfair share of the benefits (Pafuri Camp, South Africa).
- **Sustaining meaningful community benefits** and positive community perceptions in the long term (Phinda, South Africa).
- **Establishing joint ventures has high associated transaction costs**, particularly where community members have a low basic understanding of tourism and hospitality, and basic education (Anvil Bay, Mozambique).
- **JV partnerships are only a success if the business is profitable**, otherwise the accumulated losses have to be shared according to the shareholding. The private sector bears the cost of losses because communities are often unable to so (Ndzou Lodge, Mozambique; Damaraland, Namibia).
- **Risk with community equity loans**, and rights potentially lost by community members (Anvil Bay, Mozambique).
- **High infrastructure and equipment maintenance costs in rural areas**, which are often borne by the private sector (Covane Lodge, Mozambique; !Xaus, South Africa).
- **Access to infrastructure in remote areas**, including the road network (Ndzou, Mozambique; Chemucane, Mozambique; Nkwichi, Mozambique; Bisate, Rwanda).
- **Increased HWC** where conservation has improved wildlife populations (Damaraland, Namibia; Bisate, Rwanda).

Overall, there is little value in establishing a community and/or JV tourism operation which tourists do not know about (because of poor promotion); cannot reach (because of poor infrastructure); where the establishment is product-led rather than demand-led (because no market research was done); where a low level of service is given (because of poor training); and which does not make a profit (because expectations remain unrealised, and third parties have to subsidise the operations in the long term) (Spenceley & Snyman, 2017a). Some of the pros and cons identified for different partnership models are described in Table 75.

## 6.6. Lessons Learned

Professionals working on PA tourism constantly face trade-offs and need to find ways to balance optimising the quality of visitor experience and generating revenue for conservation management, with the integrity of the ecological resource base (Spenceley & Snyman, 2017a).

Lessons learned from the case studies include the following:

- **PAAs can identify and partner with established responsible companies**, and/or nurture emerging enterprises, through reliable, accountable and transparent

**Table 75.** Pros and cons for the private sector of different partnership models.

| Partnership model | Potential pros | Potential cons |
|---|---|---|
| **Joint Venture** | Smaller share of profits; social benefits; empowerment benefits; access to different areas. | More complex; potential conflict between stakeholders; sharing of profits. |
| **Public Private Partnership** | Access to PAs (often exclusive). | Government complacency in partnership to abide by contract terms; potential conflict between stakeholders. |
| **Pure private sector** | Simple agreement; greater share of profits; exclusive access. | Can be costly to perform all functions. |
| **Tripartite** | Diversity in product; social benefits; empowerment benefits; access to different areas. | Highly complex; potential conflict between stakeholders. |

concession and partnership processes (Mombo, Botswana).

- **Government investment can generate a positive return** for government if managed commercially (!Xaus, South Africa).
- **Commercial success** provides revenues that can be used to invest in conservation, environmental technologies and community development (Mombo, Botswana).
- **Volatile external factors** can have a major impact upon success, and a strong and flexible relationship is required with the lender (Bale Mountain Lodge, Ethiopia).
- **Investment in conservation and in environmentally sound technologies**, as well as the employment of additional staff for park management and environmental education programmes, raises investment and operational costs considerably, making it difficult to compete with other tourism enterprises (Chumbe, Tanzania).
- **A comprehensive stakeholder engagement plan is needed**. Identify clearly who the relevant communities and other stakeholders are early in the process, and define and communicate clearly what community and other benefits are likely, and what is actually shared (Witsieshoek, South Africa; !Xaus, South Africa; Nkwichi, Mozambique; Vumbura, Botswana; Bisate, Rwanda; Chumbe Island, Mozambique).
- **Community members need a greater understanding of the tourism business** and the implications of shareholding to community income (Damaraland, Namibia; Sabyinyo, Rwanda).
- **Community trusts need to have a logical, systematic and informed decision-making framework** (which includes community input and is transparent and accountable) to prioritise and allocate revenue to benefit the community, as well as conservation (Sabyinyo, Rwanda).
- **Realistic expectations** among the community must be set at the start and throughout the process, and the non-tangible benefits as well as the cash benefits should be made clear (Pafuri Camp, South Africa).
- **Inter- and intra-community conflict poses a risk** to JV partnerships and a cohesive, stable community structure is important (Doro Nawas, Namibia).
- **Establishing environmental education programmes** enables a wide cross-section of society (e.g. schoolchildren, teachers, fishers) to visit and gain awareness of the importance of nature in their everyday lives, and the importance of conservation areas and the ecosystem services supported (Chumbe, Zanzibar; WS's CITW programme).
- **Offering internships** can be beneficial both for local students and members of the community to gain experience in hospitality, and also to provide lodges with a spare set of hands during busy periods, as well as creating a pool of potential employees (Ruzizi, Rwanda).
- **Providing philanthropic benefits** to communities separately to the commercial business (Nkwichi, Mozambique; Ngala, South Africa; Phinda, South Africa).
- **Regular meetings with partners** (e.g. PAAs, community members) and a transparent sharing of information including financial results can go a long way to overcoming the challenge of 'misinformed beliefs' (Witsieshoek, South Africa; King Lewanika, Zambia; Mkulumadzi, Malawi).
- **Never promise anything which you cannot deliver** – it is negative to relations in the long run (Bale Mountain Lodge, Ethiopia).
- **To avoid user conflicts**, it is easier to preserve an area that is not used intensively for subsistence or other economic endeavours by local communities (Chumbe, Tanzania).
- **Models evolve over the years, and success is underpinned by strong and mutually beneficial long-term relationships, commitment and trust** between private companies, PAAs and local communities (Phinda, South Africa; Ndzou, Mozambique; Ngala, South Africa; Rocktail Bay, South Africa; Simien Lodge, Ethiopia; Bale Mountain Lodge, Ethiopia; Chumbe, Tanzania; Thawale, Malawi).
- **Establishing JV partnerships has high transaction costs** (time, money) (Ndzou, Mozambique) and carries risk for all partners (Doro Nawas, Namibia).
- **Development of JVs between community members and the private sector, and preferentially employing local people**, is an important way to build local capacity

and reduce poverty in remote and marginalised areas (Anvil Bay, Mozambique).

- **Longer concession leases**, with appropriate exit clauses for underperformance by concessionaires are favourable to operators, as they allow higher levels of capital investment and greater likelihood of recouping this investment (Singita, South Africa; Chumbe, Tanzania).
- **Private investors are not usually rural development experts** and may need supplementary technical support from others (e.g. NGOs) (Pafuri Camp, South Africa).
- **Private partners need to integrate rural development and community empowerment** into their business approach. If not, the benefit-sharing and joint management are perceived as burdens that slow the business (Pafuri Camp, South Africa).
- **Rehabilitating unviable CBT enterprises** with donor finance coupled with private (rather than community) management can be viable if the conditions are right (Covane Lodge, Mozambique; Witsieshoek, South Africa; !Xaus, South Africa).

## 6.7. References

Akama, J.S. (1996) Western environmental values and nature-based tourism in Kenya. *Tourism Management*, 17(8), 567–574.

Akama, J.S. (2004) Neocolonialism, dependency and external control of Kenya's tourism industry: a case study of wildlife safari tourism in Kenya. In Hall, C.M. & Tucker, H. (eds) (2004) *Tourism and postcolonialism: contested discourses, identities and representations*, pp. 140–152. Routledge, London.

Ashley, C. & Haysom, G. (2008) The development impacts of tourism supply chains: increasing impact on poverty and decreasing our ignorance. In Spenceley, A. (ed.) (2008) *Responsible tourism: critical issues for conservation and development* (pp. 129–156). Earthscan, London.

Ashley, C. & Mitchell, J. (2007) *Assessing how tourism revenues reach the poor.* ODI Briefing Paper No. 21. Overseas Development Institute, London.

Ashley, C., Mitchell, J. & Spenceley, A. (2009) *Opportunity study guidelines*. International Trade Centre's Export-Led Poverty Reduction Program, UNCTAD, Geneva.

Ashley, C., Roe, D. & Goodwin, H. (2001) *Pro-poor tourism strategies: making tourism work for the poor – a review of experience*. Pro-Poor Tourism Report No. 1. The Russell Press, London.

Belisle, F.J. (1983) Tourism and food production in the Caribbean. *Annals of Tourism Research,* 10(4), 497–513.

Belisle, F.J. (1984) Tourism and food imports: the case of Jamaica. *Economic Development and Cultural Change*, 32, 819–842.

Bennett, O., Roe, D. & Ashley, C. (1999) *Sustainable tourism and poverty elimination: a report for the Department for International Development*. Deloitte and Touche, IIED and ODI, London.

Bovarnick, A., Fernandez-Baca, J., Galindo, J. & Negret, H. (2010) *Financial sustainability of protected areas in Latin America and the Caribbean: investment policy guidance*. United Nations Development Programme (UNDP) and The Nature Conservancy (TNC), New York.

Britton, S. (1982) The political economy of tourism in the Third World. *Annals of Tourism Research,* 9(3), 331–358.

Brohman, J. (1996) New directions for tourism in Third World development. *Annals of Tourism Research,* 23(1), 48–70.

Buckley, R. (2010) *Conservation tourism*. CAB International, Wallingford, UK.

de Kadt, E. (ed.) (1979) *Tourism: passport to development?* Oxford University Press, New York.

Eagles, P.F.J. (2013) Role of ecotourism in preserving natural areas and biodiversity. In Bricker K., Black, R. & Cottrell, S. (eds) (2013) *Sustainable tourism & the Millennium Development Goals: effecting positive change* (pp. 169–184). Jones & Bartlett Learning, Burlington, MA.

Emerton, L., Bishop, J. & Thomas, L. (2006) *Sustainable financing of protected areas. A global review of challenges and options*. IUCN, Gland, Switzerland.

GTZ (German Technical Cooperation) (2007) Value links manual: The methodology of value chain promotion, 1st edn. GTZ, Eschborn.

Hall, C. (ed.) (2007) *Pro-poor tourism: who benefits? Perspectives on tourism and poverty reduction*. Channel View Publications, Clevedon, UK.

Kirsten, M. & Rogerson, C.M. (2002) Tourism, business linkages and small enterprise development in South Africa. *Development Southern Africa,* 19, 29–59.

Mbaiwa, J.E. (2003) The socio-economic and environmental impacts of tourism development on the Okavango Delta, north-western Botswana. *Journal of Arid Environments* 54(2), 447–467.
Mbaiwa, J.E. & Darkoh, M. (2009) The socio-economic impacts of tourism in the Okavango Delta, Botswana. In Saarinen, J., Becker, F., Manwa, H. & Wilson, D. (eds) *Sustainable tourism in southern Africa: local communities and natural resources in transition* (pp. 210–230). Channel View Publications, Clevedon, UK.
Meyer, D. (2007) Pro-poor tourism: from leakages to linkages. A conceptual framework for creating linkages between the accommodation sector and 'poor' neighbouring communities. *Current Issues in Tourism*, 10(6), 558–583.
Mitchell, J. & Ashley, C. (2010) *Tourism and poverty reduction: pathways to prosperity*. Earthscan, London.
Mowforth, M. & Munt, I. (2009) *Tourism and sustainability: development and new tourism in the Third World*, 3rd edn. Routledge, London.
Rogerson, C. (2012) Tourism–agriculture linkages in rural South Africa: evidence from the accommodation sector. *Journal of Sustainable Tourism*, 20(3), 477–495.
Rylance, A. & Spenceley, A. (2016) Applying inclusive business approaches to nature-based tourism in Namibia and South Africa. *Tourism: An International Interdisciplinary Journal*, 64(4), 371–383.
Rylance, A., Snyman, S. & Spenceley, A. (2017) c area management in southern Africa. *Tourism Research International*, 21, 139–149.
Rylance, A., Spenceley, A., Mitchell, J. & Leturque, H. (2009) *Training module for agriculture*. International Trade Centre, Geneva.
Saarinen, J. (2009) Conclusion and critical issues in tourism and sustainability in southern Africa. In Saarinen, J., Becker, F., Manwa, H. & Wilson, D. (eds) (2009) *Sustainable tourism in southern Africa: Local communities and natural resources in transition* (pp. 269–286). Channel View Publications, Clevedon, UK.
Scheyvens, R. (2002) *Tourism for development: empowering communities*. Prentice Hall, London.
Scheyvens, R. (2007) Exploring the tourism–poverty nexus. *Current Issues in Tourism*, 10(2–3), 231–254.
Scheyvens, R. (2011) *Tourism and poverty*. Routledge, New York.
Scheyvens, R. & Biddulph, R. (2017) Inclusive tourism development. *Tourism Geographies* 20(4), 589–609, doi: 10.1080/14616688.2017.1381985.
Spenceley, A. (2008) Local impacts of community-based tourism in southern Africa. In Spenceley, A. (ed.) (2008) *Responsible tourism: critical issues for conservation and development* (pp. 285–303). Earthscan, London.
Spenceley, A., Rylance, A., Nanabhay, S. & van der Watt, H. (2016) Operational guidelines for community based tourism in South Africa. Department of Tourism, Republic of South Africa.
Spenceley, A., Snyman, S., and Eagles, P. F. J. (2017) Guidelines for tourism partnerships and concessions for protected areas: Generating sustainable revenues for conservation and development, Report to the Secretariat of the Convention on Biological Diversity and IUCN.
Spenceley, A. (2017) Tourism concession guidelines for transfrontier conservation areas in SADC, Summary, June 2018.
Spenceley, A. & Meyer, D. (2012) Tourism and poverty reduction: theory and practice in less economically developed countries. *Journal of Sustainable Tourism*, 20(3), 297–317.
Spenceley, A. & Snyman, S. (2017a) Protected area tourism: progress, innovation and sustainability. *Tourism and Hospitality Research*, 17(1), 3–7.
Spenceley, A. & Snyman, S. (2017b) Can a wildlife tourism company influence conservation and the development of tourism in a specific destination? *Journal of Hospitality and Tourism Research* 17(1), 52–67, doi: 10.1177/1467358416634158.
Stone, L.S. & Stone, T.M. (2011) Community-based tourism enterprises: challenges and prospects for community participation – Khama Rhino Sanctuary Trust, Botswana. *Journal of Sustainable Tourism*, 19(1), 97–114.
Tewes-Gradl, C., van Gaalen, M. & Pirzer, C. (2014) *Destination mutual benefit: a guide to inclusive business in tourism*. GIZ, Frankfurt.
Torres, R. (2002) Toward a better understanding of tourism and agriculture linkages in the Yucatan: tourist food consumption and preferences. *Tourism Geographies*, 4, 282–306.
Torres, R. & Momsen, J.H. (2004) Challenges and potential for linking tourism and agriculture to achieve pro-poor tourism objectives. *Progress in Development Studies*, 4(4), 294–318.
Wardle, C., Buckley, R., Shakeela, A. & Castley, J.G. (2018) Ecotourism's contributions to conservation: analysing patterns in published studies. *Journal of Ecotourism* 1–31, doi:10.1080/14724049.2018.1424173.
Wearing, S. & McDonald, M. (2002) The development of community-based tourism: re-thinking the relationship between tour operators and development agents as intermediaries in rural and isolated area communities. *Journal of Sustainable Tourism*, 10(3), 191–206.
Wilkinson, P.F. (1987) Tourism in small island nations: a fragile dependency. *Leisure Studies*, 6(2), 127–146.
World Bank Group (2014) Getting financed: 9 tips for community joint ventures in tourism. Available at https://openknowledge.worldbank.org/handle/10986/21698.

# 7

# Conclusion

This book has provided comprehensive documentation of the role of the private sector in tourism in Africa and has described the various ways that the private sector can engage in tourism. Our case studies have provided a detailed review of the various models/options used by the private sector to engage in tourism in conservation areas in Africa including, among others, pure private sector ownership, joint ventures (JVs), tripartite agreements and government leases. We also described the processes used to develop these partnerships from start to finish as well as best practices for the private sector engaging in tourism. The book provides guidance for establishing partnership models, and the roles of various stakeholders within these, as well as ideas for maximising benefits, financially, socially and environmentally.

## 7.1. Overview of Findings from the Case Studies

The case studies reviewed institutional issues, economic, socio-cultural and environmental impacts of the tourism operations.

### 7.1.1. Institutional issues

The two main institutional arrangements explored were: private and JV ownership models (see Figure 5, p. 94). We observed simple arrangements (e.g. a single company that owns and manages a lodge, based on leased private or government land) and more complex models with private sector JV partnerships and public–private partnerships (PPPs). Among community JVs, there was a high degree of complexity in some of the institutional arrangements, particularly where there had been a land restitution situation (e.g. in South Africa). In some instances, governments had provided land tenure to communities to give them preferential access to wildlife resources and tourism opportunities (e.g. Mozambique, Namibia). In almost all case study examples, there were two or more stakeholders engaged, highlighting the complexity of private sector tourism in conservation areas. Appropriate policy and institutional support is important to allow for these complex relationships and to enable them to thrive. Many of the case study examples align with Bramwell and Lane's (2000) observation that leveraging the strengths of all stakeholders can create a competitive advantage. This does, however, require time and energy which needs to be accounted for in the tourism development process. Some case study examples also mentioned the need for clear processes for conflict management and mitigation to ensure prompt resolution of conflicts between stakeholders should they arise. Long delays in sorting out conflicts can negatively impact on the private sector tourism business

© S. Snyman and A. Spenceley (2019). *Private Sector Tourism in Conservation Areas in Africa* (S. Snyman and A. Spenceley)

(e.g. the intra-community conflict in Doro !Nawas Conservancy discussed in Case Study 22).

A number of financing options were used for capital investment for the enterprises reviewed. Sources included development banks (e.g. World Bank Group, African Development Bank), impact investment vehicles (e.g. African Wildlife Capital), non-governmental organisations (NGOs) (e.g. African Parks, African Wildlife Foundation, Africa Safari Foundation), government grants and private investment. The growth of impact investment vehicles in particular demonstrates how innovative 'green' financing options are being used to leverage funds from socially orientated investors to reduce financial risks of the private sector working in remote areas of Africa. It was also shown that it is possible to use a number of different financing options for one tourism operation in order to diversify risk, though this does increase complexity.

### 7.1.2. Economic considerations

The case studies examined financial impacts in relation to lease payments paid to communities. The eight enterprises paying lease fees to government collectively paid USD 2.3 million per year, while eight enterprises with community leases collectively paid USD 1.1 million to the landowners. A number of different approaches to calculating the lease fees were used, which included fixed annual lease fee, percentage of turnover or profit and bednight fees. It is difficult to establish a 'best practice' in this regard, and better to provide a range of options that new partnerships could explore. A combination of different forms of lease fee could assist with reducing risk for both the lessee and lessor (e.g. a combination of fixed and variable – see Box 8 for more details on this).

It is often argued in the literature that tourism in conservation areas employs a large number of expatriates and limits employment of local people to menial jobs (e.g. Barber & Pittaway, 2000; Mbaiwa, 2003, 2005). However, the case study examples consistently illustrate more local people being employed than expatriates, and show that they are empowered to fulfil management roles. The enterprises reviewed employed 1,588 people and at least 1,210 (76%) of these came from local communities. Collectively, the tourism businesses spent USD 15 million in 2017 on wages for local people. Some of the enterprises also demonstrated substantial contributions to the empowerment of their staff, through training and advancement within the company. The indirect and induced impacts of these wage payments are likely to be extensive in the rural communities surrounding most conservation areas (see Snyman, 2017, for more on tourism staff spending in rural areas).

### 7.1.3. Social considerations

The social impacts reviewed included local procurement, cultural tourism (mostly through village visits) and philanthropic contributions.

The value of local procurement by the enterprises ranged from nothing to over USD 300,000 per annum. Collectively, 13 enterprises spent USD 8.2 million on the procurement of local products and services each year. However, it is notable, and in line with previous literature, that there are considerable challenges for remotely based tourism operations to procure locally. This is particularly because of constraints in the availability of goods, reliability, quality, lack of local skills or capital, transport, health and safety concerns, prices and economies of scale (Rogerson, 2012; Rylance, Spenceley, Mitchell & Leturque, 2009). Despite the challenges, some enterprises helped build capacity and provided equipment to local enterprises, so that they can provide them with a better quality of product (e.g. Witsieshoek, Anvil Bay, Ruzizi). Other enterprises (Ruzizi, Simien Lodge, Bisate) supported the establishment of community cooperatives to assist local suppliers of goods and services to develop economies of scale and to better manage quantity and quality of products.

Donations were also channelled to local communities, sometimes by philanthropic programmes established by the companies (e.g. andBeyond's Africa Foundation, the Wilderness Safaris, Children in the Wilderness and Wilderness Wildlife Trust, and Singita's Singita Community Development Trust). Over extensive periods of time, these foundations generated substantial impacts in rural areas, particularly in the realms of education, health and small business development. As discussed in Chapter 1, tourism can in this way stimulate investment in infrastructure and livelihood opportunities, both directly through the tourism business and indirectly through philanthropy. Many of the case studies emphasised the need to work closely with community stakeholders to align objectives, manage expectations and promote the sustainability of projects.

A number of the operations included, where possible, the option of a visit to a local community village. Such visits sometimes included a direct fee paid to the community by each guest visiting (Satao Elerai), others included contributions in kind through mechanisms such as 'Pack for a Purpose' and also through channelling guest donations to specific community development projects. A total of USD 1.3 million per annum was contributed by 14 tourism operations to various community development projects in villages in or adjacent to conservation areas. Such investment over and above lease fees and the payment of wages and salaries can have significant local economic impacts, stimulating economies and resulting in numerous induced and indirect impacts.

#### 7.1.4. Environmental considerations

While some of the enterprises provide substantial lease fees to protected area authorities (PAAs), there is no guarantee that these are reinvested in the specific protected area (PA), directly in conservation or management. Often the system is dependent on government policy and regulations that provide the enabling environment for conservation finance. However, several companies employ major conservation programmes as part of their business model. Multi-country operation such as AP, WS and andBeyond have established globally significant programmes to conserve endangered species and extensive conservation landscapes. Support of biodiversity conservation by the private sector can be through investment in anti-poaching activities, relocation and restoration of wildlife, and supporting research and monitoring. The presence of tourism operations in conservation areas can also often act as a deterrent to poachers (this has been evidenced in Kafue National Park in Zambia, where there is less poaching in areas where the tourism operations traverse).

There have also been considerable efforts to reduce the environmental footprint of tourism. This includes the use of renewable energy (particularly solar power); reducing solid waste (through recycling and reducing use); and reducing the volume of water used (including in single-use plastic bottles). Company approaches to monitor and improve their performance include environmental audits, either through PA requirements (e.g. environmental audits by South African National Parks – SANParks) or applying international processes (e.g. the Global Reporting Initiative by WS). Some have also used an independent third party certification scheme to provide their claims of sustainable practices with credibility (e.g. !Xaus Lodge and Vumbura Camp and Little Vumbura).

Most case study examples used a combination of promoting positive environmental impacts through investing in, and supporting, biodiversity conservation and mitigating and/or minimising negative environmental impacts, through managing environmental systems, such as waste, water or energy.

## 7.2. General Conclusions

Based on the literature review, case study analysis and the authors' experience in tourism in conservation areas in Africa, below are some broad conclusions highlighting the responsibility of the various stakeholders engaged in tourism.

### 7.2.1. Importance of sustainable partnerships

Multi-stakeholder partnerships and collaborations related to tourism in conservation areas have a unique complexity as they bring together numerous stakeholders, often with divergent objectives, which are often in competition. For example, a private sector stakeholder looking simply to maximise profits may have competing objectives to a conservation agency whose primary focus is the conservation and/or preservation of natural resources, which can often be negatively impacted by tourism in one way or another. Developing these partnerships into sustainable, positive relationships takes time, and it requires the management and acceptance of others' objectives and contributions to the partnership. In most cases there will also be necessary compromises from all stakeholders to allow the relationship to grow and benefit the greater good, rather than any selfish desires or needs. What has been shown in this volume is that complex partnerships can work and provide benefits, economically, socially and environmentally. This finding is in line with that of the UNWTO (2014) study which highlighted that wildlife watching tourism benefits a wide range of stakeholders, especially national parks, local tourism providers and the local community, and also offers a wide range of employment areas for the local community.

### 7.2.2. Responsibility of private sector tourism business

A growing number of private sector tourism businesses (andBeyond, Asilia, Singita, WS) are investing a large amount in the sustainable development of their businesses, investing in measuring, monitoring and reporting at economic, environmental and social levels. WS has published an annual integrated report since 2011 and in 2018 andBeyond published its first impact report. Asilia also publishes an annual positive impact report. The WS integrated report provides a detailed analysis of all measures of the business, from financial, to social, cultural and environmental (including biodiversity conservation and environmental management systems). Austin, Epler Wood and Leonard (in press) recently released information on this level of reporting in tourism and the transparency offered by it. This needs to become the norm among tourism businesses if we are to understand both the positive and negative impacts that tourism has in conservation areas and to manage it accordingly for long-term sustainability.

The development of benchmarks related to various sustainability indicators is important to set standards and ensure effective monitoring and evaluation of tourism in conservation areas. Asilia, Singita and WS are currently (in 2018) working together on a benchmarking initiative to develop standards for various environmental management systems (EMSs), and community and conservation indicators, with the aim to continuously improve processes and systems to mitigate and minimise negative impacts, and to promote positive impacts on the environment.

As mentioned in Chapter 1, the case studies presented in this volume are not exhaustive and, in most cases, provide examples of best practice or represent private sector tourism businesses who are well respected in the industry and who offer examples of best practice. The threat of unsustainable operations to the long-term sustainability of conservation areas should not be denied and efforts should be made to assist such conservation areas by building their capacity, knowledge and skills to sustainably manage tourism in their conservation areas. Tools such as those discussed by Spenceley *et al.* (2017) and others are useful in assisting governments to assess, manage and monitor tourism in their PAs. Allowing tourism to be operated unsustainably in conservation areas is short-sighted and will ultimately impact negatively on local communities, governments and the private sector business. Private sector tourism in conservation areas should be held accountable for its operations and the management and monitoring of them. Saying this, the private sector should not have its hands tied, inhibiting the successful operation of the business (i.e. through onerous, time-consuming reporting or processes), but should be empowered, enabled and encouraged to manage the business successfully and sustainably. A number of the case studies in this volume mentioned restrictive government policies, or the lack of supportive policies, which inhibited the operation of their businesses. Close collaboration between government and the private sector is essential for the long-term sustainable growth and development of tourism: seeing each other as partners, rather than the traditional adversarial approach, will go a long way to maximising benefits and promoting long-term, sustainable growth in tourism in conservation areas.

Twining-Ward, Li, Bhammer and Wright (2018) highlighted that wildlife tourism is a powerful tool which countries can leverage to grow and diversify their economies, while protecting their biodiversity and meeting several Sustainable Development Goals (SDGs). They went further in saying that it is also a way to engage tourists in wildlife conservation and inject money into local communities living closest to wildlife. This aligns with many of the findings in the case studies, where the private sector tourism operators are actively engaging tourists in conservation and community development initiatives.

Twining-Ward *et al.* (2018) also emphasise that their study showed sustainably run tourism operations have led to increased investments in PAs and reserves, a reduction in poaching, an increase in, and opportunities for, rural communities to improve their livelihoods through tourism-related jobs, revenue-sharing arrangements, and co-management of natural resources. Our case studies showed similar results.

### 7.2.3. Responsibility of government

From a policy perspective, there is a need for supportive, enabling policies, governance and supporting infrastructure to allow the private sector to operate. This also means investment in capacity-building and skills development for staff working in conservation areas to allow them to manage and monitor tourism in their areas. The engagement and close collaboration of tourism and conservation ministry staff is also a requirement for long-term success. The current situation in most African countries is that tourism and conservation are managed separately by governments, with little engagement between the two government departments, and little synchronicity of policies. This hinders progress and creates numerous obstacles to the sustainable development of tourism in conservation areas. Cross-sectoral engagement of government departments is essential for the successful development of sustainable tourism. This includes engagement with immigration and customs departments whose management of visa allocations and import restrictions can impact on tourism both positively and negatively. For example, a recent (2017) decision by the Rwandan government to issue visas on entry to the country for all visitors (including those who required one prior to entry in the past) is likely to have a hugely positive impact on tourism, allowing for easier, less time-consuming access (Republic of Rwanda, 2017). Supportive government staff, policies and governance can enhance the relationship between private sector tourism businesses and government and result in a win–win situation for both parties as government will, in turn, receive more taxes from successful private sector businesses and often more revenue from an increase in tourism numbers to successful tourism businesses. The building of relevant and sufficient capacity and skills in government, NGOs, communities and the private sector cannot be emphasised enough. Governments need to ensure that they have clear, updated tourism and conservation policies, which emphasise the development of sustainable tourism, collaboration and the engagement of different stakeholders to ensure more inclusive tourism and conservation models.

Governments also have a role to play in terms of maintaining and effectively managing the conservation areas which fall under their jurisdiction. Many operators mentioned the negative impact of poaching on their business. This is in line with the UNWTO (2014) study which also found that poaching has a negative impact on the tourism experience. As found in the case studies in this volume, UNWTO also found that tour operators can play an important role in raising awareness of poaching and (co)-funding anti-poaching initiatives (see Case Study 5 and Case Study 17).

### 7.2.4. Responsibility of NGOs

In general, NGOs that assist communities and governments in terms of tourism are largely development NGOs with little, if any, experience in tourism. This can lead to a number of issues, including a lack of understanding of the requirements of tourism, setting unrealistic expectations and initiating tourism businesses in areas, or using models, which are unlikely to be sustainable or to succeed. Private sector tourism businesses on the other hand, though having the correct tourism skills, are generally not development or conservation organisations and, therefore, need the engagement of conservation and development stakeholders to ensure a balanced approach to tourism and engagement in their areas of operation. Recently, a number of private sector tourism businesses have, however, invested in funding conservation and development human capital to ensure a more balanced approach to business (Singita, andBeyond, WS). Ideally, this should become the norm, with tourism in conservation areas having the correct balance of skills and experience in terms of the tourism business, conservation and socioeconomic development. Until that time, it will be a necessity for stakeholders to collaborate and form partnerships as evidenced in this volume. The complexity of a number of the partnerships outlined in this volume highlights the complexity of tourism in conservation areas in Africa. Balancing environmental, social and economic objectives will be the only way that tourism in conservation areas is going to survive and thrive. This requires an investment of time, capital (both financial and human), resources and a balancing of needs, expectations and requirements.

### 7.2.5. Responsibility of local communities

Local communities have the responsibility to request and, where necessary, demand that they are empowered through the provision of the correct skills, knowledge and experience related to tourism to be able to engage more equitably with the private sector, as well as government and NGOs. Communities should have a clear understanding of their objectives in terms of engaging in tourism, as well as related timelines. They should take initiatives to engage with private sector tourism businesses through internships and learnerships, especially with youth in the community (see Case Study 2 in this volume). Requesting this as part of a partnership agreement would go a long way to develop the required community skills, knowledge and capacity.

## 7.3. Lessons Learned

The case studies revealed a series of successes and challenges, which are summarised in Table 76.

Lessons learned from the case studies include the following:

- PAAs can create positive partnerships that provide positive conservation and local economic development returns, including through business expenditure, profit-sharing and philanthropy. They can even reinvigorate ailing businesses run by government or communities.
- Establishing sustainable investments in rural areas can be relatively expensive, due to transaction costs, volatile external factors and the high transaction costs of JV partnerships.
- Comprehensive stakeholder engagement plans are needed, with regular meetings with partners, and clear and realistic targets for what can be delivered.
- Capacity-building and training is often needed for community members so that they understand tourism better, have realistic expectations and can avoid and mitigate conflict. This includes environmental education programmes to gain awareness of the importance of nature in their everyday lives, and the importance of conservation areas. However, private investors are not usually rural development experts, and may need supplementary technical support from others.
- Models evolve over the years, and success is underpinned by strong and mutually beneficial long-term relationships, commitment and trust. This means that long lease or concession periods allow higher levels of capital investment and conservation investment.

In line with the World Bank Group (2017), the case study examples illustrated that private sector tourism operations in conservation areas in Africa can be labour intensive, facilitate new infrastructure development and help to fund conservation. Also, in line with Christie *et al.*'s (2014) 10 main reasons to develop tourism in Africa discussed in Chapter 1, the case studies show that tourism can, and does, spur economic development, create jobs, empower marginalised populations and promote PPPs.

The extensive contribution of the private sector to government through lease fee payments shown in the case studies could, if the lease fees were reinvested and used efficiently, provide a partial solution to the underfunding of PAs discussed in Chapter 1. Revisiting the allocation of tourism funds received to specific PAs or conservation projects should be considered to ensure better funding for PAs.

## 7.4. Future of Tourism in Conservation Areas in Africa

For the foreseeable future, it is unlikely that tourism in conservation areas will be successful and

**Table 76.** Types of successes and challenges of tourism operations in PAs.

| Successes | Challenges |
|---|---|
| • Transformation of dilapidated community owned lodges into commercially viable enterprises.<br>• Partnerships with local communities.<br>• Long-term technical support and commitment.<br>• Meaningful financial returns provided to community members.<br>• Meaningful improvements in local communities, including in health and education.<br>• Increased environmental awareness among communities.<br>• Sponsorship of academic research on wildlife and conservation.<br>• Improved conservation, wildlife management and protection in natural areas.<br>• Achieving independent sustainable tourism certification. | • Inconsistent government policies and legislation.<br>• Volatile business and security environments.<br>• PAA does not fully understand tourism.<br>• Misinformed beliefs among community members about the profitability of tourism.<br>• Unrealistic expectations of the size of financial benefits.<br>• Perceptions of community members that biodiversity and nature conservation are a problem, particularly where human–wildlife conflict (HWC) increases when conservation has improved wildlife populations.<br>• Misalignment of expectations between commercial tourism operator and conservation management teams.<br>• Challenges in coordination of local people, government departments and non-profit organisations.<br>• Recruitment of community members because of low literacy and education levels in rural areas, coupled with attrition rates among female employees following maternity leave and loss of trained employees to other companies.<br>• Transparency and accountability of community trusts' financial management combined with conflict created by benefit-sharing.<br>• High associated transaction costs associated with JV creations.<br>• Risks with community equity loans.<br>• High infrastructure and equipment maintenance costs in rural areas. |

sustainable without the engagement and involvement of the private sector along with a number of other stakeholders specialising in other areas such as conservation and development. Whether it is through the provision of capital, human resources or providing knowledge and experience, there is a need to engage the private sector and from there to develop the skills and experience needed in government, local communities and, in many cases, NGOs.

Incentivising the private sector to develop sustainable tourism in conservation areas is one way that government can encourage private sector business to develop in a way that balances economics, environmental and social concerns; for example, by providing tax incentives to private sector tourism businesses that employ locally, use local suppliers of goods and services, invest in environmentally friendly technology, systems and processes, and invest in socioeconomic development projects around their areas of operation. Tax incentives could also be given to private sector tourism businesses which form partnerships with local communities, provide internships for local community members, and invest in local skills training, development and empowerment of local communities.

In order to ensure a greater likelihood of success in terms of engaging local communities in tourism businesses, it is important to allow them to walk before trying to get them to run. Insisting on local community shareholding in a business of which they have little understanding and little experience of the risks and potential challenges can be disempowering rather than having the desired empowerment benefits. Situations like this can result in unnecessary and harmful conflict which can leave communities disillusioned and, in some cases, worse off than prior to their engagement in tourism. Building the necessary tourism business skills, knowledge and experience is essential for success. The tourism industry is not the same as most other business sectors, especially tourism in conservation areas. There are complexities related to access, seasonality, infrastructure, skills to service the industry, supporting legislation related to visas and red tape, animal distributions and seasonal changes in this, all of which can be further impacted by climate change. All of these can impact both positively and negatively on a tourism business, with most being external complexities which cannot be controlled by the business. The focus, therefore, needs to be on providing a more in-depth understanding of all these potential challenges, mechanisms to manage them and processes to have in place to maximise benefits and minimise costs. All of this doesn't yet account for the high level of competition in the tourism industry, which has so many potential options for tourists to visit, globally, regionally and locally. The identification of unique selling points (USPs) and the maintenance of the integrity of conserved areas is important in ensuring a long-term competitive advantage.

Government and NGO investment in providing knowledge, skills and experience in the tourism industry specifically is the only way to ensure that local community members are empowered to engage in tourism. Providing understanding in terms of conservation and socioeconomic development would enhance this even further. A balanced approach is the only way that tourism in conservation areas is going to succeed. Epler Wood (2017) writes extensively on the potential challenges that tourism faces and the potential negative impacts that tourism can have and how these need to be accounted for and managed. Much emphasis is put on the potential positive impacts of tourism and the need to grow the tourism economy, but this will not come without complications, challenges and potential negative impacts, especially for tourism in conservation areas, and especially on a continent such as Africa, with a rapidly growing population and ever-increasing competition for land. Trade-offs are going to be inevitable and the management of these trade-offs is going to be critical in terms of long-term sustainability. Collaboration and the formation of mutually beneficial partnerships are likely to lead to greater long-term success, as illustrated by many of the case studies in this volume. Bringing together stakeholders with expertise, knowledge, skills and resources in specific areas allows for a greater chance of maximising benefits and at least satisfying all relevant stakeholders.

In her review of tourism and protected areas issues presented at IUCN World Parks Congresses in 2003 and 2014, and published in the intervening period, Spenceley (2016) demonstrated that there had been considerable research effort on: (i) sustainable use of natural and cultural diversity; (ii) sources of financial support for protected areas; (iii) supporting local and indigenous community development and poverty alleviation; (iv) co-management of protected areas; and (v) fostering attachment to heritage through visitation and conservation education. Looking forward, Eagles (2014) has suggested nine key areas for future protected area tourism research, namely: (i) visitor use monitoring; (ii) park tourism economic impact monitoring; (iii) park finance and professional competencies for tourism management; (iv) building public support; (v) visitor satisfaction; (vi) licences, permits, leases and concessions for tourism; (vii) pricing policies; (viii) management capacity; and (ix) park tourism governance. Leung *et al.* (2018) consider that protected area managers and nature conservation agencies will increasingly need to consider the implications of population growth, increasing consumption, urbanisation and climate change as they plan tourism. Future research should focus on finding a comparable way to measure tourism's contribution to PAs across Africa, as well as looking at ways to measure the induced and indirect impacts of tourism to gain a better understanding of its full role in terms of biodiversity conservation and local socioeconomic development. There should also be a focus on visitor management, understanding and consistently measuring tourism statistics, impacts of visitors on conservation areas (positive, negative, social, economic and environmental), and ways to more sustainably manage visitation to promote benefits and minimise costs to conservation areas and to communities.

Tourists travelling to visit conservation areas in Africa should ask questions to ensure that the company that they are travelling with, and whose lodges they are staying in, is operating in an economically, socially and environmentally responsible way. Through tourists demanding transparency and accountability from the private sector there will be a greater need for more private sector tourism businesses to operate sustainably, to maximise benefits to different stakeholders and to operate more inclusively.

In the final analysis, a huge amount of responsibility rests on the sustainable management of tourism in conservation areas. Not only are there the required economic and social responsibilities, but the conservation of natural resources in order to ensure the success of the business also plays a major role in the success and survival of humankind, through the provision of ecosystem services and natural resources important for survival. The sustainable development, management and monitoring of tourism in conservation areas should be a priority, with investment focused on finding and ensuring the implementation of sustainable, environmentally friendly developments with positive socioeconomic and sociocultural impacts. This is not an easy task and we should not take this responsibility lightly!

## 7.5. References

Austin, *et al* (unpublished) Quadruple bottom line sustainable business model, turbo charged by collaboration. *Business and Society*.

Barber, N. & Pittaway, L. (2000) Expatriate recruitment in South East Asia: dilemma or opportunity? *International Journal of Contemporary Hospitality Management* 12(6), 352–359. Available at https://doi.org/10.1108/09596110010343530 (accessed 12 September 2018).

Bramwell, B. and Lane, B. (2000) *Tourism Collaboration and Partnerships: Politics, Practice and Sustainability*. Channel View Publications, USA.

Christie, I., Fernandes, E., Messerli, H. & Twining-Ward, L. (2014) *Tourism in Africa: harnessing tourism for growth and improved livelihoods*. The World Bank, Washington, DC. Available at https://openknowledge.worldbank.org/handle/10986/18688 (accessed 16 June 2017).

Eagles, P.F.J. (2014) Research priorities in park tourism. *Journal of Sustainable Tourism*, 22(4), 528–549.

Epler Wood, M. (2017) *Sustainable tourism on a finite planet: environmental, business and policy solutions*. Routledge, Oxford and New York.

Leung, Y-F., Spenceley, A., Hvengaard, G. & Buckley, R. (2018) *Tourism and visitor management in protected areas: guidelines for sustainability*. Best Practice Protected Areas Guidelines No. 27, IUCN, Gland, Switzerland.

Mbaiwa, J.E. (2003) The socio-economic and environmental impacts of tourism development on the Okavango Delta, north western Botswana. *Journal of Arid Environments*, 54(2), 447–467.

Mbaiwa, J.E. (2005) The problems and prospects of sustainable tourism development in the Okavango Delta, Botswana. *Journal of Sustainable Tourism*, 13(3), 203–227.

Republic of Rwanda (2017) *New visa regime 2017*. Available at https://www.migration.gov.rw/index.php?id=283 (accessed 3 June 2018).

Rogerson, C. (2012) Tourism–agriculture linkages in rural South Africa: evidence from the accommodation sector. *Journal of Sustainable Tourism*, 20(3), 477–95.

Rylance, A., Spenceley, A., Mitchell, J. and Leturque, H. (2009) *Training Module for Agriculture*. International Trade Centre, Geneva.

Snyman, S. (2017) African tourism industry employees: expenditure patterns and comparisons with other community members. *Journal of Sustainable Tourism* 1–17, doi:10.1080/09669582.2017.1408634.

Spenceley, A. (2016) Tourism and protected areas: comparing the 2003 and 2014 IUCN World Parks Congress, *Journal of Sustainable Tourism* 17(1), 8–23.

Spenceley, A., Snyman, S. & Eagles, P.F.J. (2017) Guidelines for tourism partnerships and concessions for protected areas: generating sustainable revenues for conservation and development. Report to the Convention on Biological Diversity and IUCN. Available at https://www.cbd.int/tourism/doc/tourismpartnerships-protected-areas-web.pdf (accessed 22 June 2018).

Twining-Ward, L., Li, W., Bhammar, H. & Wright, E. (2018) *Supporting sustainable livelihoods through wildlife tourism. Tourism for development*. World Bank, Washington, DC. Available at https://openknowledge.worldbank.org/handle/10986/29417 (accessed 11 April 2018).

World Tourism Organization (2014), Towards Measuring the Economic Value of Wildlife Watching Tourism in Africa – Briefing Paper, UNWTO, Madrid.

World Bank Group (2017) Tourism for development: 20 reasons sustainable tourism counts for development. Available at https://openknowledge.worldbank.org/bitstream/handle/10986/28388/119954-WP-PUBLICSustainableTourismDevelopment. pdf?sequence=1&isAllowed=y (accessed 29 September 2017).

# 8

# Supplementary Material

The following web links include publicly available materials that can be accessed to provide more detailed information and background reading.

**Table 77.** Guidelines and tools for tourism concessions and partnerships.

| **Guidelines and tools for tourism concessions and partnerships** | |
|---|---|
| Spenceley, A., Snyman, S. and Eagles, P.F.J. (2017) Guidelines for tourism partnerships and concessions in protected areas: generating sustainable revenues for conservation and development. Report to the Convention on Biological Diversity and IUCN, June 2017. | English: https://www.cbd.int/tourism/doc/tourism-partnerships-protected-areas-web.pdf |
| | French: https://www.cbd.int/tourism/doc/tourism-partnerships-protected-areas-fr-web.pdf |
| | Spanish: https://www.cbd.int/tourism/doc/tourism-partnerships-protected-areas-es-web.pdf |

© S. Snyman and A. Spenceley (2019). *Private Sector Tourism in Conservation Areas in Africa* (S. Snyman and A. Spenceley)

**Table 77.**

| | |
|---|---|
| Thompson, A., Massyn, P.J., Pendry, J. and Pastorelli, J. (2014) Tourism concessions in protected natural areas: guidelines for managers. United Nations Development Program. | http://www.undp.org/content/undp/en/home/librarypage/environment-energy/ecosystems_and_biodiversity/tourism-concessions-in-protected-natural-areas.html |
| Spenceley, A., Nevill, H., Coelho, C.F. and Souto, M. (2016) An introduction to tourism concessioning: 14 characteristics of successful programs. World Bank Group. | http://documents.worldbank.org/curated/en/459431467995814879/An-introduction-to-tourism-concessioning-14-characteristics-of-successful-programs |
| Spenceley, A. (2014) Tourism concession guidelines for transfrontier conservation areas in SADC. Report to GIZ / SADC. | https://tfcaportal.org/sites/default/files/public-docs/tourism_concession_guidelines_sadc_tfcas_final.pdf |
| How to apply for financing. | http://www.ifc.org/wps/wcm/connect/corp_ext_content/ifc_external_corporate_site/solutions/how-to-apply-for-financing |
| The World Bank Group's Getting Financed: 9 – tips for community joint ventures (JVs) in tourism. | https://openknowledge.worldbank.org/handle/10986/21698 |
| **Guidelines and tools for community-based tourism (CBT)** | |
| Spenceley, A., Rylance, A., Nanabhay, S. and van der Watt, H. (2016) Operational guidelines for community-based tourism in South Africa. Department of Tourism: Republic of South Africa. | https://tkp.tourism.gov.za/Documents/Community%20Based%20Tourism%20Operational%20Guidelines.pdf |

**Table 77.**

| | |
|---|---|
| Linking communities, tourism & conservation: a tourism assessment process. | https://www2.gwu.edu/~iits/Sustainable_Tourism_Online_Learning/Gutierrez/Tourism_Assessment_Process_Manual.pdf |
| Sustainable tourism enterprise development: a business planning approach. | https://www.usaid.gov/sites/default/files/documents/1865/EnterpriseDev_5%5B2%5D.pdf |
| Planning for community responsible tourism development. | https://docs.wixstatic.com/ugd/ff4ce3_db01330e9fef4ed4a5b40cb00a8086a6.pdf |
| Effective community-based tourism: a best practice manual. | https://www.apec.org/-/media/APEC/Publications/2010/6/Effective-Community-Based-Tourism-A-Best-Practice-Manual-June-2010/210_twg_CommunityBasedTourismWEB.pdf |
| Handbook on community-based tourism 'How to develop and sustain CBT'. | http://publications.apec.org/publication-detail.php?pub_id=952 |
| Vietnam community-based tourism handbook: a market-based approach. | http://vietnamtourism.gov.vn/dmdocuments/CBTHandbookENonepage.pdf |

**Table 77.**

| | |
|---|---|
| ILO toolkit on poverty reduction through tourism. | http://www.ilo.org/sector/Resources/training-materials/WCMS_218361/lang--en/index.htm |
| ITC opportunity study guidelines. | www.intracen.org/uploadedFiles/intracenorg/Content/Exporters/Sectoral_Information/Service_Exports/Tourism/Opportunity%20Studies%20Guidelines%20TPRP.pdf |
| Guidelines for community-based ecotourism development. | http://assets.panda.org/downloads/guidelinesen.pdf |
| Organisation for Economic Cooperation and Development (OECD) Development Assistance Committee (DAC) criteria for evaluating development assistance. | http://www.oecd.org/dac/evaluation/49756382.pdf |
| What makes a project bankable? | https://www.slideshare.net/boundless-southern-africa/day-1-what-makes-a-project-bankable-idcmartin-potgieter |
| A guide to starting a tourism enterprise in Botswana. | http://www.the-eis.com/data/literature/CBNRM%20Support%20Programme%20paper%209.pdf |

**Table 77.**

| | |
|---|---|
| **Stakeholder relationships** | |
| Stakeholder engagement: a good practice handbook for companies doing business in emerging markets, pp. 113–114. | http://www.ifc.org/wps/wcm/connect/938f1a0048855805beacfe6a6515bb18/IFC_StakeholderEngagement.pdf?MOD=AJPERES |
| Development without conflict: the business case for community consent. | http://pdf.wri.org/development_without_conflict_fpic.pdf |
| Stakeholder communication and relationship management: training module. | http://www.nacso.org.na/resources/104-stakeholder-communication-and-relationship-management |
| The role of NGOs in facilitating tourism concessions and providing support to communities entering joint venture agreements. | https://www.slideshare.net/AnnaSpenceley/the-role-of-ngos-in-tourism-concessions-steve-collins |
| **Setting up the stakeholder structure** | |
| Legal structures commonly used by non-profit organisations. | http://www.etu.org.za/toolbox/docs/building/lrc.html |
| JVs: tips for joint venture partnerships in tourism. | http://www.nacso.org.na/resources/getting-financed-9-tips-for-community-joint-ventures-in-tourism |

**Table 77.**

| | | |
|---|---|---|
| Constitutions for non-profit organisations. | | http://www.etu.org.za/toolbox/docs/building/const.html |
| **Starting a tourism business** | | |
| Starting a tourism business. | | http://smetoolkit.businesspartners.co.za/en/tourism/starting-tourism-business |
| How to establish a bed and breakfast or guesthouse. | | https://www.westerncape.gov.za/general-publication/how-establish-various-types-tourism-businesses?toc_page=2 |
| Becoming a tour guide. | | https://smetoolkit.businesspartners.co.za/en/content/becoming-tour-guide |
| Starting a tour or tourist transport business. | | https://smetoolkit.businesspartners.co.za/en/content/starting-tour-or-tourist-transport-business |
| How to establish a tour operating business. | | http://www.zulu.org.za/archive/how-to-establish-a-tour-operating-business-F57993 |

**Table 77.**

| | |
|---|---|
| How to establish a restaurant, eating house or tavern. | https://www.westerncape.gov.za/general-publication/how-establish-various-types-tourism-businesses?toc_page=1 |
| Start-up costs for an accommodation business. | https://smetoolkit.businesspartners.co.za/en/content/start-costs-accommodation-business |
| Getting your tourism business off the ground. | https://smetoolkit.businesspartners.co.za/en/content/getting-your-tourism-business-ground |
| A guide to starting a tourism enterprise in Botswana. | http://www.the-eis.com/data/literature/CBNRM%20Support%20Programme%20paper%209.pdf |
| **Capacity-building and HR** | |
| Community tourism and enterprise training manual. | http://pdf.usaid.gov/pdf_docs/Pnadb184.pdf |
| ILO SCORE training. | http://www.ilo.org/empent/Projects/score/lang--en/index.htm |

**Table 77.**

| | |
|---|---|
| Lobster Inc. | https://www.lobsterink.com |
| **Funding** | |
| Getting financed: 9 tips for community JVs in tourism. | https://openknowledge.worldbank.org/bitstream/handle/10986/21698/959240WP00PUBL050NamibiaonlineFINAL.pdf?sequence=1 |
| UNESCO World Heritage sustainable tourism online toolkit: guide 9: securing funding and investment. | http://whc.unesco.org/sustainabletourismtoolkit/guides/guide-9-securing-funding-and-investment |
| **Sustainable tourism** | |
| Responsible tourism manual for South Africa. | http://www.kruger2canyons.org/031%20-%20Responsible%20Tourism%20Manual.pdf |
| Destination mutual benefit: a guide to inclusive business in tourism. | http://www.endeva.org/publication/destination-mutual-benefit-a-guide-to-inclusive-business-in-tourism |
| Biodiversity: my hotel in action. | https://cmsdata.iucn.org/downloads/iucn_hotel_guide_final.pdf |

**Table 77.**

| | |
|---|---|
| GeePee responsible tourism challenge. | https://bettertourismafrica.org/the-amageepee-challenge/ |
| Series of 'How to … ?'<br>Brief 1: Boosting procurement from local businesses. https://www.odi.org/resources/docs/2255.pdf<br>Brief 2: Stimulating local cultural and heritage products. https://www.odi.org/resources/docs/2257.pdf<br>Brief 3: Building local partnerships. https://www.odi.org/resources/docs/2259.pdf<br>Brief 4: Setting corporate priorities and managing internal change. https://www.odi.org/resources/docs/2261.pdf | www.odi.org.uk |
| **Marketing the venture** | |
| Community-based tourism market access programme. | https://www.researchgate.net/profile/Anna_Spenceley/publication/280319439_Welcome_to_the_community_based_tourism_market_access_manual/links/55b2862f08ae9289a0858a89/Welcome-to-the-community-based-tourism-market-access-manual.pdf |
| **Monitoring** | |
| A toolkit for monitoring and managing community-based tourism. | http://www.bibalex.org/Search4Dev/files/283814/115937.pdf |
| **Case studies** | |
| Rocktail Bay case study. | http://www.odi.org/sites/odi.org.uk/files/odi-assets/publications-opinion-files/4016.pdf |

**Table 77.**

| | |
|---|---|
| Madikwe Game Reserve, South Africa – investment and employment. | Chapter 12 in: http://books.google.co.za/books/about/Responsible_Tourism.html?id=rrGTngEACAAJ&redir_esc=y |
| Practical strategies for pro-poor tourism, Wilderness Safaris (WS) South Africa: Rocktail Bay and Ndumu Lodge – practical examples of the involvement of the communities in a public–private-partnership (PPP) tourism concession. | http://www.odi.org/sites/odi.org.uk/files/odi-assets/publications-opinion-files/4016.pdf |
| Concessions processes in South African National Parks (SANParks) | https://www.slideshare.net/AnnaSpenceley/south-african-national-parks-concessions-processes-giju-varghese |
| Concession contract management and monitoring: SANParks (presentation). | https://www.slideshare.net/AnnaSpenceley/contract-management-in-tourism-concessions-giju-varghese |

# Photo credits

| Case Study | Credit |
|---|---|
| Case Study 1 – Bisate Lodge, Rwanda | Wilderness Safaris |
| Case Study 2 – Wolwedans, Namibia | Wolwedans |
| Case Study 3 – Mombo Camp and Little Mombo, Botswana | Wilderness Safaris |
| Case Study 4 – Simien Lodge, Ethiopia | Nick Crane |
| Case Study 5 – Davison's Camp, Linkwasha Camp and Little Makalolo, Zimbabwe | Wilderness Safaris |
| Case Study 6 – Nkwichi Lodge, Lake Malawi, Mozambique | Nkwichi Lodge |
| Case Study 7 – Chumbe Island, Tanzania | Chumbe Island |
| Case Study 8 – Bale Mountain Lodge, Ethiopia | Billy Dodson |
| Case Study 9 – King Lewanika Lodge, Zambia | Time + Tide |
| Case Study 10 – Ngala Safari Lodge, South Africa | AndBeyond |
| Case Study 11 – Mkulumadzi Lodge, Malawi | Robin Pope Safaris |
| Case Study 12 – Sunbird Thawale Lodge, Malawi | Sunbird Thawale |
| Case Study 13 – Ruzizi Tented Lodge, Rwanda | Akagera Management Company |
| Case Study 14 – Singita Lebombo, South Africa | Singita |
| Case Study 15 – Africa Foundation | Africa Foundation |
| Case Study 16 – Children in the Wilderness (CITW) | Children in the Wilderness |
| Case Study 17 – Wilderness Wildlife Trust (WWT) | Wilderness Safaris |
| Case Study 18 – Singita Community Development Trust | Singita |
| Case Study 19 – Anvil Bay Chemucane Lodge, Mozambique | Anvil Bay |
| Case Study 20 – Ndzou Camp, Mozambique | Ndzou Camp/Eco-MICAIA Ltd |
| Case Study 21 – Damaraland Camp, Namibia | Wilderness Safaris |
| Case Study 22 – Doro Nawas Camp, Namibia | Wilderness Safaris |
| Case Study 23 – Witsieshoek Mountain Lodge, South Africa | Transfrontier Parks Destinations |
| Case Study 24 – Covane Community Lodge, Mozambique | Ron Olivier_ Incynq Solutions (Pty) Ltd |
| Case Study 25 – !Xaus Lodge, South Africa | Transfrontier Parks Destinations |
| Case Study 26 – Phinda Private Game Reserve, South Africa | andBeyond |
| Case Study 27 – Serra Cafema Camp, Namibia | Wilderness Safaris |
| Case Study 28 – Sabyinyo Silverback Lodge, Rwanda | The Governors' Camp Collection |
| Case Study 29 – Vumbura Plains and Little Vumbura, Botswana | Wilderness Safaris |
| Case Study 30 – Pafuri Camp, South Africa | Return Africa (Pty) Ltd |
| Case Study 31 – Satao Elerai Lodge, Kenya | Charles Grieves-Cook |
| Case Study 32 – Rocktail Camp, South Africa | Wilderness Safaris |

# Index